Seamanship

Titles in the
Fundamentals of Naval Science Series

Seamanship: Fundamentals for the Deck Officer

Lieutenant Commander David O. Dodge
U.S. Naval Reserve

and

Lieutenant Commander Stephen E. Kyriss
U.S. Navy

Naval Institute Press
Annapolis, Maryland

Fundamentals of Naval Science Series

Library of Congress Cataloging in Publication Data
Kyriss, Stephen E   1946–
   Seamanship.
   Edition for 1972 entered under title.
   Bibliography: p.
   Includes index.
   1. Seamanship. 2. United States. Navy—Officers'
handbooks. I. Dodge, David O., 1951–   joint
author. II. Title.
VK541.K94 1980   623.8′8   80-5684
ISBN 0-87021-613-9

Printed in the United States of America on acid-free paper ∞
10 9

This book is dedicated in fond appreciation to Mr. Bert C. Wylds who, as an instructor in the seamanship and navigation department and as the U.S. Naval Academy sailing master, has contributed a wealth of knowledge and experience to midshipmen and officers of the Navy. Bert helped many of us recognize and acquire the skills of the true seaman—a gift that will remain long after we have docked for the last time.

Contents

Seamanship: Fundamentals for the Deck Officer is designed to introduce the student to some of the basic knowledge required of a naval officer. The midshipman or officer candidate must acquire and demonstrate many of the skills described in this text early in his or her career.

Although intended as a revision of the *Seamanship* volume originally developed as part of the Fundamentals of Naval Science series, this text highlights and expands upon those elements of seamanship most helpful to the midshipmen and officer candidates preparing for their first at-sea cruise. The role of the enlisted seaman and his responsibilities aboard a small combatant are woven throughout the book despite its orientation toward officer education. It is hoped that *Seamanship* may continue to serve the student long after commissioning by forming the beginning of an officer's professional library.

Seamanship

Standard Pattern of Ship Organization

Basic Structure

The primary function of ships of the United States Navy is either to fight or to support combat. If a ship is to function well in combat, the crew has to be organized in such a way that it can be effectively directed and controlled.

A warship's complement is composed of such numbers, grades, and ratings of officers and enlisted personnel as are necessary to fight the ship most efficiently. The ship's organization is essentially a war organization, developed on the theory that ships should operate in peacetime with an organization that can be expanded quickly without basic change when the transition to a wartime operating condition becomes necessary. It is based on a grouping of functions and personnel that is intended to reduce to a minimum both the possible overlapping of responsibility within the command and the duplication of personnel.

A unit's organization for battle consists of functional groups headed by key officers who are at specified stations and control the activities of personnel under their direction. Such control helps to ensure the effectiveness of the organization in carrying out either the plan for battle or variations necessitated by the tactical situation.

Heading the battle organization is the commanding officer, who exercises command and whose responsibility it is, during action, to engage the enemy to the best of his ability. He is assisted by subordinate officers who have cognizance over the major control functions of the ship. Such functions include navigation, weapons, engineering and damage control, operations, and supply. These functions are divided into administrative units called departments.

The assignment of personnel to administrative departments must closely approximate the major components of the battle organization. However, to meet the requirements of sound organization, the administrative structure must allow for the performance of certain tasks that have no place in battle. In the day-to-day routine, the needs of training and maintenance are emphasized, and certain support measures are necessary for administrative reasons, and for the welfare of the crew.

Efficiency of operation is promoted when every member of the crew has a clear understanding of the functional relationships within the ship's organization. This requires that the organization be set forth in writing; otherwise, confusion and conflict can develop. Details of an organization's formal relationships are made known through both graphic and written descriptions of the various relationships and positions.

Standard Organization and Regulations of the U.S. Navy (OPNAVINST 3120.32) is the directive that governs the administrative organization of the ship, the coordination of shipboard departments, and the conduct of people on board the ship. The explanation of the administrative organization of a ship outlined in this chapter is based on the description of the delegation of executive responsibility as it is delineated in OPNAVINST 3120.32.

This basic directive includes the following: 1. description, both written and graphic, of the ship's administrative organization, from the commanding officer through the division petty officer, and of the watch organization, through all echelons; 2. organizational bills of the ship; and 3. ship's regulations. Even though it is the responsibility of higher authority to establish standard ship organization and regulations, the commanding officer of a ship is obliged to adapt the standard organization to his particular ship and to make modifications to account for variations in personnel, spaces, or equipment. Appendices and addendums may be used to include further information within the standard directive. Navy ships conform to a standard pattern of shipboard organization so that personnel can move from ship to ship and from fleet to fleet with a minimum of time required to adapt to each new organization.

Departments and Divisions of a Ship

The administrative organization for all types of ships is defined in OPNAVINST 3120.32. The five basic departments found on all U.S. Navy ships are navigation, operations, weapons (deck), engineering, and supply. The organization may include other departments to fulfill the ship's assigned tasks. Figure 1-1 shows the departments in various ships of today's fleets. The details of the organization of these departments are established for each particular type of ship so that each type may accomplish its assigned tasks effectively. The departments of a ship are organized into divisions. These divisions are established in the organization structure so that they may be assigned as units within the components of the battle organization.

Department Organization

Ship Types	Major Command Departments								Staff Depts			Special			
	Navigation	Operations	Weapons	Deck	Engineering	Air	Communications	Reactor	Supply	Medical	Dental	Repair	Ordnance	Hydrographic	Flag Division
Amphibious															
LCC	X	X		X	X		X		X	X	X				
LKA	X	X		X	X				X	X	X				
LPH	X	X		X	X	X	X		X	X	X				
LPD	X	X		X	X	X			X	X					
LST	X	X		X	X				X						
LSD	X	X		X	X				X	X					
Carriers	X	X	X	X	X	X	X5	X4	X	X	X				
Cruisers	X	X	X		X		X5	X4	X	X	X				
Destroyers	X	X	X		X			X4	X						
Mine Warfare	X	X		X	X				X						
Patrol	X	X	X		X				X						
Submarines	X	X	X		X			X4	X	X					
Auxiliary															
AD	X	X		X	X				X	X	X	X			
AE	X	X		X	X				X	X					
AFS	X	X		X	X				X	X					
AGS	X	X		X	X				X	X	X			X	
AH1	X	X		X	X				X						
AOR	X	X		X	X				X	X					
AOE	X	X		X	X				X	X					
AR	X	X		X	X				X	X	X	X			
ARC	X	X		X	X				X	X					
ARG	X	X		X	X				X	X	X	X			
ARL	X	X		X	X				X	X		X			
ARS	X	X		X	X				X						
AS	X	X		X	X				X	X	X	X			
ASR	X	X		X	X				X						
ATA	X	X		X	X				X						
ATF	X	X		X	X				X						
AV	X	X		X	X	X			X	X	X				

NOTES:

1. In hospital ships, the medical and dental departments are integrated with the hospital.

2. In small ships, the navigation department is integrated with the operations department for administration, while its men report to the navigator for technical control.

3. In small ships, supply duties may be delegated to a line officer, who will be a department head.

4. On those ships having reactors.

5. Ships with large communication installations, such as cruisers and carriers, will frequently have a communication department.

Figure 1-1. The departments in various ship types.

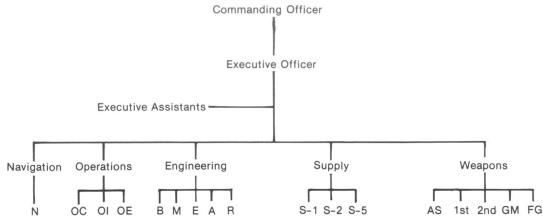

Figure 1-2. Department and division organization on board an FFG.

An example of a typical shipboard administrative organization is illustrated by Figure 1-2. It shows the structure of the departments in the administrative organization. Each department is headed by an officer known as a department head. On occasion, an officer may head more than one department or division if there are not enough qualified officers on board.

Unit Organization and Chain of Command

Any Navy organization operates on the principle of the chain of command. The shipboard chain of command is like a pyramid with the commanding officer on top and a large number of personnel on the bottom. It is structured like this:

> Commanding officer
> Executive officer
> Heads of departments
> Division officers
> Division leading petty officers
> Division petty officers
> Nonrated personnel

It has been proven time and time again that adherence to the principle of the chain of command is essential to the effective functioning of the shipboard organization. Heads of departments, for example, report to the commanding officer directly on operational matters pertaining to their department, and they report directly to the executive officer on administrative matters. Division officers, in turn, report only to their respective heads of departments on all matters pertaining to their divisions. In this way the flow of communication provides for efficient functioning both up and down the chain of command.

Commanding Officer

The responsibility of the commanding officer for his command is absolute as defined by Navy Regulations. His authority is commensurate with his responsibility, subject to the limitations prescribed by law and regulations. While he may delegate authority to his subordinates for the execution of details, such delegation of authority in no way relieves the commanding officer of his continued responsibility for the safety and efficiency of his entire command.

In the discharge of his duties, the commanding officer is assisted by the executive officer, who acts as his direct representative.

The commanding officer must exert every effort to maintain his command in a state of maximum effectiveness for war service consistent with the required degree of readiness. He issues the necessary directions to his executive officer who, in turn, with the assistance of the various department heads, prepares and conducts exercises and drills required to bring about the necessary proficiency.

A primary responsibility of the commanding officer is at all times the safety of the ship. This means issuing specific orders regarding the handling, stowage, and use of ammunition; providing for watertight integrity, which involves closing watertight doors, opening ports at sea, and other relevant matters; careful navigation; posting of proper lookouts; showing required lights; observing Rules of the Road to prevent collisions, and so on. It is manifestly impossible for the captain to attend to all these matters personally. But while the navigator, for example, is charged with the specific duty of knowing the ship's position at all times, the commanding officer nevertheless retains ultimate responsibility for safe navigation, because he is responsible for the safety and efficiency of the ship.

The details of the training and education of the ship's company are responsibilities that the commanding officer delegates to his executive officer. All ships must have an organized program for shipboard training.

During action, the commanding officer is required to engage the enemy and fight to the best of his ability.

The commanding officer's battle station is that station from which he can fight the ship to best advantage. In case of the loss of his ship, both custom and regulations require that the commanding officer ensure that abandon-ship procedures are completed and all personnel are off the ship before he leaves.

The commanding officer supervises the conduct of all persons under his command. Should he not suppress unlawful activities or conduct, he himself is subject to trial by court-martial. It is essential to efficiency and discipline that a commanding officer have the power to enforce prompt obedience to his orders. By the Uniform Code of Military Justice the power is vested in the commanding officer to impose limited punishment. This power is an attribute of command and may not be delegated to a subordinate.

If the officer regularly in command of the ship is absent, disabled, relieved from duty, or detached without relief, the command devolves upon the line officer next in grade who is regularly attached to and on board the ship, and who is eligible for command at sea (this excludes such officers as may be restricted to the performance of engineering or other special duties).

The Executive Officer

The executive officer is the commanding officer's aide or executive. His position and duties are also defined in Navy Regulations. He is the second-most senior officer on board the ship, and he would temporarily succeed the captain should the commanding officer not be able to carry out his duties. The executive officer is directly responsible to the captain for the internal administration of the ship. Subordinate officers report to the executive officer on all matters pertaining to the internal administration of the ship, and they keep him informed of any operational developments or difficulties in their area of responsibility that they have reported to the captain.

The executive officer coordinates and supervises the administration of the command, paying particular attention to training, work, discipline, safety, welfare, rights, and privileges of the crew. He makes recommendations to the commanding officer concerning each individual's performance, using fitness reports for officers and evaluation sheets for enlisted personnel. He prepares the fitness reports after the department heads have submitted their recommendations. Among his numerous other duties, the executive officer conducts regular inspections of messing and berthing facilities, regulates the leave and liberty of the crew, acts on personal requests, plans with the crew a program of recreation and athletics, and directs the ship's public affairs program.

The executive officer directs an investigation for the commanding officer when a violation of military or civil law is alleged to have taken place on board the ship and recommends the necessary action. This role applies to Captain's Mast, to formal court proceedings, to violations of safety, and to all forms of misconduct.

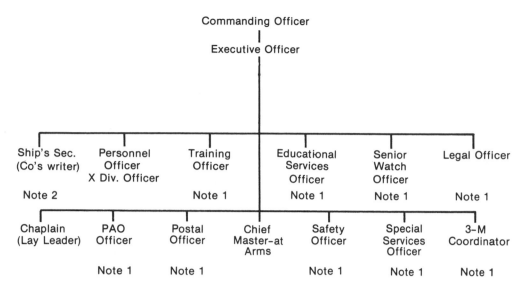

Figure 1-3. *The executive's assistants on board a ship. In small ships most of the duties are assigned as collateral duties to officers and senior petty officers.*

He is responsible for overseeing the writing, updating, and implementation of the ship's bills, although department heads are responsible for specific bills. For example, the executive officer will ensure that the first lieutenant has an up-to-date and workable Underway Replenishment Bill.

The Executive's Assistants

From the discussion of the executive officer's duties and responsibilities, it is evident that he must have some members of the crew assigned to assist him. If the ship is a large one, the executive officer will have a number of officers who are assigned to him as his special assistants. If the ship is small, the executive officer will have fewer assistants. Many duties that the executive officer delegates to officers as primary duties on a large ship will, on a small ship, be performed by officers as collateral duties. The enlisted billets assigned to assist the executive officer do not change much between large and small ships. When performing duties on a collateral basis, officers and enlisted personnel report directly to the executive officer regardless of their primary assignment on board. Figure 1-3 is an example of the executive's assistants on board a small combatant, an FF.

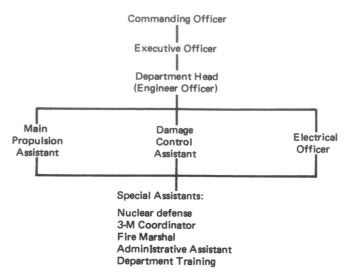

Figure 1-4. The organization of a typical department as it relates to the command structure. This engineering department corresponds to a random breakdown of the engineering department shown in figure 1-2. Any combination of duties is possible, depending on the size, class, and type of ship.

Many special or collateral duties of the executive officer are carried out by petty officers. These duties often include those of the 3-M coordinator, the welfare and recreation officer, and the chief master at arms who directs the command's master-at-arms force.

Department Organization

Figure 1-4 illustrates the standard organization of a department on a small ship. It shows the lines of authority and the relative positions of the officers in the department. (Many of the billets shown may be combined.) The structure, therefore, is adjusted to fit the needs of a particular type of ship. As will be explained in detail later, the structure employed on a particular class of ship is based on the organization for battle as expressed in the battle bill. In the engineering department of a frigate, for example, there are three primary assistants under the engineer officer: the main propulsion assistant, the damage control assistant, and the electrical officer. One or more divisions are assigned under each assistant. On board a minesweeper, however, there is one officer assigned to the engineering department. He carries all the responsibilities of his department.

Heads of Departments

The head of a department is the representative of the commanding officer in all matters that pertain to the department. All persons assigned to the department shall be subordinate to him, and all orders issued by him shall be obeyed accordingly by them.

Department heads report to the commanding officer for the operational readiness of their departments. This means that they report to him on the general condition of the equipment and spaces, including the need for major repairs, and any condition that may reduce the ship's ability to operate. They supervise a shipboard maintenance and material management system to help keep the equipment in working order.

Department heads report to the executive officer for all administrative matters and keep the executive officer informed of reports made directly to the commanding officer. There are many such administrative matters for which a department head is responsible.

1. He formulates and carries out a training program for all the personnel in his department, within the framework of the ship's training program.

2. He maintains established standards of performance and conduct, by means of drills, exercises, inspections, and other controls.

3. He prepares fitness reports and evaluation sheets on the personnel under his control. He then forwards such reports and evaluations, as well as recommendations on meritorious mast, disciplinary matters, special requests, advancement in rate and the like to the executive officer.

4. He advises the division officers of his department on matters affecting the morale or discipline of their personnel.

5. He submits a budget to the commanding officer for the maintenance and operation of his department and controls the expenditures of his department.

Division Organization

Figure 1-5 illustrates the basic organization of a division. The organization shown is often modified to meet the needs of particular divisions.

The Division Officer

The division officer is responsible for the organization, administration, and operation of his division. His duties are prescribed by U.S. Navy Regulations. The division is an administrative grouping of personnel in a department, which facilitates their employment as components of the battle organization. On occasion all the personnel of a division may be responsible for the same job, as in the case of signal-

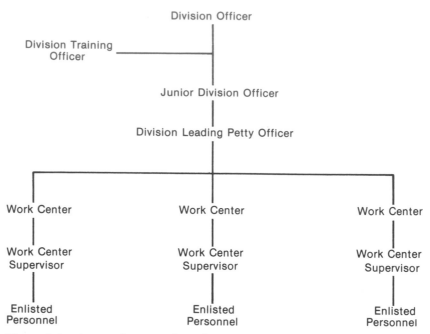

Figure 1-5. A typical pattern for a division in a small ship.

men, for example; as often as not, however, personnel in a division perform different functions and have different skills. An example might be the R Division in the Engineering Department, which includes electrician's mates (EMs), enginemen (ENs), machinist mates (MMs), machinery repairmen (MRs), and hull technicians (HTs).

The division officer directs his personnel through division petty officers. The division officer assigns personnel to watches and duties within the division and rotates them at battle stations, watches, and general duties to ensure their training and proficiency. Division training includes indoctrination of new personnel, preparation for advancement in rating, both in military and professional subjects, individual instruction in shipboard duties, and team training to fulfill operating requirements of the division.

The division officer maintains a division notebook containing personal information about his personnel, training program records, watch and battle stations, personnel qualifications, equipment custody logs, and other information that may be useful for the orientation of an officer relieving him.

The division officer forwards requests for leave, liberty, and special privileges to the department head with his recommendations. He also forwards recommendations for advancement in rate and performance evaluation marks. In order to evaluate performance, the division officer stays in close touch with the personnel in his division and also conducts periodic inspections, exercises, and musters.

Junior Division Officer

The junior division officer assists the division officer in coordinating and administering the division and develops a thorough understanding of the functions, directives, and equipment of the division in preparation for assuming the duties of the division officer.

Division Training Officer

The division training officer is responsible to the division officer for the administration of training within the division, and he coordinates the program with the departmental and overall training program of the ship. He conducts the same training program at the division level as the departmental training officer carries out for the department. The division training officer is normally the senior enlisted person in the division or the junior division officer.

Division Leading Petty Officer

A division officer generally has a number of enlisted personnel working for him. The most senior of these enlisted people normally is designated the division's leading petty officer (LPO). A chief petty officer would be termed an LCPO (figure 1-6). A leading petty officer assists the division officer in the administration, supervision, discipline, and training of personnel in the division. Under the supervision of the division officer, the LPO assigns tasks to, and oversees the performance of, work center supervisors and all other divisional personnel.

Work Center Supervisor

For administrative purposes, each of a division's rate specialties is usually organized into a subunit or maintenance group called a work center. A division, for example, that was composed of torpedomen and sonarmen would likely have two work centers. The torpedomen work center would handle assignments in their rate specialty, while the sonarmen would be responsible for maintenance and operation of the ship's sonar system.

An enlisted person in charge of a work center is known as a work center supervisor. Work center supervisors see that all maintenance-related tasks are carried out and report equipment status to the LPO who relays such information to the division officer. This high degree of organization and centralized authority is very necessary to enable the division officer to perform his many duties.

Figure 1-6. The division leading chief petty officer (LCPO) in "M" Division supervising the main engineering control throttlemen.

Ratings and Rates

A *rating* is a Navy job—a duty calling for certain skills and aptitudes. The rating of boiler technician, for example, calls for personnel who are good with their hands and are mechanically inclined. The specialty mark of each rating is included with the rating description. Specialty marks were added to enlisted uniforms in 1866. They originally represented the instrument used to perform the particular task. For example, the quartermaster has a ship's helm while a gunner's mate has two crossed cannons. The custom of representing the type of work with a specialty mark for each rating continues, but often the design has been stylized. For instance, the journalist (JO) is represented by crossed quill and scroll, and the cryptologic technician (CT) is crossed quill and spark.

A paygrade (such as E-4, E-5, E-6) within a rating is called a *rate*. Thus a boiler technician third class (BT3) would have a rating of boiler technician, and a rate of third-class petty officer (E-4).

The term *petty officer* (PO) applies to anyone in paygrades E-4 through E-9. E-1s through E-3s are called nonrated personnel. Personnel in general apprenticeships are identified as recruit (E-1), apprentice (E-2), or at the E-3 level, by their apprenticeship field—such as seaman, fireman, airman, constructionman, dentalman, or hospitalman. A person training for a specific job in paygrades E-1 through E-3 is called a striker—one who has been authorized to "strike" or train for a particular job.

Enlisted seniority is determined by time in rate and time in the Navy. If two petty officers are in the same paygrade, the one in that grade the longest is considered senior.

Ship's Bills

For special evolutions and for specific recurring tasks, the enlisted personnel on board ship are made aware of their duties and stations by rosters containing their names and job assignments. Ships' rosters of this type are called "bills," and their use is called for in the Navy's Standard Organization and Regulations Manual.

Ships' bills fall into the categories of operational bills, emergency bills, and administrative bills.

Operational bills set forth procedures and specific personnel assignments for evolutions of a periodic nature. Operational bills include the:

1. Special Sea Detail Bill
2. Underway Replenishment Bill
3. Rescue and Assistance Bill
4. Landing Party Bill
5. Visit and Search, Boarding and Salvage, and Prize Crew Bill
6. Towing Bill

Emergency bills detail the procedures and the specific assignment of personnel to perform an evolution on short notice. Such emergencies occur when there is danger of loss of life or of the ship itself. Emergency bills include:

1. General Emergency Bill
2. Man Overboard Bill
3. Nuclear, Biological, and Chemical Defense Bill
4. Emergency Destruction Bill.

Administrative bills set forth procedures and assignments for the everyday administration of the ship. The executive officer is often responsible for maintaining a number of administrative bills. Such bills include the:

1. Berthing and Locker Bill
2. Cleaning and Maintenance Bill

WATCH, QUARTER & STATION BILL

SECTION _First_ DIVISION _First_ COMPT A-303-L

COMPLEMENT | ALLOWANCE | ON BOARD | DATE 7/14/—

BILLET	NAME	BUNK NO.	LKR. NO.	RATE COMP	RATE ALL.	RATE ACT'L	CLEAN STATION	BATTLE COND. I GENL. QTRS	BATTLE COND. II	BATTLE COND. III	LANDING PARTY	EMERG. GETTING UND'WAY	WATCH AT SEA	WATCH IN PORT	SPECIAL SEA DETAIL	FIRE STATION	FIRE PROVIDE	RESCUE PARTY	RESCUE PROVIDE	COLLISION	ABANDON SHIP STATION	ABANDON PROVIDE	MAN OVERBD	SPECIAL DETAIL
H01	King, K.K.	CPO 16			BMC	BMC	in chge DC Central	in chge Rep II	in chge Repair II Hdtrs	RDC Dark	GTRD N10	in chge fo'c'sle	Repair II			PLANE CRASH	assist OinC	scene			Sta #1 muster		lower boat	
H02	Johnson, J.J.	#1	1	BM3	BM2	in chge fo'c'sle	gun capt LGMT 52	gun capt LGMT 52	Sec 1 LGMT 52	in chge fo'c'sle	BMOW watch Sec 1	PO of watch line #1	in chge line 2	scene	OBA	Boot lowering detail	G.Q.	Sta E/ Boot 1	lifeboat	Sec 1		qtrs	
H03	Peterson, P.P.	2	2	GM1	GM1	in chge ord repair	MT capt MT 51	MT capt MT 52	Sec 1	infantry chief Sec 1	Helm Sec 1	PO of watch	qtrs	Fwd mag sprinklers	scene	OBA	rescue swimmers	Armory keys	Fwd mag Sprkl	Sta E/ Boot 1		qtrs	
H04	Smith, S.S.	6	6	GM3	GM3	in chge MT 51	MT capt MT 51	MT 51	MT3	MT capt L5B2-1	in chge line 1 Sec 1	PO of watch Sec 1	in chge line 3	scene tend lines	OBA	distress ashore	Safety Oclf	Sta #1 Boot 1	rifle ammo	Boot Sec 1	rifleman Sec 1			
H05	Kash, K.K.	9	9	SN	SN	in chge A-303-L	1st load L.G. MT 51	MT 51	LGMT	1st load 55 Sec 1	line #1 Sec 1	lifeboat Sec 1	Poof watch Sec 1	line #2	scene	foam	Boot Cexswain	scene	Sta #1 Boot 1	in chge infld	Boot winch oper	
H06	Brown, B.B.	4	4	SN	SN	Gig	1st load RG MT 51	1st load MT 52 Sec1	RG	1st load leader	Fire Team Sec 1	M&B Helm Sec 1	3/B Coxn	line 1 Sec 1	scene	CO2	Boot Winch detail	G.Q.	Sta #1 Boot 1	extra water	Boot winch det. fwd fall	
H07	Able, A.A.	8	8	SN	SN	fo'c'sle	train MT 51	train MT 51 Sec 1	BAR	train MT 51	line #3 Sec 1	Bow Hook Sec 1	OOD mess Sec 1	line #3 Sec 1	scene	appl'r	Boot Bowhook	G.Q.	Sta E/ Boot 1	Blanket	Bow hook	Side boy
H08				SN		MT 32	MT 32	MT 32 Sec1	BAR	pointer MT 32 Sec1	line #2 Sec 1	Port lookout Sec1	OOD mess 2	line # Qtrs		Plane crash	M-1 rifle Ammo	G.Q.	Sta #1 Boot 1	rifle rifleman	Deck rifleman	
H09	Cool, C.C.	7	7	SN	SN	compt A-303-L	pointer MT 51 Sec 1	MT 52	pointer m-M1	phones fo'c'sk	OOD mess Sec 1	OOD mess	phones fo'c'sle	qtrs	scene		Boot Mixed detail AFTFALL	G.Q.	Sta #1 Boot 1	canned juices	Boot winch det. aftfall	
H10	Easy, E.E.	11	11	SN	SN	MT 31	1st load MT 51	MT 31 Sec 1	MT 31	1st load M-1	rifle m-M1 Sec 1	OOD bagout Sec 1	OOD mess	qtrs	scene		Rescue Survivors AMMO	G.Q.	Sta #1 Boot 1	stretcher	fo'c'sle heaving line	
H11	Fox, F.F.	13	13	SN	SA	fo'c'sle	MAG MT 51 Sec1	MT 51 Sec 1	Sec 1	hot shell MT 52	rifle man M&T	fenders Sec 1	OOD mess	fenders	qtrs		distress in anchor cable	2-15 lb CO2	G.Q.	Sta #1 Boot 1	Kapok	fo'c'sle heaving line	
H12	Delta, D.D.	5	5	SN	SA	compt A-303-L	Hot shell MT 51 Sec 1	MT 51 Sec 1	Sec 1	hot shell MT 52	assist BAR	fenders Sec 1	Sec 2	send-ers mess	scene	50' hose	Distress Ashore	50 FAT 3" line	scene lego hose	Sta #1 Boot 1		fo'c'sle graphnel boy	

Figure 1-7. Sample Watch, Quarter, and Station bill.

So that each member of a ship's crew is familiar with his own individual assignment on each of these several bills, a consolidated Watch, Quarter, and Station bill is posted in the primary working or berthing space of every division. The Watch, Quarter, and Station bill is extracted from a ship's operational, emergency, and administrative bills and conveniently displays the specific job assignments and stations of each member of a division during various situations or operations. An example of a division's Watch, Quarter, and Station Bill is shown in figure 1-7.

Summary

The purpose of this chapter has been to introduce the student to the basic structure of shipboard organization. Functions and personnel are combined in order to efficiently accomplish the myriad administrative and operational tasks assigned to a U.S. naval ship in the conduct of its mission. The ship's commanding officer exercises ultimate control, authority, and responsibility over the five major shipboard departments of navigation, weapons, engineering, operations, and supply in accordance with the Standard Organization and Regulations of the U.S. Navy (OPNAVINST 3120.32). The principle of the _chain of command_ from the commanding officer down to the lowest nonrated person is the key to effective communications and functioning within the shipboard organization. The chapter discussed the content of the various primary and collateral duties assigned to officers and senior enlisted personnel in their day-to-day supervision of the ship's activities. In conclusion, personnel watchstations for recurring tasks and special evolutions are delineated in the *ship's bills*, which can be operational, emergency, or administrative in nature.

2

The Underway Shipboard Watch and Battle Organization

Introduction

The descriptions of shipboard organization that precede this chapter have all dealt with the basic administrative structure of a ship. Beyond that framework of departments and divisions, there exists a need for another kind of organization aboard ship—the watch organization. The people who form the watch organization allow the ship to carry out important missions and to travel from one area of the world to another while continuing her normal administrative and maintenance routines. Shipboard manpower and space limitations, however, make it necessary for most crew members to be part of both the administrative organization and the watch organization.

Purpose of the Underway Watch Organization

As part of the watch organization, shipboard personnel stand watches. "Standing a watch" generally entails being in a specific location or "station" aboard ship in order to operate machinery, to observe the activities of other ships or aircraft, to provide communication services, or to coordinate the activities of various other watchstanders. Although the majority of a ship's officers and crew are part of the underway watch organization, the watches are structured so that normally only a portion of the ship's personnel are on watch at one time. This structure allows a ship to steam from ocean to ocean, to conduct surveillance, and to perform numerous other communication, logistic, and weaponry-related missions while carrying on everyday administrative and maintenance activities.

The watch organization, then, has several important and distinct purposes. Watchstanders operate or coordinate the operation of a ship's essential equipment. The watch organization provides external and internal security for the ship, as will be demonstrated shortly. Watchstanders also maintain both internal and external shipboard communications. Furthermore, the watch organization increases a ship's efficiency both by establishing a schedule for manning important

16

Figure 2-1. A view of the bridge of the destroyer USS Spruance, DD-963.

stations with fresh, alert personnel and by freeing other crew members to conduct routine business or rest.

Watch Officer

Persons in charge of various watch stations are frequently termed *watch officers*. However, an unusual aspect of this title is that a watch officer need not always be a commissioned officer. A watch officer's duties are dependent upon the particular station being manned. There are stations whose associated duties are frequently more suited to a senior enlisted man than to a commissioned officer. These stations are thus manned by enlisted watch officers.

The duties of watchstanding, especially for commissioned officers, are significantly different from those associated with departmental or divisional jobs.

For example, the gunnery division officer may find himself manning a watch officer station on the bridge of a ship and having responsibility for maneuvering in or out of port. When not on watch, he returns to his divisional duties of managing and maintaining his portion of the ship's armament.

Figure 2-2. The junior officer of the deck, conning.

There are other important differences between acting as a division officer or department head and acting as a watch officer. A watch officer can have people of various ratings from several ship departments working for him at the same time. A division officer or department head, on the other hand, supervises only those personnel assigned to his own division or department, respectively.

Officers frequently have more opportunities to exercise initiative and to demonstrate nautical skills when standing a watch. As a watch officer, a division officer or department head can qualify for greater responsibilities and authority. His professional knowledge is often vigorously tested. Thus, although the administrative and supervisory duties of a division officer or department head are extremely important, it is as a watch officer that an individual generally finds shipboard duty most rewarding.

Organizing the Watches

As long as a ship is in commission in the U.S. Navy, there will be a watch organization in effect and personnel on board to man important stations 24 hours a day. The watch organization is described in the ship's *Standard Organization and Regulations Manual* (SORM, OPNAVINST 3120.32), which allows a ship to structure the watches to be stood into distinct time periods and to organize watch personnel into teams or sections.

Watch Periods and Sections

The term *watch* is used in several ways. Usually it is thought of as any one of the periods into which the day is divided, as in the following list.

0000-0400—Midwatch
0400-0800—Morning watch
0800-1200—Forenoon watch
1200-1600—Afternoon watch
1600-1800—First dogwatch
1800-2000—Second dogwatch
2000-2400—Evening watch

The 1600 to 2000 watch is often dogged; that is, it is shortened to allow the men to be relieved to eat evening meal. This divides each 24-hour period into seven watches. Dog watches also serve to alternate the daily watch routine so that sailors with the mid-watch one night will not have it again the next evening.

A *watch section* is the term used to refer to the group or team of enlisted personnel who stand watch together as a unit, although each member of the group may be posted at a different station. A ship may have enough enlisted men to establish several sections, each of which would be numbered. When the word is passed that the first section (or the second, or the third, etc.) has the watch, each man in that section reports immediately to his watch station. This watch station might be one requiring his specialty, as a radarman operating a radar repeater, for example, or it may require the performance of a general military duty, such as that of a sentry.

Senior Watch Officer

Because commissioned officers are not designated as members of enlisted watch sections, their assignments within the watch organization are handled separately. The officer watch sections are normally comprised of most of the ship's department heads and division officers. The commanding officer and the executive officer stand no watches.

The most senior officer qualified and designated to stand watch is given the administrative title and collateral duty of *senior watch officer*. He is responsible for the training and qualification of the other officers who stand watch. The senior watch officer assigns the other commissioned officers to a section and keeps the executive officer advised of their performance.

The specific type of watch or watch station an officer will be assigned to, when his section is scheduled to be on duty, depends upon his experience, his qualifications, and his eligibility for command. (Eligibility for command is determined by an officer's job specialty, training, and any restrictions on the types of work he is allowed to do.) Occasionally, the senior watch officer may designate a very experienced senior enlisted man as a member of an officer watch section, but only to stand a specific type of watch.

Watch Bills

Typically, a small ship will have enough personnel to establish four individual watch sections for both officers and enlisted men. As each watch time period passes, a different watch section will "relieve the watch" and assume the duties of the watch stations. This procedure allows other officers and members of the crew to come off watch to attend to their normal administrative and maintenance responsibilities. Thus, when the ship is under way, each watchstander can expect to be on watch duty six to eight hours out of every 24, in addition to his usual work.

In order to inform the members of each watch section when and where they will be standing watch, a *watch bill* is posted. The commissioned officers generally have their own bill, and the enlisted watchstanders consult the *Watch, Quarter, and Station bill* posted in their respective divisional working or berthing compartments. An example of a typical Watch, Quarter, and Station bill was shown in figure 1-7. Note that Seaman E. E. Easy is designated to stand a sea watch as a starboard lookout when watch section number one is on duty. As the reader will recall, the bill also displays the duties of each man during emergencies, special details, and various administrative assignments.

The Underway Watch Organization

The underway watch organization is generally standard from one ship to another. One ship may have a few more or a few less persons on watch than will another ship; however, these minor differences are usually dependent upon a ship's size, its current tactical operations, and perhaps its degree of automation.

The standard watch organization framework is especially useful when training new officers and enlisted crew members. It facilitates the learning process and does not require that individuals be completely retrained when transferred to another Navy ship.

Four Major Watch Stations

There are several key personnel watch assignments in the underway watch organization. In order to clarify these assignments, their respective responsibilities, and especially their relationships and interactions with one another, it is helpful to group them into four major areas or watch stations. The reader must recognize, however, that these four major watch stations encompass numerous individual stations and positions.

It is very important, too, for the reader to grasp the relationships between the key watchstanders and the commanding officer and executive officer.

The commanding officer heads the watch organization. All watchstanders are ultimately responsible to him for their performance and look to him for policy guidelines and tactical decisions.

However, because the commanding officer must attend to many other duties, he may each day appoint another very qualified officer to handle routine shipboard operational or watch-related matters for him. This officer is titled the *command duty officer* (CDO), is eligible for command at sea, and generally has the CDO watch for an entire day. He maintains close communications with the four major watch stations and is empowered by the captain to advise, supervise, and direct key watchstanders in matters concerning the general operation and safety of the ship. Many large ships have an underway command duty officer on watch whenever they are at sea. He reports to the commanding

Figure 2-3. Communication is the voice of command.

officer for the conduct of his watch and to the executive officer for affairs relating to the internal administration of the ship. Routine reports made to the captain are generally made to the CDO as well. The command duty officer has no specific watch station but usually remains in close proximity to the ship's bridge.

The Bridge and Deck Watch

The *bridge* is the primary control point from which a ship is maneuvered. Because ships were at one time steered from a specific location or deck, the bridge station is still often referred to as the deck watch. The bridge watch station is central to the underway watch organization. From the bridge the other three major watch stations are monitored and directed. The duties of the bridge watchstanders are described below.

The OOD

The individual in charge of the bridge watch station is called the *Officer of the Deck* (OOD). He is generally considered the most important person in the underway watch organization other than the commanding officer and CDO. His responsibilities are very broad, and he is actually in charge of the ship for the captain (and the CDO if one is appointed). All watchstanders report either directly or indirectly to the OOD for operational purposes. All ship's company officers, except the executive officer or other officers specified either by Navy Regulations or by the commanding officer, are subordinate to the officer of the deck. He speaks with the authority of the commanding officer, but, of course, the commanding officer remains ultimately responsible for the proper operation and safety of the ship. The OOD does not ordinarily concern himself with the administrative affairs of the ship's departments.

The officer of the deck sees that the established routine of the ship is carried out as published in the Plan of the Day along with any special orders or other written directives. He keeps the executive officer informed of any changes required in the ship's routine and advises him of any administrative matter requiring attention during the watch.

The OOD keeps himself informed on all aspects of the current operation plan with which the ship is complying and remains constantly alert for any new orders from the officer in tactical command (OTC), usually a high-ranking officer designated to direct the movements of several ships traveling together.

The officer of the deck is also responsible for issuing the necessary orders to change the course and speed of the ship. He is not authorized, however, to make any significant, lengthy course or speed alterations

Figure 2-4. The officer of the deck takes a reading on a gyro repeater.

without notifying the commanding officer of his actions. The OOD must keep himself informed of the operating condition and capabilities of the engineering plant and its associated propulsion equipment, and he should always advise the person in charge of the engineering watch stations of any anticipated changes in power requirements.

The OOD must know the navigational position of his ship and be aware of all other hazards to the safety of the vessel. He employs any means that are available to him for detecting and avoiding danger from grounding or collision. When there is imminent danger of grounding or collision, he takes immediate action to minimize and localize any damage that might occur. The OOD must know the Rules of the Road and comply with them, and when steaming in formation with other ships, it is his duty to ensure that his ship keeps her assigned station.

The officer of the deck promptly reports to the commanding officer all matters which might affect the safety of the ship, the crew, or other ships traveling in company. These matters include such things as: the proximity of land, shoals, buoys, discolored water, and wrecks; marked changes in the barometer; the force or direction of the wind; the state of the sea; all changes of formation course or speed ordered by the officer in tactical command; and all serious accidents.

Routine Reports   Other routine reports are made to the commanding officer by the OOD's bridge messenger or similar representative. These reports include the twelve o'clock report and any unusual circumstances or departure from the planned ship's routine.

As general guidance, the OOD reports to the commanding officer all occurrences worthy of his notice and to the executive officer all matters of a purely administrative nature. When a CDO is appointed or when a flag officer is embarked, similar reports are usually made to them.

Relationship of OOD To Other Officers

As was mentioned earlier, the command duty officer under way, when appointed, is authorized to advise and direct the OOD in matters concerning the general operation and safety of the ship. That authority is also shared by the executive officer, who is further authorized to relieve the OOD and assume charge of the bridge if he judges such action to be necessary. The CDO can relieve the OOD in this manner only if he has the prior written consent of the commanding officer to exercise such judgment. The commanding officer can, of course, direct and relieve the OOD whenever he wishes.

One other officer sometimes has this unusual relationship with the officer of the deck. The navigator routinely advises the OOD of a safe course to steer, and the officer of the deck must regard such advice as sufficient authorization to change the ship's course. The OOD must, however, report the change to the captain at once. Additionally, if the navigator has been granted proper authority in a standing written directive from the commanding officer, he may relieve the OOD and assume charge of the bridge if he determines that emergency maneuvering is necessary for the safety of the ship, and if he judges that he will be better able to navigate the ship than will the officer of the deck.

Thus, the commanding officer, executive officer, and navigator (conditionally) have authority to assume charge of the bridge anytime such action is deemed warranted.

Relieving the Watch

Near the end of each watch, word is passed for the next watch section to replace those now on station. Watches must be relieved on time. Officially, the watch change occurs 15 minutes before the hour, but watchstanders should be completing the relieving process at that point. Thus, relieving on time does not mean relieving at the exact minute the watch changes, but slightly earlier, from 5 to 15 minutes, depending on the type of watch and the routine of the particular ship. This time difference is essential so that the relief can receive information and instructions from the man he is to relieve on watch, as well as from other sources, such as the the combat information center (CIC), the navigation chart, logs, status boards, captain's night orders, standing orders, and any other directives containing information necessary to run the watch. Furthermore, the new watchstanders must take time to let their eyes adapt to night vision after sunset.

When reporting directly to the officer to be relieved, an officer will salute and say, "I am ready to relieve you, sir." The officer being relieved returns the salute and states that he is ready to be relieved (if he is). That officer then passes on to his relief any pertinent instructions or information relating to the proper standing of the watch.

When the relief is sure that he understands the conditions and any instructions given to him, he salutes again, saying, "I relieve you, sir," to which the officer being relieved responds, "I stand relieved," returning the salute. On the bridge, the officer relieved then announces to the watch section that, "Mr. _____ has the deck," or "Mr. _____ has the deck and the conn," as the case may be. Immediately thereafter, the man assuming the duty is completely responsible for the watch. The new OOD, upon assuming the watch, announces to the watch sections, "This is Mr. _____, I have the conn," or "This is Mr. _____, I have the deck and the conn." If the captain is on the bridge, the new OOD will, upon relieving his predecessor, salute the commanding officer and report that he has assumed the watch.

This procedure is standard throughout the Navy and is important for the newly commissioned officer to master.

The JOOD

The OOD's principal assistant on the bridge is the *junior officer of the deck* (JOOD). He assists the OOD in carrying out the duties of the watch in any way the OOD desires. He answers the radio telephone, breaks coded messages, etc. At the same time, it is one of the JOOD's first concerns to learn as much as possible about standing deck watches so that he can qualify to be an officer of the deck in his own right. As part of that learning process, the OOD often gives to the junior officer of the deck the *conn*; that is, the authority to order course and speed changes. The OOD should always retain the *deck*, that is, the authority and responsibility for the bridge and the ship. On some ships, the OOD is assisted by another junior officer who may be assigned as junior officer of the watch (JOOW). The JOOW duties are usually similar to those of the JOOD.

The BMOW

The rest of the bridge watch station personnel are enlisted men who have various duties and responsibilities. These enlisted personnel, while under the authority of the OOD, are managed and supervised by the watch section's *boatswain's mate of the watch* (BMOW).

The BMOW is the OOD's principal enlisted assistant. It is his responsibility to see that all the individual deck watch stations are manned and that all men in the previous watch section have been relieved. Although it is the responsibility of a man's division officer and petty officers to properly instruct him prior to assigning him to a watch section for duty, the BMOW must verify that every man in his bridge section has been properly trained. It is also up to the BMOW to remind

Figure 2-5. A boatswain's mate piping a call.

the OOD of announcements to be made over the ship's public address system. The BMOW makes announcements in compliance with the Plan of the Day, but must obtain permission from the OOD before doing so. A BMOW must be a qualified helmsman and should have adequate experience on the bridge to be of assistance to the OOD during emergencies.

The QMOW

Most of the enlisted personnel assigned to deck watches and the bridge station come from the deck or weapons department. However,

Figure 2-6. A quartermaster of the watch.

the *quartermaster of the watch* (QMOW) is assigned from the navigation department. He maintains the ship's log (which is a legal record) and assists the OOD in navigational matters. He plots the ship's course on the bridge's navigational chart and advises the OOD concerning weather and shipping likely to be encountered. The QMOW also aids the OOD by keeping the navigator up to date on the ship's position.

Figure 2-7. The helmsman and lee helmsman.

The QMOW alerts the navigator and the OOD to any significant course and speed changes required and informs them of any navigation aids available to the ship. The QMOW is expected to be a qualified helmsman and regularly supervises the training of other helmsmen.

The Helmsman

The *helmsman*, also called the steersman, is normally assigned from the weapons or deck department. He is responsible for steering the ship as ordered by the officer who has the conn. This conning officer is of course, normally the OOD or JOOD.

The Lee Helmsman

The *lee helmsman* is usually a seaman from the weapons or deck department and is responsible for transmitting ship's speed and direction orders to the engineering watch personnel as he receives them from the conning officer. The orders are transmitted from the bridge to the engineering spaces primarily by use of the *engine order telegraph* (EOT). The lee helmsman also mans the 1JV, the maneuvering and docking sound-powered telephone circuit. This circuit puts him in communication with all the individual watch stations involved in the safe maneuvering of the ship. Thus, if the EOT malfunctions, he can transmit engine orders verbally. The lee helmsman ensures that the engine orders are recognized and properly answered by the engineering personnel. Some ships with automated methods of speed and direction control on the bridge may not require a lee helmsman station.

Messenger

The *messenger of the watch*, normally a young seaman from the deck department, along with the other enlisted watchstanders, reports to the BMOW for the performance of his duties. He is a very useful member of the watch and may be given assignments by the BMOW or OOD. He runs messages, wakens watch reliefs, delivers routine reports, and relieves lookouts, the lee helm, or helm—all as the OOD directs, allowing other watchstanders to rotate among the individual stations.

Lookouts

Navy radar and sonar gear can detect many things, but there are some things that may escape detection because of their size, aspect, altitude, or because of the weather. Such things as smoke, small navigation markers, objects close to the ship, flares, or men in the water must be reported by the *lookouts*. Additionally, lookouts perform a vital function in recognition of ship types, color of navigation

Figure 2-8.   The "eyes" of the ship, the lookout.

markers, characteristics of navigational lights, and the many other sightings that electronics cannot provide.

Lookouts on watch are under the direct charge of the boatswain's mate of the watch. He assigns them to their stations, and he must be sure that they are properly clothed, instructed, and equipped. Training of lookouts is normally the responsibility of the operations department.

The number of lookouts and how they are assigned depends upon the ship's characteristics and the number of men on board. For example, small ships generally have three men in each watch assigned to lookout duties, one man for the port side, one for the starboard side, and one as after lookout who also acts as the life buoy watch. As a life buoy watch he is equipped with a life ring, which he will throw to anyone who falls overboard. He must remain very alert for such an emergency. Each lookout is stationed at the location where he can best cover the surface and sky within his zone. Large ships take advantage of their greater number of men to obtain better coverage by stationing both surface lookouts and air lookouts.

Lookouts must listen, as well as look, to enable them to hear sounds such as whistle signals, bells, and engine noises. Aircraft, some buoys, and a man in distress can often be detected by the sounds they make.

During normal steaming, a lookout is equipped with a sound-powered telephone headset and binoculars. He reports all sightings and unusual sounds over the (JL) battle lookout circuit. Reports are made to the combat information center (CIC) and to a telephone talker on the bridge who relays the information to the OOD.

In fog or thick weather, additional lookouts should be stationed in the forwardmost part of the ship (the eyes of the ship) and on the bridge wings. The bow lookouts watch for objects ahead, and the after lookout scans for anything that might overhaul the ship from astern. Each must continually search his sector. Sometimes a swirl of wind thins the mist for a second, long enough for him to look around and possibly spot something in the nick of time.

Sound carries much farther in a fog than on clear days, so a lookout must listen closely, especially if he is in the bow, for the sound of whistles, bells, buoys, and the like. For this reason, fog lookouts do not wear sound-powered phones. A sound-powered telephone talker will man the required phones at each fog lookout station. Even the wash of water against a ship's stem carries a long distance in a fog. A fog lookout must keep alert, listening in every direction, maintaining absolute silence, and quieting anyone who makes any unnecessary noise near him. He must not wait to figure out where a sound is coming from before he reports it. Fog plays tricks in this respect. A sound may seem to come from one direction while it is actually coming from another.

Lookout Reports

All reports must be made quickly, clearly, and accurately, adhering strictly to established procedures. All visual sightings are reported in bearing and range for surface sightings, and in bearing and position angle for aircraft. The words bearing and range may be omitted from the reports.

All bearings are given relative to the ship's bow, starting at 000° and increasing clockwise through 360°. Bearings are reported in three digits, digit by digit.

Bearing	Spoken as
000°	Zero Zero Zero
010°	Zero Wun Zero
315°	Thuh-ree Wun Fi-yiv

Range of an object is given in yards and is reported digit by digit except that exact multiples of hundreds are spoken as such.

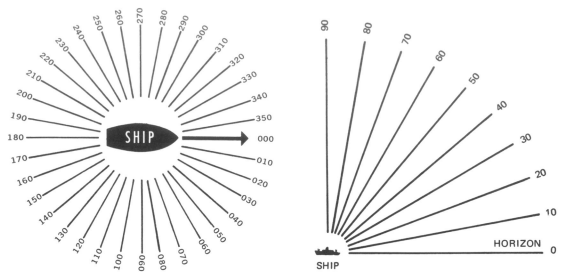

Figure 2-9. All sightings are reported in relative bearings by lookouts.

Number of Yards	Spoken as
44	Fo-wer Fo-wer
90	Niner Zero
136	Wun Thuh-ree Six
500	Fi-yiv Hundred
7,000	Seven Thow-zand

Here are some examples of visual sighting reports:

"Discolored water (bearing) Thuh-ree Fo-wer Zero, (range) Too Thow-zand." (Discolored water on a bearing of 340° relative to the bow of the ship and at a distance of 2,000 yards.)

"Aircraft Too Ate Zero, position angle Thirty, (range) Niner Thow-zand." (An aircraft bearing 280° relative to bow of ship, at an angle of 30° above the horizon, and at a distance of 9,000 yards.)

Scanning

The lookout's method of visual search is called *scanning*, a step-by-step method of searching. The lookout looks at small areas for short periods of time, then moves his eyes to another small area. Normally, the search begins at the aftermost edge of the sector assigned and continues forward in consecutive steps of five degrees. Bow and stern lookouts would begin their search at either the port or starboard limit of their sectors.

Phone Talkers

The lookouts' reports are received on the bridge by a phone talker who relays the information to the OOD. The phone talker is a vital link between the OOD and many of his information sources. Of utmost importance to every watchstander is a complete working knowledge of sound-powered telephones.

Sound-powered phones are of two types: handset and headset. In general, handset phones are used for routine ship's business. (For example, the captain calling the ship's office, or the engineroom calling the bridge.) The headset phones, on the other hand, are used for ship drills and operations.

The handset telephone looks much like a home telephone. It is held in one hand with the receiver next to one ear and the mouthpiece in front of the mouth. There is a button on the bar between the receiver and mouthpiece, and this button has to be pressed before talking. It should be held down only when in use, otherwise the mouthpiece picks up other noises in the area. This added noise makes it difficult for men on other handsets to understand one another.

When not in use, the handset phone rests in its bracket. This is a spring and level device attached to the bulkhead that keeps the phone from getting jarred loose. When fitting it into the bracket, it must fit securely, or it could fall out and be damaged.

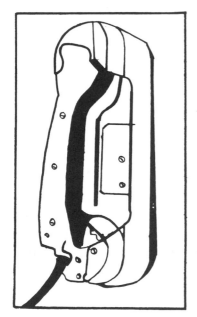

Figure 2-10. Sound-powered handset, (left). Sound-powered headset, (right).

The headset telephone is somewhat more complicated than the handset, but it has special advantages. Though it is carried around in the area of the station, the talker's hands are free for other uses except when depressing the mouthpiece button to talk). The phone is built around a breastplate. Supported on the chest by cloth neckstraps, the breastplate bears a yoke which, in turn, mounts the mouthpiece. The earphones are supported by a metal or fiber headband. The mouthpiece and the earphones are connected by cords (rubber-insulated wire) to the junction block on the breastplate. From the bottom of the junction block runs the lead cord. This cord may be 15, 25, 35, or even 50 feet in length, depending on the needs of that station. It ends in a metal plug called a jack which is plugged into a jackbox on the bulkhead in order to gain access to a phone circuit.

Sound-powered telephone circuits provide means for communication between selected battle stations grouped on established circuits. No dialing is necessary: when you plug into one of these circuits, you immediately have communication with anyone who is plugged in on the same circuit.

Sound-powered telephone circuits vary in number according to the size and mission of the ship. Circuits are designated by standard symbols, each symbol consisting of two, three, or possibly four letters. The sound-powered telephone circuits found aboard most ships include:

> JA Captain's battle circuit
> JL Battle lookouts circuit
> 1JV Maneuvering and docking circuit

When talking on a sound-powered telephone, it is important to relay information in an orderly fashion. *Most* sound-powered telephone messages have three parts:

1. The name of the station being called.
2. The name of the station doing the calling.
3. The message itself.

These three parts must be spoken in the order given. Call the station that the message is for, identify your own station, and finally, give the words of the message itself. Dangerous confusion can result if this order is not maintained. A typical message would go like this: "Bridge, forecastle; anchor ready for letting go."

Messages must be acknowledged as soon as understood. To acknowledge, you identify your station and say, "Aye, aye." This way, the sender knows that you have received and understood the message. If, for example, your station is forecastle, say "Forecastle, aye, aye"—not just "Aye, aye." (Forecastle is pronounced fo'c's'le.)

When a message is very important, the sender may want to make sure that it has been received correctly. In this case, the sender will ask the receiving station to repeat the message back to him. The message would then be repeated back by the receiving station word for word.

In talking, leave out unnecessary words. Words like "Please" and "If you don't mind" merely lengthen the message and slow things up. If a message is a long one, it should be broken into parts to make it clearer.

When messages are being sent and the control station has a more important message to get through, the control talker says, "Silence on the line." All other stations must then stop talking.

The Combat Information Center Watch

The *combat information center* (CIC) watch station is often referred to as the nerve center of the ship. It is in CIC that much of the ship's electronic surveillance, communications, and tactical planning are done. A wide range of electronic equipment is installed in CIC: radar, sonar, electronic warfare intercept receivers, radio and visual communications, display screens, and computers. Numbers and specific types of equipment installations differ from ship to ship; but the mission of CIC to collect, process, display, evaluate, and disseminate information from sources both inside and outside the ship does not change. The responsibilities of the combat information center watchstanders are described below.

The CICWO

The *combat information center watch officer* (CICWO), is in charge of CIC during his watch and is responsible for the proper and timely performance of its mission. The CICWO is normally a commissioned officer, but a senior enlisted CIC watchstander may at times be designated as the CIC watch officer, especially on small ships. It is the responsibility of the CIC watch officer to ensure (1) that radar and sonar operators are detecting and reporting air, surface, and subsurface contacts within the capabilities of their equipment; (2) that plotters are obtaining accurate solutions to contact tracking problems; (3) that voice radio and telephone circuits are properly manned; and (4) that a CIC navigational plot is maintained as a backup to that of the bridge's QMOW.

The CICWO also is required to review, evaluate, and disseminate operational information received in the combat information center by means of voice radio, radar, sonar, electronic warfare equipment,

Figure 2-11. Keeping watch. Crewmen aboard the amphibious cargo ship USS El Paso (LKA 117) keep up with landing craft operations by radar, charting moves on the plotting table in the ship's combat information center.

visual lookouts, direction finders, various television detection and display devices, and messages.

The CIC watch officer makes numerous recommendations to the officer of the deck, including suggestions for maintaining station in a formation, avoiding navigational hazards and collisions, and changing course or speed as necessary to accomplish a maneuver.

Enlisted Watch Supervisor

Assisting the CIC watch officer in supervising the equipment operators and in maintaining various CIC logs is the combat information center *enlisted watch supervisor*. The enlisted watch supervisor is a relatively senior enlisted man who ensures that CIC personnel on watch perform their jobs in a professional manner, and when necessary, he operates equipment, plots, and works maneuvering problems himself to facilitate the flow of information. The logs kept for and by the enlisted watch supervisor serve as complete and accurate written chronological accounts of both routine and unusual events pertaining to a CIC watch. The enlisted watch supervisor, because of his experience, is often further able to assist the CIC watch officer by participating in the evaluation of information to be passed to the OOD.

In some newer ships the CIC is organized into modules, each of which is specialized in electronic warfare, or antisubmarine warfare, or antiair warfare, etc. A *module supervisor* may be assigned for each of those areas. Their activities are coordinated and supervised by the CICWO.

CIC Enlisted Ratings

Personnel with various enlisted ratings perform duties in the combat information center from time to time. Some of the most common of those ratings are mentioned below.

Operations Specialist (OS): OSs operate radar, navigation, and communications equipment; keep logs; detect, track, and plot ships, planes, and missiles; maintain CIC displays and status boards; work maneuvering board problems; and break coded radio transmissions for the OOD.

Sonar Technician (ST): STs operate and repair sonar equipment; detect and track underwater objects; repair antisubmarine warfare fire-control equipment; maintain and operate underwater communications equipment; maintain and operate the ship's depth sounder for safe navigation; and provide some ocean meteorological information to the OOD and QMOW.

Electronic Warfare Technician (EW): EWs operate and maintain various electronic equipments that intercept and interpret incoming electronic signals to determine their source; they operate equipment designed to prevent or increase the difficulty of electronic spying by enemies; maintain and operate equipment used to disrupt enemy electromagnetic transmissions; and provide repair services for various other electronic equipments requiring their expertise.

The Communications Watch Station

Communications are a vital part of any ship operation. Most communication between ships is by radiotelephone, radioteletype, or visual means.

The CWO

The watchstander responsible to the OOD for the proper performance of the ship's communication equipment and for the proper receipt and transmission of visual and written messages is the *communications watch officer* (CWO). In large ships, junior commissioned officers from the operations department are frequently assigned CWO watches. In small ships, however, the watch is generally stood by an operations department senior enlisted petty officer or chief with a radioman rating.

The CWO ensures that voice radio circuits are properly set up for use by the OOD and CIC watch personnel. He also ensures that all outgoing and incoming radioteletype message traffic is in the correct form, promptly handled, and efficiently distributed.

Visual communications are the responsibility of the CWO, as well. A visual watch section composed of signalmen mans the ship's signal bridge to send and answer flashing lights, signal flaghoists, and

Figure 2-12. The communications watch in radio central.

Figure 2-13. *A signalman third class aboard the attack carrier* USS John F. Kennedy *(CVA-67) looks through the ship's binoculars.*

semaphore messages as directed by the officer of the deck. The communications watch officer monitors the performance of the signal bridge watch and directly supervises the radiomen in the ship's main communications compartment, radio central.

Radio Watch and Signal Bridge Supervisors

The specific duties of enlisted personnel assigned communications duties (radio operators and signalmen) vary according to the size, location, and mission of a ship. During the period of his watch, the communications watch officer is assisted by other senior petty officers in the supervision and control of the signal bridge and radio central. One such assistant is the *radio watch supervisor* who monitors the frequencies in use, inspects message traffic and logs to detect errors by his operators, and takes immediate action to notify the CWO, the bridge, and the operations department officers in the event of any equipment failure.

Another assistant to the CWO is the *signal bridge supervisor*. This supervisor keeps the other signalmen informed as to the location of ships to or from which messages may be sent, ensures that watchstanders know the meanings of all signals, and maintains all visual equipment ready for use.

The Underway Shipboard Watch and Battle Organization   **39**

The Engineering Watch Station

Providing a ship's propulsion, electrical power, fresh water, and the prevention of flooding, fire, and associated emergencies are the responsibilities of the engineering watch. However, the specific duties associated with the various positions manned by the engineering department are dependent upon the nature of a ship's propulsion plant equipment. New gas-turbine ships have different engineering requirements than do conventionally powered steam ships or ships with nuclear propulsion plants. Despite such differences, the engineering watch must be alert and responsible to the power and maneuvering demands of the bridge.

The EOOW

The engineering watch station is managed and supervised during each underway watch time period by an *engineering officer of the watch* (EOOW). This position requires much experience and is especially critical to the safe operation of the ship. The EOOW is generally a senior engineering enlisted petty officer or chief designated as qualified to stand EOOW by the engineering department head. During his watch, the EOOW is responsible to the officer of the deck for the proper operation of the ship's engineering plant.

Figure 2-14. Making sure all systems are operating properly in the engineering spaces is the job of the EOOW.

The EOOW ensures that all orders from the officer of the deck are promptly acknowledged and executed. He is required to report immediately to the OOD and to the engineering officer any casualty to, or shut down of, a major machinery unit that directly affects available propulsion power, ship control, offensive or defensive capability, or habitability of the ship.

The engineering officer of the watch must keep himself informed of the ship's power requirements for all operations, current and future. The EOOW must also ensure that all engineering watchstanders and patrols are alert for emergencies and that they maintain proper ship security. The EOOW is further required to see that the engineer's bell book and other engineering logs are kept correctly.

Sounding and Security Patrol

In order to be sure that the ship is maintaining as high a degree of watertight integrity below the waterline as possible, a *sounding and security patrol* watchstander walks a continuous circuit about the ship, checking and rechecking for flooding, especially in unmanned spaces. In addition, this engineering department petty officer takes periodic soundings of designated ship tanks and spaces to determine the amount of fuel or water they contain. He checks damage-control closures and stays alert for evidence of sabotage, thievery, fire, and fire hazards.

This watch is maintained while under way and when in port. The sounding and security patrol makes periodic reports of his findings to the OOD or his representative and alerts the ship should any emergency arise.

After Steering Watch

Another watch of some importance is the one stood in after steering. This watch station, although technically the responsibility of the engineering department, is operationally connected with the bridge. From the after steering compartment, watchstanders monitor the steering engines, and in the event of a steering casualty or a bridge equipment malfunction, the watch can remotely take over steering control from the bridge helmsman, as directed by the OOD.*

A quartermaster from the navigation department normally stands this watch. As a qualified helmsman, he is able to control the ship properly from the after steering position and can understand helm orders from the bridge relayed to him over the 1JV sound-powered telephone circuit.

A Machinist's Mate (MM) or Electrician's Mate (EM) from the engineering department is often stationed in after steering as part of

Figure 2-15. Crewmen man their duty stations in the command and control center of the destroyer USS Spruance *(DD-963).*

the watch. This individual aids in switching steering units and handles emergency electrical or mechanical repairs to the steering equipment.

Special Faith and Trust

It is important to remember that the OOD is responsible to the commanding officer for the coordinated action of all the watch stations and for the safe and proper operation of the ship. A CICWO, CWO, and EOOW assist the officer of the deck in carrying out the ship's assignments during each underway watch. The special faith and trust the captain places in the OOD to protect the ship and to manage the ship's watch stations extend to every watchstander. Each job and position in the watch organization is important to success.

Watch Conditions of Readiness

The core of the shipboard watch organization is considered to be the four watch stations just discussed—the bridge watch, the CIC watch,

*On many newer ships, after steering is not manned except during certain critical evolutions (e.g. during underway replenishment, maneuvering in or out of port). At other times engineering watch personnel are only seconds away should after steering be required to take steering control.

the communications watch, and the engineering watch. A ship's watch organization does retain the flexibility to change its shape to some degree, however, depending on the likelihood of encountering an enemy threat.

A ship's watch organization is thus structured and governed by *watch conditions of readiness*. These watch conditions of readiness represent different degrees of battle preparedness that a ship must be able to meet. Watch conditions of readiness are prescribed by higher level commanders and may be upgraded by a ship's commanding officer, if necessary.

Along with a ship's watch condition of readiness, which affects the number of positions manned by the crew and the weaponry prepared for use, a ship sets a certain *material condition of readiness*. These material conditions of readiness concern the closing and opening of watertight doors and hatches and are discussed in detail in chapter 12.

The basic underway watch conditions of readiness are:

> Condition IV—Peacetime cruising
> Condition III—Wartime cruising
> Condition II—Modified general quarters
> Condition I—General quarters

The following paragraphs provide a more detailed description of how each watch condition of readiness affects the watch organization.

Condition IV

During Watch Condition of Readiness IV, peacetime cruising, the four major watch stations are manned for routine operations. Normal underway maintenance is carried out, and none of the ship's weaponry

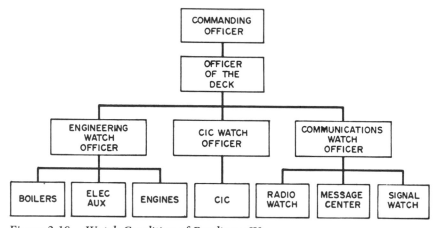

Figure 2-16. Watch Condition of Readiness IV.

systems are manned. The material condition of readiness is a modified condition *Yoke*. The bridge watch is alert, but expects no enemy attack. This watch condition of readiness is the one under which U.S. Navy ships most frequently operate.

Condition III

Watch Condition of Readiness III, wartime cruising, is established when it is likely or possible that a ship may encounter sudden enemy attack. During this watch condition, CIC and the other watch stations are manned by additional personnel. These added watchstanders give each station an increased degree of readiness and upgrade the capability to respond to an attack. CIC, for example, can handle and evaluate more vital information, if necessary.

Weapons Control Officer

The ship's essential maintenance and administrative routines continue during Watch Condition of Readiness III; however, a portion of the ship's weapons systems are manned and ready for action. An officer is thus required to coordinate and directly supervise the employment of the weaponry, when ordered to do so. This weapons liaison or *weapons control officer* is an addition to the basic watch organization. He normally mans the 1JC sound-powered telephone circuit to communicate with both CIC and the weapon stations.

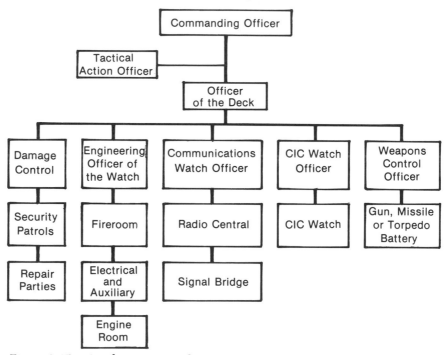

Figure 2-17. Condition III Watch.

Tactical Action Officer

Because of the necessity for rapid defensive reaction against an urgent threat encountered during wartime cruising conditions, and because the commanding officer himself cannot possibly be on the bridge 24 hours a day to direct such a sudden emergency response, the chief of naval operations has authorized a ship's commanding officer to assign an experienced officer to a watch position for that specific purpose. This officer, the *tactical action officer* (TAO), is responsible for the operation of the ship's combat systems when hostile forces are engaged. He initiates a response against an urgent threat through the weapons control officer and as quickly as the situation permits, informs the commanding officer and the OOD of such action. The TAO has the authority to direct the OOD as necessary to counter a hostile threat.

As the executive officer and the department heads of a small ship are the most experienced officers, they are normally the only officers designated by the captain to stand a tactical action officer watch. The TAO stands his watch where he is best able to direct the action, usually in CIC. During this watch condition, the CICWO is subordinate to the TAO and assists him as directed. During certain operations, the TAO may be called the *evaluator* or may be assisted by an additional watch-stander with that title.

Damage Control Watch Officer

During operations requiring the increased readiness of Condition III, enemy attack is possible and, as a result, so is damage to your ship. Material condition Yoke is normally set during this watch condition; however, in order to limit and repair any damage suffered, the Condition III watch organization also requires that a damage control team must be on station and ready for action. This team is directed by a *damage control watch officer* from DC Central, the onboard headquarters for damage control activity. The damage control assistant (DCA), a division officer in the engineering department, is usually designated to stand this watch.

Conditions II and I

During Watch Condition of Readiness I, general quarters, a ship's entire complement of officers and enlisted personnel are stationed so that every weapons system and watch position is fully manned. The ship is completely ready to engage hostile forces. Material condition Zebra is set, giving the ship maximum protection from the spread of fire and flooding.

During long periods of general quarters, a ship's commanding officer may establish Watch Condition of Readiness II, modified general

Figure 2-18.   The evaluator is the hub and directing force of the CIC team.

quarters, if he does not anticipate immediate hostilities. Modified general quarters is set to allow a brief, on-station period of relaxation for the crew or to allow battle messing.

The watch organization for Conditions I, II, and III is essentially the same. The major watch stations themselves remain unchanged. During Watch Condition of Readiness I or II, however, there are more individual positions to be manned. As mentioned, *all*, rather than a portion, of the ship's weapons and surveillance systems are manned. Additional damage control teams are also required.

A ship's department heads usually play a more significant role in the Condition I and II watch organization. The specific duties assigned to a department head during these conditions differ from ship to ship; nevertheless, there are some commonalities.

The captain takes his place as head of the watch organization and directs the battle from the bridge or from the combat information center. The executive officer will normally assume the duties of the tactical action officer unless the commanding officer desires him to assist the OOD on the bridge.

The navigator assumes his position on the bridge to provide information to the captain and the officer of the deck. The operations department head may assume the duties of OOD, act as TAO, or provide control for both CIC and the comunications watch station, according to the wishes of the commanding officer.

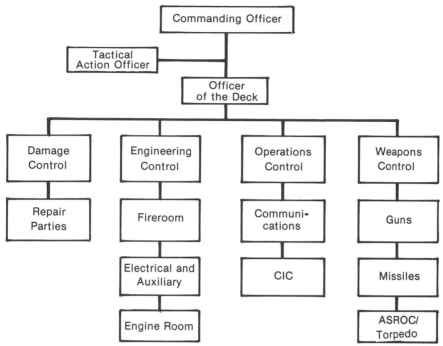

Figure 2-19. Condition I Watch.

The engineering officer normally provides supervision of the engineering watch along with the EOOW, or he may direct the damage control teams from DC Central with the DCA as his assistant. The head of the weapons or deck department usually acts as weapons control officer. He ensures that orders from the TAO and the commanding officer are properly understood and expeditiously carried out.

Regardless of the specific duties assigned to his officers, the commanding officer attempts to use their skills to best advantage during general quarters.

Summary

Watchstanders provide the necessary security for, or operate the essential equipment of, a ship. The underway watch organization provides the greatest degree of efficiency for ship operations and, when appropriate, allows the normal maintenance and administrative routines of the ship to continue.

The major underway watch stations are common to most ships, as are the ship departments discussed in the first chapter. It is important, therefore, to understand the underway watch organization, to know the watch conditions of readiness that alter its shape, and to become extremely familiar with the duties of certain watchstanders and the organizational relationships among them.

3

In-Port Watch Organization and Shipboard Etiquette

Introduction

Even when a ship is in port, a watch organization is necessary. Shipboard security, administrative details, and the formal welcoming of visitors to the ship are all tasks performed by the in-port watch organization.

The basic in-port watch organization is structured to meet a watch condition of readiness, as are underway watches. *Watch Condition of Readiness V*, peacetime in port, demands that a ship be continually manned by enough people to handle common emergencies and to get the ship under way if necessary.

During unusual circumstances or in wartime, additional watches may be added to the in-port watch organization to increase security, to protect against sabotage, and to man certain weapons systems.

When at sea, and especially when in port, the watch organization is often required to observe certain formalities of shipboard etiquette. The important ceremonies, honors, and customs which play a part in shipboard etiquette are discussed in the closing pages of this chapter.

The In-Port Watch Organization

When in port, watchstanders are grouped into watch sections just as they are when under way. An in-port watch section is officially on duty, however, for a full 24 hours. During that time, even though he may not always be manning a particular watch position, a watchstander must remain aboard the ship. Each morning a fresh watch section assumes the "duty," and the previous day's watchstanders are freed for normal activities and responsibilities.

Command Designated Watches

To understand more clearly the operation of the in-port watch organization, it is useful to consider a watch as one of two kinds: *a command designated watch* or a *departmental watch*.

A command designated watch has duties and responsibilities clearly associated with the entire ship. A departmental watch, on the other hand, has more limited duties and is generally the responsibility of, or oriented to, the functions of a single shipboard department.

The Command Duty Officer in Port

Most ships require the *command duty officer* (CDO) in port to be a commissioned officer, eligible for command at sea. The CDO is designated for a particular day's duty by the commanding officer and during that 24-hour period, acts as a deputy to the ship's executive officer. He assists the executive officer in carrying out the daily routine and supervises the officer of the deck or quarterdeck watch officer in matters concerning the safety and general work of the ship. He has authority to relieve the quarterdeck watch officer if necessary. In the temporary absence of the executive officer, the CDO will assume and carry out the duties of the executive officer.

The CDO is required to make and receive various routine reports during the day. The command duty officer is also responsible for keeping the executive officer and the commanding officer informed of any matters that may affect the normal operation of the ship. To carry out this responsibility, the CDO must remain knowledgeable as to the

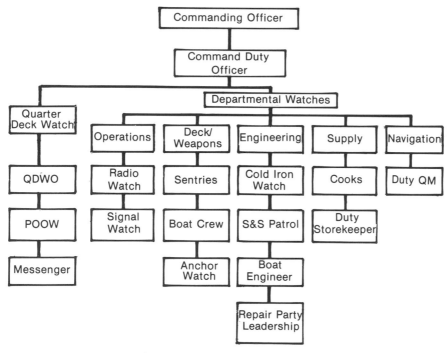

Figure 3-1. In-port watch organization.

ship's current position (in an anchorage), any unusual strain on the ship's lines (when moored), the operational status of the engineering plant, any matters affecting the internal administration of the ship, and every aspect of the ship's safety and security. To obtain such information, the CDO keeps in close communication with the in-port OOD and conducts frequent personal inspections of the ship to check its condition.

The In-Port OOD

When in port, the primary watch station is shifted from the bridge to the ship's quarterdeck. Although the commanding officer may designate any part of the ship as the quarterdeck, the quarterdeck is normally regarded as the ceremonial entrance and exit point of the ship and is generally located on the main deck near the gangway. The quarterdeck is afforded the same degree of formal respect one would exhibit to the ship's commanding officer. It is marked off by appropriate lines, deck markings, decorative cartridge cases, or fancy work and is always kept particularly clean and ship-shape. Men not on duty should stand clear of the quarterdeck. The dignity and appearance of the quarterdeck is a symbol of the quality of a ship and her crew.

The quarterdeck is manned 24 hours a day by an *in-port officer of the deck* (OOD), who is also appropriately termed the *quarterdeck watch officer* (QDWO). The QDWO may be a commissioned officer or a petty officer. Despite his official rank, the QDWO is a designated representative of the commanding officer and is subject only to the orders of the commanding officer, executive officer, and command duty officer. In the performance of his duty, the in-port OOD speaks with the authority of the commanding officer. He is essentially in charge of the ship during a given four-hour watch period.

The quarterdeck watch officer is responsible to the CO and CDO for the safety and security of the ship. He keeps them informed of the condition of all mooring lines or anchoring equipment in use, passes up tide and weather information, and oversees the operation of the ship's boats according to a published departure and arrival schedule.

The quarterdeck watch officer ensures that all sentries and patrols are properly posted and alert. He is given the additional responsibilities of supervising the proper performance of the signal bridge watch personnel and for carrying out the routine of the ship as published in the Plan of the Day. The in-port OOD's primary tool for fulfilling this latter task is the ship's 1MC, the multichannel general announcing system. The QDWO uses the system to keep the crew informed of unusual occurrences and the times of routine events. The QDWO also

Figure 3-2. A petty officer of the watch supervises the enlisted watchstanders on deck. He stands his watch on the quarterdeck.

has access to the nearby general, chemical, and collision alarms with which the ship may be alerted to an emergency.

The in-port OOD is also responsible for the rendering of side honors and honors to passing ships, as discussed in the last part of this chapter.

Other Quarterdeck Watchstanders

Assisting the in-port OOD on the quarterdeck are generally two to three other watchstanders. A *junior officer of the deck* (JOOD) may be assigned if the ship has enough personnel. He aids in the supervision of the quarterdeck as directed and has the same relationship to the OOD as he would during an underway watch.

The *petty officer of the watch* (POOW), is the QDWO's primary enlisted assistant. He is usually stationed near the gangway leading from the ship to the pier. He inspects all packages brought aboard the ship, ensures that all personnel boarding or leaving the ship have proper identification, aids the QDWO in management of the ship's boat schedule, makes announcements, and checks the ship's mooring when appropriate. The POOW also instructs and supervises the quarterdeck messenger and any personnel assigned sentry duty.

The petty officer of the watch sometimes is required to keep a deck log, a chronological record (by watches) that describes any circumstance of interest concerning the ship and its crew. Most ships require that the POOW be armed with a .45-caliber pistol for increased quarterdeck security.

In addition to the QDWO, the JOOD (if assigned), and the POOW, the quarterdeck watch will normally include a *messenger of the watch*. The messenger, usually a very junior enlisted man, must be familiar with the various departments of the ship and recognize key ship's company personnel. He is often required to deliver messages, wake members of the crew for night watches, and assist the POOW with his many duties.

Each messenger, petty officer of the watch, JOOD, and quarterdeck watch officer stands a four-hour watch. At the end of the watch, fresh watchstanders assume the responsibilities of the quarterdeck. The quarterdeck watchstanders and other personnel in a watch section are assigned their specific watch positions, duties, and time periods either by a watch bill published by the CDO, a list in the ship's Plan of the Day, or by the appropriate Watch, Quarter, and Station Bill.

Departmental Watches

Besides those watches which have command-designated responsibilities, there are other watches that are generally manned from, or have duties limited to, a single ship's department. These *departmental watches* and watchstanders are a vital portion of any in-port watch section.

Department Duty Officers

If they are not assigned to the watch section required to remain aboard that day, most department heads, division officers, and crew members go on liberty or go home when in port. Each department thus has a "duty" department head in that day's watch section designated to handle affairs when the official department head is not on board the ship. *Department duty officers* are junior officers, senior petty officers, and CPOs who, in the absence of the regular department heads, are responsible to the command duty officer for all matters affecting their departments.

Department duty officers are held responsible for the proper performance of other watchstanders in their departments. The weapons or deck duty officer, for example, would be responsible for the performance of all deck department sentries in the watch section. He would ensure that only qualified personnel were assigned such duties, and he would monitor their actions on watch. The engineering duty officer, on the other hand, would ensure that all in-port engineering watches were properly manned.

The ship's *eight-o'clock reports*, which describe general departmental readiness, are normally made by a ship's department head to the executive officer each evening just before 2000. In the absence of those officers, the reports are made by the department duty officers to the command duty officer. The CDO accepts the reports and ensures that the commanding officer and executive officer receive them upon their return to the ship.

In each day's watch section, divisional affairs are handled (in the absence of the responsible division officer) by a *division duty petty officer* (PO). Division duty POs represent their division officers and ensure that all divisional watches and responsibilities are properly carried out. The division duty POs report to the duty department heads any problems or abnormal circumstances encountered.

Weapons/Deck Department Watches

The weapons or deck department has responsibility for manning several different watches. The more important and most common of these watches are described below.

Security Watches and Sentries Various security watches and nearly all sentries are assigned from the weapons or deck department. They are posted to increase the physical security of the ship and its contents. These watchstanders are guided by written instructions that specify the limits of their post, the steps to be taken in case of alarm or a breach of security, and how and when to use assigned arms (rifle or nightstick). In addition, sentries must know how to challenge boats in order to identify occupants before a boat comes alongside.

Other duties include making periodic reports to the in-port OOD or to a roving patrol, protecting classified material security, ensuring the

Figure 3-3.   A sentry watch on a pier.

security of weapon stowage magazines, and being alert for signs of sabotage or unauthorized boarding.

Boat Crews   Each day's watch section generally has a boat crew or crews assigned from the deck department. Every crew, however, will also have a boat engineer from the engineering department to make emergency engine repairs.

Boat crews are especially important when a ship is at anchor, since the boats provide the primary means of transportation for the ship's crew. The boat crew is responsible for the boat's care and all her equipment. The crew operates the boat in accordance with an established arrival and departure schedule and is subject to the orders of the quarterdeck watch officer.

Anchor Watch When a ship is at anchor, frequently there is both an in-port OOD and a quarterdeck watch officer on duty. The OOD stands his watch on the bridge to check the position of the ship in the anchorage and to ensure that the anchor is not dragging. The quarterdeck watch officer is assigned to the quarterdeck with his normal duties.

Figure 3-4. A boat crew taking their shipmates to port.

Assisting the in-port OOD or QDWO in determining the status of the anchor, its chain, and any associated lines is the duty of the ship's *anchor watch*. This watchstander is posted on deck in the immediate vicinity of the anchor equipment or ground tackle. He maintains a continuous watch on the anchor chain and, primarily through experience, determines the amount of strain on the chain and the direction in which it seems to be pulling or tending. Conditions are periodically reported to the QDWO or the in-port OOD by sound-powered telephone.

Operations Department Watches

The ship's operations department normally has the primary responsibility of maintaining the ship's communications capability when in port. At least two watches are usually associated with this duty. Both are described below.

Radio Communications Watch   Whether anchored or in port, a ship continually receives messages containing important and up-to-the-minute information on various subjects. The radio communications watch has the responsibility of maintaining the voice communication circuits; sending, receiving, and distributing written radioteletype messages; and alerting the command duty officer if any significant communications equipment problems develop. The radio communications watch is under the supervision of the operations department duty officer.

Signal Watch   The signal bridge of the ship is usually manned during daylight hours when in port. The signal watch sends and receives flashing light messages, makes certain that required flags and pennants are displayed, and hoists other visual signals as appropriate. The signal watch is also under the supervision of the operations duty officer but frequently receives orders directly from the QDWO.

Navigation and Supply Department Watches

The specific watches manned by the navigation and supply departments vary from ship to ship; however, those mentioned below can be found with some frequency.

Duty Quartermaster   A quartermaster of the watch or duty quartermaster is more necessary when a ship is anchored than when it is moored to a pier. He maintains a deck log, assists in determining the ship's position in an anchorage, and keeps an eye on weather reports. Even when moored, however, a duty quartermaster is a valuable

Figure 3-5. *A Navy signalman, well trained in the art of visual communications, uses a flaghoist.*

addition to the watch section. He aids the CDO and QDWO in rendering honors to passing ships or dignitaries and assists with morning and evening colors.

Duty Storekeeper and Cooks The supply department has personnel in each in-port watch section assigned to carry out cooking and various other supply-related duties. The duty storekeeper, for example, is responsible for receiving foodstuffs or other materials delivered to the ship, and if any equipment casualties are suffered during the day, he determines whether repair parts are available.

Engineering Department Watches

Exactly what watches are manned by the engineering department when in port is very much dependent upon what engineering equipment is to be operated during that time. If the engineering plant is to continue producing steam and electricity for the ship, a number of watches, including a damage-control watch, fireroom watch, auxiliary watch, engineroom watch, and electrical watch may be required. If the ship receives power from the pier, however, fewer watches are needed. The watches commonly required during this latter condition are described below.

Cold Iron Watch   A ship whose main machinery is inactive or which does not have an auxiliary equipment watch on duty, stations a *cold iron watch*. "Cold iron" refers to the nonoperating status of the boilers and turbines. This watch consists of a man or men from the engineering department who are required to check all machinery spaces for fuel or water leaks, improperly operating auxiliary equipment, rags or tools left adrift, and any other hazards. The cold iron watch makes periodic reports to the quarterdeck watch or to the *sounding and security patrol*. The duties of the sounding and security patrol were described in chapter 2.

Emergency Parties   Even when a ship is in port, it is still necessary to maintain an ability to fight fire, to combat flooding, and to provide assistance to other units in the vicinity. Crew members from various departments compose ship's emergency parties: a repair party, fire party, rescue and assistance party, etc. The engineering department, however, frequently provides the majority of those personnel and, under the direction of the command duty officer, conducts periodic drills to determine and maintain readiness. A senior petty officer in the engineering department is generally designated as leader of an emergency party.

In-Port Watch Organization Summary

The principal and guiding consideration for manning the watch during Condition of Readiness V is the need to have enough men on board to allow the command duty officer and the in-port OOD to operate the ship and cope with such emergencies as fire or flooding. The CDO and the in-port OOD are not equipped to fight the ship with the watch or duty section alone. However, in an emergency situation in port, the command duty officer has the option of holding every man on board, regardless of his duty status. During any emergency, the crew is expected to augment the day's watch section. If the captain is not

Figure 3-6. A repair party practices fire fighting.

aboard, the command duty officer is expected to use every means to locate and inform him of any emergency affecting his ship.

Shipboard Etiquette, Custom, and Ceremony

An important part of sea power is the representative function that a naval ship plays in foreign ports on behalf of her country. It is a visible symbol of national power. In 1946, when President Truman wished to express support for Turkey at a time when that country was under considerable pressure, the USS *Missouri* (BB-63) was sent to Turkey carrying the body of the recently deceased Turkish Ambassador to the

United States. This purely ceremonial task was chosen by Secretary of the Navy James Forrestal to demonstrate clearly to Russia our support for Turkey. This point was made and reinforced the following year with the Truman Doctrine.

Maritime nations have employed their navies for centuries in the conduct of diplomacy as well as in battle. As a result, naval ceremonies and honors are an important part of many foreign missions. American commissioned ships practice essentially the same etiquette, ceremonies, and formal honors as the ships of other navies.

Customs, less formal in nature than honors, form the major portion of ceremonial functions. Customs include such things as raising and lowering flags, or dressing ship. It is difficult to separate custom in the Navy from everyday life aboard ship. Even the actions of greeting seniors, saluting, and leaving or boarding the ship are customs that may properly be called ceremonial functions.

Salutes and Personal Etiquette

The rules for military etiquette are founded in custom and tradition, and their strict observance forms an important factor in the maintenance of discipline. These evidences of respect and courtesy are observed equally by all officers and men in the U.S. Navy. As a rule, the junior is the one to take the initiative.

Personal salutes and other marks of respect are extended to officers of the armed services of the United States in uniform (in civilian clothes, if recognized); to high-ranking dignitaries of the United States government; and to officers in the armed services and high-ranking dignitaries of foreign nations. Naval officers do not normally salute when uncovered or when they are inside the ship.

On board ship, men salute their officers and say, "Good morning, sir," when first seen each day. They salute flag officers, the commanding officer of the ship, and all officers from other ships on every occasion of meeting them, passing near to them, or being addressed by them.

Customs of Formal Address

Officers are always addressed and referred to by their title or rank, such as "Admiral," "Captain," or "Commander." If several officers of the same rank are together, it is proper to use both title and name, such as "Admiral Taylor" or "Captain Smith," to avoid confusion. Warrant officers are addressed in the same manner as officers. Midshipmen and aviation cadets are addressed as "Mister" or "Miss."

By tradition, the commanding officer of any ship or station, no matter what his rank, is addressed and referred to as "Captain." The executive officer, likewise, is "Commander." Other captains or commanders in the same command should be addressed by rank and name.

An officer in the Medical or Dental Corps is addressed and referred to by title, or as "Doctor." A chaplain may be called "Chaplain," no matter what his rank. An officer below the rank of admiral who is in command of a squadron, task unit, or convoy of ships is customarily addressed and referred to as "Commodore." The actual rank of commodore, between the ranks of captain and admiral, is not used in peacetime.

A chief petty officer is addressed as "Chief Petty Officer Smith," or more informally as "Chief Smith," or as "Chief" if you do not know his name. But in recruit training, all chiefs acting as company commanders

Figure 3-7. Saluting is a sign of respect.

rate "Mister" and "sir." Master and senior chief petty officers are customarily addressed and referred to as "Master Chief Smith," or "Senior Chief Smith," or as "Master Chief" or "Senior Chief" if you do not know their names.

Other petty officers are addressed and referred to by their specific rates. "Nonrated" personnel—in paygrades E-1 through E-3—are addressed and referred to as "Seaman Wells," or Fireman Clifton," regardless of their specific paygrade.

In civilian life it is customary to introduce men to women, and young people to older ones. The same general rules are followed in military life, except that in most cases, rank establishes the order of introduction: introduce the junior to the senior, regardless of either one's sex. Navy personnel, regardless of rank or sex, are introduced to a chaplain.

Flags and Flag Etiquette

Customs regarding flags are numerous and quite explicit. Crises have been known to develop over disrespect to a national ensign. For nearly two-hundred years, the "Stars and Stripes" has served as a symbol of our country. Because it represents our country, we owe it every respect and honor to which it is entitled.

During the ceremony of hoisting and lowering the national ensign, or when the ensign is passing in a parade or review, all persons who are not part of a military formation stand, face the colors, and come to attention. Men of the armed services in uniform render the hand salute.

When a number of flags, including the ensign, are flown from adjacent poles or masts, the ensign is hoisted first and lowered last. Ordinarily, no other flag should be placed to the right of the ensign—that is, to the flag's right—although certain situations require it, as when the national ensigns of the United Nations are displayed together.

If the ensigns of two or more nations are displayed, they are flown at the same height from separate masts, and are approximately equal in size. International custom forbids flying one nation's ensign above that of another nation.

The signal bridge watch is responsible for the maintenance of flags and pennants and ensures that the proper codes and signals are displayed as directed by the OOD.

Morning and Evening Colors

The ceremonial function of hoisting the national ensign at 0800 and lowering it at sunset in port is referred to as *morning* and *evening* *colors.* U.S. Navy Regulations prescribe the procedures for morning and evening colors. When there is more than one ship in port, all ships follow the motions of the senior officer present afloat (SOPA). Five minutes before colors the prep pennant is closed up. For morning colors the prep pennant is then lowered to the dip* position at 0800. The petty officer of the watch or bridge watch blows one blast on a hand whistle over the 1MC, all hands topside come to attention, and if in uniform and covered, they salute in the direction of the national ensign. The national ensign and union jack are closed up smartly. "Carry on" is executed by three short blasts of the hand whistle and prep is simultaneously hauled all the way down.

At evening colors, the same procedure is followed except that at sunset the national ensign is lowered ceremoniously. If there is a band, the ensign is lowered so as to be completely lowered at the same moment the music ends. The boatswain's mate of the watch, petty officer of the watch, or signal bridge watch blows three blasts on the hand whistle over the 1MC to secure from colors, and the prep pennant is hauled down.

Ships under way do not hold morning or evening colors, but do fly a "steaming" ensign at the gaff from sunrise to sunset. If the commanding officer or SOPA so authorizes, the steaming ensign may be lowered when out of sight of land and shipping to reduce wear and tear. The union jack is not flown at sea.

Union Jack

The *union jack* is a replica of the blue, star-studded field in the corner of the national ensign. It symbolizes the union of the states of the United States. Each star represents a state, but not a particular state.

When a naval ship is at anchor, the union jack is flown from the jackstaff in the bow of the ship from 0800 to sunset. In addition to flying from the jackstaff, the union jack is also hoisted at the yardarm when an onboard general court-martial or a court of inquiry is in session.

When displayed from the jackstaff, the union jack is half-masted if the national ensign is half-masted. The union jack is not dipped when the national ensign is dipped.

The union jack is issued in several sizes, but when flown at the jackstaff, it must be the same size as the union of the ensign flown at the flagstaff.

*The dip position of a flag or pennant is approximately ¾ of the way up the mast.

Figure 3-8. A crewman is ready to lower the union jack.

Shifting Colors

When mooring and unmooring, the colors are shifted from the gaff on the mast to the flagstaff on the stern, or the other way around. The jack is raised or lowered simultaneously on the bow. There is probably no activity afloat which results in more anguish for a commanding officer and officer of the deck than does this evolution. When mooring and unmooring, the ship is normally being observed from many quarters. More can be observed about a ship's smartness, discipline, professional performance, and her officers and crew themselves during mooring and unmooring than during any other evolution or series of evolutions. The necessity to perform all aspects of mooring and unmooring perfectly can never be over-emphasized.

On unmooring, the instant the last mooring line leaves the pier or the anchor is aweigh, the BMOW blows a long blast on a hand whistle over the 1MC and passes the word "*Shift colors.*" The jack on the jackstaff forward and the national ensign on the flagstaff aft, are hauled down smartly. At the same instant, the "steaming" ensign is hoisted on the gaff, and the ship's call sign and other signal flags are hoisted or broken. The national ensign is never broken.* On mooring, the instant the anchor is let go or the first mooring line (not heaving line) is made fast on the pier, the BMOW performs the same actions as for unmooring. At this signal, the ship's call sign and the steaming ensign are hauled down smartly, and the union jack and ensign are hoisted fore and aft.

Half-Masting the Ensign

The custom of flying the ensign at half-mast is observed as a tribute to the dead. The Navy has specific rules for all occasions of half-masting the ensign. They are as follows:

1. Whenever the ensign is to be half-masted, it first is closed up and then is lowered to the half-mast position. The same procedure is used when lowering the ensign from half-mast; it first must be closed up and then lowered.

2. On Memorial Day, the ensign is flown at half-mast from 0800 until completion of the 21-gun salute fired at 1200, or until 1220 if no salute is fired.

During burial at sea, the ensign is at half-mast from the beginning of the funeral service until the body is committed to the deep. A longer period for displaying the ensign at half-mast may be prescribed, according to circumstances, by the senior officer present.

Dipping

Merchant ships "salute" Navy ships by *dipping* their ensign when they pass close to a Navy ship. The procedure is as follows: the merchant ship will haul its ensign to half-mast, and the Navy ship will, when at or near the closest point of approach, haul its ensign to

---

*Breaking a flag or flaghoist refers to a sudden, manipulated unfolding of the flag after it has been hoisted.

Figure 3-9. *Full-dressed ships.*

half-mast, hold it for a few seconds, then close it up. The merchant ship will then close up its ensign.

When a merchant ship of any nation (recognized diplomatically by the United States) salutes a ship of our Navy by dipping her national ensign, the salute is returned by the U.S. Navy ship, dip for dip.

If the original salute is given before 0800, or after sunset in port, or at any other time when the ensign is not displayed, the Navy ship hoists her colors, returns the salute, then hauls down the colors after a short interval. An ensign displayed at half-mast is closed up before a dip is answered. Ships of the U.S. Navy dip the national ensign only to return such salutes. U.S. Navy ships are forbidden to answer the salute of ships flying the colors of a nation not recognized diplomatically by the United States.

Dressing and Full-Dressing Ships

U.S. Navy Regulations prescribe that commissioned U.S. Navy ships will be *full-dressed* on Washington's birthday and Independence Day, and will be *dressed* on other national holidays.

When dressing ship, the largest national ensign the ship has is flown from the flagstaff. Except as prescribed for a ship displaying a personal flag or command pennant, a national ensign also is displayed from each masthead. The national ensigns at the mastheads are uniform in size. If there is a substantial difference in heights of mastheads, however, a variation in the size of the national ensigns is appropriate.

When the ship is full-dressed, the mastheads are dressed as described in the preceding paragraph, and a rainbow of signal flags is displayed from stem to stern. They should reach from the foot of the jackstaff to the mastheads and then to the foot of the flagstaff.

When dressing or full-dressing the ship in honor of a foreign nation, the national ensign of the nation replaces the United States national ensign at the main (or at the masthead of a single-masted ship).

If circumstances necessitate half-masting the national ensign when the ship is dressed or full-dressed, only the national ensign at the flagstaff is half-masted.

When full-dressing is prescribed, the senior officer present may direct that dressing be substituted if, in his opinion, weather conditions make it advisable. Under such circumstances, he also may direct that the ensigns be hauled down from the mastheads after they are hoisted.

When prescribed, the ship will be dressed or full-dressed from 0800 until sunset. Dressing ship is accomplished simultaneously with morning colors. Under way, ships are not dressed or full-dressed.

Command Pennants

An officer below flag rank, when in command of a force, flotilla, squadron, carrier division, cruiser division, or aircraft wing, flies a broad command pennant (white with blue stripes top and bottom). An officer in command of any other unit, such as an aircraft squadron, flies a burgee command pennant, which is white with red stripes top and bottom.

Personal Flags of Navy Flag Officers

When a flag officer of the Navy—a commodore, rear admiral, vice admiral, admiral, or fleet admiral—assumes command of a fleet or a unit of a fleet, his personal flag is hoisted and kept flying until he turns over his command to his successor. If he is absent from his command for a period exceeding 72 hours, his flag is hauled down.

The flag officer's flag is displayed from only one ship or station at any one time. It is flown at the main truck by the ship he is aboard. Normally, no personal flag or pennant is shown at the same masthead with the national ensign. When a double display is required, the personal flag or pennant should be flown at the fore truck. When a single-masted flagship is dressed or full-dressed, however, the personal flag or pennant is hoisted at the starboard yardarm.

During a gun salute, the ensign is displayed at the main truck. Any personal flag is lowered clear of the ensign.

If two or more ships of the Navy are together in port, the senior officer present afloat pennant (starboard pennant) is displayed from the ship in which the senior officer present afloat is embarked, except when his personal flag clearly indicates his seniority. It is displayed from the inboard halfyard of the starboard main yardarm.

Absence Indicators

When a commanding officer or any flag officer is absent, an *absentee pennant* is flown. The absence of an admiral or unit commander, whose personal flag or pennant is flying, is indicated by the "first substitute indicator," flown from the starboard yardarm. The "second substitute," flown from the port yardarm, indicates that the chief of staff is absent. The *third substitute*, also flown from the port yardarm, indicates the absence of the commanding officer. (If the CO is to be gone more than 72 hours, then the pennant is used to show the absence of the executive officer.) The "fourth substitute" means that the civil or military official whose flag is flying (such as the Secretary of Defense) is absent. It is flown from the starboard yardarm.

Table 3-1. Use of substitute pennants for absentee indicators

Sub.	Indication	Where normally displayed	Absentee
1st	Absence of an official from his ship for a period of 72 hours or less	Starboard main yardarm (outboard)	Absence of a flag officer or unit command whose personal flag or command pennant is flying in this ship
2nd	Same as 1st substitute	Port main yardarm (inboard)	Absence of chief of staff
3rd	Same as 1st substitute	Port main yardarm (outboard)	Absence of captain (executive officer if captain is absent for a period exceeding 72 hours)
4th	Same as 1st substitute	Starboard main yardarm (inboard)	Absence of civil or military official whose flag is flying in this ship

Commission Pennant

Every Navy ship in commission flies a *commission pennant* except when it is replaced by a personal flag or a command pennant. It is a long, thin pennant with a blue field studded with stars and has alternate red and white stripes as if it were a triangle cut at random from the ensign. The number of stars and stripes have no special significance.

Figure 3-10. Crewmen prepare to raise the commissioning pennant during commissioning ceremony.

The commission pennant is flown at the after truck of a naval ship or, if a mastless ship, at the highest and most conspicuous point of hoist. It also is flown from the bow of a boat when a commanding officer, not entitled to a personal flag, is embarked on an official visit.

The commission pennant is not a personal flag, but sometimes it is regarded as the personal symbol of the commanding officer. Along with the ensign and the union jack, it is half-masted upon the death of the commanding officer of the ship.

Church Pennant

The *church pennant* is the only flag ever flown over the national ensign at the same point of hoist. It is displayed only during church services conducted by a chaplain, both ashore and afloat.

Boarding and Leaving a Navy Ship

A large ship will usually rig two gangways or brows to the pier when in port. Small ships commonly use one. The forward gangway or the starboard one is usually reserved for officers, while the after or port gangway is used by enlisted men. The officer of the deck or his representative will be on duty at the gangway to greet every person who is boarding or leaving the ship.

When an officer desires to leave his own ship and if the national ensign is flying, he will step to the QDWO, salute him, and say, "I have permission to leave the ship, sir." Before arriving on the quarterdeck, the officer in question will have obtained permission from his department head or the executive officer, the appropriate senior required in this particular instance. When the QDWO has said "Very well," or "Very good," and has returned the salute, the officer will then turn aft to face the ensign, when it is flying, and salute; the QDWO returns the salute for the national ensign. The officer then leaves the ship.

In the reverse procedure, when an officer desires to return on board his own ship, he will, upon reaching the quarterdeck, first face aft, if the ensign is flying, and salute; the QDWO will return the salute. Then the officer will turn to the QDWO, salute him, and say, "I report my return aboard, sir." The QDWO will return the salute saying, "Very well," or "Very good."

When going aboard a ship other than his own, an officer or enlisted man must obtain permission to board from the ship's QDWO. The person will first stand at the gangway and salute the ensign if it is flying, then turn to the QDWO, salute, and say, "I request permission to come aboard, sir."

On leaving a ship he has been visiting, a man will go first to the QDWO, salute, and say, "I request permission to leave the ship, sir."

Figure 3-11. Displaying the church pennant.

After the QDWO has said, "Very well" or "Permission granted" and has returned the salute, the officer or man will step to the gangway and if the ensign is flying, salute in its direction before leaving. The QDWO again returns the salute for the national ensign.

Figure 3-12.   An officer of the deck tending the gangway of his ship.

Crossing Nests

Destroyers and smaller ships sometimes tie up in *nests* (clusters) alongside a tender or pier, and a man may have to cross several ships to get to his own. The usual quarterdeck procedure described for boarding and leaving a ship does not apply when crossing a ship, but there is still a procedure to be followed. On boarding the inboard ship, salute the colors and the quarterdeck, and request "Permission to cross" of

Figure 3-13. *A nest of destroyers.*

the quarterdeck watch. Do not salute the quarterdeck or colors on leaving. Repeat this procedure on each ship until you reach your own. Going from your ship in a nest to the pier or tender, the procedure is reversed; after leaving your own ship, request permission to cross from the quarterdeck watch on each inboard ship.

Formal Honors

Formal honors are rendered during unusual or infrequent circumstances requiring the participation of the entire ship's crew, or at least a major portion of it. These honors can require parading the crew at quarters, parading of the guard of the day or full guard, sideboys,* manning the rail, or they can involve gun salutes.

Parading

The crew will normally be paraded at quarters when entering and leaving foreign ports, returning to homeport from a long cruise, departing from homeport for an extended deployment, or when the commanding officer deems that military smartness and/or circumstances warrant parading the entire crew. On all other occasions, in lieu of parading the entire crew at quarters, the guard of the day is paraded in a conspicuous place on the weather decks. A destroyer guard of the day consists of eight men under the command of a petty officer as squad leader. The required "full" guard for this type of ship is

*Sideboys are non-rated men who attend a gangway, in numbers prescribed in Navy Regulations, upon the arrival and departure of visiting senior officers or dignitaries for whom side honors are rendered. For example, a formal visit to a ship by a Navy captain requires the presence of four sideboys.

twelve men with an officer in command, assisted by a senior platoon petty officer.

Entering and leaving homeport as a matter of routine, and entering and leaving other U.S. ports when the visit is operational rather than ceremonial, are examples of when parading the entire crew at quarters is unnecessary. The crew or guard, as appropriate, is paraded at quarters for fifteen minutes prior to reaching or after leaving the berth unless local SOPA instructions direct otherwise. Ranks are not broken until the bridge orders details to stand by their lines, boat booms, or gangways, as appropriate. Quarters may be dispensed with during hours of darkness.

Side Honors

Side honors are those honors normally accompanying the official visit of a military or civilian dignitary, or as part of a formal inspection.

On the arrival and departure of civil officials and foreign officers, and of United States officers when directed by the senior officer present, the side is piped and the appropriate number of sideboys paraded, with a boatswain's mate, in two rows on either side of the gangway so that the visitor passes between the ranks of sideboys. Most ships smaller than cruisers have sideboy watches only on special occasions. Sideboys are not paraded on Sunday nor between sunset and 0800 on other days.

Manning the Rail

Manning the rail is an honor given to visiting officers or dignitaries. It is an all-hands evolution in which all weather-deck rails are manned by the ship's company in single rank, at as equal intervals as possible. The men in ranks do not salute.

Gun Salutes

Gun salutes for officers and officials who are entitled to 17 or more guns are fired on the occasion of each official visit of the individual concerned. (An official visit is a formal visit of courtesy requiring special honors and ceremonies.) Gun salutes prescribed for officers and officials entitled to 15 guns or less are not fired unless ordered by the senior officer present or higher authority.

The interval between guns in salutes normally is five seconds.

During a gun salute, persons on the quarterdeck or in the ceremonial party, if ashore, render the hand salute; other persons on deck, or in the vicinity of the ceremonial party, if ashore, stand at attention.

Officers being saluted render the hand salute during the firing of the gun salute.

Figure 3-14. Manning the rail.

No salutes are fired between sunset and sunrise, and except when international courtesy requires, no salutes are fired before 0800 or on Sunday. When an official visit is made on a Sunday by a person entitled to a gun salute, the salute is fired immediately after colors on Monday, if the visitor is still aboard.

Passing Honors

Passing honors are those honors, except gun salutes, rendered by ships and boats when ships, officials, or officers embarked in boats pass (or are passed) close aboard. Close aboard generally means passing within 600 yards for ships, and within 400 yards for boats. To ensure that appropriate honors are given, these distance limitations should be interpreted liberally.

Passing honors are exchanged between ships of the U.S. Navy, between ships of the Navy and the Coast Guard, and between U.S. ships and most ships of foreign navies passing close aboard.

The table below shows the steps involved in passing honors. Steps one, two, and three should be accomplished in sufficient time to permit the accomplishment of step four just before the ships are at their closest point of approach.

Passing honors are initiated by the "junior" ship or boat. The seniority of a ship is determined by the rank of the commanding officer, unless a more senior officer or civil official is embarked.

Table 3-2. Passing Honors

Step	Officer of the Deck of Junior Ship	Officer of the Deck of Senior Ship	Bugle Call	Battery or Hand Whistle
1	Sounds "attention" starboard (port)		"attention" starboard (port)	1 short whistle (stbd) 2 short whistles (port)
2		Sounds "attention" starboard (port)	"attention" starboard (port)	1 short whistle (stbd) 2 short whistles (port)
3	Sounds "hand salute" (guard presents arms and band sounds off if required)		1 short note	1 short whistle
4		Sounds "hand salute" (guard presents arms and band sounds off)	1 short note	1 short whistle
5		Sounds "TWO" (in 3 seconds or after band sounds off)	2 short notes	2 short whistles
6	Sounds "TWO"		2 short notes	2 short whistles
7		Sounds "carry on"	"carry on"	3 short whistles
8	Sounds "carry on"		"carry on"	3 short whistles

The seniority of U.S. naval officers is determined by a lineal number assigned to each officer. If necessary, a ship may consult a register of such numbers or the appropriate fleet administrative organization notice kept on the bridge or quarterdeck.

Figure 3-15.   A gun salute is fired from a carrier during a port visit.

Bridge Customs

Just as the quarterdeck is the center of most ceremonial functions when a ship is in port, so the bridge is when at sea. However, since the men on the bridge are primarily concerned with operating and navigating the ship, the actual ceremonial functions associated with the bridge are kept to a minimum. To maintain the sanctity of the bridge, many ships require all nonwatch personnel to request permission from the OOD to come on the bridge, accompanying such a request with a salute. Most ships require any crew member coming on the bridge to be in a proper and seaman-like uniform and to remain covered.

If the commanding officer comes on the bridge, his presence is announced (to the bridge watch). Officers, and on some ships senior enlisted men, will make it a point of greeting him at this time. If the captain leaves the bridge, his departure is also formally announced (e.g., "The captain has left the bridge").

Shipboard Etiquette Summary

Shipboard etiquette, custom, and ceremony are an important part of life aboard Navy ships. The courtesies and honors described in this chapter are meticulously practiced, since they are often considered indications of the smartness and professionalism of the ship and the crew themselves. Strict observance of military etiquette not only increases the discipline aboard ship, but it also forges a strong sense of self-respect within the officers and the crew.

4

Small Boat Seamanship

Introduction

The term *boat* refers to small craft that are limited in their use by size. Usually they are incapable of making regular, independent voyages of any length on the high seas. Small vessels carried aboard a ship, which are lowered to perform various ship's tasks and evolutions, are known as ship's boats.

The distinction between a ship and a boat is largely one of size, but there is no well-defined line of demarcation.

Small-boat seamanship encompasses much more than a knowledge of the kinds of boats in operation in the Navy. Boat crews are responsible for the upkeep of their craft, and must receive training in a number of other areas. Some of the techniques to be mastered require much practice and experience before a boat crewman can become accomplished in his work. The more important of these skills include:

- Steering a compass course;
- Using relative and true bearings;
- Knowledge of Rules of the Road;
- Knowledge of buoys;
- Knowledge of the small-boat engine;
- Line handling;
- Hoisting and lowering methods; and
- Boat etiquette.

At one time or another almost every Navy man will be embarked in a boat either as a passenger, an officer-in-charge, or as a member of the boat crew. These jobs are both challenging and rewarding and demand a thorough knowledge of boat seamanship and seamanship in general.

Boats of the Fleet

Boats can be grouped or classified in many ways. For our discussion it is helpful to the reader to consider two broad categories of boats: standard (shipborne) boats and combatant craft.

Standard Boats

Most standard boats are referred to by their length and type; for example: "26-foot motor whaleboat." But boats may also be referred to by their function.

For many, many years the motor whaleboat, motor launch, and motorboat filled the requirements for ships' boats. The motor whaleboat, used primarily as a lifeboat, still retains its place aboard most ships. Recently, however, motor launches and motorboats have been giving way to utility boats and personnel boats, respectively. Various standard boats are described below.

Motorboats (MBs)

Motorboats are fast, decked-over boats with closed compartments forward and aft, and open cockpits amidships, where coxswains steer by wheel. The closed compartments are roofed over by rounded metal canopies. MBs are used mainly for carrying officers. Enlisted passengers, when aboard, occupy the forward cabin. MBs are 35 and 40 feet long, are diesel-powered, and are generally painted haze grey.

Figure 4-1. A boatswain's mate steadies a Jacob's ladder to the bow of the captain's gig.

Barge

A *barge* is a deluxe motorboat assigned to a flag officer (admiral) for his personal use. Barges have black hulls and white canopies.

Gig

A *gig* can be any boat designated for the personal use of a commanding officer, a chief of staff, a squadron commander, or a division commander. In many cases the gig is a motorboat; on a small ship, it may be a motor whaleboat.

Motor Whaleboats (MWBs)

These round-bottomed, double-ended, 26 feet long, diesel-powered boats are used as lifeboats and shipboard utility boats. Many small ships use them as gigs and officers' motorboats, in which case they have metal or canvas canopies.

Figure 4-2. A motor whaleboat.

Motor Launches (MLs)

These are heavy-duty, square-sterned boats. They are 40 and 50 feet long, diesel-powered, with removable seats (thwarts). MLs are used for hauling liberty parties and stores.

Personnel Boats (PERs)

These are fast, V-bottomed, double-ended, diesel-powered 28- and 40-foot boats with enclosed passenger spaces, specifically designed to transport officers, although smaller types are used for shore party boats, lifeboats, and mail boats. A 40-foot boat will carry a maximum of 43 persons. Smaller types have only one closed compartment.

Wherries

A *wherry* is a boat with a square stern and a round-bottom and is designed to be rowed or powered by an outboard motor. A wherry may

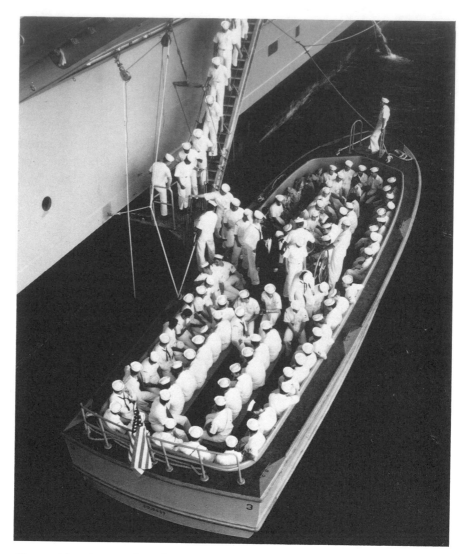

Figure 4-3. A motor launch.

be 12-, 14-, or even 16-feet long. A single wherry is often the only boat aboard a small naval vessel.

Utility Boats (UBs)

These boats, varying in length from 22 to 65 feet, are generally used as cargo and personnel carriers or as heavy-duty work boats. Many have been modified for survey work, tenders for divers, and mine-sweeping operations. A 50-foot UB will, under ideal weather conditions, carry 146 men, plus crew. The largest UB, a general-purpose work boat with a 24,000-pound carrying capacity, is steered from a pilot house.

Punts

Punts are small, open, square-ended boats, either rowed or sculled by oar over the stern. They are used primarily for working along the waterline of a ship in order to paint or clean the ship's sides.

Combatant Craft

Combatant craft are boats specifically designed for combat roles, and include patrol craft, riverine and SEAL support craft, amphibious warfare craft, and those craft devoted to mine countermeasures. Examples of each of these craft are described below.

Patrol Craft

65-Foot Sea Specter Patrol Boat The 65-ft. PB is the newest, most advanced small Patrol Boat in the U. S. Navy inventory. It was designed as a high-speed weapons platform for the Naval Inshore Warfare

Figure 4-4. A personnel boat.

Figure 4-5. A utility boat.

forces, capable of carrying a variety of U.S. or foreign weapons in a number of alternative locations. A modular payload concept is incorporated, allowing the craft to be adapted to a variety of missions in deep rivers, harbors, coastal or open sea environments. Missions envisioned include patrol, surveillance, interdiction, fire support against ashore and afloat targets, and insertion/extraction of special warfare groups. The main deck of the craft is reinforced in vital areas so that future mission capabilities may include use of antisubmarine sonar or torpedoes, mine laying, mine detection and mine sweeping.

The craft is powered by three high-powered, lightweight diesels providing speeds significantly higher than any other U.S. Navy patrol boat of this size. Fuel and accommodations will permit unsupported missions of up to five days. Multi-frequency communications, high-resolution surface-search radar and reasonable stability in moderately heavy seas will permit day/night, all-weather operations. The all-aluminum craft was designed with a low silhouette, low radar cross section and extremely low acoustic noise level to preclude ready detection.

The armament of the patrol boat can include four .50-caliber machine guns and two or more mortars.

36-Foot Sea Fox   The 36' Sea Fox was developed to fill the special requirements of the Naval Special Warfare Groups (NSWGs). The first production model is scheduled to reach the fleet in the early 1980s. It may differ slightly from the drawings.

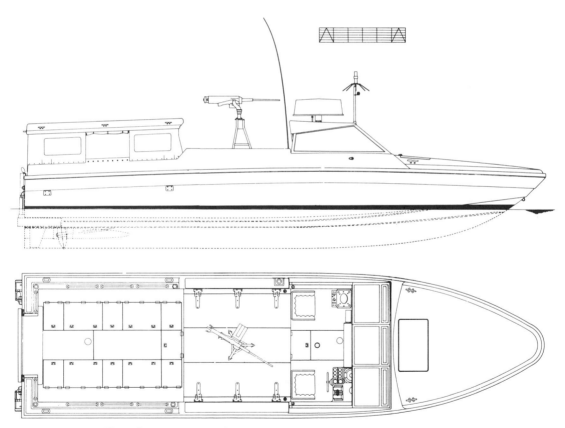

Figure 4-6.   Profile and arrangement of 36' SWC(L) Sea Fox class.

The Sea Fox will feature high-powered diesel engines, an abundance of electronic gear, and will be capable of surviving high sea states. The armanent of the Sea Fox will consist primarily of .50-caliber machine guns. Its low profile will make it very difficult to detect as it approaches an enemy shore.

Amphibious Warfare Craft

LCM   The LCM(6), popularly known as "Mike 6," was designed to transport cargo, troops, or vehicles from ship-to-shore, shore-to-shore, or in retrograde movements during amphibious operations. These boats are capable of carrying thirty-four (short) tons of cargo or eighty troops. The LCM(6) has been used, in addition, for various types of utility work in harbors. They have also been converted to flame-thrower craft, helicopter platforms, refuelers, and mine-sweepers for riverine warfare. They have been converted, as well, for use as ferries, pusher boats, and diving salvage boats for harbor work. These boats are light enough to be carried to oversea destinations as deck cargo aboard larger vessels or in the well decks of LSDs and LPDs.

This versatile craft is a shallow-draft boat constructed to the standard of commercial materials and equipment. Its design lends itself to mass production in relatively short building periods. The high stability of the LCM(6) allows it to sustain extremely heavy damage without loss of the craft.

Mine Countermeasures Craft

MSL   MSLs can be carried aboard amphibious ships for assault mine-sweeping of moored, magnetic, or acoustic mines during amphibious assault operations.

Figure 4-7.   A 56' LCM(6) MOD2 landing craft, mechanized.

Figure 4-8. A 36' minesweeping launch (MSL).

The MSL's are small, shallow-draft craft of glass-reinforced plastic construction for mine countermeasures in the shallow waters of rivers and harbors. They can carry chain-drag minesweeping gear for bottom mines detonated remotely from shore, moored contact minesweeping gear, and acoustic or magnetic mine countermeasures gear. The small size of the craft permits only one type of gear to be carried at one time.

With the restructuring of the Navy's mine countermeasures forces, the MSLs have been stripped of their sweep gear and are being employed as utility launches and training craft.

Boat Crews

Most boats have permanent crews assigned to them. The size of the crew varies, depending on the type and size of the boat. A typical crew consists of a coxswain, engineer, bowhook, and sternhook. In addition to a requirement that every member of a boat's crew be a qualified swimmer, each crewman must have a number of important skills. Following the individual narrative devoted to each member of a boat's crew, is a description of those skills and other knowledge essential to that crewman's performance.

Coxswain

The *coxswain* is generally considered to be in charge of his boat and her crew. He is, however, subject to the orders of the boat officer (if one is assigned) and the most senior line officer embarked in his boat. The coxswain drives the boat and issues orders to the crew from his station at the helm.

A coxswain's responsibilities are considerable. He must be completely familiar with everything relating to the care and handling of his boat. He must know the physical characteristics of his boat—its dimensions, draft, and the cargo and passenger capacities in both fair weather and foul. Knowing the boat's dimensions and draft will allow him to avoid narrow berths and shallow water. The cargo and passenger capacities are normally stamped on the boat label plate, and it is most important that they not be exceeded. The maximum capacity includes the boat crew and assumes that all passengers are seated in the cockpits. During heavy weather, in particular, overloaded boats or boats with an unevenly distributed load swamp easily.

The coxswain ensures that his crew and all passengers wear lifejackets in heavy weather. In the past, Navy boats have swamped, and although the boats usually did not sink, lives were lost (generally because overconfident swimmers left the boat). In the event a boat is swamped, all hands should remain with the boat where the strong can assist the weak. It is much easier for rescue boats to find one large group than it is for them to locate two or three dozen scattered individuals.

Normally, the boat coxswain and his crew complete an *underway check-off list* prior to getting under way. The check-off list includes every important equipment check and preparation that must be made before operating the boat. The underway check-off list is a valuable tool and an element of safety that should not be overlooked.

The OOD or quarterdeck watch officer (QDWO) is responsible for the safe loading of the boat when it loads at the ship. When loading ashore, the coxswain assumes responsibility unless a beach guard or other individual has been specifically assigned that duty. The coxswain's experience and safety recommendations should always be considered, however.

The coxswain has responsibility for his boat's cleanliness and readiness for service. He must keep abreast of the condition and completeness of the boat equipment, and should report all deficiencies (when discovered) to the boat officer, the responsible division officer, and the officer of the deck.

The boat coxswain is responsible, too, for the appearance and behavior of his boat crew, and must ensure that they always conduct themselves in a seamanlike manner. Coxswains and boat crews are representatives of their ship and should, for that reason, take pride in their own appearance and the "image" presented by their boat. The efficiency and smartness of a ship's boats and boat crew reflect the standards of the ship to which they belong.

Along with his many responsibilities, a boat coxswain has considerable authority. Subject to the orders of the officer of the deck, the senior line officer embarked, and the boat officer (when assigned), a coxswain has full charge of his boat and its crew. Passengers, regardless of rating or grade, must cooperate fully with him and obey his orders. The coxswain ensures that all passengers are seated properly and remain so, that they keep their hands and arms off the gunwales, and that boat etiquette is observed at all times. He enforces the no-smoking regulation. He has the authority to quell any disturbance, and if unable to do so, he can request assistance from the senior officer or petty officer embarked. The coxswain reports any disturbance or unusual occurrence to the OOD immediately upon return to the ship.

Bowhooks and Sternhooks

A *bowhook* and *sternhook* are also members of a small boat's crew. Their titles refer to the boat hooks which they sometimes use to help dock the boat. The bowhook and sternhook must set themselves the task of acquiring all the knowledge necessary to operate the boat, in the event that one of them should be required to relieve the coxswain in an emergency. When the boat is in operation, the bowhook should always be forward acting as a lookout, keeping watch for any floating object that might damage the boat.

Both the bowhook and sternhook should be ready at all times to fend off the boat from contact with other boats or with the gangway or landing. Positioning a boat's *fenders* is thus one of their more important tasks. Fenders are shock-absorbing devices used to cushion any contact between a boat and a pier or ship's side. Fenders may be constructed of rubber, manila, or nylon, and may be of various shapes and sizes. A boat will normally carry several small fenders to protect her sides during landings.

Boat Engineer

The *boat engineer*, generally a member of the engineering department, aids the coxswain by maintaining the boat's engine. A proper monitoring of engine pressures, temperatures, and water flow enables the engineer to detect malfunctions quickly before serious damage is done. If emergency repairs of adjustments are required, the boat

Figure 4-9. A bowhook.

engineer has that responsibility. Unless the situation dictates differently, only the boat engineer should work on the engine.

Boat Officer

During heavy weather, fog, low visibility, and at other times deemed necessary, an officer or chief petty officer is assigned as a safety observer to each ship's boat and is known as a *boat officer*. A boat officer has authority over the coxswain. He does not assume the coxswain's responsibilities, and he rarely relieves him of his normal duties. The boat officer, however, may relieve or direct the coxswain as he sees fit in order to ensure that safety precautions are followed and the boat safely navigated. The situation is somewhat like the relationship between the officer of the deck and the commanding officer on the bridge.

The coxswain and the boat officer together are responsible for the boat and for the safety and welfare of the crew and passengers. However, U.S. Navy regulations state that the senior line officer, embarked and eligible for command at sea, has authority over all persons in the boat and has the ultimate responsibility for the safety and management of the boat. The boat officer is responsible for keeping the senior line officer embarked informed of any unusual circumstances or difficulties affecting the boat's safe operation. If no senior line officer is embarked, the boat officer retains ultimate responsibility for the craft.

The Small Boat Engine

Small boats are generally powered by either a gasoline or diesel engine. Both types convert thermal energy to mechanical energy through a process of internal combustion.

The general trend in the Navy is to install diesel engines rather than gasoline engines unless special conditions favor use of the latter. Although gasoline engines are convenient because of their small size, diesel engines tend to be more efficient, and their fuel is less dangerous to store and transfer.

The chief danger of a gasoline engine lies in the highly explosive fumes from her fuel. Those fumes can travel along a current of air, and like a powder train, lead a blast or flame back to the source of supply and send the whole works skyward. The fumes are heavier than air, and may hang around indefinitely, even in the bilges of an open boat. Before starting a gas engine, every space subject to the accumulation of vapor must be thoroughly ventilated.

Most Navy powerboat engines are very simple to operate. Direction of propeller motion is controlled by a clutch lever, which moves in a fore-and-aft line through about 20° of the arc of a circle. When the lever is midway between its extreme forward and extreme after positions, the clutch is out; in other words, the propeller shaft is disengaged from the engine. Pushing the clutch lever forward engages the propeller ahead, so that the boat is driven forward. Pushing the clutch lever aft engages the propeller astern, so that the boat backs. Propeller speed in either direction is controlled by a throttle, which is usually in the shape of a small hand-operated lever, moving in a vertical line: up for faster, down for slower. Pushing the throttle all the way down shuts off the engine.

In the motorboat, in new personnel and utility boats, and in most landing craft, the coxswain operates the boat's engine(s) himself: the clutch lever and throttle are so situated with reference to the wheel that the coxswain can operate both of them as he steers. In some older boats and launches, however, the engine is located amidships, with the coxswains's station aft at the tiller. In this type of craft the boat engineer operates the engine, in accordance with orders received from the coxswain.

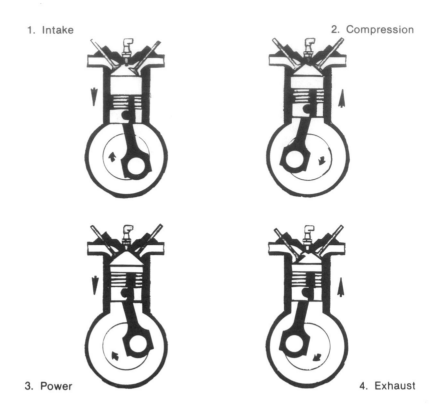

1. Intake   2. Compression

3. Power   4. Exhaust

Figure 4-10. A gasoline engine combustion cycle.

Gasoline and Diesel Engine Operation

Gasoline and diesel engines differ principally in that the former has a carburetor and a "spark ignition" system. The fuel and air for the gasoline engine is mixed in the carburetor. This mixture is drawn into the cylinders where it is compressed and ignited by an electric spark.

The diesel is commonly known as a compression-ignition type engine. The diesel engine takes in atmospheric air, compresses it, and then injects the fuel into the combustion space. The heat generated by compressing the air (over 1000° F.) ignites the fuel, hence the term "compression ignition."

The operation of an internal combustion engine of the reciprocating piston type (diesel and gasoline) involves the admission of fuel and air into a combustion space (cylinder) and the compression and ignition of the charge. The resulting combustion releases gases and greatly increases the temperature within the space. As temperature increases, pressure increases and forces the piston to move. This movement is transmitted through a series of parts to a shaft. The resulting rotary motion of the shaft is used for work; thus, heat energy is transformed into mechanical energy. In order for the process to be continuous, the expanded gases must be removed from the combustion space, a new charge admitted, and then the process repeated.

In the study of engine operating principles, starting with the admission of air and fuel and following through to the removal of the expanded gases, it should be noted that a series of events takes place in the cylinder of an engine for each power impulse transmitted to the crankshaft. These events always occur in the same order each time the cycle is repeated. The number of events occurring in a cycle of operation will depend upon the engine type—diesel or gasoline. The difference in the events occurring in the cycle of operation for these engines is shown in the following table.

Table 4-1. Cycles of Operation for Diesel and Gasoline Engines

Diesel Engine	Gasoline Engine
Intake of air	Intake of fuel and air
Compression of air by piston (producing heat)	Compression of fuel-air mixture by piston
Injection of fuel	Spark ignition and combustion (increasing temperature)
Heat ignition and combustion (increasing temperature)	Expansion of gases (increasing pressure, moving piston)
Expansion of gases (increasing pressure, moving piston)	Removal of waste
Removal of waste	

As shown in the table, the principal difference in the cycles of operation for diesel and gasoline engines involves the admission of fuel and air to the cylinder. While this takes place as one event in the operating cycle of a gasoline engine, it involves two events in diesel engines. Thus, insofar as events are concerned, there are six main events taking place in the diesel cycle of operation and five in the cycle of a gasoline engine. However, even though all of these events take place during every cycle of operation, the number of piston strokes required to carry out the various events may differ.

Piston Stroke Cycles

All reciprocating internal combustion engines operate on either a 2-stroke or a 4-stroke cycle. A stroke is a single up or down movement of the piston, or the distance a piston moves between limits of travel. The number of piston strokes occurring during any one series of events required to perform a cycle determines whether it is a 2-stroke (one power stroke every crankshaft revolution) or 4-stroke (one power stroke for every two crankshaft revolutions) engine.

Four-Stroke Cycle   In a 4-stroke diesel cycle, the first piston stroke (the intake stroke) is downward and allows air to enter the cylinder. As the crankshaft completes one revolution, the piston makes its second stroke (an upward stroke) and compresses the air in the cylinder. The third piston stroke (downward) occurs after the heated air has ignited the injected fuel. This third stroke is the power stroke that keeps the crankshaft turning. The fourth piston stroke, the exhaust stroke, is again an upward one that forces the burned gases out of the cylinder through an exhaust valve. The crankshaft has thus completed two revolutions, the piston has made four strokes, and the cycle begins anew.

Two-Stroke Cycle   Two-stroke-cycle diesel engines are widely used by the Navy. Although some gasoline engines operate on the 2-stroke cycle, their use is limited principally to small outboard motors and some small motorcycles.

Every second stroke of a 2-stroke-cycle engine is a power stroke. The strokes between are compression strokes. The intake and exhaust functions take place rapidly at the bottom of each power stroke. With this arrangement there is one power stroke for each revolution of the crankshaft, or twice as many as in a 4-stroke cycle engine.

The steps in the operation of a 2-stroke-cycle engine are shown in figure 4-11. The cylinder has exhaust valves but no intake valves. Instead it has holes or ports in the cylinder wall near the lowest point of the piston's travel. As the piston nears the bottom of the power stroke, shown in (a) of figure 4-11, it uncovers these intake ports. Air delivered under pressure by a blower (air pump) forces air in through the intake ports, and the burned gases are carried out through the exhaust valve. This air scavenging operation takes place almost instantly and corresponds to the intake and exhaust strokes of the 4-stroke cycle.

In (b) of figure 4-11, the piston is moving upward on the compression stroke. The exhaust valves and the intake ports are now closed and the piston is compressing the air trapped in the combustion chamber. At the top of the stroke, (c) of figure 4-11, fuel is sprayed into the cylinder where it is ignited by the hot compressed air. The power stroke has started. Hot expanding gases force the piston back down.

In (d) of figure 4-11, the piston is moving downward, completing the power stroke. The exhaust valve now opens and the intake ports are uncovered, allowing more scavenging air to force the burned gas from the cylinder.

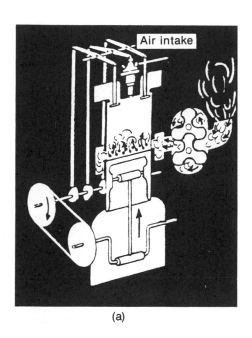

(a)

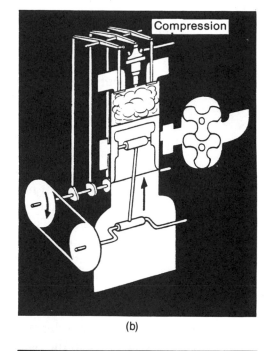

(b)

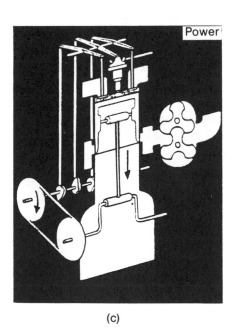

(c)

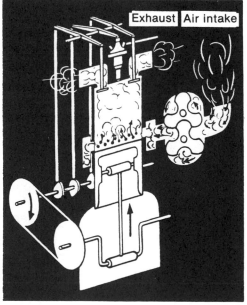

(d)

Figure 4-11. 2-stroke diesel cycle.

You might expect a 2-stroke-cycle engine to develop twice as much power as a 4-stroke-cycle engine. Such is not the case, however, because some of the engine's power is required to drive the blower and some is lost due to the position of the intake ports at the cylinder bottom. Nevertheless, 2-stroke-cycle diesel engines give excellent service.

Small-Boat Line Handling

When approaching a ship's gangway in a small boat, the bowhook should be ready to use his boat hook to snag the boat line from the ship and secure it to a cleat on the bow. On approaching a pier landing, the bowhook is responsible for throwing the boat's bow line to someone on the pier so that it may be secured to a cleat or set of bitts. However, should a line handler not be on the pier, the bowhook should be ready to spring ashore smartly with one end of the bow line and take a turn on the nearest cleat. The bowhook must exercise great caution as he jumps, even though the boat may be very near or perhaps touching the landing. Sometimes a line may foul and restrict the movement of the line handler so that he falls short of his mark.

The sternhook, likewise, should be ready to jump ashore to make the boat's stern fast. Frequently, though, the stern is some distance from the landing, and the sternhook may have to move closer to the bow to be able to reach the pier. The sternhook, it is humorously said, should never try a leap that is going to take two jumps—for obvious reasons.

The sternhook ordinarily does not carry the stern line when he jumps ashore. It usually is not safe, since the distance he must cover is greater than that of the bowhook and, again, the line may foul. The stern line is passed to the sternhook once he is ashore.

When the boat is about to get under way, both the bowhook and sternhook must be at their lines, ready to cast off and jump aboard. They should never cast off, however, without orders from the coxswain. He frequently must use the boat's lines to aid in maneuvering to clear the landing. When not in use, a boat's lines should be neatly stowed on deck or put away.

Line-Handling Commands

Considering the importance of line handling in both landing a boat and getting her under way, it is not surprising to note that the coxswain issues all line handling commands to the bowhook and sternhook. They should never put over or take in the boat's lines without the coxswain's permission.

In order to avoid dangerous misunderstandings or misinterpretations, line-handling commands are standardized, and each one has a

Figure 4-12.   Handling a small boat's lines and fenders.

very specific meaning. Several of the most commonly used commands
are listed below with their definitions.

"Put over the (bow or stern) line." Meaning pass the line to the pier,
place the line around the cleat, but take no strain.

"Take a strain on the (bow or stern) line." Meaning put the line under
tension.

"Hold the (bow or stern) line." Meaning do not allow any more of
that line to pay out; take enough turns on the cleat to prevent slippage
even though the risk of parting the line may exist.

"Check the (bow or stern) line." Meaning put a heavy tension on the line, but tend the line and allow some slippage if it looks as if it may part.

"Slack the (bow or stern) line." Meaning take all the tension off the line and let it hang slack, but not in the water.

"Cast off the (bow or stern) line." Meaning remove the line from the cleat and throw it to the boat. This command is given to someone *on the pier*.

"Take in the (bow or stern) line." Meaning retrieve the line and bring it back on deck. This command is given to someone *on the boat*.

There are other standard line-handling commands, but they are easily learned and are covered in greater depth in chapter 6.

Line-Handling Safety

A brief word about boat line-handling safety must be mentioned at this point. Lines on board a boat may seriously injure an unwary seaman. Lines can burn or wrap around a human body and actually sever a limb or finger. Respect lines and handle them with caution. Learn these important points:

- Never put feet or hands in the bight (loop) of a line.
- Lines not in use should be carefully made up and stowed clear of walkways.
- Never stand in the snap-back path of a line under such strain that it might part.
- Never grab a line as it runs through a chock.
- Never place your fingers between a line and a cleat.

Small Boat Handling

Prerequisites to becoming a competent boat handler include an understanding of the forces that influence boat movement and the ability to use those forces to advantage. The coxswain must know the maneuvering characteristics of his boat, the effects of propellers and rudders, and the effects of various sea and wind conditions.

Forces Affecting Boat Movement

A variety of forces influence a boat's movement through the water. It is convenient to think of these forces as being either controllable (i.e., under the control of the coxswain) or noncontrollable (i.e., outside the influence of the coxswain).

Controllable Forces

Controllable forces are those over which the boat coxswain has command. His skill in bringing these forces into play will usually determine how well the boat is maneuvered. Controllable forces include the following:

Propellers Generally speaking, a boat is moved by forces resulting from pressure differences. For all practical purposes, water is incompressible; therefore, when force is applied to a propeller or screw, high- and low-pressure areas are created on opposite sides of the propeller blades. This force, called *propeller thrust*, is transmitted along the propeller shaft in the direction from the high-pressure area toward the low-pressure area. When the propeller is rotating clockwise, the low-pressure area is on the forward face of the blade, resulting in forward movement of the boat.

Side Force Next in importance to propeller thrust is *side force*, which tends to move the boat's stern sidewise in the direction of propeller rotation.

The upper blades exert a force opposite to that of the lower blades, but the lower blades are moving in water of greater pressure. Consequently, the force of the lower blades is greater. It is as though the lower blades were touching the bottom and pushing the stern to the side (figure 4-13). When going ahead the stern tends to starboard, and

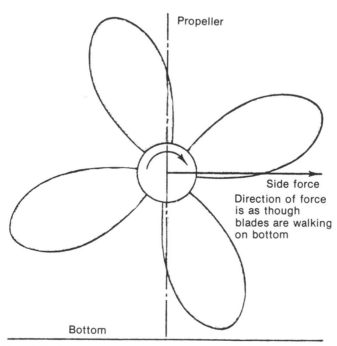

Figure 4-13. Side force.

when backing, to port. Side force is greatest when the boat begins moving from a stationary position, or nearly so, and decreases rapidly as the boat's speed increases. Side force is greater when backing than when going ahead.

Screw Current *Screw current*, caused by the action of a rotating propeller, consists of two parts. The portion flowing into the propeller is the suction current, and the portion flowing away from the propeller is the discharge current. Suction current is a relatively minor force in boat handling. Discharge current is a major force in two main respects: it is a strong force acting on the rudder with the screw going ahead; and it is a strong component of side force when the screw is backing because of the discharge current acting against the boat's hull.

Rudders Single-screw ships and boats have a single rudder mounted directly behind the propeller. Twin-screw ships and boats usually have a rudder mounted directly behind each propeller, but some have a single rudder mounted between and just abaft the propellers.

Basically, a rudder is used to attain or maintain a desired heading. The force necessary to accomplish this is created by dynamic pressure against the surface of the rudder. The magnitude of this force and the direction in which it is applied produces the rudder effect that controls stern movement and, through it, the boat's heading. Factors having a bearing on rudder effect include rudder size, rudder angle, rudder location, boat's speed, direction of propeller rotation, headway, stern-way, suction current, discharge current, and side force. The diverse effects of all of these factors can be lumped together under a single term, *resultant force*, that indicates the direction and amount of thrust exerted on a boat's stern.

Resultant force can be shown by a vector diagram of side force, rudder force, and propeller thrust. Examples of the nearly infinite number of combinations for a single-screw vessel are shown below. The vectors are not to scale, being merely representative of how resultant force is derived.

As might be surmised from studying the resultant vectors in the diagrams, a single-screw vessel is most difficult to maneuver at very low speeds where rudder effect is minimal, while at the same time propeller side force is greatest.

One of the most notable characteristics of a single-screw boat or ship is its tendency to back to port. Four distinct forces affect a boat's steering when backing:

1. The discharge current from the propeller. This tends to throw the stern to port.

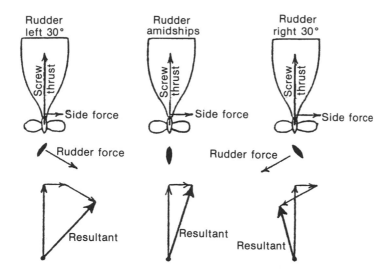

(a) Boat starts ahead from being dead in the water, RPM for 5 knots.

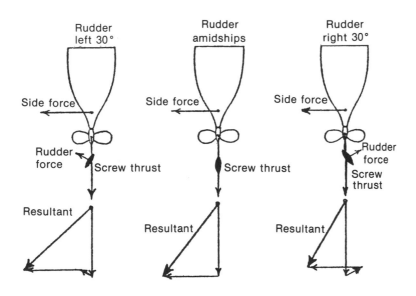

(b) Boat starts astern from being dead in the water, RPM for 5 knots.

Figure 4-14. A. Boat starts ahead from being dead in the water, RPM for 5 knots.
B. Boat starts astern from being dead in the water, RMP for 5 knots.

2. The suction current caused by the propeller drawing in water from astern, which adds to the steering effect of the rudder, although not by any great amount.

3. The sidewise pressure of the blades, which forces the stern to port.

4. The normal steering effect of the rudder.

When a single-screw boat first starts to back, the steering effect of the rudder is negligible. The suction current tends to force the stern to the side on which the rudder is placed. The propeller discharge and sidewise pressure both force the stern to port. Even with a hard right rudder, the boat will usually back to port because the suction current force is less than the combined effect of the propeller discharge and sidewise pressure from the blades.

As a boat gathers sternway, the steering effect of the rudder increases. All four of the above forces combine to make the stern go rapidly to port if the rudder is hard left.

Usually, after the boat is moving rapidly astern, it will be possible to steer the stern to starboard if the rudder is put hard right. In this case, the combined force of the suction current and the steering effect overcomes the combined effect of the sidewise pressure of the blades and the discharge current of the propeller. (See figure 4-15.)

Mooring Lines and Anchors   Mooring lines allow a boat coxswain to carry out maneuvers alongside a pier or landing that would otherwise be extremely difficult or impossible. By *springing* on a mooring line, that is, using a line to restrict the forward or aft movement of the boat, a coxswain is able to swing the bow or stern away from a landing and (1)

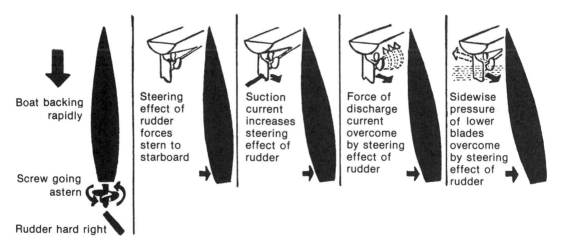

Figure 4-15.   *Boat backing rapidly, rudder hard right.*

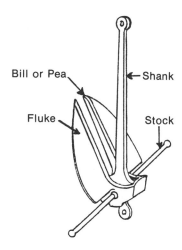

Figure 4-16. *Lightweight type (LWT) anchor.*

overcome any disadvantages associated with a screw that causes the boat to back to port or (2) avoid hazards associated with restricted maneuvering space.

Anchors, too, can be used to aid or restrict the movement of a boat. A boat coxswain can use his anchor to help the boat maintain an advantageous position or resist the effects of wind and current.

When operating in heavy seas a *drogue* or sea anchor is a handy device for a coxswain to have aboard. A drogue or sea anchor is a cone-shaped canvas bag about two feet wide at the mouth and approximately four and one-half feet long. It is towed open-end foremost so as to offer resistance. The towline is made fast to the open end of a sea anchor, and a tripping line is secured to the pointed end. The drogue fills with water and tends to slow down the forward movement of a boat. The most important use of the drogue is in keeping a boat at right angles to a sea. The bow of a small boat can be kept toward the seas by securing the drogue line forward. The drogue's resistance to the water then causes the boat to heave to.

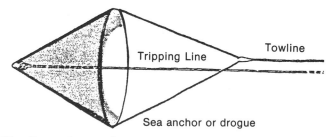

Figure 4-17. *Sea anchor or drogue.*

If the drogue no longer is needed, the towline is let go and the tripping line is held. This action causes the sea anchor to lose its resistance and enables the crew to haul it aboard with relative ease.

Noncontrollable Forces

Noncontrollable forces are those forces over which the boat coxswain has no influence. They include physical restrictions on a boat's maneuverability and various environmental factors. Our discussion of these forces must be general in nature because boat-handling conditions are seldom the same from one day to the next. Nevertheless, an understanding of the effects of the winds, currents, seas, and confined waters is essential to the successful boat coxswain.

Wind   The effect of wind will vary with the design and draft of a boat. A boat with high freeboard will be more affected than one that is low in the water. If the boat has a high bow or superstructure forward, wind will have a greater influence on the boat's bow than it will elsewhere. This may prove helpful under certain conditions, but at other times will be a serious handicap. Its principal effect is to make it difficult to bring the boat up into the wind. In going astern, most ships and boats have a tendency to back into the wind. Therefore, when turning in a confined space with the wind on one bow, the turn should be made away from the wind.

The wind can be particularly troublesome when making a landing. If the boat has a large sail area (superstructure) forward, it may be very difficult to get alongside a pier when the wind is offsetting (coming off the pier).

Current   Just as wind affects the sail area, currents work against the underwater portion of the hull. Unlike the wind, however, the effects or even the presence of an ocean current may be unknown for a considerable time. In inland waters, on the other hand, the effects of tidal and river currents usually are quite evident; if not compensated for, the boat may run aground.

Thus, a coxswain should attempt to determine the existence and influence of any set and drift. *Set* is the direction and *drift* is the speed a vessel is being offset from her course whether by current, wind, or a combination of the two. Knowing the set and drift, a compensating course and speed can be determined that will keep the boat on its proposed track.

In general, a boat that is heavily laden and has low freeboard reacts more to the current, while a light vessel with high freeboard is influenced more by the wind.

Seas It is best to avoid operating boats when the weather is poor and the seas are high. However, a coxswain and crew must be able to handle their boat and get to safety if a sudden squall hits.

One of the more risky situations arises when a powerboat is running before a sea. When the hull is lifted by the stern, there is danger that steerageway and power may be lost when the screw and rudder are clear of the water. The boat may then swing around broadside to the seas. The coxswain must call upon all his skill and adroitness in the use of the rudder to keep the stern to the mountains of water that sometimes are encountered when the going gets rough. It is often helpful to reduce speed and to allow large swells to roll by. In extreme cases, a drogue or sea anchor may be used.

Running into a sea is less hazardous, but not without peril in bad weather. Reduced speed lessens the strain on both engine and hull. To this end the throttle should be adjusted so that the bow rises with oncoming waves instead of driving into them. Taking the seas on either the port or starboard bow is sound seamanship, too, because some of the pitch is lessened by this method.

Avoid the trough except in an emergency. When moving broadside to waves, turn the wheel momentarily, so as to take larger wave crests on the windward bow, and return to the course when conditions permit.

Pier Space and Water Depth Boat coxswains generally have little influence over the pier space or maneuvering area in which they must operate, and they have even less control over the depth of the water in which they must travel. For these reasons it is especially important for a coxswain to know his boat's width, length, and draft, and he must be sure of the surrounding water depth. Grounding a vessel is one of the most serious consequences of poor seamanship.

Another potentially disastrous after-effect of inexperience or irresponsible boat handling is caused by too much speed in confined waters. As a boat increases speed, she starts sinking lower in the water, and distinct bow and stern waves are formed. The bow and stern are relatively level until the speed reaches a certain point, at which time the bow starts rising and the stern sinks. This effect is known as *squatting*. As speed increases past the critical point, the bow wave moves aft, the stern sinks farther, and the boat is, in effect, riding on her own bow wave. The height of the stern wave that travels along with the boat also increases as the boat moves with greater speed.

In shallow water, squatting is more pronounced and can become a serious problem at high speeds because the stern may sink several feet below normal. Whereas at slow speed there might be three feet of water under the propellers, at high speed there might be only two feet, making it possible to damage the propellers if the boat suddenly moves over a very shallow area.

Additionally, a coxswain's high speed and resulting stern wave and wake, although not a menace to his own boat, may cause extensive damage to shore structures, induce heavy rolling in anchored vessels, and break other boats loose from their moorings.

Boat-Handling Pointers

In operating a small boat, as in steering a ship, one of the most important points to remember is that the stern (not the bow) moves first when the wheel is turned and the rudder is put over. It is also important to remember that the boat turns much faster at high speed than at low speed.

As a reminder, all single-screw boats have right-handed screws, turning in a clockwise direction going ahead, when viewed from astern. For this reason, the side force of the screw when going ahead tends to walk the stern to starboard when the boat is gathering headway. This screw action means that your boat always makes a faster turn to port than to starboard when gathering headway.

When beginning to back, however, the stern tends to walk to port, no matter how much rudder you put on to the right. If you have to back a long stretch in a straight line, back with a hard right rudder. Your boat should straighten out if you develop enough momentum (sternway).

One of the first pointers you must learn about your boat is how fast she will back down to a stop. Reverse engine is the only brake you have, and boats vary widely in backing power. If your boat is not a good backer, you must cut your engine a long way off from your landing, otherwise you'll go right by, with your engine backing full, and wind up among the pilings.

Landing Alongside and Getting Under Way

A landing is usually made by running either the boat's starboard or port bow alongside the ship or pier at which you wish to dock. The approach should be made slowly and at an appropriate angle. The coxswain can then back down to bring the boat to a stop in the best position.

It's always easier to go alongside port-side-to than starboard-side-to, because when you put your port bow alongside and start to back, the side force of the backing screw on the stern will walk your after end nicely alongside. In the starboard-side-to landing, however, the same propeller effect sends the stern farther off. Thus, if you have to go starboard-side-to, remember that you must come alongside much straighter, under as little headway as possible, so that little backing down will be necessary. (See figure 4-18.)

Whenever current is a factor in a landing, you should usually make your approach into it, so that the landing is made with the bow against the current. It is extremely difficult to get alongside going with the current, because a following current makes rudder effect very erratic, or reduces it to nil.

Tie up your boat with a bow line leading forward and stern line leading aft. Never have both lines leading in the same direction.

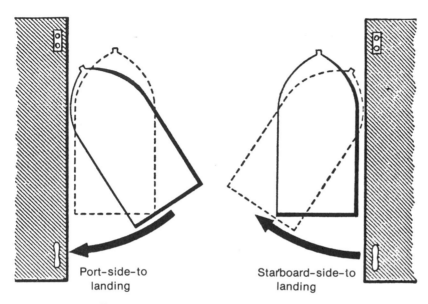

Port–side-to   Starboard–side-to
   landing   landing

Figure 4-18. Effect of backing propeller in coming alongside.

In getting under way from a starboard-side-to landing, usually it is best to back until the stern has walked itself away from the dock. If you have no room astern, hold the bow in with the bow line and go ahead slowly with hard right rudder. When your stern is well out, shove off forward and go ahead with left rudder, but not so much rudder as to send the stern against the dock. If you try to get under way from alongside by immediately going ahead and turning the rudder away from the pier, gangway, or ship's side, the stern will hit hard alongside.

The best way to get under way from a port-side-to landing is also to get your stern out first, but backing the engine here only tends to send it against the dock. It is better to spring ahead on the bow line with a hard left rudder, and your stern will walk out without difficulty. (See figure 4-19.) In both illustrative cases, the bowhook must do all he can to keep the bow off the pier or protect it with a fender.

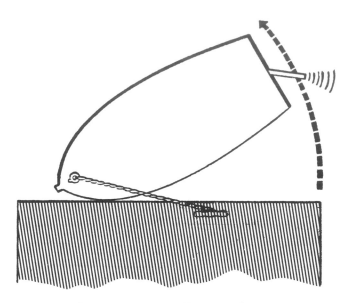

Figure 4-19. Using a bow spring to get off a port-side-to landing.

Man-Overboard Recovery

A potential emergency common to both ships and small boats is losing a man overboard. Additionally, small boats are often the means used to recover a shipboard sailor or downed pilot from the water.

Upon seeing a man go overboard from the boat or upon hearing a call for such assistance, a crew member should immediately alert the boat coxswain by shouting, "Man overboard, port side" (or starboard side, depending on where the man fell). The crew member should simultaneously make every attempt to toss a life ring to the man. It matters not whether the individual in the water is a good swimmer; often a man is injured by his fall and would find it difficult to stay afloat without the life ring. The crew member should keep the man in sight at all times and point in his direction so that others may spot him.

It is not always necessary in a small boat, but it is generally considered wise for the coxswain, upon hearing "Man overboard," to turn the boat toward the direction in which the man fell (e.g., right full rudder for a man overboard, starboard side). The purpose of this maneuver is to move the boat's screw away from the man should he not already be past the stern.

To alert other craft in the area of the emergency so that they may stay clear, sound six or more short blasts on the boat's horn or whistle. If the boat is configured to do so, display the appropriate visual signals as well. By day hoist the OSCAR flag; at night display two vertical pulsating red lights, or fire one white rocket (a Very light).

There are various man-overboard recovery methods that can be used with a small boat, but only one, the *Anderson turn*, will be described here. The Anderson, or circular, turn is a relatively simple maneuver in a small boat primarily because of a boat's tight turning characteristics and maneuverability. The Anderson turn is an appropriate recovery method if visibility is such that the man lost overboard can be kept in sight at all times.

To make an Anderson turn, the coxswain puts the rudder over in the direction toward which the man fell and increases the boat's speed to complete a circular turn quickly. When about two thirds or so of the way around, he should reduce the boat's speed and begin to back down as he nears the man. (Backing is the boat's brake, or course.) Full rudder should continue to be used until very near the man.

To pick the man up on the boat's starboard or port side is the decision of the coxswain. If heavy winds would tend to push the boat away from the man and make the recovery more difficult, the coxswain may wish to maneuver the boat between the man and the wind. Ordinarily, however, the coxswain will decide to recover a man overboard on the side of the boat which affords him greatest visibility. Keeping the man in sight is the safest procedure.

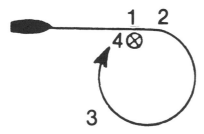

Figure 4-20.   1. *Put the rudder over full in the direction corresponding to the side over which the man fell.*
2. *When clear of the man, increase the speed.*
3. *When about two-thirds of the way around, reduce speed, back the engine to stop near the man.*
4. *Pick the man up on the side of the boat offering least difficulty and greatest safety.*

Steering a Boat by Compass

Standard boats and combatant craft practically always are equipped with a compass. The coxswain uses this instrument more than any other device in piloting his craft to its destination.

A compass is simply an instrument that tells you the direction you are heading. It tells you where north is, so you can measure all other directions from that one fixed point or direction.

Compasses are of two main types: *gyroscopic* and *magnetic*. The gyrocompass works on the gyroscopic principle of a spinning top; the magnetic compass is affected by the magnetic field of the earth. In each instance the compass card points toward the north. From the compass card, directions can be taken in degrees or in such terms as north, south, southwest, and so on. The Navy expresses direction in degrees, saying that the direction or course is 000°, 180°, or 225°, instead of north, south, or southwest.

Gyrocompass

The gyrocompass is unaffected by magnetic influence. When in proper running order, it points constantly to the *true* rather than to the *magnetic* North Pole. Although it may have a slight mechanical error of 1° or 2°, corrections are computed easily and remain constant for any heading, so that the error does not interfere in any way with the instrument's practical value.

Considering the gyro's advantages, you may wonder why the Navy doesn't heave all the magnetic compasses over the side and relieve everyone of the necessity of learning the principles of using them. Despite the excellence of the gyro mechanism, however, the magnetic compass—not the gyro—is standard on board ships and boats of the Navy.

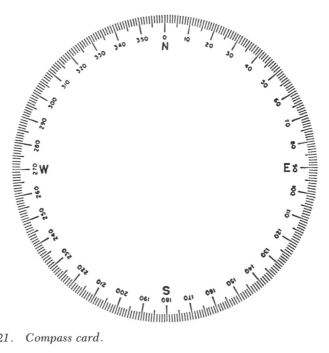

Figure 4-21. Compass card.

This is because the magnetic compass operates through the attraction exerted by the great natural magnet, the earth. Since the earth is absolutely certain to continue to function as a magnet, the magnetic compass will never go out of commission as a result of any failure of its source of power. On the other hand, the gyrocompass is powered by electricity. If the power should be cut off, the gyro would be absolutely useless. It is an extremely complicated and delicate instrument, and sometimes is subject to serious mechanical failure. An impaired gyro, for instance, may become erratic after the ship makes a series of sharp turns at high speed. This does not mean, however, that great confidence cannot be placed in a gyro. When running properly, it can be depended upon to point faithfully and steadily to true north. But the magnetic compass remains the always reliable standby, constantly checking the gyro's performance, and ready at all times to take over if it fails.

Magnetic Compass

The magnetic compass consists of a magnetized compass needle attached to a circular compass card. The compass card is divided into 360 degrees and is numbered all the way around in a clockwise direction. The card and needle are supported on a pivot that is set in a cast

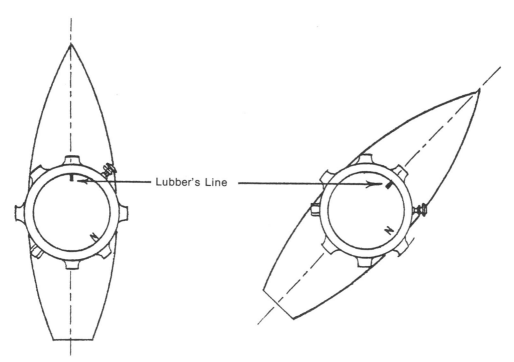

Figure 4-22. Lubber's line.

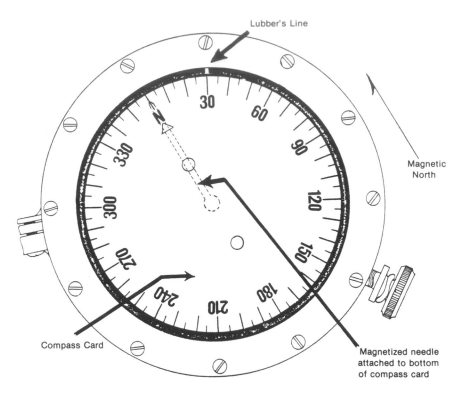

Figure 4-23. Compass card showing lubber's line.

bronze bowl filled with a liquid. This liquid buoys up the card and magnet, tending to take some of the load off the pivot, thereby reducing the friction and letting the card turn more easily on the pivot. At the same time, the liquid slows the swing of the card and brings it to rest more quickly. Marked on the compass bowl is a line, called the *lubber's line*, which agrees with the fore-and-aft line of the ship or boat. By reading the compass card direction, lined up with the lubber's line, you can tell the direction in which the boat is heading. Remember, though, that the card remains stationary. It always points at the magnetic pole. When you are steering, always remember that the ship turns UNDER the card.

Magnetic Compass Error Since the earth's magnetic pole is approximately 400 miles from the geographic north pole, there is usually a difference of several degrees between true north and magnetic north. This angular difference between true north and the earth's magnetic field, with which the magnetic compass aligns itself, is called *variation*. The amount of variation experienced depends upon the observer's geographic location.

The motor and the metal used in boat construction may cause another difference in magnetic compass readings. The influence of metal or electrical fields may prevent a magnetic compass needle from aligning itself parallel to the earth's magnetic field. The error that results is called *deviation*. Deviation is seldom a significant problem in Navy boats if the compass is mounted well forward of the motor and away from any electrical fields caused by wiring. All metal objects, however, including the anchor, should be kept as far from the compass as possible.

Variation and deviation will cause a boat's magnetic compass to differ or "error" from true north. Corrections can be applied to a magnetic reading to convert it to a true reading if such is necessary.

Bearings

Accurately measuring or obtaining the correct direction is clearly an important skill for any coxswain to develop. As you have read, the compass indicates direction and helps to establish a course for your boat to steer.

In modern navigation, the direction to any object is called its *bearing*. Bearings are given in degrees (as are courses) and are measured clockwise, usually from a compass. For clarity, a bearing, of course, is

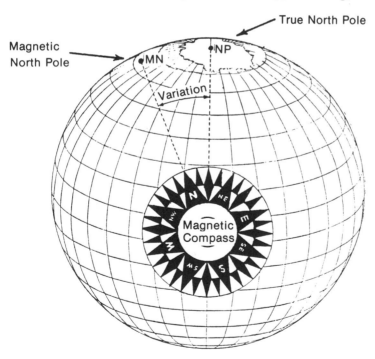

Figure 4-24. *The angular difference between true north and the earth's magnetic field is called variation.*

always expressed in three figures, regardless of whether three digits are required. For example, the bearing 45° is not (forty-five), but 045° (zero four five), and due north can be stated as bearing 000° (zero zero zero).

There are actually two kinds of bearings frequently used in the Navy. These are *true bearings* and *relative bearings*. True bearings to objects can be obtained directly from a gyrocompass or from a magnetic compass (after applying the appropriate corrections for variation and deviation). True bearings are based on a circle of degrees with true north as 000°T (or 360°T); east as 090°T; south as 180°T; and west as 270°T.

Gryocompass repeaters on the bridge wings of a ship are most often used to determine the true bearing to an object. Movable sighting vanes placed on the face of the compass are aimed at an object in the same manner in which rifle sights are lined up. The bearing to the object is then merely read from the designated point on the compass card.

Relative bearings, on the other hand, are used to locate quickly, or indicate the position of, an object in relation to your own ship or boat without the aid of a compass, as do shipboard lookouts. Lookouts and boat coxswains know that relative bearings are based on a circle drawn

Figure 4-25. Gyro repeater and sighting vanes.

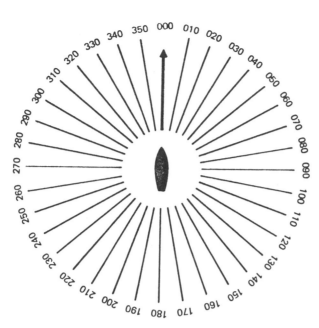

Figure 4-26. Relative bearings, measured clockwise from the ship's head, locate an object in relation to the ship. They have nothing to do with geographical directions.

clockwise around the ship or boat itself, with the bow as 000° relative, the starboard beam as 090°R, the stern as 180°R, and the port beam as 270°R. Thus, if a ship is on a course true north (000°), another ship sighted dead ahead would bear 000° true and 000° relative. But if the ship were on a course true east and sighted a ship dead ahead, the sighted ship would bear 090° true but would still be dead ahead or 000° relative.

Both true and relative bearings are used by coxswains to navigate their craft and to aid in avoiding collisions with other vessels. By monitoring the bearings to other ships and boats and noting the changes or lack of change of those bearings, a coxswain can determine if it is necessary to maneuver to avoid trouble. A well-known thumb rule concerning bearings and other vessels is "constant bearing and decreasing range means collision unless things change."

Basic Rules of the Road

With a view to avoiding collisions at sea, the maritime countries have adopted a system of International Rules of the Road (1972 COLREGS). These Rules comprise a uniform set of traffic regulations that apply to vessels of all nations while navigating the high seas. Vessels operating

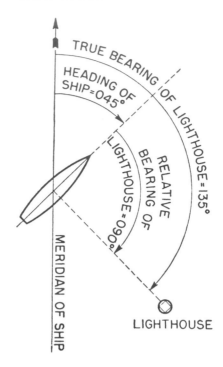

Figure 4-27. True and relative bearings.

in U.S. inland waters conform to U.S. Inland Rules of the Road.* Navy small craft operate most frequently in waters where U.S. Inland Rules apply. The applicable coverage, according to the clearly defined Rules, is as follows:

> "All harbors, rivers, and inland waters of the United States, except the Great Lakes and their connecting and tributary waters as far east as Montreal, Canada, and the Red River of the North and rivers emptying into the Gulf of Mexico."

Inland Rules of the Road vary from International Rules chiefly by the addition of certain extra precautions. In general, the Rules of the Road describe situations where one vessel must take necessary action to keep clear of another. This is termed *giving way*. The other ship, at the same time, is required to maintain her course and speed and thus is termed the *stand-on* vessel. There are three basic maneuvering situations involving risk of collision. Each is described below.

---

*These rules are presently being revised to conform more closely to the International Rules and will probably be in effect in 1982.

One thing to keep in mind is that a power-driven vessel must always keep clear of a vessel under sail, except when being overtaken by the latter and except when the power-driven vessel is restricted to a narrow channel.

Overtaking Situation

Any vessel, even a sailing vessel, overtaking another from astern must keep clear of the vessel being overtaken. Inland Rules require that steam vessels must not pass from astern without an O.K. by whistle of the vessel ahead. If you intend to pass to starboard, you sound one short blast (about one second in length) on the vessels's whistle or horn; should you intend to pass to port, you sound two short blasts. If the other ship answers with the same number of blasts, go ahead and pass. If she thinks it's dangerous for you to pass her at that point, she replies with no less than four short rapid blasts, in which event you positively are forbidden to pass her. The short rapid blasts are commonly called the danger signal.

Under International Rules, there are similar passing signals for overtaking a vessel in a narrow channel. The danger signal under the International Rules (five or more short blasts) is, however, more appropriately referred to as the "doubt" signal. It may be sounded by any vessel doubting the actions or intentions of an approaching ship or boat.

Meeting or Head-on Situation

The meeting situation is said to exist between two vessels when their bows are pointed at one another (or are nearly so), and the distance between them is decreasing. To clarify, as two ships approach each other on essentially reciprocal courses, the meeting situation would exist if each vessel could see the masts or masthead lights of the other

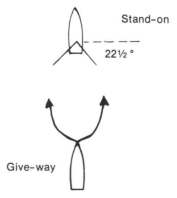

Stand-on

22½ °

Give-way

Figure 4-28. Overtaking situation.

ahead and in line or nearly in line with her own. At night each ship would see both side lights of the other vessel.

The Rules of the Road require both vessels in this situation to give way. Each ship or boat should alter her course to starboard to leave the other on her port side as they pass.

In international waters, when a vessel changes its course to starboard during a meeting situation, a single short blast (about one second in length), should be sounded on the vessel's whistle or horn. This sound serves as a signal to the other ship or boat that a starboard course alteration has been made.

In inland waters there is also an exchange of sound signals between two meeting vessels. One vessel proposes a port (side) to port (side) passage by sounding one short blast on the whistle or horn, and the other vessel agrees to such a passage by repeating the same signal, one short blast. If one vessel fails to respond, does not understand the other's intentions, or does not agree to the proposed passage, the danger signal (four or more short blasts) should be sounded.

A starboard to starboard passage is legal under Inland Rules, but prior to the passage, two short blasts must be sounded by both vessels. Such a passage generally is not made unless the vessels are so far to the right of one another that maneuvering is unnecessary for a safe passage.

It is important to remember that signals must be given in plenty of time to be effective, and that nearly all head-on collisions occur because one vessel fails to alter course when necessary or alters course to the left in violation of the Rules of the Road.

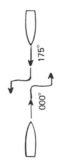

Figure 4-29.   Meeting situation.

Crossing Situation

When two vessels are approaching each other in such a way as to risk collision (i.e., there is no appreciable change in the bearing), and they are not considered to be in a meeting or an overtaking situation, they are considered to be in a crossing situation. That means they are approaching each other either obliquely or at nearly right angles.

The Rules of the Road state that when two vessels are crossing so as to involve risk of collision, the vessel to the right is the stand-on vessel and is obligated to maintain her course and speed. The other ship or boat is considered the give-way vessel and must stay clear of the stand-on vessel. The give-way vessel keeps out of the way by slowing, stopping, backing, or by changing course (the usual procedure).

In a crossing situation the usual procedure is for the give-way vessel to alter course to starboard to pass astern of the stand-on vessel. In international waters the give-way vessel would sound one short blast indicating she was carrying out such a maneuver.

In inland waters the stand-on vessel may sound one short blast indicating her intention to maintain course and speed. The give-way vessel would respond with one short blast indicating agreement and her intention to keep clear by coming right, slowing, stopping, or backing down as necessary.

In international or inland waters, if one vessel fails to understand the movements or intentions of the other, the danger signal should be sounded.

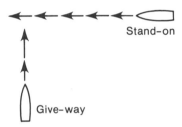

Figure 4-30. Crossing situation.

The question of increasing speed and crossing ahead of a slower moving stand-on vessel is frequently asked. This maneuver is sometimes an option of the OOD or boat coxswain, but it is one that should be considered carefully, because the Rules of the Road do not recognize its legality if a collision occurs. If any doubts exist as to the safety of such a maneuver or if it is likely to worry or embarrass the other vessel, crossing ahead should not be attempted. It would be a good idea for a ship's OOD to seek the advice of the CO or for a boat's coxswain to check with the boat officer before crossing ahead of a stand-on vessel.

General Prudential (Special Circumstances) Rule

Whether a situation between two vessels is characterized as overtaking, meeting, or crossing depends upon the relative positions of the two ships or boats *when they initially sight each other (visually, not on radar*). The nautical Rules of the Road associated with those situations are designed to provide guidance for the two vessels in order to avoid collision.

Nautical Rules of the Road are actually laws and should be regarded as such. However, when the risk of collision exists between more than two ships at the same time, a strict adherence to the rule for one maneuvering situation may cause a disaster as another situation unfolds.

For example, if a vessel were required by one situation to maintain course and speed and by another situation (involving a third vessel) to alter course to avoid collision, then certainly she could not do both. The *General Prudential* (Special Circumstances) *Rule* allows a departure from the commonly observed maneuvering rules in this and certain other situations. The General Prudential Rule gives a vessel the right to use good nautical sense to avoid collision when more than one contact is encountered at the same time or when other special circumstances dictate.

Rule of Good Seamanship

Another important rule of a general nature is the *Rule of Good Seamanship*. The Rule of Good Seamanship states that nothing in the Rules of the Road shall exonerate any vessel from the consequences of neglecting to comply with any precaution normally called for in the practice of good seamanship. Such things as carrying the proper lights and signals or keeping a proper lookout for danger are practices of this type.

Lights

United States Navy boats carry lights as prescribed in the International and Inland Rules. The lights required under both sets of rules differ slightly, but in simplest terms, they are:

- A red side light on the boat's port side forward.
- A green side light on the boat's starboard side forward.
- A white light on the boat's stern.
- A white light in the highest, forwardmost location, if such a light can be mounted.

These running lights must be bright enough to be visible for prescribed distances and must be screened in such a way that each light can be seen only from certain aspects. For example, your boat's stern light should not be visible to another vessel off your port bow. The other boat should be seeing your red port side light. That light tells her your relative position and in what direction you are heading.

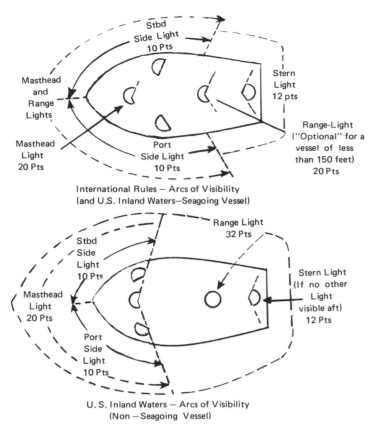

Figure 4-31. *Lights for a power-driven vessel under way.*

During daylight hours, when visibility is good, it is fairly easy to recognize a situation that exists between two boats. But at night, with only the running lights to indicate relative positions, it is more difficult. Thus, a boat's coxswain and crew must exercise additional caution when operating at night or during reduced visibility.

Reduced Visibility and Fog Signals

In fog, mist, falling snow, heavy rainstorms, or any other condition similarly restricting visibility, whether by day or night, a power-driven vessel must sound various signals to alert other vessels as to her presence.

Under International Rules, a power-driven vessel under way and making way through the water must sound a prolonged blast (4 to 6 seconds in length) at intervals of not more than 2 minutes. If the vessel is under way with no way on, two prolonged blasts, with an interval of about 1 second between, are sounded every 2 minutes.

Under Inland Rules, a prolonged blast is sounded at intervals of not more than 1 minute.

A vessel at anchor in international waters must sound a bell located in the forepart of the vessel for a period of about 5 seconds at intervals of not more than 1 minute. In addition, a gong or other instrument with a distinct tone (that cannot be confused with the bell) must be sounded at the same intervals for the same period of time from the after part of the vessel. The sounding of the gong immediately follows the bell signal. Inland Rules require only the bell signal at intervals of not more than 1 minute.

In addition to the regulation fog signal, the Navy sometimes sounds another fog signal while at anchor. This additional signal consists of sounding (immediately following the sounding of the bell forward) the number of strokes necessary to indicate the last two digits of the ship's hull number. Boat coxswains learn the calls of the various ships and thus can work their way through the fog to and from their destinations.

Speed in Fog

Under conditions of reduced visibility, every vessel is required to proceed at a safe or moderate speed. Moderate speed, as defined by the courts, is "any speed which will enable a vessel to stop within half the distance of visibility." Obviously, this interpretation is necessary in order to allow a vessel on an opposite course to have an equal distance to stop after the vessels sight one another.

Under International Rules, any vessel hearing, apparently forward of her beam, the fog signal of another vessel whose position is either unknown or might cause close quarters, must reduce her speed to the minimum required to stay on course or if necessary, take all way off, and in any event, navigate with caution until the danger of collision is over. Similar rules apply on inland waters.

U.S. Buoyage System

The system of buoyage used in United States waters has been devised for the purpose of guiding ships in channels, warning them away from sunken dangers, and leading them to anchorage areas. Buoys may be of various sizes and types, but their distinctive coloring indicates their purpose, regardless of their shapes and sizes.

Lateral and Cardinal Buoyage Systems

Most maritime countries use either the lateral or the cardinal system of buoyage. Some countries assign both systems.

The lateral system is used on all navigable waters of the United States. In this system the coloring, shape, and lighting of buoys indicate the direction to a danger relative to the course that should be followed. Thus, a buoy that should be kept on the port hand lies between the vessel and the danger when the buoy is approximately abeam to port.

In the cardinal buoyage system, the coloring, shape, and lighting of buoys show the direction to a danger relative to the buoy itself.

Types of Buoys

Although a buoy's type generally does not have a special navigational significance, it may help toward its identification and purpose.

The principal types of buoys are described below:
- Spar buoys are large logs, trimmed, shaped, and appropriately painted. They may also be of metal, constructed in the familiar spar shape.
- Can and nun buoys are cylindrical and conical, respectively.
- A bell buoy has a flat top, surmounted by a framework in which is housed a bell. Most bell buoys are sounded by the restless motion of the sea, but a few are operated automatically by gas or electricity.

Figure 4-32. U.S. buoys.

• A gong buoy is similar to a bell buoy, except that it has a series of gongs, each with a different note.

• A whistle buoy usually is cone-shaped, and carries a whistle, also usually sounded by the sea's motion. Some whistle buoys are equipped with horns sounded at regular intervals by mechanical means.

• A lighted buoy carries batteries or gas tanks, and is surmounted by a framework supporting a light.

• A combination buoy is one in which are combined a light and sound signal, such as a lighted bell, gong, or whistle buoy.

Color of Buoys

The colors of buoys have a direct connection with navigation. Red buoys mark the right-hand side, and black buoys the left-hand side of a channel, coming from seaward. The expression "red-right-returning" is a great help in remembering this color-direction scheme for buoys.

Red channel buoys usually are cone-shaped nun buoys; black channel buoys are cylindrical can buoys. This situation is about the only one where a buoy's shape is of any significance, and even here the rule is not controlling. Either can buoys or nun buoys may be replaced with spar buoys of proper color. It is the color that counts. Sometimes red and black buoys are painted white on top, but this color merely makes them easier to see at night.

Black and red horizontally banded buoys mark obstructions. They may be passed on either side. But, unless you know the dimensions of the obstruction, it is best to keep well clear of such a buoy. Although these buoys may be passed on either side, sometimes—for various reasons—the channel on one side is preferable to the channel on the other side. If the top band on the buoy is red, the preferred channel is to the left of the buoy, coming from seaward; if the top band is black, the preferred channel is to the right.

Black and white vertically striped buoys mark the middle of a channel or fairway. Yellow buoys mark quarantine anchorages. Buoys with black and white horizontal stripes are commonly used to mark fishtrap areas; as another example, a white buoy with a green top usually marks a dredging area.

Lighted Buoys

Green lights are used only on black channel buoys; red lights, only on red channel buoys. In other words, a green light on a channel buoy means the left side of the channel, coming from seaward. A red light means the right side. When a light of considerable brilliance is required, a white light may be (and frequently is) substituted for either the green or the red light. White lights are the only lights used on the black and white vertically striped buoys that mark the middle of a channel or fairway.

Numbers on Buoys

Red buoys, which mark the right side of a channel, bear even numbers, starting with the first buoy from seaward. This maritime situation is practically the only one where anything to starboard has an even number. Black channel buoys, to the left of the channel coming from seaward, have odd numbers. Both a number and a letter or two appear on some channel buoys.

Banded or striped buoys do not have numbers, but some bear letters for identification purposes.

Fallibility of Buoys

Buoys frequently drag their moorings in heavy weather, or they may be set adrift when run down by passing vessels. Light buoys may have their lights go out of commission. Whistles, bells, and gongs, that are sounded by the sea's motion, may fail to function in smooth water. Consequently, although they are valuable aids to navigation, buoys cannot be depended upon exclusively. Ship OODs and boat coxswains must be very aware of the fallibility of buoys.

Boat Hoisting and Lowering Equipment

Heavy boats on large men-of-war are generally handled by powerful boat cranes which hook on to slings attached to hoisting eyes built into strong parts of a boat's framing. Boats are more often handled in the destroyer Navy, however, by using *davits*. Davits are the strong mechanical arms from which a boat hangs while being raised from or lowered to the water.

The purpose of the davits is to swing the boat out from its stowage place to a point from which it may be lowered, and the reverse of this process when she has been hoisted up again. The actual hoisting or lowering is done by means of tackles called boatfalls, which run from the davit heads to the boat's bow and stern.

There are various designs in davits to accommodate the needs of a ship's boats and ship's structure. This discussion will cover only a few types of boat davits.

Types of Davits

Radial Davits

Radial or *round bar davits* rarely are used in the Navy today and are being phased out of service. When the boat is in the stowed position of

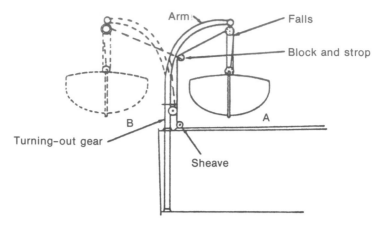

Figure 4-33. Radial davit.

radial davits, the davit arms point inboard. (See figure 4-38.) To get the boat out to the lowering position, it must be swung aft until the bow of the boat will clear the forward davit. Next, it must be swung out, forward, and then aft to the lowering position. Before swinging the boat out, it usually is necessary to hoist it high enough for the keel to clear the skids.

Quadrantal Davits

Quadrantal davits are used chiefly on merchant vessels. The boat rests in chocks under the davits. Outboard sections of the chocks usually are hinged so that once the weight of the boat is off them, they can be laid flat on the deck, making it unnecessary to raise the boat high enough to clear them in their normal position. Turning the crank that operates the worm gear raises the boat sufficiently high to clear the flattened chocks. Continued cranking racks the boat out to the lowering position. The boat then is lowered away, as with radial davits.

Crescent Davits

The *crescent davit* and other makes of hinging-out davits (which have largely superseded radial and quadrantal mechanical davits) have been used in all classes of naval vessels, including combatant ships. They generally handle boats of 26 to 30 feet and up to 13,500 pounds. In this type of davit, the arms usually are crescent shaped and are racked in and out by means of a sheath screw that may be operated by handcrank or by power. (See figure 4-34.)

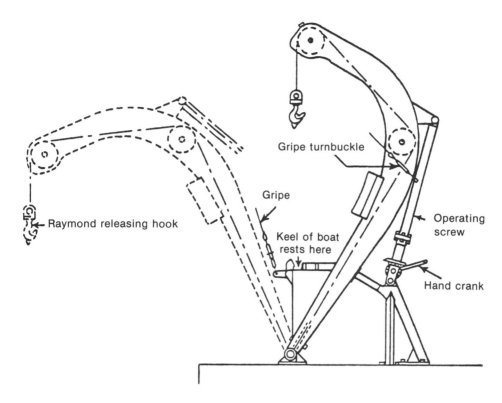

Figure 4-34. Crescent davits.

Gripe turnbuckle

Gripe

Raymond releasing hook

Keel of boat
rests here

Operating
screw

Hand crank

Gravity Davits

Gravity davits are most commonly found on newer vessels. They consist of two trackways and davit arms fitted with rollers which travel in the trackways. An electric-powered two-drum winch, located in the immediate vicinity of the davits, provides power to hoist the boats. Cranks can be attached to the winch for manual hoisting.

Power is not required to lower boats. The boat lowers by gravity as it is suspended from the falls, and the descent speed is controlled with the boat-davit winch manual brake. Gravity davits are rigged in such a way that when the falls are raised to the davit arms, continued heaving pulls the davit arms up to the stowed position. Keeper bars then may be placed across the trackway, and the falls slacked off, allowing the davit arms to rest against the keeper bars.

Several types of gravity davits are used. Depending on design, a pair of modified davits can handle one to four boats and are designated as single-, double-, or quadruple-bank davits. These are mainly used with amphibious craft.

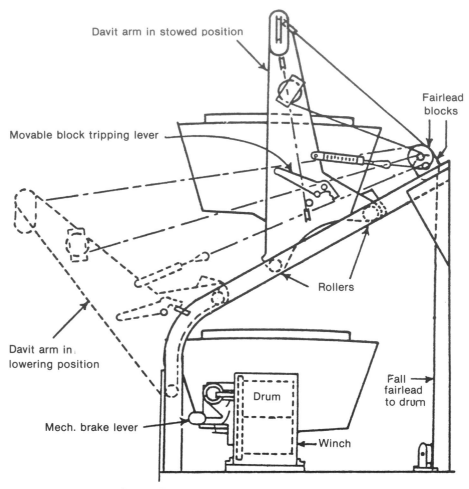

Davit arm in stowed position

Movable block tripping lever

Fairlead blocks

Rollers

Davit arm in lowering position

Mech. brake lever

Drum

Winch

Fall fairlead to drum

Figure 4-35. Welin trackway gravity davit.

A single-arm gravity davit, being introduced on DD-, CGN-, and FFG-type ships, allows superior boat-handling operations. It also allows rescue-boat handling in higher sea states than are considered safe with conventional double-arm davits.

Lowering Boats in Davits

Regardless of when or how a boat is lowered into the water, the coxswain is responsible for making the boat ready and getting the crew into the boat. He must make sure the engineer checks the fuel and tests the engine. He must check the boat plugs to ensure watertight integrity, and make sure that the regular boat equipment is in the boat. Also, he must see that any required slings are rigged and that fenders are in place. Each member of the crew wears his life jacket when a boat is being lowered.

When the boat is ready in all respects and the crew is aboard, the coxswain reports to the boatswain's mate in charge, who checks to see that the boat is not overloaded and then gives the order to begin lowering. The boat is lowered with the stern slightly lower than the bow to prevent the bow from digging into a wave and upending the boat.

Once the boat is waterborne, the orders "Cast off aft" and "Cast off forward," are given. First the after fall is released, then the forward fall. Falls are pulled clear of the boat by means of the frapping lines. Each man in the boat must keep a monkey line or lifeline in hand for safety

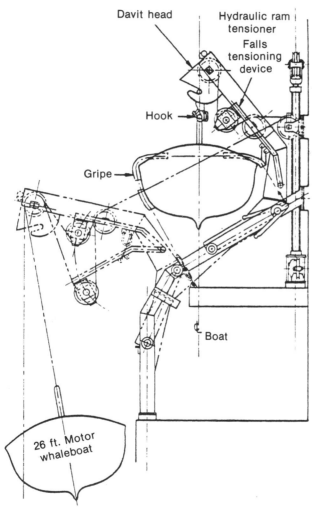

Figure 4-36. Single-arm trackway gravit davit.

during lowering and hoisting operations (figure 4-37). During lowering, the monkey lines are allowed to hang over and outside the inboard side of the boat. This prevents them from becoming fouled around a leg or other object in the boat, and also makes it unnecessary to clear them from the boat once it is waterborne.

Figure 4-37. Monkey lines will save a man from falling with a boat if it slips in the davit.

Raising Boats in Davits

Raising or hoisting a boat with davits is essentially the reverse of the lowering process. However, there are often times when a boat must be raised with the ship itself under way. A slight amount of headway on

Figure 4-38. Raising a motor launch.

the ship (approximately 5 knots is the maximum safe speed under calm sea conditions) is actually helpful to the boat crew in hooking up the boat. The boat is not so much at the mercy of wind and waves while under way.

When recovering a boat while under way, the men on the ship's deck should have everything ready in advance. Equipment that might be in the way is removed, fenders are rigged, the davits are swung out, the boat falls are lowered and held at the ship's side with frapping lines, and the winch or davit power is tested.

As the boat approaches, the ship makes a lee in the water; that is, it turns and moves slowly ahead in such a way that the boat coming alongside is protected as much as possible from the wind and sea and so that the ship has a minimum roll. When the boat comes alongside, the *sea painter* (a bow line of sorts) is passed to the bowhook, and he drops the eye over an inboard cleat. Then the forward fall is passed to the bowhook. When the forward fall is secure, the after fall is passed to the coxswain. When both falls are secured, the slack is hauled out of them, and the boat is carefully raised.

Ready Lifeboat

Navy regulations require that a ship at sea have at least one boat rigged and ready for lowering, to be used as a lifeboat. The ship's Boat Bill specifies the exact condition in which the lifeboat must be and the items of equipment that must be in the boat.

Periodically (at least once each day), the lifeboat coxswain musters the boat crew, checks the boat and gear, has the engine tested, and reports its condition to the officer of the deck. If the boat must be used, the boatswain's mate of the watch takes charge of lowering the boat.

When a man goes overboard, and it is necessary to use a boat to recover him, every man must know the recovery procedure. This is particularly important in cold water where a man lost overboard can live only a few minutes. Time must not be lost fumbling around trying to get the boat in the water.

Boat Etiquette

There are many excellent reasons for observing boat etiquette in the U.S. Navy. It is a tradition that has been passed along through the years from the days when John Paul Jones was sailing the seas.

A knowledge and observance of proper boat etiquette mark a crew as well trained and smart. The customs that have been established promote the smooth loading of passengers, help govern boat traffic, and expedite the movement of boats at gangways and piers. Proper boat etiquette is a sign of good seamanship. It also makes a lasting impression on all who observe it. Clean boats and sharp, courteous crews draw favorable comments.

The following few rules of boat etiquette, established by custom and regulations, should serve as your guide to proper conduct when in boats. Observe them closely, and insist that others in your boat do likewise.

Boat Salutes

Hand salutes are rendered to boats carrying officers and officials in much the same way as salutes would be made when passing such individuals walking on land. Junior boats salute the senior first, and the senior returns the salute. It is not the size or type of boat, but the rank of the officer aboard that determines a boat's seniority. Thus, a small whaleboat carrying a commander is senior to a large boat that is carrying a lieutenant. Usually it is possible to tell by the officer's uniform or by the flag flown which boat is senior. In cases of doubt, however, it is best to go ahead and salute.

Boat salutes are rendered by a boat's coxswain and by the senior officer embarked. The engine of the junior boat should be idled during the salute, and after the return of the salute, speed may be resumed. Coxswains always rise to salute unless it is dangerous or impractical to do so. Officers generally do not rise to salute, but do so from a seated position if visible to the other boat.

During morning or evening colors, a boat's engine should be idled or stopped and the clutch disengaged. The boat officer (if assigned) and the coxswain stand at attention and salute in the direction of the ceremony if it is possible to do so without losing control of the boat.

If a boat is carrying an officer or official for whom a gun salute is being fired, the coxswain slows the engine, disengages the clutch, and turns the boat so that it is parallel to the saluting ship. During the salute, only the person honored rises.

A coxswain in charge of a boat salutes when officers enter or leave his boat if the situation allows. For example, when a boat is alongside a ship's accommodation ladder, the coxswain oftentimes is too busy maintaining control of the boat to salute.

Finally, men working in a boat or working on the ship's side from a boat do not salute unless "Attention" is sounded.

Courtesy Aboard Boats

Through the years, certain courtesies have come to be recognized by the crews and passengers of boats. The basic rule in Navy manners, as in civilian life, is to make way for a senior quickly, quietly, and without confusion.

The procedure for boarding and leaving boats is as follows: Juniors board boats first, and leave after seniors, unless the senior officer gives orders to the contrary. The idea is that the senior officer should not have to wait in a boat for anyone. The senior gets out first, because normally his business is more important and pressing than that of the men of lower rank. Generally, seniors take the seats farthest aft; in boats with no officers embarked, the after part of the boat (or stern sheets) is usually reserved for chief petty officers.

Subject to the requirements of the rules for preventing collisions, junior boats must avoid embarrassing senior boats. At landings and gangways, juniors should give way to seniors. Juniors should show deference to their seniors at all times by refraining from crossing the bows of their boats or ignoring their presence.

Under ordinary circumstances, enlisted men maintain silence when they are passengers in boats with officers aboard.

Boat Flag Etiquette

The national ensign and personal flags and pennants of officers are properly displayed from small boats as described below.

National Ensign

The national ensign is displayed from boats of the Navy at the following times:

1. When under way during daylight in a foreign port.
2. When ships are required to be dressed or full dressed.
3. When going alongside a foreign vessel.
4. When an officer or official is embarked on an official occasion.
5. When, in uniform, a flag or general officer, a unit commander, a commanding officer, or a chief of staff is embarked in a boat of his command or in one assigned to his personal use.
6. At such other times as may be prescribed by the senior officer present.

Inasmuch as small boats are a component of a vessel, they follow the motions of the parent vessel regarding the half-masting of colors.

Personal Flags and Pennants

When embarked in a boat of the naval service on official occasions, an officer in command, or a chief of staff when acting for him, displays from the bow of the boat his personal flag or command pennant or, if not entitled to either, a commission pennant.

An officer entitled to display a personal flag or command pennant may display a miniature of such flag or pennant in the vicinity of the coxswain's station when embarked on any except official occasions in a boat of the naval service.

Hailing an Approaching Boat

With the heavy boat traffic in some harbors and anchorages, it is important for a quarterdeck watch officer to have as much advance notice as possible of whom an approaching boat may have embarked. The QDWO must know the rank of the senior officer embarked so that he may be received with the appropriate ceremonies. When an officer is embarked in a boat and his rank or the occasion does not authorize a personal flag, or at night when it cannot be seen, other means of identification must be used.

Boat Hails and Replies

A boat approaching a ship at night is hailed as soon as it is within hearing distance by the petty officer of the watch or the QDWO, with "Boat ahoy." Answering hails by the coxswain, to give an indication of who is embarked in the boat, are shown in Table 4-2.

During daylight, the QDWO hails a boat with a clenched fist, and the coxswain of the boat will indicate the rank of the senior person in the boat by holding up the number of fingers equal to the number of side boys rated by that person. A wave-off from the coxswain would indicate no officers rating side boys are embarked.

Flagstaff Insignia

Because an officer's personal flag may be obscured or difficult to see when flown from a small boat, boat hails are often used to determine an embarked officer's rank. Another method of obtaining the same information is to observe the insignia fitted at the peak of a boat's flagstaff. It may be visible even though the flag or pennant is not.

The various flagstaff insignia, their uses, and the number of side boys associated with each are noted below.

Bow Insignia

Barges employed by flag officers are distinctively marked as are the gigs used by the commanding officers of ships or by chiefs of staff. These marks also help the QDWO recognize approaching visitors.

The bow of a barge carries the flag officer's stars in chrome, while the stern carries the official abbreviated title of his command, for example, CinCLantFlt, in gold letters.

On gigs for unit commanders below flag rank, the bow has a broad or burgee command pennant painted on it with accompanying squadron or division numbers in the center of the pennant. The stern carries the

Figure 4-39. The national ensign is displayed from U.S. Navy boats.

official abbreviation of the command in gold letters. Gigs assigned to commanding officers of ships have their bows fitted with the ship's name or the ship's hull number in chrome, with a chrome arrow running through the markings fore and aft. A gig for a chief of staff is marked on the bow with the abbreviated title of the command in chrome, with the arrow bisecting these markings running fore and aft.

Small Boat Safety

A boat is a convenient means of transportation for the sailor, and it may be his only means of survival in case of casualty to his ship. A boat,

Table 4-2. Boat Hails

Officer or Official	Coxswain's Reply
The President or Vice President of the United States	"United States"
Secretary of Defense, Deputy or Assistant Secretary of Defense	"Defense"
The Secretary, Under Secretary, or Assistant Secretary of the Navy	"Navy"
Chief of Naval Operations, Vice Chief of Naval Operations	"Naval Operations"
Fleet or Force Commander	"Fleet" or Abbreviation of Administrative Title
A General Officer	"General Officer"
A Chief of Staff	"Staff"
A Group Commander	"_____GRU_____" (Type) (Number)
A Squadron Commander	"_____RON_____" (Type) (Number)
A Division Commander	"_____DIV _____" (Type) (Number)
A Marine Officer Commanding a Brigade	"Brigade Commander"
A Commanding Officer of a ship	"_____" (Name of Ship)
A Marine Officer Commanding a Regiment	"Regimental Commander"
Any other Commissioned Officer	"Aye, Aye"
Other officers (not commissioned)	"No, No"
Enlisted Men	"Hello"
A boat not intending to go alongside, regardless of rank of passenger	"Passing"

however, can also be a source of potential danger if proper and sane precautions are not taken during operations. The primary concern in the use of boats is the safety of the men; concern for the equipment is

Table 4-3. Side Boys Required for Each Rank of Visitor

Personage	Flagstaff Insignia	Side Boys
President	Spread eagle	8
Secretary of Defense	Spread eagle	8
Secretary of the Navy	Spread eagle	8
Fleet Admiral	Spread eagle	8
Chief of Naval Operations	Spread eagle	8
Admiral	Halberd	8
Assistant and Under Secretaries of the Navy	Halberd	8
Vice Admiral	Halberd	8
Cabinet officers	Halberd	8
Commodore and Rear Admiral	Halberd	6
Captain	Gilt ball	4
Commander	Gilt star	4
Officer of lower rank	Flat truck	2

Figure 4-40. A sharp-looking boat crew.

secondary. It is necessary both for the safety of all crew members and for the safety of the boat that the following basic precautions be strictly adhered to:

(a) Boats must always be properly loaded for the sea state. Never overload a boat. In heavy weather, most of the weight should be loaded in the stern.

(b) Inherently buoyant lifejackets, equal in number to the capacity of the boat, must be readily available in the boat at all times. Make sure that lifejackets are always kept dry. Lifejackets should always be worn during adverse weather conditions, including reduced visibility.

(c) Never smoke in an operating boat. The smoking lamp must be out in the vicinity of any boat being refueled. Never refuel with passengers aboard.

(d) Make sure that fire extinguishers are in place and charged before operating your boat.

(e) Do not operate a boat with defective bilge pumps. If, during engine operation, it is observed that excessive leaks occur, stop the engine immediately; correct the cause of the leak before restarting the engine.

Summary

The moment you are appointed duty as a boat coxswain or boat officer will probably be one of the first times in your life you are handed so many responsibilities, and you should be thoroughly impressed by them.

You must be completely familiar with everything relating to the care and handling of the boat. You must know its physical dimensions, handling characteristics, the Rules of the Road, how to steer, how the engine operates, boat etiquette, and every aspect of boat safety.

Every member of a boat crew has an important job and must function as part of a team. Many of the seamanship skills developed aboard small boats prove invaluable in the operation of ships.

5

Ship Characteristics and Basic Shiphandling

Basic Nautical Terminology

In some respects a ship is like a building. It has outer walls (forming the *hull*), floors (called *decks*), inner walls (called *partitions* and *bulkheads*), corridors (called *passageways*), ceilings (called *overheads*), and stairs (called *ladders*). But, unlike a building, a ship moves around—so new terms for directions and for getting around have to be learned. When going up the stairs from the dock to a ship, the *accommodation ladder* is used to go on board; what might be an entrance hall or foyer in a building is the *quarterdeck* on a ship.

The forward part of a ship is the *bow*; to go in that direction is to go *forward*. The after part is the *stern*; to go in that direction is to go *aft*. The top, open deck of a ship is the *main deck*. Anything below that is *below decks* and anything above is *superstructure*. The forward part of the main deck is the *forecastle* (pronounced "fōc' sle"); the after part is the *fantail*. To proceed from the main deck to a lower deck you go *below*. Going back up again is going *topside*. Facing forward on a ship, the right side is *starboard*, the left side is *port*. An imaginary line running full length down the middle of the ship is the *centerline*. The direction from the centerline toward either side is *outboard*, and from either side toward the centerline is *inboard*. A line from one side of the ship to the other runs *athwartships*.

Basic Ship Structure

The hull is the main body of the ship. Structurally it is a big box girder, similar to a bridge. *Shell plating* forms the sides and bottom, and the *weather deck* or *main deck* forms the top. The intersection of the weather deck with the shell or side plating is called the *deck-edge* or *gunwale* (pronounced "gunnel"). The intersection of the side plating with the bottom plating is called the *bilge*.

The shape and construction of the hull depends on the type of ship. Ships designed for high-speed operations—destroyers, frigates, and cruisers—have long, narrow hulls with fine lines and rounded bilges. Aircraft carriers and auxiliary ships have hulls with square center sections, vertical sides, and flat bottoms for greater carrying capacity.

140

Submarines, designed to operate underwater, have hulls that are generally rounded in sections, like an egg, because that shape withstands great pressure.

Most ships have unarmored hulls. The hull consists only of the basic shell plating. Ships with armored hulls have a waterline armor belt of very thick steel running fore and aft to protect enginerooms and magazines from torpedoes or shellfire, and thinner armor steel plates on one or more decks to protect against bombs and shells.

The *keel* is the backbone of the hull. (Figure 5-1 shows the hull and other structural members discussed in this section.) It usually looks like an I-beam running the full length of the ship with heavy castings fore and aft called *stem* and *stern posts*. *Frames*, fastened to the keel, run athwartships and support the watertight skin or shell plating. Most ships built for the Navy also have longitudinal frames running fore and aft. The longitudinal and athwartships frames form an egg-crate structure in the bottom of the ship called the *double bottom*. *Deck beams*, *transverse bulkheads*, and *stanchions* support the decks and help strengthen the sides against water pressure. The framework is assembled by electric-arc welding, which is lighter than riveting.

Compartments are the rooms of a ship. Some compartments are called rooms, such as *wardroom, stateroom, engineroom*, but generally speaking, you don't use the word "room." You don't refer to the space where the crew sleeps as the bedrooms, nor the place where they eat as the dining room. They are called *berthing compartment* and the *messdeck*, respectively.

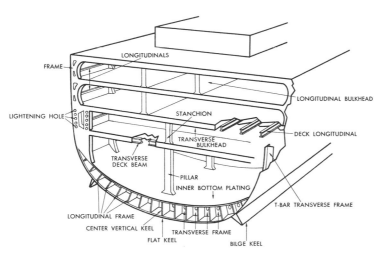

Figure 5-1. A ship's deck is strengthened by transverse beams and longitudinal girders.

The decks of a ship divide it into tiers or layers of compartments, in the same way the floors of a building divide it into stories. The deck normally consists of steel plates, strengthened by transverse (athwartships) deck beams and longitudinal (fore and aft) girders. Decks above the waterline are usually cambered, or arched, to provide greater strength and to drain off water.

Decks are named by their position in the ship and their functions (Figure 5-2). For purposes of compartment identification, decks are also numbered. The *main deck* is the uppermost of the decks that run continuously from bow to stern. The *second, third*, and *fourth* decks are continuous decks below the main deck and are numbered in sequence from topside down.

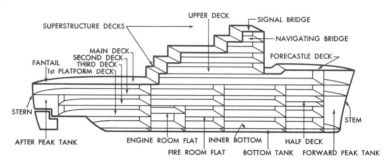

Figure 5-2. Decks are named and numbered by their position and function on a ship.

A partial deck above the main deck is named according to its position on the ship. At the bow it is called a *forecastle deck*, amidships it becomes an *upper deck*, and at the stern it is a *poop deck*. The term *weather deck* includes all parts of the main, forecastle, upper, and poop decks that are exposed to weather. A partial deck between two continuous decks is referred to as a *half deck*. A partial deck below the lowest continuous deck is a *platform deck*.

The top deck of an aircraft carrier is the *flight deck*. The deck below it, where aircraft are stored and serviced, is the *hangar deck*.

The quarterdeck is not a true deck or structural part of the ship, but merely a location designated by the commanding officer as the ceremonial entrance and exit point for the ship.

Compartmentation and Watertight Integrity

If a ship were built like a rowboat, one hole below the waterline could sink it. To prevent this from happening, naval ships are built with watertight bulkheads, which divide the hull into a series of watertight

Figure 5-3. *Aboard an aircraft carrier, the main deck is the flight deck, and the superstructure is called the island.*

compartments. By shutting compartments off, any flooding experienced aboard ship can be limited to a few spaces. Cargo ships have widely spaced bulkheads in order to provide large hold areas. Ships designed to carry troops or passengers have smaller holds, and much of the interior is divided into smaller living compartments.

Ship Characteristics and Basic Shiphandling   **143**

Watertight doors and *watertight hatches* allow access through all bulkheads and decks. Any ship could be made virtually unsinkable if it were divided into enough watertight compartments, but too much compartmentation may interfere with the arrangement of mechanical equipment and with the ship's operation.

Large ships have outer and inner *double bottoms*. These are divided athwartships and longitudinally into tanks, which are used for fuel oil, boiler feed water, fresh water, or sea-water ballast. In armored hulls the double-bottom compartmentation may extend past the turn of the bilge (where the bottom meets the side of the hull) and all or part way up the side, as protection against torpedoes and other weapons.

Tanks at the extreme bow and stern, called the *forward peak* (or *forepeak*) tank and the *after peak* (or *aftpeak*) tank, are used for trimming the ship. Sometimes they may carry potable (drinking) water.

A strong watertight bulkhead at the after side of the forepeak tank is called the *collision bulkhead*. If one ship rams another head on, the bow structure would collapse to a point, hopefully, somewhere forward of the collision bulkhead, thus preventing flooding of compartments aft of it.

All tanks are connected to a pumping and drainage system so that fuel, water, and ballast may be transferred from one part of the ship to another or pumped overboard.

Maintenance of *watertight integrity* is a function of damage control (Chapter 12). All doors and hatches through watertight bulkheads or decks must also be watertight. Wherever water, steam, oil, air piping, electric cables, or ventilation ducts go through a watertight bulkhead or deck, the hole is plugged by a stuffing tube, pipe, spool, or other device to prevent leakage. All watertight doors and hatches carry markings that determine when they may and may not be opened.

Compartment and Deck Numbering

Trying to find your way around a ship that is several hundred feet long, with many decks, is like trying to get around in a strange town where the street signs have been torn down. This is why the compartment numbering system was devised. It gives each compartment an "address," so that you can go directly to any designated compartment—once you understand the system.

Every space aboard ship (except for minor spaces, like peacoat, linen, and cleaning-gear lockers) is assigned an identifying letter-number symbol, which is marked on a label plate secured to the door, hatch, or bulkhead of the compartment.

The compartment numbers contain the following information: deck number, frame number, relation to the centerline of the ship, and use of the compartment.

The *deck number* is the first part of the compartment number. Where a compartment extends to the bottom of the ship, the number assigned to the bottom compartment is used.

The *frame number*, the second part of the compartment number, is found at the forward end of the bulkhead of a compartment. If the bulkhead is between frames, the frame number is forward of the bulkhead.

The third part of the compartment number refers to the compartment's relation to the centerline. Compartments located on the centerline carry the number 0. Those to starboard have odd numbers, while those to port have even numbers. Where two or more compartments with the same deck and frame number are entirely to starboard or port of the centerline, they are numbered consecutively odd or even, from the centerline moving outboard. Thus, the first compartment outboard of the centerline to starboard is 1, the second is 3, and so on. The first compartment outboard of the centerline to port is 2, the second is 4, and so on.

When the centerline of the ship passes through more than one compartment, the compartment having that portion of the forward bulkhead through which the centerline of the ship passes, carries the number 0, and the others carry the numbers 01, 02, 03, etc.

The fourth and last part of the compartment number is the letter that identifies the compartment's primary use. On dry- and liquid-cargo ships, a double-letter identification designates cargo-carrying compartments as follows:

A Dry stowage—storerooms, issue rooms, refrigerated compartments.

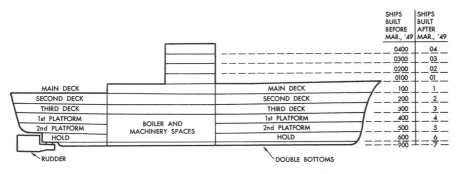

Figure 5-4. *Compartment and deck numbers are assigned starting with the main deck.*

AA Cargo—cargo holds, cargo refrigerated compartments.

C Ship and fire-control operations—CIC, plotting rooms, communication centers, radio, radar, sonar operating spaces, pilothouse.

E Engineering control centers (manned)—main propulsion spaces, boiler rooms, evaporator rooms, steering-gear rooms, auxiliary machinery spaces, pumprooms, generator rooms, switchboard rooms, windlass rooms.

F Oil Stowage (ship's use)—fuel oil, diesel oil, and lubricating oil compartments.

FF Oil stowage (cargo)—all types of oil in cargo.

G Gasoline stowage (ship's use)—tanks, cofferdams, trunks, and pumprooms.

GG Gasoline stowage (cargo)—all gasoline in cargo.

K Chemicals and dangerous materials (other than oil and gasoline)—stowage, either for ship's use or as cargo.

L Living spaces—berthing and messing spaces, staterooms, washrooms, heads, brigs, sickbays, hospital spaces, passageways.

M Ammunition—magazines, handling rooms, turrets, gun mounts, shell rooms, ready service rooms, clipping rooms.

Q Spaces not otherwise designated—shops, offices, laundry, galley, pantries, unmanned engineering or electrical spaces.

T Vertical access trunks—escape trunks or tubes.

V Voids—cofferdam compartments (other than gasoline), void wing compartments, wiring trunks.

W Water—drainage tanks, fresh-water tanks, peak tanks, reserve feed-water tanks.

Hull Reference Terms

Ballast: Weight added in a ship's inner bottom to balance her topside weight, or to keep her down in the water under light loads. Some ships carry permanent concrete ballast. Others pump salt water into tanks for the same purpose.

Bilge Keels: Long, narrow fins fitted to both sides of the hull at the turn of the bilge to prevent the ship from rolling.

Bulwarks: Vertical extensions above the deck edge of the shell plating. Bulwarks are built high enough to keep men and equipment from going overboard.

Draft: The vertical distance from the waterline to the keel. Draft is measured in feet and inches, by scales marked on the hull at the stem and stern post. Draft numbers are six inches high and spaced six inches apart. The bottom of each number indicates foot marks, the top indicates half-foot marks.

Freeboard: Vertical distance from the waterline to the weather deck.

Lifelines: Light wire ropes supported on stanchions. They serve the same purpose as bulwarks.

Propeller Guards: Steel braces at the stern, directly above the propellers. They prevent the propellers from striking a dock, pier, or another ship.

Stem: The point of the hull at the bow, where port and starboard sides meet.

Stern: The point of the hull at the after end, where both sides of the ship meet.

Trim and List: *Trim* refers to the relation between the fore-and-aft draft. A ship properly balanced fore and aft is "in trim"; otherwise she is "down by the head" or "down by the stern." *List* refers to athwartships balance. A ship with one side lower than the other has a "starboard list" or "port list." List is measured in degrees by an inclinometer, mounted on the bridge, exactly on the centerline of the ship.

Waterline: The line where the hull meets the surface of the water.

Superstructure

The superstructure includes all structures above the main deck. The superstructure will vary according to the type of ship, but all ships have a wheelhouse, bridge, signal bridge, chart room, combat information center, radio room, and probably a sea cabin or emergency cabin for the captain. (These are discussed later in this chapter.)

The superstructure is topped off by the *mast*. In its simplest form, a mast is a single pole, fitted with a yardarm (spar) that extends above the ship and carries flag halyards and navigational and signal lights. Generally, a mast consists of several structural members in tripod form. In addition to the usual yardarm, the mast may support various electronic devices, radar antennas, and radio aerials.

On older ships, and particularly on small escort and patrol craft, the mast is a distinct feature. If the ship has two masts, the one forward is called the *foremast*, the one aft, the *mainmast*. On single-masted ships, the mast, whether forward or amidships, is usually part of the super-structure and is simply called "the mast."

The top of a mast is called the *trunk*. The top of the forward mast is the *foretrunk*, while the top portion of the main mast is the *maintrunk*. The *pigstick* is a slender vertical extension above the mast from which is flown the ship's commission pennant or an admiral's personal flag. The *gaff* extends abaft the mainmast. It is from the gaff that the national ensign is flown when the ship is under way.

The small vertical spar at the bow and the slightly raked one at the stern are called the *jackstaff* and *flagstaff*, respectively. When a Navy

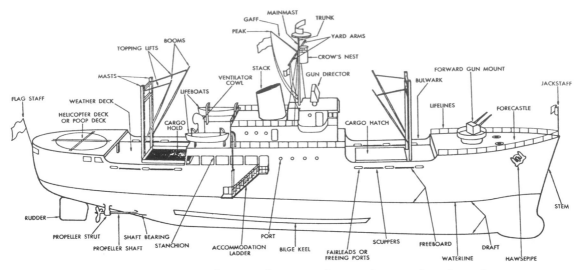

Figure 5-5. These are the principal parts of a typical auxiliary ship.

ship is at anchor or moored, it flies the union jack on the jackstaff and the national ensign on the flagstaff from 0800 to sunset.

The *stack* of a ship serves the same purpose as the smokestack on a power plant ashore. It carries off smoke and hot gases from the boilers, and exhaust from the diesel engines. (Nuclear-powered ships do not need stacks, since their reactors produce no smoke or gas.) Some diesel-powered ships have their exhaust on the sides. On some new ships the masts and stacks have been combined to form large towers called *macks.*

Propulsion Plant

A typical steam propulsion plant consists of *boilers, main engines, reduction gears, propeller shafts*, and *propellers*. There are many variations, involving turboelectric drive, direct diesel drive, diesel-electric drive, and gasoline engines. Nuclear-powered ships have steam propulsion, but the steam is produced in a reactor instead of in oil-fired boilers.

A *boiler* consists of a box-like casing containing hundreds of water-filled steel tubes. These tubes are arranged so that heat from the *fireboxes* passes over them. Fuel oil, heated and sprayed into the fireboxes under high pressure, burns intensely, turning the water into steam. The steam then flows through pipes to the turbines. *Forced-draft blowers* increase the air pressure—either in the *firerooms* where the boilers are mounted, or in the boilers themselves—for better combustion. Fresh water used in the boilers is made from salt water by *evaporators* and *condensers*.

148 Seamanship

A *turbine* consists of a revolving rotor, with several rows of blades mounted in a steam-tight casing with several rows of stationary blades. Rotor and casing blades are set in alternate rows. Thus, as the steam passes through the turbine, each row deflects the steam to the next row. Most turbines have both high pressure (HP) and low pressure (LP) stages. After steam has passed through both stages, it is cooled, condensed into water, and then returned to the boilers.

Turbines cannot be reversed, so to reverse the shaft, a *backing turbine* has to be installed, or else one section of the main turbine called an *astern element* is fitted inside a separate casing. Because backing turbines or astern elements have fewer rows of blades than the main turbine, they produce less power. A ship never has as much power for backing down as she has for going ahead.

Reduction gears connect turbines and shafts. They are required because turbines operate most efficiently at several thousand rpm, but propellers are not very effective above 400 rpm. Reduction gears reduce the turbine RPMs to a point where they efficiently rotate the shafts.

Propellers drive the ship. All aircraft carriers and most cruisers have four propellers. Most older destroyers have two, as do older submarines. Some newer destroyer types and most nuclear submarines have one propeller. Ships are classed as four-screw, twin-screw, or single-screw types. Newer single-screw-type ships have adjustable-pitch propellers. With this type of propeller, instead of reversing the direction of rotation to back down, the curvature of the blades is reversed.

For relatively small ships that need no more than 5,000-6,000 horsepower, diesel engines are frequently used. Diesels are lighter, take up less space, and are more efficient than steam turbines. The diesel can be coupled directly to the shaft through reduction gears and perhaps a clutch; or it can drive a generator which produces current for the main drive.

Nuclear Power Plant

A nuclear power plant uses a reactor (instead of oil-fired boilers) to provide heat for the generation of steam. The primary system is a circulating water cycle, consisting of the reactor, loops of piping, primary coolant pumps, and steam generators. Heat produced in the reactor by nuclear fission is transferred to the circulating primary coolant water, which is pressurized to prevent it from boiling. This water is then pumped through the steam generator and back into the reactor by the primary coolant pumps. It can then be reheated for the next cycle.

In the steam generator, the heat of the pressurized water is transferred to a secondary system, where water is turned into steam. This secondary system is isolated from the primary system.

From the steam generator, steam flows to the engineroom where it drives the turbogenerators that supply the ship with electricity and the main propulsion turbines that turn the propeller. After passing through the turbines, the steam is condensed, and the water is fed back to the steam generators by feed pumps.

The generation of nuclear power does not require oxygen. Thus, submarines can operate completely submerged for extended periods of time.

During the operation, because there are high levels of radiation around the reactor, men are not permitted to enter the reactor compartment. Heavy shielding protects the crew so that they receive less radiation than they would from natural sources ashore.

Nuclear power plants give a ship the advantage of unlimited endurance at high speed. Instead of refueling every few thousand miles, as oil-burning ships must do, a nuclear-powered ship can operate for years on one reactor core. This means that they require far less logistical support. Such ships can be better sealed against NBC attack, and they emit no corrosive stack gas. As of 1 January 1979, the Navy had a total of 124 nuclear-powered ships in service; of this number 113 were submarines, and the remaining 11 were surface ships—3 carriers and 8 cruisers.

Steering

Any ship or boat is steered by a rudder. The rudder is controlled by a tiller in an open boat (such as a motor whaleboat or motor launch), and by a wheel in the cockpit of a larger boat or on the bridge of a ship. In a boat, the motion of the wheel is transmitted to the rudder by a cable or shaft. On a ship the rudder is turned by an electric or steam steering engine in the steering-engine room. This electrical or hydraulic engine is controlled by the wheel on the bridge.

A rudder acts by the force of water pushing against one side of it. There is no rudder action when the ship is motionless. The greater the speed, the greater the effect the rudders have. That's why they are usually mounted just astern of the screws, where the wash pushes directly against them. When a ship is backing down, the propeller wash goes forward and the rudder has very little effect, especially at slow speeds.

To prevent loss of control in case of damage to the bridge (sometimes called the main conn), there is usually a second steering wheel mounted elsewhere (called the secondary conn). If that wheel is disabled, the ship can be hand-steered by several persons using special gear in the after steering room.

Ship Control

Among the important functions performed on the bridge is that of maneuvering the ship. The conning officer must be thoroughly familiar with the maneuvering characteristics of his ship and with equipment and personnel available to assist him. (He also must be aware of the capabilities and limitations of the engineering plant.)

Of the enlisted bridge watchstanders only two members are directly involved with ship control: the helmsman, who steers the ship; and the lee helmsman, who operates speed control equipment. In some cases one man performs both functions.

When issuing ship control orders, the conning officer must ensure that he has been heard and understood. All orders must be given in standard phraseology, otherwise confusion may result. A new order should never be given until the previous one has been acknowledged. Departure from these procedures has been a direct cause of accidents.

Bridge Equipment

A variety of equipment is available to assist the conning officer in directing the movements of his ship. Specific equipments vary in design, and their physical locations vary from ship to ship, but most bridges have apparatus for:

1. Steering.
2. Indicating ship's heading, speed, and rudder angle.
3. Indicating relative wind direction and speed.
4. Transmitting engine orders to enginerooms.
5. Indicating propeller revolutions.
6. Taking bearings and ranges.
7. Plotting ship's position and course.
8. Controlling external lights.
9. Communicating internally and externally.

On many ships, most of the ship's control equipment is contained in two consoles located near the center of the pilothouse. These are steering control console (figure 5-6) and the ship control console (figure 5-7). Newer ships may have only one console.

Course Control

Standard phraseology governing orders to the helmsman (also called steersman) is required so that he will understand and promptly execute

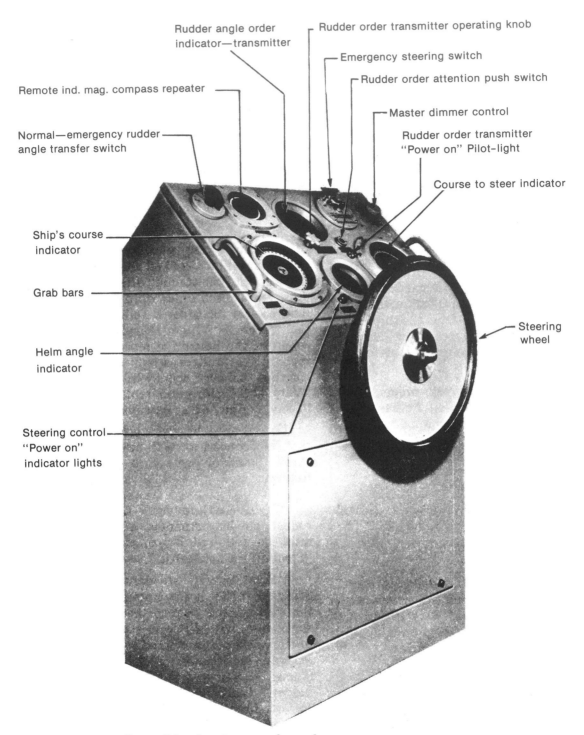

Rudder angle order indicator—transmitter

Rudder order transmitter operating knob

Remote ind. mag. compass repeater

Emergency steering switch

Rudder order attention push switch

Normal—emergency rudder angle transfer switch

Master dimmer control

Rudder order transmitter "Power on" Pilot–light

Course to steer indicator

Ship's course indicator

Grab bars

Steering wheel

Helm angle indicator

Steering control "Power on" indicator lights

Figure 5-6.   Steering control console.

152   Seamanship

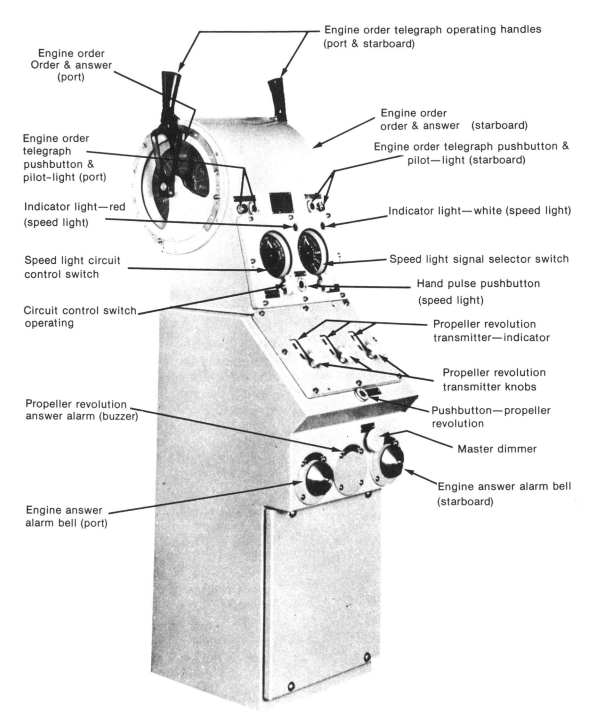

Engine order telegraph operating handles
(port & starboard)

Engine order
Order & answer
(port)

Engine order
order & answer   (starboard)

Engine order
telegraph
pushbutton &
pilot–light (port)

Engine order telegraph pushbutton &
pilot–light (starboard)

Indicator light—red
(speed light)

Indicator light—white (speed light)

Speed light circuit
control switch

Speed light signal selector switch

Circuit control switch
operating

Hand pulse pushbutton
(speed light)

Propeller revolution
transmitter—indicator

Propeller revolution
transmitter knobs

Propeller revolution
answer alarm (buzzer)

Pushbutton—propeller
revolution

Master dimmer

Engine answer alarm bell
(starboard)

Engine answer
alarm bell (port)

Figure 5-7. Ship control console.

the wishes of the conning officer. The helmsman must repeat each order word for word and must report when the ordered action is completed. If the order is "Right standard rudder," for example, the helmsman repeats the order, then reports, "My rudder is right standard, sir." The conning officer acknowledges by replying, "Very well." (He never replies, "All right," or "Okay," or any other unseamanlike remark.)

Orders must be given loudly and clearly so that all concerned will hear and understand them. Standard orders to the helm are as follows:

"Right (left) rudder." Apply right or left rudder an indeterminate amount. The order must be followed by another order, such as "Steer on the lighthouse."

"Right (left) standard (full) rudder." Standard rudder is the amount required to turn the ship on her tactical diameter. The rudder angle varies with different speeds and from ship to ship. Full rudder normally is that required for reduced tactical diameter. Maximum rudder (about 35°) is ordered by "Right (left) hard rudder." Hard rudder risks jamming the rudder against its stops and is used only in an emergency.

"Right (left 5) (10, etc.) degrees rudder." The order is normally followed by a new course to steer, such as "Steady on course 265." If no course is specified, the helmsman should call out the heading in 10° increments, such as "Passing 150, sir, passing 160, sir," until a course order is given. The helmsman should follow this same procedure for standard and full rudder commands if no course is given.

"Increase your rudder to _____ degrees." Increase the rudder angle to cause the ship to turn more rapidly.

"Ease (your) the rudder." Decrease the rudder angle. The exact amount may be ordered by "Ease (your rudder) to _____ degrees."

"Rudder amidships." Put the rudder on zero angle (centerline it).

"Meet her." Use the rudder as necessary to check, but not stop, the ship's turn. The order is given to prevent the ship from swinging past her new course.

"Steady"; "Steady as you go"; "Steady as she goes." Steer the course on which the ship is heading when the order is given. If the ship is turning, the helmsman notes the heading and brings the ship back to that course. His reply should be "Steady as she goes; course _____, sir."

"Shift your (the) rudder." Move the rudder to the same angle in the opposite direction from where it now is set. The order is given, for example, when the ship loses headway and gathers sternway, to keep her turning in the same direction. It may be given only when a specific rudder angle order is in effect.

"Mind your helm (rudder)." This order is a warning to steer more exactly.

"Nothing to the right (left)." "Nothing to the right (left) of (degrees)." Do not let the ship's head swing past the course indicated.

"How is my rudder?" or "How are my engines?" A query from the conning officer to ensure the proper placement of the rudder or the proper speed or direction of the engines.

"Mark your head." A command from the conning officer to which the helmsman replies by reporting the course on which he is actually steering at that instant.

"Keep her so." Steer the course just reported by the helmsman, such as when he replies to a query on the ship's heading.

"Very well." This is the reply by the conning officer after a report by the helmsman.

The helmsman usually steers by the gyrocompass repeater; but in the event of a gyro failure, he uses the magnetic compass. Therefore, whenever he comes to a new course, he should check the magnetic compass heading against that of the gyrocompass. For example:

Conning officer: "Left standard rudder; come to course 075."
Helmsman: "Left standard rudder, aye sir, come to course 075."
Conning officer: "Very well."
Helmsman: "Steady on course 075, sir, checking 076."
Conning officer: "Very well."

Speed Control

Engine and propeller speed control are exercised through the ship control console (figure 5-7) manned by the lee helmsman. Electromechanical devices used are the engine order telegraph and the propeller revolution indicator-transmitter. (Propeller, or shaft, revolutions are commonly referred to as turns.)

The engine order telegraph is circular, with duplicate dials, (for twin-engine ships) divided into sectors for flank, full, standard, two-thirds, and one-third speeds ahead; stop; and one-third, two-thirds, and full speeds astern. Hand levers are set to the desired speed sector, which causes pointers in the engineroom to respond accordingly. Answering pointers on the telegraph indicate that the enginerooms are acknowledging the order.

Ahead speeds are based on a prescribed standard speed. If standard speed is 15 knots, for example, then one-third and two-thirds speeds are 5 knots and 10 knots, respectively. Full speed is 20 knots and flank speed is 25 knots. There is no standard astern speed; the orders refer to the amount of backing power to be used.

A more precise control of speed is accomplished with the shaft rpm indicator. Two rows of numbers appear in three small windows, with the upper row indicating actual propeller speeds. When the conning officer orders a change in rpm, the lee helmsman sets the desired figures in the lower row of numbers by means of hand knobs. When the upper row of numbers responds in kind, the engineroom has acknowledged the order.

In maneuvering situations, such as when approaching a pier, the rpm indicator usually is set on 999 to inform the engineroom that the ship is on special "maneuvering bells." Thereafter, speed changes are ordered strictly via the engine order telegraph, and the throttleman will make the standard number of turns prescribed for each bell.

As with orders to the helm, there is a prescribed procedure for giving and acknowledging orders regulating the engines. A speed order consists of three parts: the engine(s) affected, direction, and speed. The lee helmsman repeats and simultaneously executes the order. When the pointers on the telegraph indicate compliance by the engineroom, he so reports.

Some typical orders are:

Conning officer: "Port engine ahead one-third, starboard engine back one-third."

Lee helm: Repeats order and sets telegraph levers to appropriate positions. "Port engine answers ahead one-third, starboard engine answers back one-third, sir."

Conning officer: "All engines ahead standard."

Lee helm: "All engines ahead standard, aye, sir."

Conning officer: "Very well."

If the speed of only one engine is changed, it is a good practice to have the lee helmsman report the condition of both engines. This helps the conning officer keep in mind what his engines are doing.

Conning officer: (All engines are already ahead one-third.) "Port engine stop."

Lee helm: "Port engine stop, aye, sir."

Lee helm: "Port engine answers stop, sir. Starboard engine is ahead one-third."

Conning officer: "Very well."

Tables listing the revolutions required for each knot of speed are part of the ship's tactical data folder and are also posted near the lee helm. When a general speed order, such as "Ahead full," is given, the lee helmsman rings up the order on the telegraph, then sets the corresponding number of turns for that speed on the shaft rpm indicator. Thereafter, to increase or decrease speed, while remaining within the speed range set on the telegraph, the proper order is "Indicate _____ _ revolutions (or turns)," rather than "Add two," or "Take off four." There are times when the conning officer will not have the speed table at hand and, not wanting to rely on memory, will order "Indicate turns for _____ knots." The lee helmsman checks the table, sets the rpm indicator, reports "_____ turns indicated for _____ knots, sir," and then "Engineroom answers _____ turns for _____ knots, sir."

In an emergency the normal acceleration/deceleration table may be bypassed in order to change engine speed and/or direction as quickly as possible. In response to "All engines back full emergency," the lee helmsman rings up "back full" several times in rapid succession on the EOT.

Modern Installations

Modern bridge design can reduce manning levels through the use of automated equipment. Figure 5-8 illustrates a design prototype of the integrated bridge console, a major component of the Integrated Bridge System (IBS) to be installed in new frigates. Actual installations will in all likelihood differ in detail, but not in capabilities.

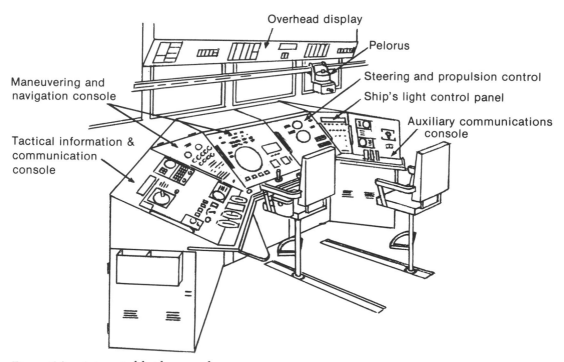

Figure 5-8. Integrated bridge console.

The IBS reduces the bridge watch to three men (not counting a signalman and a lookout): OOD, quartermaster, and helmsman. Only two men are required to operate the controls. Main components of the console are as follows:

1. Anticollision system. Automatically tracks surface targets and displays information to avoid collision; acts as a piloting aid to avoid navigational hazards; and performs many of the computations now done on a maneuvering board, such as station changing courses.

2. Automatic open-sea navigation. Continuously updated direct readout of the ship's latitude and longitude using the OMEGA system.

3. Autopilot. Permits both remote control steering from CIC and automatic steering to preset courses.

4. Integrated communications system. All means for internal and external communications are in one unit readily available to the OOD.

5. Alarm status board. Immediate reading on all the ship's alarms (flooding, fire, propulsion or steering casualty, etc.).

6. Automatic logging system. A digital recorder logs all collision avoidance and piloting decisions. The system has a continually running voice tape recorder and provides a printout of all course and speed changes, hourly positions, and water depths.

Engine and propeller orders are transmitted by a single-lever control operated by the helmsman. There also is a weapons advisory panel which monitors weapons safety.

Basic Shiphandling Principles

Prerequisites to becoming a competent shiphandler include an understanding of the forces that influence ship movement and the ability to use them to advantage. The conning officer must know the maneuvering characteristics of his ship, the effects of propellers and rudders, and the effects of various sea and wind conditions. Other factors, such as the use of mooring lines and ground tackle to assist in maneuvering, are described in chapter 6.

Controllable Forces

The primary controllable forces available to the shiphandler, specifically propeller and rudder effects, were previously addressed in detail in the discussion of small boat shiphandling. The general principles of propeller thrust, discharge current, side force and rudder force apply equally to fleet ships and small boats. In the majority of single-screw ships, clockwise propeller rotation results in forward movement with attendant side force imparted. The direction of the side force is simply a function of propeller rotation, whereas the magnitude of this force varies with the type of propeller and hull configuration as well as the speed of propeller rotation relative to ship speed.

When a single-engine ship moves at low speed, there is a tendency for the stern to swing to one side or the other. This is due to a greater side effect set up by the propeller. The blades below the shaft get a better bite in the denser water and push the stern sideways. This effect is even more noticeable when the ship is backing down, because the propeller wash is moving forward and exerts no force on the rudder.

In a twin-screw vessel with fixed pitch propellers, the starboard screw rotates clockwise and the port screw counterclockwise to obtain forward movement (just the opposite when both engines are backing). When both propellers are driving ahead or astern in this manner, side forces are effectively canceled out. With twin screws opposed, (one driving ahead and one driving astern) side forces are enhanced, and a *twisting* effect is imparted on the ship, all other forces remaining constant. The combined effects of propeller thrust, discharge current, side force, and rudder force combine to produce a resultant force which indicates the direction and amount of thrust exerted on the ship's stern. Resultant force vectors were illustrated in the previous chapter.

Noncontrollable Forces

Most noncontrollable forces, those over which a shiphandler has no control, were discussed in chapter 4. The reader is reminded, however, that weather, sea conditions, wind, ship loading, and hull conditions vary greatly from day to day, and as a result, every shiphandling evolution involves separate and distinct factors that must be identified and considered by the conning officer. If the necessary precautions are taken, a seaworthy vessel with power properly handled will have no difficulty riding through the worst weather likely to be met. In extreme weather, however, a shiphandler's goal may simply be to maintain *steerageway*, *stability*, and *buoyancy*.

Maneuvering Characteristics

This topic must be general in nature because no two vessels will respond exactly alike to the same maneuvering orders. Additionally, the same vessel will react differently under different environmental and physical conditions (some of which are discussed later in this chapter).

Several characteristics, however, must be understood to become a competent shiphandler. Basically, these characteristics are related to how a vessel responds to various rudder and engine orders. This discussion assumes ideal shiphandling conditions—no wind, current, or other factors that might influence ship movement.

Pivot Point

A ship's pivoting point is a point on the centerline about which the ship turns when the rudder is put over. The pivot point scribes or marks the ship's turning circle.

A ship's pivoting point is nearly always about one-third the ship's length abaft her bow when moving ahead, and at or near her stern when moving astern. The location of the pivoting point will vary with ship's speed, an increase in speed shifting the pivoting point in the direction of the ship's movement. In restricted waters the conning officer must always bear in mind the position of his pivot point before starting a turn. This is especially important when moving ahead to prevent the stern from swinging into an undesirable location, such as a pier.

Turning Circle

A ship's turning circle is the path followed by the ship's pivot point when making a 360° turn. Its diameter varies with rudder angle and speed. With constant rudder angle, an increase in speed results in an increased turning circle. Very low speeds (those approaching bare steerageway) also increase the turning circle because of reduced rudder effect.

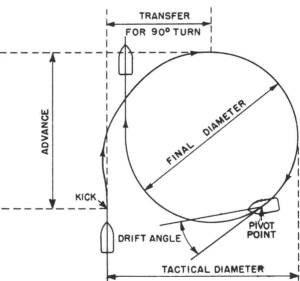

Figure 5-9. Turning circle.

Knowledge of the turning characteristics of one's ship is essential to safe shiphandling, particularly when in restricted waters. Figure 5-9 illustrates a representative turning circle. Definitions of the various elements follow:

Advance—Distance gained toward the direction of the original course after the rudder is put over.

Transfer—Distance gained at right angles to the original course when turning. Figure 5-9 shows transfer for a 90° turn. For a 180° turn, transfer equals tactical diameter.

Tactical Diameter—Perpendicular distance between the path of the ship on the original course and the path of the ship when a 180° turn has been completed with a constant rudder angle. The standard tactical diameter is prescribed in current tactical orders. It is important that the rudder angle to obtain this diameter be known by the conning officer. For example, standard tactical diameter is normally attained on a typical frigate-type ship using standard rudder at a speed specified in the ship's tactical characteristics. Reduced tactical diameter is attained using full rudder at the same speed.

Standard Rudder—Rudder angle necessary to turn the ship in the prescribed tactical diameter.

Final Diameter—Diameter of the circle which ultimately will be scribed by a ship that continues to circle with a constant rudder angle.

Kick—Swirl of water toward the inside of the turn when the rudder is put over. Also, the momentary movement of the ship's stern toward the side opposite the direction of turn.

When the rudder is put over in making a turn, the stern is forced away from the direction of the turn. For several lengths the ship turns very slowly from her original course, because of momentum. She then commences to gain ground in the new direction, moving sidewise through the water to a considerable degree. This naturally results in loss of speed and is why, when a column turn is made, a vessel gains rapidly on the ship ahead while that ship is turning, but loses this distance during her own turn as the first ship completes her turn and steadies on the new course.

A ship's turning data also should be known and certain key values committed to memory. The minimum turning diameters at 10, 20, and 30 knots should be remembered, and the turning diameters for 10, 20, and 30 degrees rudder should be memorized for a speed of 15 knots. The *rate* of turn in degrees per second using 30 degrees rudder at 20 knots is useful for solving maneuvering board problems when the turning circle has to be taken into account.

Calibration and Surge Rate

One of the first steps in accurate shiphandling is to calibrate the ship so that the conning officer knows average turning rates and reaction times in a variety of frequently used engine and rudder combinations.

The distance required to come to a stop when going ahead at various speeds while using various backing powers is vital information for the conning officer. For instance, the distance the ship moves before stopping when "Back one third" is ordered while going ahead at five knots should be kept in mind, because it is very useful when going alongside or making a buoy. And the distance the ship moves ahead before coming to rest when "Back two thirds" is ordered at 15 knots is vitally important knowledge when recovering torpedoes or picking up a downed aviator. A conning officer should familiarize himself with these values to be sure he is ready for emergencies. It will pay dividends later in accurate shiphandling.

The amount the ship "surges" during a speed increase or decrease should be remembered. Perhaps the best way to explain the meaning of "surge" is to give a typical example. Suppose our ship is making 20 knots and is coming up from behind to join a column of ships proceeding at only 10 knots. We accordingly drop our own speed to 10 knots. But by the time our ship slows down from 20 to 10 knots, we will have closed up on the ship ahead of us in column by perhaps an additional 350 yards. In other words, in slowing from 20 knots to 10 knots we have closed by 350 yards, or 35 yards per knot of speed change. We call this ratio the surge or surge rate, and the example given is about typical of the average frigate.

Maneuvering a Single-Screw Vessel

A single-screw vessel is the most difficult to maneuver, particularly at very low speeds where rudder effect is minimal, and propeller side force is greatest. The following discussion covers four cases that illustrate the effects of the controllable forces reviewed earlier in this chapter.

Ship and Screw Going Ahead

When the ship is dead in the water and the propeller starts turning ahead, the screw current hits the rudder and causes the ship to turn the way the rudder is put over. As the ship gathers way, the effect of this screw current diminishes. The normal steering effect of the rudder then controls the ship's head.

When the ship is proceeding ahead in the normal manner and the rudder is suddenly put over to one side or other, she will first fall off away from the side on which it is desired to go. The stern goes away most, but the whole ship is thrown more or less to this side. The ship advances along the line of the original course two or three lengths before she commences to gain in the desired direction. In this case, the speed has little effect on the amount of advance, but the more speed, the faster the turn will be executed. So if you attempt to avoid a danger suddenly discovered two or three ship lengths ahead, you will probably fail. Of course, if you wish to avoid a moving object while making considerable speed, the time of turning may be to your advantage.

Ship and Screw Going Astern

In this case, maneuvering is more complicated because the effect of the propeller is as important as that of the rudder. As in the case illustrated in the previous chapter concerning a small boat with a single screw, the discharge current and side force imparted by the propeller forces the stern to port. When the ship first begins to back, the stern will go to port regardless of the position of the rudder. As the ship gathers sternway, and the rudder is put hard right, the stern will usually swing to starboard, but if the rudder is put left, the stern will go rapidly to port. The stern will back into the wind under all conditions except when the speed of the ship is very slow or the wind is quite light.

Ship Going Ahead, Screw Going Astern

Knowledge of ship reaction in this situation is particularly important with respect to emergency shiphandling. It is assumed by those who have not studied the question that the rudder will continue to affect the ship's head in the usual way as long as the ship has headway. This is not the case. New forces are brought into action when the screw starts backing.

If the rudder is left amidships (after the screw starts backing) the head will fall off to starboard because propeller side force and discharge current are the only forces affecting the stern, and both are forcing the stern to port.

If the rudder is put hard right, the ship will change course to starboard at first. The bow may continue going to the right, but it will stop, then slowly swing to port as the ship slows, then gathers sternway. (See figure 5-10.)

If the rudder is put hard left the ship's head will go slightly to port at first, but as the speed decreases the head will start falling off to starboard.

Ship Going Astern, Screw Going Ahead

In this case, the following forces influence the steering of the ship: (1) the discharge current from the propeller, part of which acts inboard on

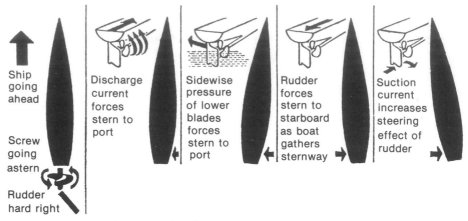

Figure 5-10. Ship going ahead, screw going astern, rudder hard right.

the rudderpost, forcing the stern to port; (2) the side force of the blades; and (3) the direct steering effect of the rudder.

If the rudder is amidships, the side force of the blades and the discharge current striking the rudderpost counterbalance each other, and it is impossible to predict which force will be the stronger.

If the rudder is put hard right, the discharge current opposes and greatly exceeds the forces of the steering effect and side force. The stern goes off to port rapidly.

If the rudder is put hard left, part of the discharge current that strikes the rudderpost and the steering effect are overcome by the other component of the discharge current and the side force. The stern then swings rapidly to starboard.

Throughout this discussion, a single-screw ship with a right-handed propeller is assumed. It must be remembered that it is possible for a ship not to act as described here. Differences in the trim, wind, sea, tidal current, size of rudder and propeller, etc., all produce new forces or modify existing forces. However, if the cases shown are thoroughly understood, it will greatly simplify the estimation of the effect of noncontrollable forces.

Maneuvering a Twin-Screw Vessel

Maneuvering a ship having twin propellers and rudders is relatively easy in comparison to maneuvering a single-screw ship. Using various rudder-propeller combinations, practically any maneuver can be accomplished, including *turning the ship in her own water* (making no headway). As previously noted, the blades of the starboard propeller are so pitched that forward motion is imparted to the ship as the propeller turns clockwise. Similarly, forward motion is caused by the port propeller as it turns counterclockwise. In turning to the right, the starboard propeller exerts a force tending to move the stern in that direction. This force is counteracted, however, by the fact that the port propeller tends to move the stern to the left. These side forces are greatest when the ship is just getting under way, and become practically negligible when a normal cruising speed is attained. Nevertheless, they are of great importance in handling the ship around a pier or when turning in confined waters.

Disregarding all other factors, if both screws are working ahead at the same speed, the vessel will move forward on a straight course. Similarly, if both screws are backing at the same speed, the ship will move astern on a straight course.

The propellers of a twin-screw vessel are offset from the centerline. Therefore, when one screw is working singly, or when both screws are working in the same direction at different speeds or are working in opposite directions, a turning moment is set up that will change the heading of the vessel.

One Screw Working Singly

If the starboard screw is working ahead and the port screw is stopped, the stern will swing to starboard. Similarly, if the port screw is working ahead and the starboard screw is stopped, the stern will swing to port. If the starboard screw is backing and the port screw is stopped, the stern will swing to port. If the port screw is backing and the starboard screw is stopped, the stern will swing to starboard.

Screws Working in Same Direction at Different Speeds

When both screws are working ahead at different speeds, the stern will swing to the side of the screw working at the higher speed. Thus, if the starboard screw is working ahead at standard speed and the port screw is working ahead at two-thirds speed, the stern will swing to starboard. When both screws are backing at different speeds, the stern will swing in the direction of the slower screw. Thus, if the starboard screw is backing at full speed and the port screw is backing at two-thirds speed, the stern will swing to port. The sharpness of the turn will vary with the difference in speed between the two screws. The greater the difference in speed, the sharper the turn.

Screws Working in Opposite Directions

When the screws are working in opposite directions, the bow will swing toward the side of the screw that is backing, and the stern toward the side of the screw that is working ahead. Thus, with the starboard screw working ahead and the port screw backing, the bow will swing to port and the stern to starboard. Obviously, the turning effect will be much greater than in any of the situations discussed previously. Whether the ship will have headway or sternway will depend upon the relative speed and power of the two engines and the amount of way upon the ship when the operation was begun.

A ship may be turned on her heel when dead in the water by using full rudder in the desired direction of turn, going ahead two-thirds on the outboard engine, and backing two-thirds on the inboard engine.

Emergency Shiphandling—Man Overboard

An emergency that may occur at any time at sea is the loss of a person overboard. Often, especially at night or in very cold waters, only immediate action can save the person. All conning officers, therefore, must be familiar with recovery procedures to the point that their reactions will be automatic.

Of the several methods of recovery by a ship, the one used depends on a variety of conditions: daytime or nighttime, visibility, sea conditions, availability of other units for assistance, and elapsed time after the accident. Two other factors are the type of formation in which the ship is steaming and whether it is peacetime or wartime.

Before discussing shipboard procedures, it should be mentioned that, depending on availability, tactical situation, and flying conditions, a helicopter may be used to assist in the recovery. Surface ships must keep clear of a helicopter actually rescuing personnel.

Standard Procedures

Anyone sighting a person overboard must sing out, "Man overboard, (port/stbd) side," and must ensure that the bridge receives the report. If near a lifebuoy, he should throw it overboard as near the person as possible.

The lifebuoy (after lookout) watch throws over the appropriate day or night marker (smoke or flare, respectively) and a lifebuoy whether or not he sees the person. If he sights the person, he should throw additional life rings and markers. (If highly volatile fuel might be in the water, or if in darkened ship condition, flares are not used.)

Upon receipt of the report, the OOD takes the following steps:

1. Maneuver the ship according to prescribed doctrine. This usually entails putting the rudder full over toward the side from which the person fell in order to swing the stern away from him. However, the value of this maneuver depends on time late for receipt of the report, the point of the ship from which the person fell, and the ship's speed.

2. Notify CIC and have the word passed twice over the 1MC: "Man overboard, (port/stbd) side". All hands in the (designated) section assigned to the man-overboard detail man their stations on the double.

3. Sound six or more short blasts on the whistle and make the appropriate visual signal: by day, the OSCAR flag., by night, two red pulsating lights or a white rocket (Very pistol).

4. Notify ships in company and the OTC by the quickest means permitted under the communication policy in force.

5. Inform the commanding officer, the executive officer, and the flag duty officer if appropriate.

6. Take steps to keep the person in sight. Normally a lookout is posted in the eyes of the ship.

7. Establish communications with the deck recovery detail, and keep them informed of the side to be used for recovery.

8. Use searchlights as the situation permits.

Upon receipt of the report in CIC, the dead-reckoning tracer (DRT) is shifted to the 200-yards-per-inch scale and the ship's position is marked. Because of the time delay involved, an estimate of the person's position is made, based on ship's speed and time late. That point is marked back along the ship's track, and the DRT plotter commences reporting the bearing and range of the man's probable position to the bridge and the lookouts.

There are a number of methods of recovering a man overboard (see diagrams and descriptions following). The three most often used are: the Anderson turn, which is the fastest but requires skillful shiphandling; the Williamson turn, for night or low visibility; and the racetrack turn for quick recovery when proceeding at high speed in clear weather. Very large ships often use a small boat to recover a man from the water. Small vessels also use a boat when the sea is very rough and there is little chance of getting the ship close alongside the man. Under any conditions, the OOD should see to it that swimmers with life-jackets and tending lines are ready to go into the water.

Regardless of which recovery method is used, the same basic principles apply. Full rudder should be used to swing the stern away from the man. If the shaft on the side toward the man can be stopped before he reaches the screws, this should be done. If it cannot be done, which is likely, the recovery should be continued without attempting to stop the screws.

Man-overboard maneuvering for naval vessels involved in tactical evolutions can be found in ATP-1, Volume I, Chapter 5. Of specific importance are the instructions for column formations. In this situa-

METHOD AND PRIMARY USE	DIAGRAM (SHIP ON COURSE 090; NUMBERS REFER TO THE EXPLANATION)	EXPLANATION	ANALYSIS	
			ADVANTAGES	DISADVANTAGES
WILLIAMSON TURN 1. USED IN REDUCED VISIBILITY BECAUSE IT MAKES GOOD THE ORIGINAL TRACK. 2. USED WHEN IT IS BELIEVED THAT A MAN FELL OVER-BOARD SOME TIME PREVI-OUSLY AND HE IS NOT IN SIGHT.	⊗ = MAN	1. PUT THE RUDDER OVER FULL IN THE DIRECTION CORRE-SPONDING TO THE SIDE OVER WHICH THE MAN FELL. STOP THE INBOARD ENGINE. 2. WHEN CLEAR OF THE MAN, GO AHEAD FULL ON ALL ENGINES, CONTINUE USING FULL RUDDER. 3. WHEN HEADING IS 60° BEYOND THE ORIGINAL COURSE, SHIFT THE RUDDER WITHOUT HAVING STEADIED ON A COURSE. 60° IS PROPER FOR MANY SHIPS, HOWEVER, THE EXACT AMOUNT MUST BE DETERMINED THROUGH TRIAL AND ERROR (50° FOR YP₄). 4. COME TO THE RECIPROCAL OF THE ORIGINAL COURSE, USING FULL RUDDER. 5. USE THE ENGINES AND RUDDER TO ATTAIN THE PROPER FINAL POSITION (SHIP UPWIND OF THE MAN AND DEAD IN THE WATER WITH THE MAN ALONGSIDE, WELL FORWARD OF THE PROPELLERS).	1. SIMPLICITY, THE REASON WHY IT IS TAUGHT ON YP DRILLS. 2. MAKES GOOD THE ORIGINAL TRACK IN THE OPPOSITE DIRECTION, EXCEPT FOR THE EFFECTS OF WIND AND CURRENT.	1. SLOW 2. TAKES THE SHIP A RELA-TIVELY GREAT DISTANCE FROM THE MAN, WHEN SIGHT MAY BE LOST.
ANDERSON TURN USED BY DESTROYERS, SHIPS WHICH HAVE CONSIDERABLE POWER AVAILABLE AND RELA-TIVELY TIGHT TURNING CHARAC-TERISTICS.		1. PUT THE RUDDER OVER FULL IN THE DIRECTION CORRE-SPONDING TO THE SIDE OVER WHICH THE MAN FELL. STOP THE INBOARD ENGINE. 2. WHEN CLEAR OF THE MAN, GO AHEAD FULL ON THE OUT-BOARD ENGINE ONLY. CONTINUE USING FULL RUDDER. 3. WHEN ABOUT TWO-THIRDS OF THE WAY AROUND, BACK THE INBOARD ENGINE 2/3 OR FULL. ORDER ALL ENGINES STOPPED WHEN THE MAN IS WITHIN ABOUT 15 DEGREES OF THE BOW, THEN EASE THE RUDDER AND BACK THE ENGINES AS REQUIRED TO ATTAIN THE PROPER FINAL POSITION (AS FOR THE OTHER METHODS). 4. MANY VARIATIONS OF THIS METHOD ARE USED, DIFFERING PRIMARILY IN RESPECT TO THE USE OF ONE OR BOTH ENGINES, AND THE TIME WHEN THEY ARE STOPPED AND BACKED TO RETURN TO THE MAN AND TIGHTEN THE TURN. THE VARIATION USED SHOULD REFLECT INDIVIDUAL SHIP'S CHARACTERISTICS, SEA CONDITIONS, PERSONAL PREFER-ENCES, ETC.	THE FASTEST RECOVERY METHOD.	1. REQUIRES A RELATIVELY HIGH DEGREE OF PROFI-CIENCY IN SHIPHANDLING BECAUSE OF THE LACK OF A STRAIGHT-A-WAY APPROACH TO THE MAN. 2. OFTEN IMPOSSIBLE FOR A SINGLE PROPELLER SHIP.
RACETRACK TURN (TWO 180° TURNS) USED IN GOOD VISIBILITY WHEN A STRAIGHT FINAL APPROACH LEG IS DESIRED.		1. A VARIATION OF THE ONE TURN METHOD WHICH PROVIDES A DESIRABLE STRAIGHT FINAL APPROACH TO THE MAN. 2. PUT THE RUDDER OVER FULL IN THE DIRECTION CORRE-SPONDING TO THE SIDE OVER WHICH THE MAN FELL. STOP THE INBOARD ENGINE. 3. WHEN CLEAR OF THE MAN, GO AHEAD FULL ON ALL ENGINES, CONTINUE USING FULL RUDDER TO TURN TO THE RECIPRO-CAL OF THE ORIGINAL COURSE. 4. STEADY FOR A DISTANCE WHICH WILL GIVE THE DESIRED RUN FOR A FINAL STRAIGHT APPROACH. 5. USE FULL RUDDER TO TURN TO THE MAN. 6. USE THE ENGINES AND RUDDER TO ATTAIN THE PROPER FINAL POSITION (SHIP UPWIND OF THE MAN AND DEAD IN THE WATER WITH THE MAN ALONGSIDE WELL FORWARD OF THE PROPELLERS).	1. THE STRAIGHT FINAL AP-PROACH LEG FACILITATES A MORE CALCULABLE AP-PROACH. 2. THE SHIP WILL BE RETURNED TO THE MAN IF HE IS LOST FROM SIGHT. 3. REASONABLY FAST. 4. EFFECTIVE WHEN THE WIND WAS FROM ABEAM ON THE ORIGINAL COURSE.	SLOWER THAN THE ONE TURN METHOD.

Figure 5-11. Methods of man-overboard recovery.

tion, the ship that loses the man takes action to avoid him, as do the others, odd-numbered ships in the column clearing to starboard, and even-numbered ships clearing to port. The ship in the best position to recover the man does so, and keeps the other vessels informed of her actions.

The man should be recovered in the shortest possible time. Large ships usually use the Williamson method. Small ships, in good weather, use the racetrack method. At night or in low visibility, the Williamson turn, though not the fastest recovery method, must be used to bring the ship back along her track. No matter what method is used, the desired final position is beam to the wind slightly to windward of the man, with all way off. When in this position, the ship provides a lee for the man and, since she will make more leeway than he will, she will drift toward, rather than away from, him. When picking up a downed pilot, it is important that the man be kept *forward* of the main condenser injection intakes, particularly if there is a possibility that he still has a parachute attached; a parachute can clog the intakes, which are ordinarily aft of the midships section, on either side. In her final position, the ship should have the man just off her leeward bow.

Summary

The capable mariner must know his ship. This chapter has addressed basic nautical terminology and basic ship structure. The junior officer should be conversant on the structural characteristics of his ship as well as on the general compartmentation and deck locations. Ship control spaces, such as the bridge and after steering, were discussed with a primary focus on the equipment and procedures used in shiphandling. Basic shiphandling terms and principles were discussed with particular emphasis on the controllable and noncontrollable forces involved in any shiphandling evolution. A thorough understanding of the various forces that act upon the ship is the cornerstone of effective shiphandling. Unless the conning officer thoroughly understands the forces that come to play on his ship, how they act, and how they can be controlled, efficient and safe shiphandling is not possible. Shiphandling is an art that is learned primarily through experience. Even those who have spent many years at sea do not claim to have mastered it completely. Shiphandling proficiency requires constant analysis, study, experiment, and practice.

6

Mooring and Anchoring

Mooring

To bring a ship to a mooring in a smart, seamanlike manner is the mark of an efficient shiphandler. To accomplish such an evolution takes planning, advance preparation, training, and the teamwork of all of the crew. A sound knowledge of deck equipment, deck fittings, and the proper use of mooring lines is vital to the successful accomplishment of any mooring or anchoring evolution. Mooring to a pier and getting under way from a pier are the most basic, yet extremely critical, evolutions performed by the conning officer and the deck department.

Deck and Pier Fittings

It is important to know the different deck and pier fittings that may be used when mooring and unmooring. These fittings consist of such devices as cleats, bitts, bollards, chocks, and towing pads (illustrated in figure 6-1).

A cleat is a device consisting mainly of a pair of projecting horns used for belaying a line or wire. Bitts are cylindrical objects made of steel and implanted in the deck. They are usually arranged in pairs, each pair mounted on a separate footing.

A bollard is a strong cylindrical upright on a pier, around which the eye or bight of a ship's mooring line is placed.

A chock is a heavy fitting, with smooth surfaces through which mooring lines are led. Mooring lines are run from bitts on deck through chocks to bollards on the pier when the ship is moored. Chocks are of three types:

1. Open chock: A mooring chock, open at the top.
2. Closed chock: A mooring chock closed by an arch of metal across its top.
3. Roller chock: A mooring chock that contains a roller for reducing friction.

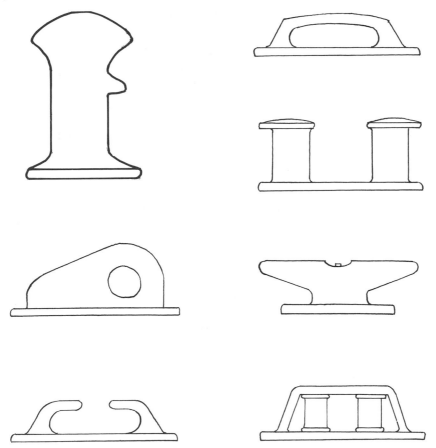

Figure 6-1. *From top to bottom: a bollard; towing pad eye; open chock; closed chock; bitts; cleat, roller chock.*

A towing pad is a large pad eye of extra strength which is used in towing operations.*

Mooring Lines

Ships are moored to piers, wharfs, and other ships with a set of mooring lines that vary according to the size and character of the ship (figure 6-2). In general, mooring lines must satisfy two requirements. First, they must be as light as possible for ease in handling, and second, they must be strong enough to take considerable strain during moor-

*A pad eye is a right-angled trunnion mounting, welded to the deck, with a hole in the upright plate through which attachments or line can be reeved. It is used to secure a rig or line to the deck.

ing, unmooring, and heavy weather, since they are the means by which a ship is held in place. The following table gives some idea of the size of fiber line, manila and synthetic fiber, used as mooring lines aboard various ship types:

	Natural Fiber	Synthetic Fiber (nylon, dacron)
MSO and smaller	5"	3-½" and 4"
DD, FF	6"	5"
CG	8"	6"
LPD, LKA, LPH and LSD	8"	6"
AOE, AOR	8"	6"
CV	10"	8"

Figure 6-2. A cruiser moored with six lines doubled up.

Mooring lines are generally classified according to their use as bow lines, stern lines, breast lines, or spring lines. The *bow* line is the mooring line that runs through the bull-nose or chock nearest the eyes of the ship and holds the bow in. The corresponding line used to secure the stern is the *stern* line. A breast line is led nearly perpendicular from a ship to the pier, controlling the distance of a part of the ship from the pier. *Breast* lines are called bow, waist, or quarter breasts. Where there is a considerable rise and fall of tide, breast lines are undesirable due to their short scope and consequent need for constant attention and readjustment. A *spring* line leads obliquely to the pier and controls the fore-and-aft position of the ship with respect to her berth. Spring lines leading forward away from the ship, at an angle with the keel, are *forward (bow, quarter,) or waist springs*. Spring lines leading aft are *after (bow, quarter,) or waist springs*. Two spring lines, leading in opposite directions in the same vicinity, act as breast lines from the pier to the ship. *Springing* is a term applied to the use of spring lines to move the ship in toward the pier by surging forward or aft against a line which leads obliquely to the pier.

Ships are normally moored with six and sometimes seven mooring lines, the lines being numbered, from forward aft, on *the ship* as shown in figure 6-3. A ship may use fewer or more lines as necessary, in which case the numbers are changed accordingly.

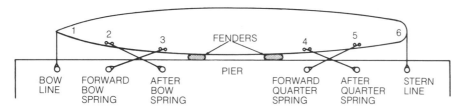

Figure 6-3. Proper positions for mooring lines of a destroyer.

Well in advance of mooring, the lines are faked down, fore and aft (if practicable), each near the chock through which it will pass. The end with the eye is passed through the chock and the loop laid back over the lifeline.

When the ship is secured, the mooring lines are normally doubled up which means that a bight of line is passed to the pier or another ship, giving three parts of line each taking an equal strain, instead of only one part. Figure 6-4 shows a correctly secured mooring line which has been properly "doubled up." Notice that the strain is equally divided among each part of line.

Figure 6-4. Correctly doubled mooring line.

Rat Guards

When moored to a pier, rat guards are always put on mooring lines to prevent rats from climbing aboard on them. These rat guards consist of a circular galvanized metal disk, made in halves, which can be lashed together on the lines. They usually dip toward the center, and the concave side faces the pier (figure 6-5). Chafing gear, usually canvas secured by small stuff, is applied to the mooring lines before attaching rat guards.

Heaving Lines

Heaving lines, bolos, and line-throwing guns play an important part when going alongside. The speed with which the lines are sent to the pier is often critical, especially in strong winds or currents. When a successful throw has been achieved, a heaving line can then be bent to the mooring line that is needed first. The heaving line is bent on to the eye of the mooring line. Hawsers should have short messengers attached to them so that the heaving line does not part during delivery to the pier. This measure will in turn alleviate the problem of the heaving line jamming between the eye of the hawser and the bollard.

Under difficult conditions it is best to bend the heaving lines for the additional mooring lines to the first line that goes over, instead of making further attempts to heave them over.

In addition to normal heaving lines, it is very useful to have bolo lines ready both fore and aft. They usually consist of a padded lead weight attached to the end of a nylon shot line. With a bolo, a skillful sailor can reach to fully twice the distance of a normal heaving line, and because of its weight, a bolo is much more effective in the wind than a normal heaving line. The bolo is hazardous, however, especially when used where there are large numbers of people on the dock. For this reason, its use is discouraged or sometimes prohibited by some commanding officers. Bolos are therefore used as back-ups to the heaving line.

Owing to the danger it poses to people on the pier, the line-throwing gun is seldom used in mooring, although it is used extensively in underway replenishment. In mooring, it is only used under extremely

Figure 6-5. A rat guard.

adverse conditions, when the heaving line or bolo will obviously not be effective, or when they have already failed. Men on the pier or on the other ship are told to take cover before the line is fired.

Dipping the Eye

If two mooring lines are placed over the same bollard, the second one is led up and through the eye of the first, before placing it over the bollard. This makes it possible for either line to be cast off independently of the other and is called dipping the eye.

Fenders

A fender is a shock-absorbing device used to cushion the shock of contact between a ship and pier or between ships. Fenders are a matter of concern to the deck seamen and the officer bringing a ship alongside. The most frequently used ship fender is a pneumatic fender made of inflatable rubber, about four feet long and three feet in diameter. It should be lowered to a point just clear of the water at the extreme beam amidships. This fender is normally the only one the ship rides against when alongside another ship, and the perfect maneuver in mooring ends with a gentle "one point" landing on this fender.

In addition to the fender amidships, a number of additional cylindrical fenders, depending on the size and type of ship, are kept ready on the forecastle and on the fantail. These are normally smaller pneumatic fenders or "home made" manila fenders about four feet long and a foot in diameter. On board a destroyer, it is normally desirable to place one of these with its top about one foot above the deck edge just forward of the forecastle windbreak and another similarly placed abreast the after end of the deckhouse. Other cylindrical fenders are kept available for "immediate use" to protect the forecastle and the propeller guards as may be necessary.

Finally, several ball fenders made of manila are kept ready for placement at any other point of contact between the side of the ship and the pier. These are not as dependable as the cylindrical fenders, because they are more easily squeezed out from between the ships, but they are easier to handle and can be put in place quicker than heavier types.

Camels

A camel is a heavy floating raft of metal or timber used to fend a ship off a pier or wharf. It can be from 10 to 60 feet in length and 3 to 20 feet in width. Its purpose is to separate the ship from the pier face in order to prevent contact between it and the ship's side or projections from the ship's side, such as screw guards.

Camels serve another very practical purpose. They allow the ship's crew to clean and paint the ship's sides down close to the waterline when the ship is moored alongside a wharf, pier, or another ship.

Standard Commands to Line Handlers

In giving orders to the line handling stations, it is mandatory that the orders have the same meaning on the forecastle as was intended by the conning officer. In addition, all orders must be obeyed promptly. The following examples and definitions are in common use in the fleet and form the basis for all orders to line handlers. In these orders the lines are referred to by number—"hold one, slack two, check three"—because numbers are shorter and more precise than names. Once the ship is secured and the use of each line becomes definite, the lines are frequently referred to by name.

Stand by your lines—Man the lines and stand ready to cast off.

Pass one—Pass line number one on to the pier, place the eye over the appropriate bollard, but *take no strain*.

Take in the slack on three (or number three)—Heave in on number three line but do not take a strain.

Take a strain on one—Put line number one under tension.

Slack one—Take all tension off of line number one and let it hang slack, but not in the water.

Ease one—Let number one line out until it is under less tension, but not slacked.

Take number two to the capstan—Lead the end of line number two to the capstan, take the slack out of the line, but *take no strain*.

Heave around on two—Apply tension on number two line by hauling on it with capstan.

Avast heaving—Stop the capstan, or stop pulling in.

Hold what you've got—Hold the line as it is. If the line is on a bollard or cleat, two or three turns are taken.

Hold five—Do not allow any more line to go out on number five, even though the risk of parting the line may exist.

Check five—Put a heavy tension on number five line but not to the breaking point, tending the line so it will not part.

Surge five—Hold moderate tension on number five line, but allow it to slip enough to permit movement of the ship (used when moving along the pier to adjust position).

Double up—Pass an additional bight on all mooring lines, or line indicated, so that there are three parts of each line to the pier.

Single up—Take in all bights and extra lines so there remains only a single part of each of the normal mooring lines.

Take in all lines—Used when secured with your *own* lines, it means to have all lines cast off from the pier and brought on board.

Take in one (or number one)—When used by the officer in charge on the forecastle, it is preceded by the commands "slack one" and "cast off one" and means merely to retrieve line number one and bring it back on deck.

Cast off all lines—When secured with your *own* lines, it is a command to *those tending the mooring lines on the pier or on another ship* to disengage or throw off the lines from the bollards or cleats. When secured with *another* ship's lines in a nest, it means to cast off the ends of her lines and allow the other ship to retrieve her lines.

Often the ship must move up the pier or wharf in short steps, and then the command is given, "Shift lines on the dock forward (or aft)," or, "Walk number one forward (or aft)." Supplementary information about the distance of the move is also sent down from the bridge. Caution is used in this movement, since control of the ship's position is still being exercised by the use of the mooring lines.

If the ship's auxiliary deck machinery is to be used to haul in on a line, the command is given, "Take one (number one) to the capstan." This may be followed by, "heave around on one (number one)" and then, "Avast heaving on one (number one)."

Line-Handling Safety Precautions

Under no circumstances stand in the bight of a line or on a taut fall.

Don't try to check a line that is running out rapidly by stepping on it.

When handling lines, the standing part is coiled or faked down to prevent fouling in case the line runs out rapidly.

Nylon, dacron, and other synthetic-fiber lines are widely used for mooring and rigging. These lines are characterized by high elasticity and a low friction. The following rules apply:

An extra turn is required when securing to bitts, cleats, capstans and other holding devices;

When easing out from holding devices, use extreme caution because of the high elasticity, rapid recovery, and low friction;

Nylon line, on parting, is stretched 1-½ times its original length and snaps back. Do not stand in the direct line of pull of nylon line when heavy loads are applied.

Shiphandling Considerations

Bringing a ship to a successful mooring requires a great deal of skill on the part of the shiphandler and all other persons involved in the evolution. Many elements enter into the problem, such as individual ship characteristics, wind direction and strength, and currents. Basically, however, making a good mooring depends on the proper use of rudder and engines and on using assistance from other forces, such as mooring lines and tugs.

This discussion mainly concerns twin-screw ships. For single-screw vessels there are any number of methods for accomplishing the required evolution, depending primarily on the type of ship. What works with one type may not be effective for another type or even for different classes of the same type. Some frigates, for example, have a single rudder, while others have twin rudders, making their handling characteristics quite different. It is in the handling of single-screw ships that knowledge of the forces described in the previous chapter is of prime concern.

The mooring methods described are not the only ones or even the best ones for all occasions. Under strong wind and/or current conditions, for instance, single-screw and large twin-screw ships should use tugs. *Crenshaw's Naval Shiphandling* illustrates and describes many examples of actual mooring problems and their solutions.

Mooring to a Pier

The experienced shiphandler will bring his ship alongside the pier by making judicious use of rudder and engines, placing as little strain as possible on the mooring lines. Nonetheless, the function of the various lines must be understood thoroughly, because they are extremely important in mooring the ship without damage to her or the dock. Various mooring situations are described below.

No Set On or Off the Pier   In the absence of a set (wind or current) on or off the pier, a twin-screw vessel can be moored equally well to either side. Lines and fenders are made ready, and the mooring is approached at an angle of 10° to 20°. Only sufficient speed to maintain steerageway is needed. Engines should be stopped, and the bow allowed to approach fairly close to the pier, at which point the rudder is put over in the direction away from the pier.

This latter action will bring the stern in so the ship is parallel with the wharf. Headway is then stopped by backing the outboard engine. If the ship has reached a parallel position before she loses her headway, it will be better to back both engines to prevent the stern from swinging into the pier.

A single-screw vessel will have little difficulty making a port-side-to landing. When the bow has been eased in alongside the berth, the engine is reversed, and propeller side force will bring the stern in.

For a landing to starboard, the single-screw vessel should approach the pier at a shallower angle and at a slower speed. The stern line should be put over as soon as possible because, when the engine is backed, the side force will push the stern away from the pier.

Being Set On   Making a landing when being set on may be a dangerous operation requiring skillful handling and quick action. In going alongside under such conditions, it is usually best to bring the ship to a stop parallel to the pier, with half a beam's width of open water between. The current or wind will push the ship in. The set may be strong enough, however, to cause damage when the vessel comes up against the pier. This can be overcome by bringing the ship in faster, canting the bow outward, and when close to the pier, backing down full on the inboard propeller. The increased speed cuts down the effectiveness of the set, while backing the engine straightens out the ship, stops the headway, and creates a wash to cushion her against the pier. Needless to add, such an operation requires good judgment and timing.

Being Set Off   If the current or wind is such as to set the ship off, the approach should be made at a fair angle with considerable speed. Lines must be passed as soon as possible, and the stern brought in by putting the rudder away from the pier. Headway is stopped by backing the outboard engine. This also helps to bring in the stern, but it is often necessary to back down on a forward quarter spring while holding the head by the bow line and bow breast. If the set is strong, careful handling is needed to prevent parting the lines.

Current From Ahead   When the current is running parallel to the face of the pier, it is best to go alongside against the set. In this way the ship can maintain steerageway. The approach should be slow with reference to the pier, and on a parallel heading. It is dangerous in this case to come in at an angle because the current may force the bow in against the pier. The ship is brought above the point of mooring, and her lines are passed to the pier before stopping her headway. Bow lines are put over first, and the vessel is then allowed to drift in on her forward spring lines. The rudder is used to swing the stern, and strain on the lines is prevented, if necessary, by an occasional kick ahead on the engines. (See figure 6-6.)

If the current is very strong, it is possible to drop the outboard anchor at a point above the pier, and to spring in on a forward bow spring while veering chain.

Current From Astern   Bringing the ship alongside with a following current is always difficult and often dangerous. If space permits, it is

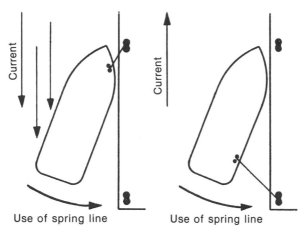

Figure 6-6. Making use of current.

much better to come about and meet the current as previously discussed. In case this is not possible, the best procedure may be to let go an anchor and wait for the ship to swing around, thus approaching the pier against the current.

When it is necessary to moor with the current from astern, it is essential that the stern line and after quarter spring be secured first. When this has been done, the strain on these lines will spring the ship in to the wharf. It must be remembered that the speed of the vessel relative to the pier will be greater than its velocity through the water. This places a severe strain on the lines, which must be overcome by backing the engines. If the engines are backed before the lines are passed, however, a loss of steerageway will result which may prove disastrous. Thus, it can be seen that the entire operation involves careful timing and instantaneous decision.

Clearing a Pier

Getting under way from a mooring alongside a wharf is usually easier than making a landing. If there appears to be no set on or off the pier, it is necessary only to single up and slack off the remaining lines. Observation will show whether or not a current is operating. The vessel may drift out, in which case all that need be done is to take in all lines and proceed to get under way. If she does not drift off, however, the stern can be kicked out by going ahead slowly on the outboard engine while taking a strain on the after bow spring. As the stern swings out, the bow will come up against the pier and must, of course, be protected by fenders. As soon as the stern is well clear, take in all lines and back out, steering with the engines until sufficient sternway for the rudder to take effect is obtained.

Mooring and Anchoring   **181**

Being Set On   This is probably the most difficult situation in getting under way. If the set is strong, large vessels usually require tugs in order to get clear. If tugs are not available, it is necessary, as previously described, to spring the stern out and then to take the ship out astern. In backing out, it is necessary to use plenty of power on the inboard engine. This serves to keep the stern clear, but again the bow will be set upon the pier and fenders must be carefully tended. In order to reduce the effective time of the set, the outboard engine also should be backed and the ship taken out as rapidly as possible.

Being Set Off   When the current tends to cause the ship to drift away from the wharf, it is usually quite easy to get clear. It is only necessary to take in all lines and allow the set to move the ship out to a position where she can get under way.

Current From Ahead   If the ship at her mooring is headed into the current, the usual method of getting clear is to let the bow swing out while taking a strain on a forward quarter spring. The vessel can then be taken out ahead. If the stern is close to the pier, it will be best to go ahead on the outboard engine first so there will be no danger of fouling the inboard propeller. It may be necessary to hold the head with a bow breast while slacking quarter spring until the stern is clear. In using the bow breast, the bow must be kept farther out than the stern, or the breast line will spring the ship back into the pier.

It is sometimes necessary to go out astern even with a current from ahead. This will be true when wind prevents the bow from falling off and holds the ship's head in against the pier.

Current From Astern   When the current is running parallel to the wharf in the direction of the ship's head, it is relatively easy to get under way. By taking a strain on the after bow spring, the stern can be eased out on a quarter breast until the ship is pointed as desired. By backing down, the vessel can then be taken out astern.

Anchoring

A ship is anchored when it is held in position by an anchor on the bottom, and moored when it is made fast either to a buoy or a pier. A ship is moored to a buoy by anchor chain, but moored to a pier by mooring lines. A discussion of anchoring or mooring to a buoy is impossible without an understanding of the deck machinery and equipment involved in such an evolution. *Ground tackle is the collective term applied to all the equipment used in anchoring.* It includes the anchors themselves, their anchor cables (sometimes called chain),

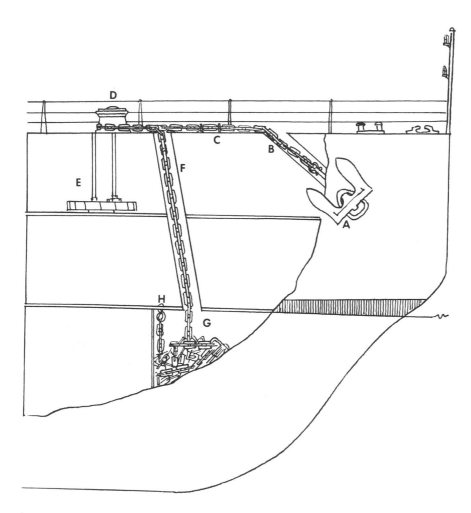

Figure 6-7. The chain locker. A, starboard anchor; B, hawsepipe; C, chain stopper; D, windlass; E, windlass room; F, chain pipe; G, chain locker; H. bitter end secured.

connecting fittings, the anchor windlass, and all the devices used in securing (housing) the anchors in their hawsepipes. Before foundries produced anchor chain as we know it, anchors were raised and lowered by fiber hawsers and later wire rope. Thus, the large pipe through which the cable passes from the deck to the ship's side is called a hawsepipe. The hawsepipe must not be confused with the chain (or spill) pipe through which the chain runs from the windlass down to the chain locker (figure 6-7). In addition to these structural fittings, other connecting fittings or appendages of the ship's ground tackle include *detachable links, bending shackles, mooring shackles, mooring swivels, shackle tool sets, clear hawse pendants, dip ropes, chain stoppers, wrenches for chain stoppers, outboard swivel shots, chain cable jacks, mooring hooks, and anchor bars.* The more important of these will be covered in some depth below.

Anchors

Anchors in use in the Navy today can, in general, be grouped according to type as follows: *patent* or *stockless anchors, mushroom anchors,* and *lightweight type* or *stock in crown anchors*. *Patent* or *stockless anchors*, the type of anchor shown in figure 6-8, have been adopted on most combatants principally because of ease of stowage and handling. Because of the absence of the stock, these anchors can be raised directly into the hawsepipe. The arms of this kind of anchor are pivoted upon the shank and swing up to 45 degrees on either side to permit the anchor to dig into the sea bottom. A distinct disadvantage of the patent anchor is its tendency to disengage its flukes by gradually turning over. In addition, it tends to clog with mud, and should it roll out in this condition, the flukes may be up at such an angle as to prevent their taking a new bite. In this case the only resistance to dragging is the weight of the anchor and chain on the bottom. When the possibility for such an occurrence exists, the ship must be prepared to take immediate action either by using its engines and/or by dropping another anchor.

The *mushroom anchor* (figure 6-9) was at one time issued to submarines. Its rounded surface allowed it to be carried against a submarine's smooth hull. The mushroom anchor is used primarily today to anchor buoys, small boats, and special barges.

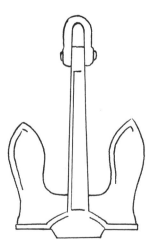

Figure 6-8. Patent or stockless anchor.

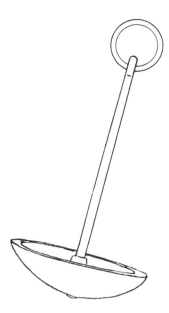

Figure 6-9. A mushroom anchor.

The *lightweight (LWT)* anchor, with the stock in the crown, is a comparative newcomer to the Navy. Two of these are shown in figure 6-10. The *Northill* anchor is a small-boat anchor. The *Danforth* anchor's original use was for small boats and stern anchors on landing craft and ships, but they also are used as a bow anchor on destroyer-type ships. The Danforth anchor is comparable in strength and holding power to a stockless anchor of approximately two times its weight. Other advantages of the lightweight anchor are that the length and sharpness of its flukes enables it to dig in faster and easier. In addition, its lighter weight requires lighter and less costly anchor-handling gear. Further, the stock through its crown is an effective anti-rolling rod and does not interfere with stowing it in the hawsepipe. Under a steady strain, this anchor tends to bury itself deeper in the bottom. In fact, difficulty in breaking it free from the bottom when heaving in is sometimes a disadvantage.

Chain and Appendages

Modern Navy anchor chain is made of dielock or high-strength welded steel. The size of the link is designated by its diameter, called *wire diameter*. Wire diameter is the diameter of a link measured at its point of contact with the adjacent link. All links are studded; that is, a solid piece is either forged or welded in the center of the link. These studs eliminate the danger of the chain kinking and the pounding of

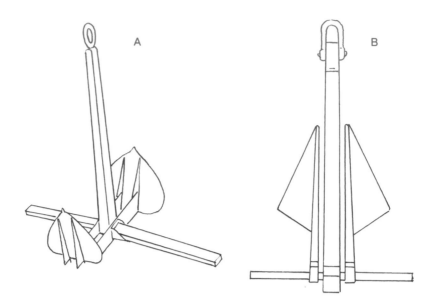

Figure 6-10. Lightweight anchors of the Northill (left) and Danforth (right) type.

links on adjacent links. To give some idea of the weight of a large anchor chain and anchor, a single link of the USS *John F. Kennedy*'s chain weighs 360 pounds, and each of its anchors weigh 30 tons.

An anchor chain is made up of several smaller lengths of chain called *shots*. Standard shots of chain, 15 fathoms in length, are connected to each other by special *detachable links*. Such links are constructed so that they may be disassembled, allowing shots of chain to be removed and replaced. Detachable links serve another purpose. Their different colors allow quick determination of how much chain is paying out. The detachable links and their adjacent links on both sides are marked in accordance with table 6-1. By observing these markings a crewman is

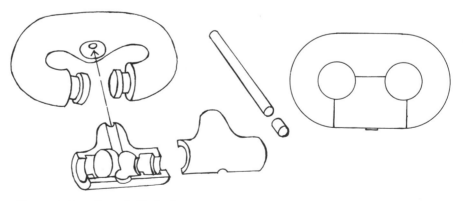

Figure 6-11. Detachable link.

Table 6-1. Method used to mark anchor chain.

Shot Number	Color of Detachable Link	Number of Adjacent Links Painted White	Turns of Wire on Last White Links
1 (15 fathoms)	Red	1	1
2 (30 fathoms)	White	2	2
3 (45 fathoms)	Blue	3	3
4 (60 fathoms)	Red	4	4
5 (75 fathoms)	White	5	5
6 (90 fathoms)	Blue	6	6

able to tell when the desired length of chain is deployed. Each shot of chain is marked in this manner except the last two. Each link of the entire next-to-last shot is painted yellow; the last shot is entirely red. These last two shots give warning of the approach of the bitter end of the chain.

Figure 6-12. Riding and housing chain stoppers are made up of a turnbuckle inserted in a short section of chain, with a slip or pelican hook attached to one end of the chain and a shackle at the other end.

Chain Stoppers

Riding and housing chain stoppers are made up of a *turnbuckle* inserted in a short section of chain, with a slip or pelican hook attached to one end of the chain and a shackle at the other end (figure 6-12). The *housing stopper*, which is bent to the anchor chain when the anchor is housed ready for sea, is the one nearest the hawsepipe; any others are

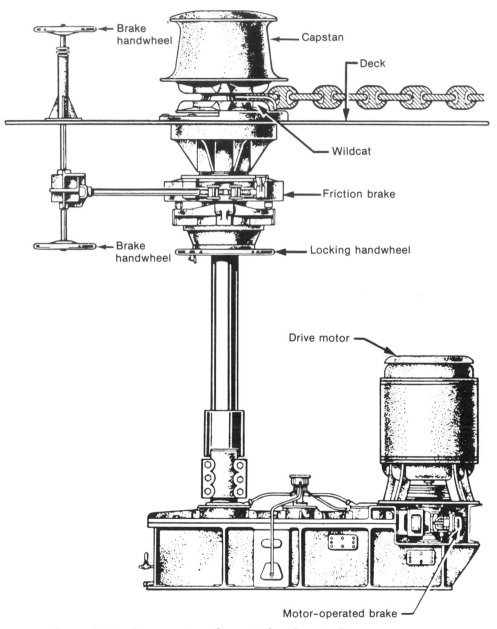

Figure 6-13. *Cutaway view of a vertical anchor windlass.*

referred to as *riding stoppers*. These last-mentioned stoppers are used for holding the anchor taut in the hawsepipe, for riding to an anchor or holding an anchor when an anchor chain is disconnected for any reason. When in use, a stopper is attached to the chain by straddling a link with the tongue and strongback of the pelican hook. When riding to an anchor with more than one stopper on the chain, the strain must be equalized between the stoppers by adjusting the settings of the turnbuckles.

Anchor Windlass

An anchor windlass is the machine used to hoist a bow anchor or warp a ship into position alongside another ship or pier. Stern anchors are handled by a stern anchor winch. There are two types of windlasses: the verticle shaft type and the horizontal shaft type. Although the basic principle of operation is the same for both types of windlass, the method of letting go and raising the anchor differs. Also, the fact that a vertical shaft windlass usually is much farther aft than a horizontal shaft windlass causes a certain difference in the make-up of the chain.

Nomenclature and Functioning

Figure 6-13 shows a vertical shaft anchor windlass of the electric-hydraulic type. The parts above the deck are the friction brake hand-

Figure 6-14.   *The crew of a multilateral-force ship using the capstan independently of the wildcat.*

Figure 6-15. A horizontal shaft anchor windlass.

wheel, machine control, *capstan*, and *wildcat*. (The proper naval term for the line-handling drum on the anchor windlass is *warping head*. Usage, however, has given authority to the word *capstan*.) All the remaining machinery is located below the main deck in the anchor windlass room.

The drum, located just below the capstan, is called a wildcat and contains teeth that engage the links of the anchor chain. By turning the locking handwheel in the windlass room, the wildcat may be engaged to the shaft for raising the anchor, or disengaged from the shaft prior to letting go (dropping) the anchor. When using the capstan, as when mooring to a pier (figure 6-14), the wildcat is disengaged, and in order to prevent it from rotating, the friction brake is set up by the brake handwheel on the main deck or in the windlass room. With the friction brake off and the wildcat disengaged, the wildcat can rotate independently of the shaft. This is the arrangement when the anchor is dropped. Most large combatant ships have a separate anchor windlass for each bow anchor. Some small ships, like FFs, have a single anchor windlass and are equipped with some means for removing one anchor chain from the windlass and engaging the other.

The horizontal shaft windlass is depicted in figure 6-15. For this type of windlass, all of the machinery is above deck. Two wildcats are on the shaft, one for each bow anchor.

The Anchor Detail

The first lieutenant is in charge on the forecastle while anchoring and weighing anchor. Aboard most ships his assistant is either the ship's boatswain or a chief boatswain's mate. In their absence, the senior boatswain's mate aboard is his assistant. A man from the auxiliary machinery division (A or R division) and an electrician's mate from the E or R division of the engineering department are in the anchor windlass room to take care of any mechanical or electrical failure that may occur. The first lieutenant has a telephone talker on the 1JV sound-powered telephone circuit to relay orders and information between the forecastle and the bridge and other line-handling stations.

Taking Soundings

As a ship proceeds toward her anchorage she will always take *soundings*, that is, measure the depth of water during her approach. Soundings may be taken with the *hand lead*, frequently called a *leadline*, or with the electronic depth sounder.

With the ship making 12 knots, a good leadsman can get reliable soundings down to about seven fathoms. At slower speeds, of course, the lead has time to sink farther before the ship moves up to it, allowing even deeper soundings. Before heaving, the leadsman takes station in the *chains*, which on most ships is a platform projecting over the side at the after end of the forecastle. The marker is read when the lead is on the bottom and the line is hauled taut, up and down (figure 6-16).

Making the Anchor Ready for Letting Go

On ships with two anchor windlasses, both ship's anchors are made ready for letting go. The anchor detail receives certain information from the bridge prior to anchoring. For example, the bridge will designate what anchor (port or starboard) is to be used. Nonetheless, both anchors are made ready for letting go to the farthest extent possible in the event one fouls, or one is needed to slow the ship in an emergency. In addition, the bridge will inform the forecastle of the depth of water at the anchorage. The depth of water is needed by the anchor detail to determine the amount of chain the ship will ultimately veer out. The bridge will also tell the forecastle what sort of holding ground (mud, sand, etc.) the anchor will dig in to, as this will indicate

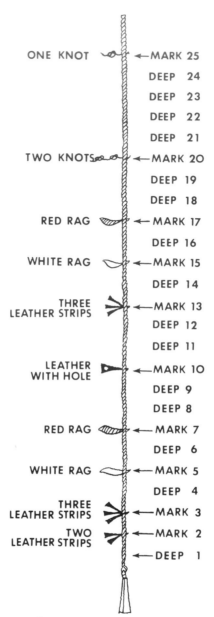

ONE KNOT ← MARK 25
DEEP 24
DEEP 23
DEEP 22
DEEP 21
TWO KNOTS ← MARK 20
DEEP 19
DEEP 18
RED RAG ← MARK 17
DEEP 16
WHITE RAG ← MARK 15
DEEP 14
THREE
LEATHER STRIPS ← MARK 13
DEEP 12
DEEP 11
LEATHER
WITH HOLE ← MARK 10
DEEP 9
DEEP 8
RED RAG ← MARK 7
DEEP 6
WHITE RAG ← MARK 5
DEEP 4
THREE
LEATHER STRIPS ← MARK 3
TWO
LEATHER STRIPS ← MARK 2
← DEEP 1

Figure 6-16. Leadline markings.

how well the anchor can be expected to hold. For example, a sandy bottom is considered to be good holding gound for an anchor.

The exact procedure may vary for making the anchor ready for letting go, but in general the following tasks must be performed: the anchor windlass is tested; the anchor is walked out of the hawsepipe using the wildcat to ensure it will not hang up in the pipe; the brake is set; and the wildcat is disconnected. In addition, all stoppers but one, the housing stopper, are disconnected prior to letting go. The anchor buoy line is attached to one of the anchor flukes. The buoy so attached is used to mark the location of the anchor while the ship moves around it, and to aid in locating it if the chain should part or be slipped in an emergency. Another task prior to letting go is to inspect the chain locker for any such loose gear as hand tools that might become wedged in the chain pipes or come flying out, endangering the men on deck. When the anchor is ready for letting go, that fact is reported to the conning officer on the bridge. While the anchor detail gets the ground tackle ready, distances to the anchorage are relayed to the first lieutenant from the bridge.

Techniques of Anchoring

Although anchoring is a relatively simple operation, several preparatory actions must be taken by various groups of people involved in the evolution.

Information must be compiled by the navigator, including: anchorage assignment, location, and dimension; water depth; tidal data; type of bottom; proposed track to the anchorage; current and wind direction and velocity; and landmarks for fixing the ship's position.

On the bridge and in CIC piloting teams must be set. Using visual bearings and radar ranges and bearings, respectively, to they must determine the ship's position and any set and drift. On the forecastle the anchor detail makes the anchor ready for letting go as previously described.

Approaching the Anchorage

A direct approach to the anchorage is not always possible due to such factors as other ships at anchor, wind and current, and hazards to navigation. For our purposes, however, a straight run with no set and drift is assumed.

On a chart, the navigator plots range arcs along the approach track at 100-yard intervals outward from the letting-go circle to 1,000 yards, then at ranges of 1,200, 1,500, and 2,000 yards. As the ship nears the anchorage, speed is gradually reduced until the engines are stopped. At 1,500 yards, for example, speed might be 10 knots, and at 1,000 yards, 5 knots. Between 300 and 500 yards, the engines are stopped, and the ship coasts into the anchorage. Speeds and distances will vary from ship to ship, of course, since they are dependent on ship characteristics, sea and weather conditions, the desires of the captain etc.

Whenever possible the navigator should establish a landmark (head-mark) on which to lay out his approach track. It should be in line ahead with the center of the anchorage. He should establish another land-mark on or near the beam for determining when to let go the anchor (the letting-go bearing).

During the approach the conning officer is responsible for remaining on track, using the headmark as a reference. A bearing taker should call out bearings to the landmark on the beam. (Additionally, the navigator may make recommendations based on his fix information.) Ideally, the ship will pass through a point that is on both the head bearing and the letting-go bearing, at which time the anchor is let go. The ship should be moving (usually backing) when the anchor is dropped. This keeps the chain from piling up. Piling may damage the chain, and if the pile is on top of the anchor, the chain might foul the anchor. Further, moving aft is a precaution against damaging such things as the sonar dome with the anchor chain. At the command "Stand By," the brake is released and two seamen, one with a maul, take stations at the stopper. Men manning the brake must wear goggles for protection against flying chips of debris. When the command "Let Go" is given, one seaman pulls the pin from the stopper's pelican hook. The seaman with the maul knocks the bail off the tongue of the pelican hook and steps clear. This method is preferred to dropping the anchor by use of the brake, since a brake can freeze or become fouled. The seaman tending the anchor buoy tosses the buoy over the side. At the same instant the colors are shifted, the jack is closed up, and the anchor ball is hoisted on the mast indicating the ship is anchored.

The anchor chain goes rattling out with a roar, until an instant of slackening speed indicates that the anchor has hit the bottom. At this instant, the man on the brake begins to set up on it. The chain is stopped completely by applying the brake. The anchor is then set by backing down with the engines. The amount of chain let out before setting the anchor depends upon the depth of the water, the type of bottom, and the type of anchor. Then the brake is eased off, and the chain is *veered* (allowed to run out by slackening the brake) until the desired scope has been reached.

As each chain marking passes the wildcat, the report is made to the conning officer "(number) fathoms on deck." An alternative report is "(number) fathoms at the water's edge." To report the length of chain veered out is called reporting the *scope* of chain. In addition, the direction the chain is tending is indicated by pointing the arm and/or reporting "Chain tending (number) o'clock." The amount of strain on the anchor chain (light, medium or heavy) is also indicated. A typical anchor report would be: "chain tending three o'clock, medium strain,

75 fathoms at the water's edge. These reports are of the utmost importance to the conning officer to enable him to maneuver the ship properly. For example, if the chain tends around the stem, the situation is reported to the bridge. In this situation, when the chain is making a sharp bend around the ship's stem, damage to one or more chain links or to some underwater hull appendage is likely to result.

Figure 6-17. An anchor being let go with anchor buoy line attached.

Detachable links are particularly susceptible to damage in this fashion. A heavy strain at 12 o'clock might be an indicator that the anchor is dragging.

When the desired scope of chain is out, the brake is set again and the order is given to "Pass the stoppers." The stoppers are applied, the strain on each is equalized, and the chain is slacked between the anchor windlass and the first riding stopper.

Scope of Chain

A ship will normally anchor in water less than 20 fathoms, and under favorable conditions will use a scope of chain which is between five and seven times the depth of the water. However, if a ship at anchor is subjected to heavy weather, a strain much stronger than normal is placed on the chain and the catenary of the chain is decreased. More and more of its length lifts off the bottom as the strain increases. Since much of the holding power of an anchor is due to the heavy chain lying on the bottom, it is important to have more chain out than usual during heavy weather. Otherwise, the anchor drags before developing the full safe load on the chain. If the scope is too long, however, the breaking strain is reached before the entire length of chain lifts off the bottom, and the chain will part. While it is a common rule among seamen to use a length of anchor chain five to seven times the depth of water, the following table is a much more accurate guide:

Depth of Water in Fathoms	Recommended Scope (D is depth in fathoms)
up to 10	3D
10 to 15	4D
15 to 20	5D
20 to 30	6D
over 30 fathoms	7D

The above table applies when moderately severe weather conditions are to be expected. In extremely high winds a longer scope of chain is necessary to take advantage of the maximum holding power of the chain and anchor.

Weighing Anchor

Preparations for weighing anchor, are, in general, the same as for anchoring except that, in addition, a wash down hose is rigged and a grapnel is supplied for retrieving the anchor buoy. The hose is used to wash the mud and sand from the chain and anchor as they are being heaved in. Also, men with paint pots are placed at appropriate intervals to repaint the markings on the chain. Some links of each shot are tested by striking them with a hammer. All links are tested if the chain was subjected to a heavy strain. If a link rings, it is all right; but if it sounds flat, further examination is necessary. When all is in readiness, the report "Ready to heave in" is made to the bridge. On the command "Cast off your stopper and heave around" or simply "Heave around," the stopper is cast off by engaging the windlass, releasing the brake, and taking enough strain on the chain to slacken the stoppers. Now the stoppers can be disconnected and heaving commenced. As the chain comes aboard, it passes along the deck and down into the chain locker. Periodic reports are made to the bridge concerning the amount of chain still out, for example, "Forty-five fathoms at the water's edge," the direction it *tends* and the strain on the chain, *light, moderate, heavy,* or *no strain.* With this information, the conning officer can relieve the windlass and chain of considerable strain by the judicious use of the engines and rudder.

Frequently, the command "Heave around to short stay" is made. *Short stay* (figure 6-18) is the condition when the anchor is about ready to break out. When the flukes have broken out and the crown is still resting on the bottom, the anchor is said to be *up and down.* When free of the bottom, the anchor is *aweigh* and the ship is under way. Each of these conditions is reported to the conning officer. When the anchor comes into view and its condition can be noted, the report is made to the bridge, "Anchor in sight, clear (or fouled) anchor." An anchor is clear when nothing can prevent the ship from proceeding on her way in safety. An example of a fouled anchor might be if the ship's anchor is fouled in another ship's chain. The report "Anchor clear of the water," is also made. The anchor is reported as *housed* when the shank is in the hawsepipe and the flukes are against the ship's side. The bridge will then direct, "Secure the anchor for sea" or "Make the anchor ready for

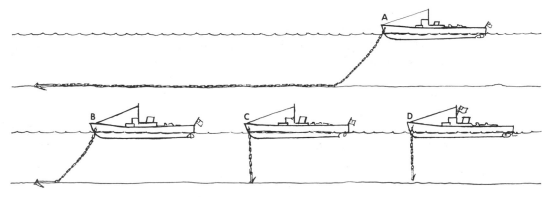

Figure 6-18.   *The stages of weighing anchor. A, anchored; B, at short stay; C, up and down; D, aweigh.*

letting go." When an anchor is secured for sea, the stoppers are passed and the turnbuckles tightened and strain equalized between them. The chain is slacked between the wildcat and the first riding stopper. The brake is set, and the wildcat is disengaged.

Precautions for Maintaining Anchorage

A vital duty of the watch on an anchored ship is checking to see if the anchor is dragging. This is especially important when conditions make dragging a definite possibility. Poor holding ground, deep water, a strong wind or current, or any combination of these mean that bearings and ranges must be taken frequently to check the ship's position.

Bearings on objects on the land are the best indicators of whether or not the anchor is dragging, but the ability must be acquired to distinguish between the change of bearing caused by a swing and that which indicates a change of position resulting from dragging. Immediately action has to be taken as soon as the anchor starts to drag. It may be necessary only to veer more chain to allow the anchor to get another bite in the bottom. However, when a ship is in a crowded anchorage or near a lee shore (one which is downwind from the ship) or shoal water, and dragging, another anchor would normally be dropped at once. If a gale or hurricane is blowing or imminent, it will probably be necessary to heave around and get under way. Preparations for getting under way are made in any event, and signal is made at once to warn ships to leeward or downstream that they may have to get out of the way.

Under normal circumstances, with the chain veered to proper scope, it should hang in a slight catenary (downward curve). If it is taut, there is a good chance that the anchor is dragging or about to drag. When an anchor drags on a hard bottom, there is usually a loud rumbling sound forward to indicate the fact. If it is sliding noiselessly along an ozzy bottom, tremors and vibrations may be felt by placing a foot on the chain.

In severe weather a ship will ride better and easier to a single anchor veered to a long scope than she will to two anchors. However, if extra holding power is needed, another anchor should be dropped. In cases of extreme necessity both anchors should be put down, their chains veered to maximum scope, and the tension on them eased as much as possible by the use of the ship's engines. It has been demonstrated more than once that even these measures will seldom make it possible for a ship to hold off a shore in the face of winds and seas of hurricane force and size. If hurricane weather is expected, the best evasive action is to get under way and get as much sea room as possible before the violent part of the storm arrives.

Mooring to a Buoy

Ships, particularly destroyer/frigate types, frequently moor to a buoy. A buoy mooring is safer in a storm than anchoring because the buoy is secured to the bottom by a very strong chain attached to several anchors, with little chance of dragging. Two methods of mooring to a buoy are discussed: the ordinary and the trolley.

A pad eye on the top of a mooring buoy contains a large ring to which a ship shackles her anchor chain. Small ships, such as minesweepers, formerly were moored by the bight of the chain, with the end secured back on deck. This practice, although it provided a convenient means for a quick release, often bent the chain and has been discontinued.

Upon approaching the buoy for an ordinary moor, the ship lowers a boat containing a buoy party of three or four men, each wearing a lifejacket. The ship reduces headway so as to come to a dead stop with her bow half a ship's length from the buoy. The boat brings her stern under the ship's bow. The end of a 5-inch dip rope and the end of a 2½-inch messenger are lowered to the boat, together with the eye of a 1¾-inch wire, containing a mooring hook or a shackle large enough to engage the ring of the buoy. The boat proceeds to the buoy, and two men get on the buoy. The buoy party secures the wire to the ring of the

Figure 6-19.   The Special Sea and Anchor Detail moor the ship to the buoy.

buoy by means of the mooring hook or the shackle. The dip rope is passed through the ring and bent to the messenger, which is used to haul the end of the dip rope back on board. The buoy party gets back into the boat while the ship hauls her bow over the buoy. The men must not remain on the buoy during this process, because the buoy always cants and at times spins. Figure 6-19 shows men on the Special Sea and Anchor Detail bending the buoy wire on the buoy.

The chain to be used already has been disconnected from its anchor, and the mooring shackle secured to it be means of a detachable link. One end of the dip rope is bent to the chain just above the shackle, and the other is led to the capstan. By walking out the chain and heaving on the dip rope, the shackle is maneuvered out to the buoy. When the end of the chain is in position, the buoy party should be ready to secure it to the ring. When this is done, they cast off the wire, and the moor is complete.

The trolley method is a simpler method for easing out the end of the chain to the buoy by letting it slide down the wire shackled to the buoy. One or more shackles over the buoy wire are used as trolleys. The chain is connected to these trolleys by means of short wire straps passed around studs of the chain links (figure 6-20). The first trolley is connected to the fourth or fifth link, providing enough chain for the men on the buoy to complete the moor without difficulty.

Other preparations on deck are much the same as for the ordinary method of mooring to a buoy, except that sufficient chain for the maneuver is roused up and allowed to hang in a bight over the side during the approach, and it is not necessary to use a dip rope. An

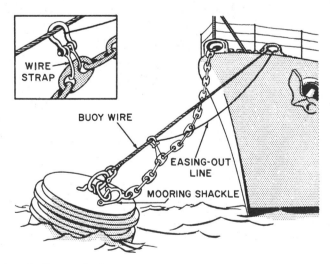

Figure 6-20. Trolley method.

easing-out line is used to control the travel of the chain during the mooring operation and prevents the bitter end of the chain from dropping into the water during the approach.

Once the buoy wire is secured, it is heaved taut and kept that way. The chain is allowed to slide down the wire by slacking off on the easing-out line, and the mooring shackle is secured to the ring of the buoy. The wire is slacked and cast off, and the moor is complete.

On ships with unusually large and heavy chain, it is a good idea to pass a line from the deck through the ring of the buoy and secure it to the mooring shackle or the first link. Then, by using this line and the easing-out line, the men on deck are able to assist those on the buoy to get the mooring shackle into position.

To unmoor, a buoy party is put aboard the buoy to unshackle the chain. First, however, they run a slipwire through the buoy ring and back to the deck so that the ship rides to the bight of the wire. A strain is taken on the wire, the chain is unshackled and heaved in, and the party returns to the ship. When ready to get under way, the end of the slipwire is let go and the wire is heaved in.

Shiphandling Techniques when Mooring to a Buoy

Mooring to a buoy requires considerable expertise on the part of the conning officer (see figure 6-21). When about 500 yards from the buoy and making about 5 knots, put the buoy party in the boat, lower it, and have it come up under the bow. The boat can be put in the water safely by a competent crew at speeds up to 10 knots, but since the boat can make only about 6 knots, the ship must proceed slowly enough to allow the boat to gain its position on the bow and ahead.

At 200 yards, stop the engines, pass the buoy line and messenger to the boat, and send the boat out ahead with the buoy line. The boat should reach the buoy about 50 yards ahead of the ship, and the men can be on the buoy securing the buoy line by the time the ship is brought gently to a stop.

The ideal buoy approach puts the bullnose *abreast* the buoy, about 10 yards to one side, with the ship heading into the wind or current so that she can be maintained in this position while the buoy line is being secured to the buoy. Bringing the buoy up abreast the bow is absolutely essential in many ships if the maneuver is to be controlled from the bridge, because the high flared bow of some of the newer ships completely masks the surface of the water ahead for a hundred yards or more. As soon as the buoy line is secured to the buoy, we should heave in until the buoy is close to the bow.

By keeping the buoy abreast the bow instead of dead ahead, the conning officer can see the buoy at all times and thus can handle the

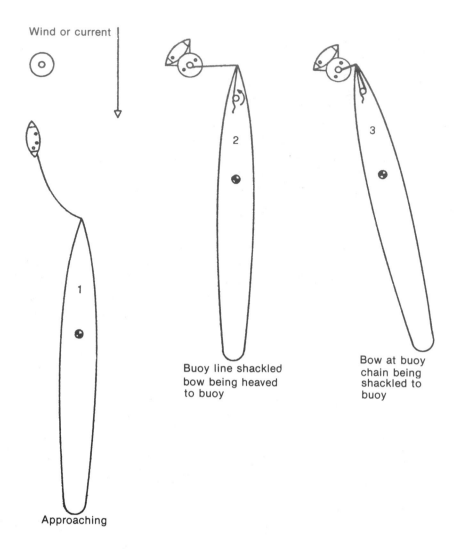

Wind or current

1

Approaching

2

Buoy line shackled
bow being heaved
to buoy

3

Bow at buoy
chain being
shackled to
buoy

Figure 6-21. *Maneuver in snatching a buoy by the trolley-line method.*

situation easily. Once the line has been secured to the buoy, it is usually advisable not to use the engines again until the chain has been securely shackled to the buoy, as the bow can generally be heaved to the buoy with the anchor windlass alone. There are times, of course, when the engines must be used to keep the bow close to the buoy, but the use of the engines should be kept to a minimum.

Throughout the maneuvering the ship must be handled with great care. It takes two seamen to handle the line and the mooring shackle at the buoy, and while these men are on the buoy the ship must not be allowed to surge against the buoy line or to brush against the buoy. It is surprising to see how readily a ship can pull a buoy under. It takes only a slight brush to spin the buoy and endanger the men on it.

Never allow the boat to get *between* the buoy and the ship. A sudden surge or a parting line here could spell tragedy. *Always* remove the men from the buoy before taking any considerable strain. Under normal conditions the ship's bow will be drifting gently in toward the buoy while the buoy line is being secured, and so can be easily brought to the buoy with the men on the buoy. If more than a light strain is needed to work the bow to the buoy, get the men off first before taking the strain, and then put them back on when the bow is snubbed up to the buoy and the chain is ready for shackling.

When making a buoy downwind, or down-current it is usually feasible to hold the stem up into the wind or current with the engines until the ship is secured to the buoy, and then to let the ship swing, keeping the buoy out from the bow by use of the engines.

Making a buoy crosswind or crosscurrent is the most difficult way to make it. Under such circumstances we should, if possible, approach to the position described above with the wind or current dead ahead; but if this is impossible, it will be necessary to make a "flying snatch." The speed of the men on the buoy is the key to this maneuver. Approach so as to put the bow well upwind and slightly short of the buoy (to ensure that it will pass clear of the buoy as the ship is blown downwind). Use the engines and helm to twist the bow upwind throughout the operation. This will keep the bow as near the buoy as possible as the stern is swept downwind, and will give the men on the buoy a maximum opportunity to get the buoy line secured. Once the buoy line is secured, you can swing to it and eventually heave the bow up to the buoy. Care must be taken while swinging, because a parted buoy line at this time will require another approach at the very least.

Summary

The use of the anchor can be an important controllable force at the bow for the shiphandler. Letting go a single anchor is perhaps the simplest method of securing a ship to the bottom, and if the holding ground is good she should ride easily in bad weather, provided ample scope of chain is used. The disadvantage is that when anchored, a ship swings to the combined effects of the wind and current. Therefore, it is necessary to have an unobstructed area equal to a circle whose radius is the length of the ship plus the scope of chain used. The anchor should also be looked upon as the "emergency brake" of the ship. When maneuvering in shoal water or in a harbor, the anchor should be ready for use on a moment's notice. In case of an engine casualty or a steering casualty, it can stop and hold the ship to keep it from running aground.

While a ship is proceeding at normal speed it is normally quite controllable, regardless of the state of the weather, but when it is required to lie to for any reason, it is largely at the mercy of the elements. If something prevents her from proceeding to her destination in a harbor, and she is forced to stop, the anchor is the only means through which the ship can be secured and prevented from drifting with the wind and current.

As the shiphandler learns to use his anchors, he will learn that they are more than portable moorings. For instance, he often can save time and effort by spinning on his anchor instead of laboriously twisting with the engines. He can also use his anchor to control his approach when making a downwind landing. The anchor of a good shiphandler spends a lot of time on the bottom serving a useful purpose, rather than just rusting in the hawsepipe.

The junior officer must have a sound knowledge of deck equipment, deck fittings, and ground tackle in order to appreciate fully the correct techniques of mooring and anchoring evolutions. The effective use of controllable forces in shiphandling, such as the mooring lines and anchor, requires the close coordination between bridge and deck personnel. The conning officer must understand how the deck force will manipulate mooring lines, associated deck fittings/equipment, and ground tackle in response to his standard commands. This chapter has defined and illustrated the use of major deck fittings, mooring lines, and ground tackle in the variety of mooring and anchoring evolutions that the shiphandler must accomplish when going to sea.

7

Marlinspike Seamanship

Introduction

The marlinspike is a tapered steel tool used for separating strands of wire. It is one of the basic tools of the seaman, and it has become a symbol of the trade.

Marlinspike seamanship is the descriptive term for the ancient art of handling, maintaining, and working with line or rope. It includes every variety of knotting, splicing, and lashing. Marlinspike seamanship has been developed to such an extent that landlubbers are often amazed at the complicated and intricate work that can be done with rope.

The knowledge and skills required to practice effectively the art of marlinspike seamanship are extensive. The ability to properly select, care for, and use the variety of fiber and wire rope that is found aboard ships today is not easily acquired. For the deck seaman, learning how to work with rope and line is one of the first challenges faced.

Officers, too, must learn many of these skills. Proper supervision and safety during shipboard evolutions requiring the use of rope or line frequently demand that an officer make judgments based upon the fundamentals of marlinspike seamanship.

Rope and Line

A real seaman, it is said, has a loving affection for a sound piece of line or a good square knot or splice. One look at the way a man handles his line tells an oldtimer whether he's a seaman. Knowledge of marlinspike seamanship and an ability to work with rope is the real test for a deck sailor.

Actually, rope is a general term and is used in the Navy to refer to both fiber and wire. Fiber rope is called rope as long as it is still in its original coil. Once the rope has been uncoiled and cut for use for a specific purpose, such as a lifeline, heaving line, lead line, or mooring line, it is seldom again referred to as rope. Thus, most every fiber rope in use on board ship is a *line*, and referring to a ship's mooring lines as ropes or similar faux pas is a sure sign of a novice. So, a word to the wise; avoid embarrassment and call a line a line.

Figure 7-1. Line and wire rope, blocks and tackle, standing and running rigging form a matrix of the boatswain's work.

Rope made of wire or some combination of fiber and wire is generally referred to by sailors as wire rope, or just wire. Wire rope has many purposes aboard ship; flexible wire rope can be used as cable or running rigging, while stiffer wire is generally used for shrouds and stays and other such standing rigging.

Fiber Line Construction and Composition

Fiber lines are classified both by their construction and their material. The most common line constructions used in the Navy are three-strand, double-braided, and plaited.

Three-Strand Line

In *three-strand line*, fibers are twisted into yarns or threads, the yarns are twisted in the opposite direction into strands, and the strands are twisted in the first direction into ropes. The direction in which the strands are twisted determines the lay of the rope. That is, if the strands are twisted to the right, the rope is said to be right laid. Nearly all three-strand rope used aboard ship has a right-hand twist or lay.

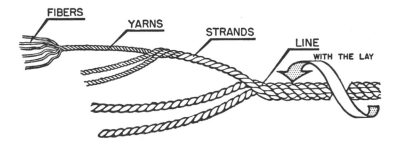

Figure 7-2. *The method of twisting to form yarn, strands, and rope.*

Variations in the lay (e.g., degree of twist) will produce variations in tensile strength, abrasion resistance, bending fatigue, and other important characteristics. For example, hard twisting increases the friction that holds the rope together and makes the rope less likely to absorb moisture. Too many twists reduce effective fiber strengths. The proper degree of twist given to a rope is generally such that the rope is from three-fourths to two-thirds the length of the untwisted yarns composing it.

On occasion, cable-laid rope is carried aboard ship for especially heavy hoisting tasks. It is made up by twisting, usually left-laid, three ropes into a cable. Cable-laid rope is used under conditions where extra elasticity and extra resistance to surface abrasion is desirable.

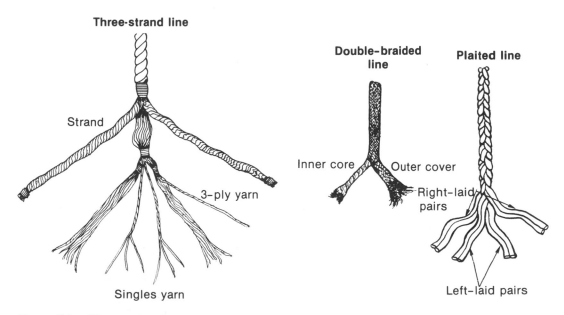

Figure 7-3. *Line construction.*

Double-Braided Line

Double-braided line, one of several kinds of braids found aboard ships, is essentially two braided ropes, one inside the other. The core is made of large single yarns in a slack braid. The cover also is made of large single yarns, but in a tight braid that compresses and holds the core. This line is manufactured only from synthetics, and about 50 percent of the strength is in the core.

Braided lines have certain advantages over twisted ropes. They will not kink, nor will they open to admit dirt or abrasives. Another advantage of braided line is that, where a load is free to rotate, the rope will not unlay (untwist). A disadvantage to braided line, however, is that the construction frequently makes it impossible to inspect the inner yarns for damage. Double-braided line is used for mooring lines, towlines, signal halyards, and many other purposes.

Plaited Line

Plaited line is made of eight strands—four right-twisted and four left-twisted. These strands are paired and worked like a four-strand braid. Thus, there are two pairs of right-laid strands and two pairs of left-laid strands formed into a rope that is more or less square. Plaited line is used for towlines, ship mooring lines, messengers, and other applications. It has many of the advantages of double-braided line but not as much strength.

Natural Fibers

Fiber rope is fashioned from both natural or synthetic (manmade) fiber material. Lines made from a variety of natural fibers (cotton, agave, jute, hemp, sisal, and abaca) have seen service in the Navy in the past, and some still are used. For example, tarred hemp is known as marline and ratline. On the other hand, sisal has been dropped from the supply system and is disappearing from our ships. Manila formerly was authorized for the general purposes sisal had served—lashings, frapping lines, steadying lines, and so on—but synthetic lines have now been substituted for manila in many applications.

Manila

Although *manila* is being slowly phased out of service in the U.S. Navy, it currently remains a very common and useful line aboard ship. Rope made from the fibers of the abaca plant (grown chiefly in the Philippine Islands) is far superior to any other rope made from natural fibers for strength, durability, ease of handling, and resistance to weather exposure. Manila in good condition is glossy, smooth, pliable, and has a brilliant sheen when new. In addition, manila line is characterized by fibers that are round, easily separated, and light in color.

Sisal, Hemp, and Jute

Sisal, made from the fibers of the sisal plant, was once frequently used as a substitute for manila, principally because it has 80 percent of manila's strength and approximately the same durability. It is recognized by its very light color, which is almost white when new. It lacks gloss, is stiff and harsh, and is easily injured by exposure to the weather.

Frequently, sisal fibers are combined with other natural fibers to produce lines of various strengths. *Composite* is a mixture of sisal and manila and has about 90 percent of the strength of manila. It also handles and looks a good deal like manila. *Sisal hemp* is made by combining sisal with fibers of the hemp plant. It has about 70 percent of the strength of manila. At one time, all lines used in the Navy were made of hemp, because the hemp plant is grown in America. Although the strength of rope made of hemp is equal to that of rope made of manila, it is seldom used today because of its poor handling characteristics. *Jute*, a course brown fiber, also has poor handling characteristics. Another of its limitations is that it readily absorbs moisture up to 23 percent of its weight. It is grown in India and is used to make burlap, wrapping paper, and a cheap grade of small cordage. It has approximately 60 percent of the strength of manila.

Synthetic Fibers

The synthetic fibers currently in use for making line are nylon, polyester (dacron), polypropylene, and polyethylene, in descending order of strength. Although synthetic lines are replacing most of the natural fiber lines in use today, manila remains a standard by which line quality may be measured. When using synthetic fiber line, safety precautions more exacting than those for manila line must be observed since, in many respects, the characteristics of synthetic line differ from those of manila line. The more important differences to be observed are listed below:

1. Due to the lower coefficient of friction of synthetic fiber line, more rapid slippage may occur. Exercise extreme care when a line is being played out or eased from securing devices (bitts, capstans, bollards, cleats, gypsy heads, etc.).

2. Synthetic line has higher breaking strengths than equal sizes of manila line. Failures of blocks, pad eyes, shackles, and line couplings can be caused by improper substitutions. Many fittings in common use in the fleet are designed for natural fiber line. For this reason, personnel should determine

the identification and capacity of all gear and fittings used with synthetic fiber line to ensure that their strengths exceed the minimum breaking strength of the rope.

3. Synthetic line has poor knot-holding characteristics. Some knots that offer good characteristics for securing manila line, such as the square knot, are not adequate for belaying or securing synthetic line. The bowline is one knot known to offer reasonable security when bending together or securing synthetic line.

4. When a synthetic line is put under load, it stretches. When the load is removed, the line recovers to its original length. Complete recovery takes time, however. If a line has been highly loaded for a long period of time, the total recovery may take as much as a month. Fortunately, most of this recovery does take place in the first several minutes after the line is unloaded. This characteristic of synthetic line is called "memory." Because of "memory," there is one situation that should be avoided when working with synthetic line. Synthetic line should not be stowed on a powered stowage drum. If a synthetic line has been under load and then is put on a powered stowage drum, where each wrap and each layer is tightly wound on the drum before the line has recovered its original length, then the line will continue to recover and shrink tighter and tighter on the drum. In several cases, this has caused steel drums to collapse.

Nylon

Nylon line is almost three times as strong as manila for a given rope size. It is smoother and easier to handle than manila and, because it is a synthetic, will not rot. Nylon should be stowed dry, however, as it can support mildew. When merely wet, nylon line has little, if any, change in length or diameter. However, nylon is quite elastic, so it is often used for mooring lines where shock absorption is desirable. Nylon also lasts nearly five times as long as does manila. Because of its high cost, though, nylon is not used for lashing and other expendable purposes. One characteristic of nylon, which can be helpful or harmful, is that it stretches more than manila when under tension. In certain applications, this can be a decided disadvantage and is one reason why nylon is never used when transferring men from ship to ship by highline. Too much elasticity and stretch can cause a man to be inadvertently dunked or lost in the swiftly moving water between two ships engaged in such transfer. Until recently, manila was the only acceptable line for use in personnel highline transfer.

Polyester

Polyester (dacron) line is almost as strong as nylon line, but has much less stretch. Therefore, dacron is used for sheets, halyards, and other applications requiring strength and minimum stretch. Like nylon, dacron will not rot and has little, if any, change in dimension when wet. The replacement line for the personnel highline, the inhaul and outhaul lines, the light-freight-transfer line, and the replenishment-at-sea messenger are made of spun polyester. The spun polyester gives the lines a "fuzzy" appearance. The highline, inhaul, outhaul, and light-freight-transfer lines are made of double-braided construction, and the replenishment-at-sea messenger is of plaited construction. (See figure 7-4). A general description of the personnel highline rigs can be found in chapter 10.

Polypropylene and Polyethylene

Polypropylene and polyethylene lines are, on the average, from one and one-half to two times as strong as manila lines of the same size. Their main advantage is that they float, making them good heaving

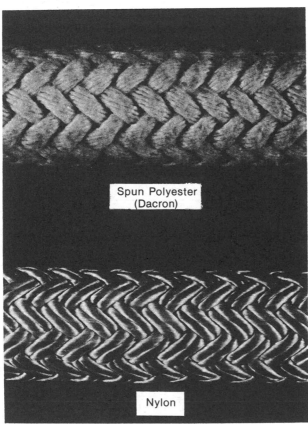

Spun Polyester (Dacron)

Nylon

Figure 7-4. Double-braided spun-polyester line for the personnel highline, the inhaul and outhaul lines, and the light freight transfer line.

lines. These lines are usually white or brightly colored. Although nylon and polyester lines exhibit almost no decrease in strength due to sunlight, polypropylene does. Polypropylene line may lose as much as 40 percent of its strength in three months when exposed to tropical sunlight, if the line is made without ultraviolet inhibitors. To reduce the effects of sunlight, ultraviolet inhibitors can be added to the line at the time of manufacture.

Table 7-1. Synthetic Fiber Line Constructions and Their Characteristics

Rope Construction	Breaking Strength	Abrasion Resistance	Stretch	Relative Cost	Unlays with Rotation Under Load
Three-Strand	Low	Best	High	Low	Yes
Double-Braided	High	Worst	Low	High	No
Plaited	Medium	Medium	Highest	Medium	No

Table 7-2. Synthetic Fiber Line Material and Their Characteristics

Rope Material	Breaking Strength	Abrasion Resistance	Stretch	Relative Cost	Resistance To Sunlight
Nylon	High	Best	High	Medium	Good
Polypropylene	Low	Poor	Medium	Low	Medium
Polyester (Dacron)	Medium	Good	Least	High	Good

Sizes and Uses of Fiber Line

When fiber rope is 1¾ inches or larger in circumference, it is classified in terms of its size and type; for example, 2-inch manila or 4-inch nylon. Such line has many uses aboard ship. For instance, natural fiber line of 2½ inches or greater is used in boat falls, cargo-boom falls, ammunition and stores falls, torpedo-handling falls, fueling-at-sea gear, and towing and mooring lines, to name a few.

The Navy seldom uses line larger than 8 inches in circumference. Any line larger than 5 inches is referred to as a *hawser* and generally is used for mooring or towing. Remember, it's the size around the line (its circumference) that is measured, not the diameter.

Synthetic line is being authorized for an increasing number of shipboard uses, such as mooring lines, boat falls, signal halyards, and running rigging. Regarding the latter use, however, note the following restrictions:

1. The line must be no less than 1 inch in circumference.

2. Nylon must not be used as replenishment-at-sea riding lines or in the riding-line tackles, because its stretch may cause the strain to be transferred to the fuel hose.

3. Nylon must not be used in torpedo-handling tackles, because it surges too easily around gypsy heads and cleats; therefore, positive control cannot be maintained.

4. Nylon must not be used in boom guys, because its stretch allows the boom heads to swing when under load.

Before using new, three-strand synthetic fiber line, it should be faked down on deck and allowed to relax for twenty-four hours. The period can be shortened to about two hours by hosing down the line with fresh water. The shorter the line, the less time the relaxing process takes; for example, a length of less than 50 feet will relax in one hour.

When wet, synthetic line shrinks slightly but does not swell or stiffen. When the line is under tension, the water squeezes out; under working loads, it appears as vapor. But because line under tension develops friction and, thus, heat, the water has a beneficial cooling effect.

Line or rope less than 1¾ inches in circumference is referred to generally as *small stuff*, and is known by the number of yarns (threads) it contains, rather than by its size. To find the number of threads in a piece of small stuff, the end of a strand is opened out, the number of yarns it contains is counted, and the result is multiplied by the number of strands.

The largest small stuff in general shipboard use is 24-thread; it has three strands, each of which contains eight threads. Other sizes of small stuff are 21-thread, 15-thread, 12-thread, 9-thread, and 6-thread. Any small stuff which is smaller than 6-thread is referred to by name rather than by the number of threads.

Marline is the most common small stuff referred to by name. It is rather roughly made up of two-strand, left-laid, tarred hemp and is not much larger than ordinary household wrapping cord. Marline is used most often when a sailor is "serving" a line, discussed later in this chapter, and for other general purposes. It is inexpensive, fairly strong, and somewhat protected from the weather by its tar.

Houseline is three-strand, left-laid tarred hemp. It is used for light seizings, light rigging, and outside work exposed to weather.

Roundline is a three-strand, right-laid, tarred hemp. It is used for seizings and servings on ships where neatness is required.

Seizing stuff is small stuff laid up right-handed by machine, like regular line, but is not much larger than fishing line. It is used for servings when a fancier job than can be done with marline is desired.

Ratline stuff is made like regular line, but is dark brown, rather course, and has little strength. It is now used primarily for snaking. (Snaking, or gunwale nettings, is the netting stretched between the deck and the bottom line of the lifelines that circle the main deck of almost all ships. It is used to prevent people and objects from being washed overboard.)

Rope yarns are used for light, temporary seizings, lashings, and whippings, and are pulled from unlaid strands of large line that has outlived its usefulness. It should be noted that in pulling a yarn from a rope, it must be pulled from the middle of the strands, away from the ends, or it is likely to tangle or foul.

Small white line or *cod line* is made from either cotton or flax and is used for lead lines and the like. In general, it is braided instead of being plain-laid, because line used for such purposes should not kink or twist.

Stowage and Care of Fiber Line

It is not news to an experienced seaman that misuse and abuse of his gear shortens its useful life. This is particularly true for rope of all types. Yet, because of carelessness and lack of knowledge, rope is the one thing that probably receives more abuse than any other equipment the seaman uses. Regretfully, rope in a doubtful condition puts lives in jeopardy. The miracle, state some sailors, is that more injuries do not occur. The next few pages of this chapter tell the fundamentals you need to know about the storage and care of fiber line.

Stowing Fiber Line

Most of the line aboard ship is stowed in the boatswain's locker—a compartment, usually forward, set aside to hold much of the line, wire, and tools used by the deck department.

Coils of rope are stored clear of the deck on shelves or platforms where they have the best chance of staying dry. They should never be covered with an accumulation of gear that might prevent the evaporation of moisture, because line composed of vegetable (natural) fiber is very susceptible to mildew and rotting.

Coils of small stuff are normally arranged along a shelf in order of size. It is common custom to set up a narrow, flat strip of wood horizontally over the shelf containing the small stuff, with a hole bored

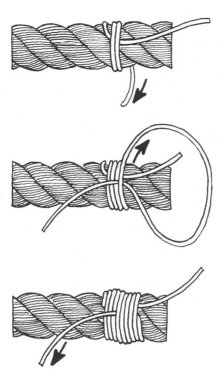

Figure 7-5. Plain whipping.

in the strip over each coil of rope. The starting end of the line is drawn up through the hole, and by putting an overhand knot in the line, the end is prevented from dropping back. This method ensures that anyone wanting a piece of small stuff need not grope around inside the coil's tunnel for the end.

Caring for Fiber Line

The bitter end of a line should always be *whipped* (wrapped) to prevent it from unlaying. One kind of whipping is a temporary plain whipping that is put on with a piece of small stuff such as rope yarn, as shown in figure 7-5. A second type of whipping is permanent whipping that is sewn with a palm and needle. It is rarely applied to any rope smaller than 1¾ inches, but is frequently used for larger lines. It is applied as shown in figure 7-6. Another method for securing the bitter end of line is to make a crown knot, as shown in figure 7-7. Crown knots generally are not recommended for shipboard use in running rigging, because the increased thickness of the bitter end tends to make them jam in blocks and cleats. A whipping or a crown knot should be put on any natural fiber line hanging loose-ended. The bitter end of nylon is normally secured by taping the end of each strand and then taping all the strands together and fusing the end of the line with a hot iron or torch. Another rule to keep in mind is that any *Irish pennant** should be cut or tucked. Observing these rules may seem inconsequential, but the smart appearance of a ship is achieved by attention to detail. The ship that takes care of detail is frequently an exceptionally high performer.

Whenever possible, wet line is dried thoroughly before stowing. Sometimes drying is not possible, as with mooring lines that must be sent below before the ship enters heavy weather. If line must be stowed wet, it should be faked out on gratings, so that it will dry as quickly as possible. It should never be covered over. Most fiber line shrinks in wet weather, and stretches again when it dries out. For this reason, secured lines, as in boat falls, must be slackened when the weather becomes damp. New line that still contains a large amount of its original waterproofing oil does not shrink as much as old line that has lost most of its oil through use and exposure.

Deterioration of most natural fiber line through use and exposure is indicated by the gradual change in its color from yellowish-white to gray. Since the surface of the line is also discolored by grime, it is usually necessary to inspect the inner parts of the line to determine its degree of deterioration. The strands must be unlayed by hand. The inner parts of the strands will then reveal any deterioration. Deterioration from use or abuse is shown by the bristling ends of broken or dislodged yarns. An overstrained line shows not only bristles but also shows a decrease in diameter. Such line must be thoroughly inspected and repaired before reuse. Men must not be permitted to go aloft or over the side using an overstrained line, as it may not carry more than a fraction of its normal safe working load.

Synthetic line that has been under heavy strain may develop glazed areas where it has worked against a bitt or a chock. This condition may be caused by rubbing against a painted surface or by fusing of the fibers from the heat of friction. In either condition, the effect on the line's strength is negligible. Synthetic line can hold a load, even though a considerable number of the yarns become worn. Where such a condition is excessive, but localized, the chafed section may be cut away and the ends spliced together for satisfactory reuse.

---

*A loose strand: any untidy object out of its normal place, particularly the end of a line that is hanging loose and is improperly stowed or dangling over the topsides.

Handling Fiber Line

Newly purchased natural fiber rope must be uncoiled from a reel by hauling on the bitter end, which is inside the center tunnel of the coil. This end must be at the bottom of the coil if it is lying down. Do not take rope off the outside, or every coil will develop a kink.

Synthetic rope on the other hand, *must be unreeled* from the outside of the coil to remain free of kinks.

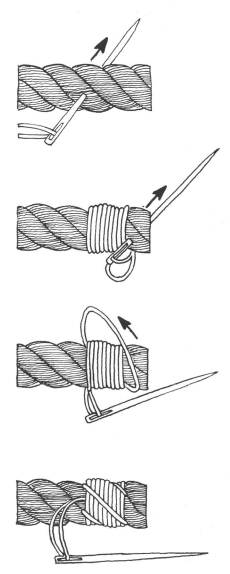

Figure 7-6. Permanent whipping.

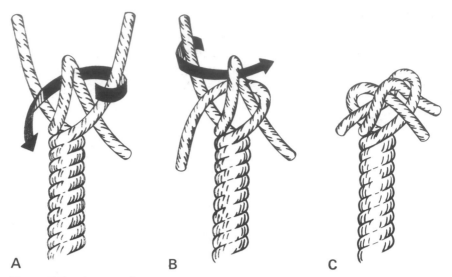

A   B   C

Figure 7-7. A crown knot.

Kinks and Heavy Strain

A line with a kink should never be placed under strain. A heavy strain on a kinked or twisted line will cause permanent distortion or damage, seriously weakening the length of rope. Figure 7-10 shows what frequently happens when a kinked line is strained. The original kink has been forced into each strand making it impossible to work out the kink.

A natural fiber line under a heavy load emits audible protests or cracking noises, as the strands of the line work against an adjacent surface as well as themselves. These telltale signs are frequently observed when maneuvering alongside a pier, or when towing. Such protests increase in intensity with the strain and serve to indicate the potential danger of a line parting. As with synthetic line, a visible sign of the strain appears in the form of a steamlike vapor if the line is wet or moist. There is little noticeable elongation with natural fiber line under a heavy strain.

Figure 7-8. Uncoiling fiber line.

Unfortunately, although synthetic lines under heavy strain decrease in diameter considerably, they give no audible indication of stress—even when about to part. For this reason, a tattletale cord should be attached to synthetic lines when they are to be subjected to strain that may exceed their safe working loads. A tattletale cord is a bight of heavy cord or light small stuff hanging from two measured points on the working line. The line, when tensioned to its safe working load, will stretch to a certain percent of its length. When this point is reached, the small stuff becomes taut, warning that there is danger of exceeding the line's safe working load.

Figure 7-9. Unreeling synthetic line.

Coiling, Faking, and Flemishing

The proper handling of fiber line is of great importance in fostering its useful life. A logical place to begin is with a discussion of how rope is measured in the Navy. The unit of length for measuring line, wire, or chain is the fathom, which is equal to six feet. When the boatswain's mate sends a seaman to the boatswain's locker for five fathoms of nine-thread, the seaman need not measure off exactly 30 feet with a tape measure. His two arms, spread wide, will approximately equal a fathom. The required number of fathoms are therefore "spread off" hand-to-hand. In measuring a long line, such as a boat fall, it is often

Figure 7-10. Result of a strong strain on a line with a kink in it.

easier and faster to lay it out in lengths along the deck until the desired total length is uncoiled.

When line is removed from the manufacturer's coil, it is made ready to use either by winding it onto a reel or by coiling or faking it down.

Figure 7-11. Coiling down a line.

Coiling down a line is laying it in circles on the deck, roughly one on top of the other. Right-laid line is always coiled down in a clockwise direction and, conversely, left-laid line should be coiled down counterclockwise.

Coiling down in the wrong direction results in annoying, unsightly, and possibly dangerous kinks and twists. Figure 7-11 shows how to coil

Figure 7-12. Faking down a line.

down a right-laid line properly. When a line is coiled down, one end is ready for running—that is, the end that was last down and hence is on top. If for some reason the bottom end must go out first, the entire coil should be overturned to free it for running. Coiling is the fastest and most common way of making up line or wire.

Faking down a line (figure 7-12) is to lay it out in long, flat rows on the deck, one alongside the other, instead of in round coils. The main advantage of working with line that is properly faked down is that it runs off with less likelihood of fouling or kinking. This method is used almost exclusively when arranging mooring lines.

A third method used aboard ships and boats for neatly handling short lengths of line, such as bitter ends of boat painters, boat-boom guys, and topping lifts, is *flemishing*. To flemish down a line is to lay it down in a completely flat coil on the deck, somewhat resembling a wound clock spring, with the bitter end in the center (figure 7-13). Right-laid line is flemished clockwise and left-laid line, counterclockwise. The line is laid down loosely, and wound tight to form a mat by placing your hands flat on the line and twisting in the direction the line is laid.

Figure 7-13. Flemishing is a traditional method of disposing ends of line on deck.

Wire Rope Construction and Composition

The basic unit of wire rope construction is the individual wire, made of steel or other metal in various sizes. These wires are laid together to form strands. The number of individual wires in a strand varies according to the purpose for which the rope is intended. A number of strands are laid together to form the wire rope itself. Wire rope is designated by the number of strands per rope and the number of wires per strand. Thus, a 6 × 19 rope has 6 strands with 19 wires per strand, but its outside diameter is the same as a 6 × 37 wire rope, which has 6 strands with 37 wires of much smaller size per strand. Wire rope made up of a large number of small wires is flexible, but the small wires break easily and the rope is less resistant to external abrasion. Wire rope made up of a smaller number of larger wires is more resistant to external abrasion but is less flexible.

The strands of any wire rope are laid up around a central core, which may be wire or fiber or merely a single strand of wire. A fiber core contributes flexibility, cushions the strands as the wire rope contracts under strain, and holds a portion of lubricant for continuous lubrication. A wire core is stronger than fiber and can be used where conditions such as high temperature would damage fiber. An end view of the arrangement of strands in wire rope is shown in figure 7-14.

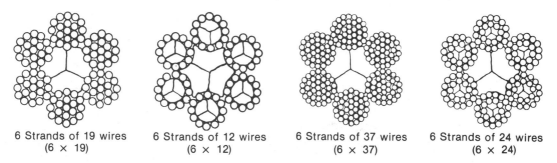

| 6 Strands of 19 wires (6 × 19) | 6 Strands of 12 wires (6 × 12) | 6 Strands of 37 wires (6 × 37) | 6 Strands of 24 wires (6 × 24) |

Figure 7-14. Arrangement of strands in wire rope.

Wire rope may be fabricated by either of two methods. If the strands or wires are shaped to conform to the curvature of the finished rope before they are laid up, the wire rope is called "preformed." If they are not shaped before fabrication, the wire rope is termed "nonpreformed." When cut, preformed wire rope tends not to untwist and is more flexible than the other.

Wire rope is made in the following grades: improved plow steel, plow steel, mildplow steel, cast steel, and—for special purposes—iron, bronze, and stainless steel.

Rust is the chief enemy of wire rope. Some wire ropes, especially shrouds, stays, and certain mooring wires, are galvanized (coated with zinc). Galvanizing protects the rope from the elements, but makes it stiffer and reduces its strength by as much as 10 percent. Galvanized rope most commonly is used for standing rigging, but also is used for some running rigging where it is not subject to much wear. Ordinarily, this rope is not used for hoisting jobs, because the constant bending and flexing as the rope runs over block sheaves and around drums causes the protective coating to crack and peel off.

As shown in figure 7-15, wire rope is layed up in various ways:

Right Regular Lay: Wires in the strands are twisted to the left; strands in the rope are twisted to the right.

Left Regular Lay: Wires in the strands are twisted to the right; strands are twisted to the left.

Right Lang Lay: Both the wires in the strands and the strands in the rope are twisted to the right.

Left Lang Lay: Both the wires in the strands and the strands in the rope are twisted to the left.

Reverse Lay: Wires of alternate strands are twisted to the right, those wires in the other strands are twisted to the left. Strands are twisted to the right.

Sizes and Uses of Wire Rope

In contrast to fiber, wire is always measured in inches by its diameter rather than by its circumference. The correct method of measuring wire rope is shown in figure 7-16. As the circumference of a circle is roughly three times its diameter, a one-inch wire is about the same size as a three-inch fiber line.

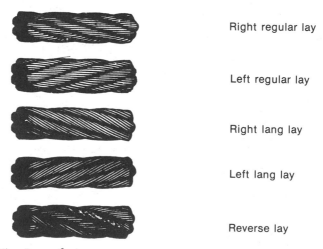

Right regular lay

Left regular lay

Right lang lay

Left lang lay

Reverse lay

Figure 7-15. Lays of wire rope.

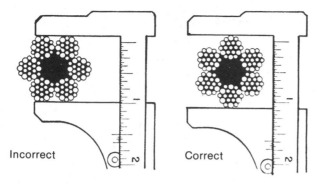

Incorrect Correct

Figure 7-16. Measuring wire rope.

Navy guidelines specify the uses that may be made of wire rope of various sizes. A few of the more common sizes and some of their uses follow:

6 × 7: Only the galvanized type is specified. It is not suitable for general hoisting, but is applicable for permanent standing rigging.

6 × 19: Size for size, this type of construction is the strongest of all the wire ropes. 6 × 19 galvanized high-grade steel wire is often used for standing rigging. Fore-and-aft supports are called *stays*, and the supports running athwartships are termed *shrouds*. Boat slings and topping lifts for booms also are frequently made of galvanized 6 × 19 wire rope. Phosphor bronze 6 × 19 rope is used for lifelines, wheelropes, radio antennas, antenna downleads, etc., where either noncorrosive or nonmagnetic properties are desirable.

6 × 37: When made of ungalvanized steel wire, this construction is flexible, making it suitable for cranes and similar machinery. It may be used for heavy hoisting. For instance, hoisting ropes larger than 1¾ inches in diameter usually are of this type. When made of galvanized steel wire, it may be used for steering gear, boatcrane falls, towing hawsers, torpedo slings, and heavy running rigging.

A very common flexible wire rope, called *spring-lay*, is composed partly of wire and partly of fiber, and therefore has substantially less strength than all-steel wire of corresponding size. However, the greater flexibility of spring-lay in handling makes it more desirable than wire when used as mooring lines and on tugboats for alongside towing. This rope coils easily and lies flat like manila, storing in 40 percent of the space of manila line having the same strength. Spring-lay, measured by its diameter, is normally found in sizes from ¾ inch to two inches. Because it is a combination of wire and fiber, rules for the care of both wire and fiber rope apply when dealing with spring-lay.

Care and Stowage of Wire Rope

Wire that has been used a long time wears like any other metal article. The outer parts of the strands begin to flatten out, and as a result the diameter of the wire decreases. Frequently, abrasion or sharp bends cause individual wires to break and bend back. These breaks are known as *fishhooks*. If several occur near each other, or several wires are broken along the wire rope's length, the safe working load has been significantly reduced. A wire that has been overstrained shows a great many fishhooks, in addition to a marked decrease in diameter where the strain occured. A wire containing fishhooks should never be used in boat falls, cargo whips, or other weight-carrying devices for handling cargo, where so much depends on the strength of the wire. Fishhooks are also dangerous because they may injure the hands of the person handling the wire.

Stowing Wire Rope

Wire rope should not be stored in places exposed to moisture or stored where acid is, or has been, kept. The importance of keeping acid or acid fumes away from wire rope must be stressed thoroughly to all hands. The slightest trace of acid coming in contact with wire rope will damage it at that particular spot. Wire rope that has given way at one point has often been found to be acid-damaged.

Rusting and corrosion of individual wires and deterioration of the fiber core sharply decrease the strength of a rope. However, it is impossible to estimate accurately the loss in strength from these effects. Prior to stowage, wire rope should always be cleaned and lubricated. If the lubricant film is applied properly and the wire is stored in a dry place, corrosion will be virtually eliminated.

Caring for Wire Rope

The importance of lubricating wire rope arises from the fact that wire is really a mechanical device with many moving parts. Each time a rope bends or straightens, the wires in the strands and the strands in the rope must slide upon each other, so a film of lubricant is needed on each moving part. Another important reason for lubrication, as just mentioned, is to prevent corrosion of the wires and deterioration of the hemp core.

Used wire ropes should be cleaned before they are lubricated. They may be cleaned with wire brushes, compressed air, or superheated steam. The object is to remove all foreign material and old lubricant from the valleys between the strands and from the spaces between the outer wires.

Lubricant may be applied with a brush, taking care to work it in well. Another method is to pass the wire rope through a trough or box containing the lubricant.

Two good lubricants for running rigging are raw linseed oil and a medium graphite grease. Raw linseed oil dries and is not greasy to handle, but graphite grease is preferable in most instances because it is highly resistant to salt-water corrosion.

Improper care, stowage, and use of wire rope are the most common causes of wire rope failure. Some examples of improper practices are listed below:

1. Using incorrect size, construction, or grade of wire.
2. Allowing wire to drag over obstacles.
3. Improper lubrication.
4. Operating over sheaves and drums of inadequate size or allowing overriding or crosswinding on drums.
5. Subjecting wire to moisture, acid fumes, or excessive heat.
6. Using improperly attached fittings.
7. Permitting wire to untwist.
8. Internal wear caused by grit penetrating between strands and wires.
9. Subjecting wire to severe overload.
10. Using wire in a kinked condition.

Handling Wire Rope

Long lengths of wire rope are usually on reels when received from a supply activity. Never try to unreel wire rope from a stationary reel. Mount the reel on a pipe or rod supported by two uprights. This method allows the reel to turn as the wire rope is pulled. Unreeling presents no problem, but spooling the wire rope back onto the reel may give you some trouble unless you remember that it tends to roll in the

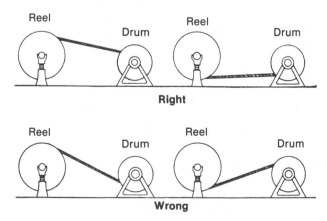

Figure 7-17. *Spooling wire rope from reel to drum.*

opposite direction from the lay. For example, a right-laid wire rope tends to roll to the left. Consequently, start a right-laid wire rope at the left and work toward the right when spooling over the top of the reel. When spooling under the reel, start at the right and work toward the left. Naturally, handle left-laid wire rope just the opposite.

If wire rope is being run off to a winch drum or another reel, run it from top to top or from bottom to bottom, as in figure 7-17.

Whenever possible, drums, sheaves, and blocks used with wire rope are placed to avoid reverse or S-shaped bends. Reverse bends cause individual wires and strands to shift, increasing wear and fatigue. Where a reverse bend is necessary, the blocks and drums affecting the reversal should be larger in diameter than ordinary, and they should be spaced as far apart as possible.

Kinks and Heavy Strain

Right-laid wire, like right-laid line, should be taken right-handed or clockwise around a gypsy head or a capstan to avoid kinking. A hard strain on a wire with a kink in it is even more disastrous than a strain on a kinked line. If a wire rope becomes kinked, never try to pull the kink out by putting a strain on either part of the wire. If a heavy strain is put on a wire rope with a kink in it, the rope can no longer be trusted.

As soon as a kink is noticed, uncross the ends by pushing them apart. (See step 1 in figure 7-18.) This method reverses the process that

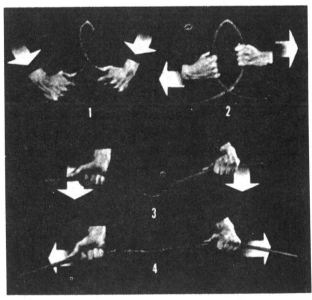

Figure 7-18. Correct way to take out a kink in wire rope.

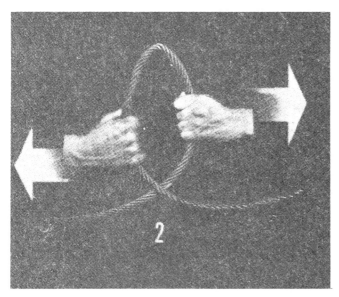

Figure 7-19. Taking out an ornery bight.

started the kink. Now, turn the bent portion over and place it on your knee or some firm object and push downward until the kink straightens out somewhat. Then lay it on a flat surface and pound it with a wooden mallet.

Coiling and Faking

Once a new coil of wire is unwound properly, it can be coiled down for running, the same as line. Because of the general toughness and springiness of the wire, a bight frequently may back up against you and try to flop the other way. When it does, don't try to yank the bight out or force it down. Slack the wire to widen the bight enough so that it may be passed under the overlapping coil and then turned as necessary to get rid of the bight. (See figure 7-19.)

When uncoiling wire rope, stand the coil on edge and roll it along the deck, uncoiling as you go, as in figure 7-20.

Wire rope that is to be made for a fast run-off, as would be required for mooring lines, highlines, and various messengers, is faked down in the same manner as line.

Natural fiber line and synthetic line generally should not be used with wire rope or spring-lay in the same chock or on the same bitts or bollard.

Synthetic rope will cut manila, and wire and spring-lay will cut both manila and synthetic lines. If you must place your mooring lines on

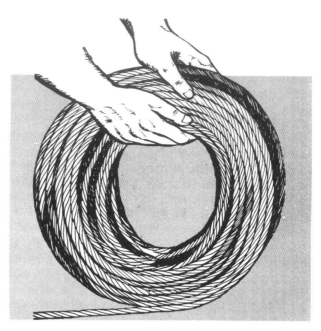

Figure 7-20. Right way to uncoil wire rope.

bollards on which another ship has dissimilar hawsers, protect your lines with plenty of canvas wrapping.

Splices

To *splice* is to join the ends of lines or wires together permanently by interlacing or intertwining the strands. To splice is also to put a loop or eye in a line or wire by tucking unlaid strands in the end under strands in the standing part or, more simply stated, bending a line back on itself to form a permanent loop at the end of a line as shown in figure 7-21. As

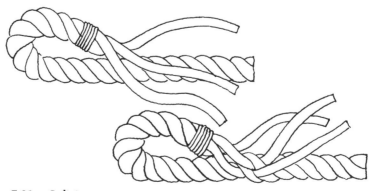

Figure 7-21. Splicing an eye.

230   Seamanship

a verb the word *splice* means the act of joining lines or wires; as a noun, it refers to the joint so made.

In joining two lines or wire ropes, either a short splice or a long splice can be used. The short splice as shown in figure 7-22 is the strongest way to join the ends of two ropes. It is stronger than the long splice, but it increases the diameter of the rope, so that it cannot be run through a block. The long splice, shown in figure 7-23, does not increase the diameter of the rope appreciably, and therefore the rope will run through a block, although its use limits the employment of the rope to but a fraction of its designed safe working load. Splicing for both fiber and wire rope is more difficult in practice than in theory; splicing wire rope is particularly difficult.

When splicing wire rope, a device called a rigger's screw (shown in figure 7-24) is often used to hold the wire for unlaying.

Two eye splices used for wire in the Navy are the Liverpool splice, considered the easiest of the eye splices to put in, and the lock-tuck splice, which is preferred by most boatswain's mates because, unlike the Liverpool, it will not pull or twist out when used to support a suspended load.

Figure 7-22. A short splice.

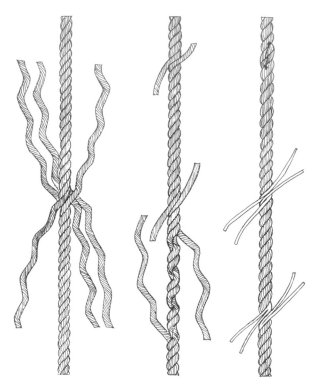

Figure 7-23. A long splice.

Seizings

Seizings are used when two lines, or two parts of a single line, are to be tied side by side permanently. This should be done with seizing stuff, which is generally right-laid, tarred hemp. For seizing small stuff, however, marline is adequate.

Many types of seizings were used for special purposes in old sailing ships, but the four described here should suffice for seamen in modern ships.

Flat seizing: This is a light seizing and is used where strain is not too great.

Round seizing: Stronger than the flat type, it is used where strain is greater.

Racking seizing: Use this type when there is an unequal strain on the two parts of the line.

Throat seizing: Throat seizing is actually a round seizing and is used whenever a permanent eye is needed in the middle of a line.

Seizings on wire rope are used in the same ways, only the seizing material is frequently annealed iron seizing wire.

Figure 7-24. The rigger's screw.

There is one other use for seizings in wire. Great care is exercised in the manufacture of wire rope to lay each wire in the strand and each strand in the rope under uniform tension. If the ends of the rope are not secured properly, the original balance of tension will be disturbed and maximum service will not be obtained, because some strands will carry a greater portion of the load than others. Before cutting wire rope, it is necessary to place at least three sets of seizings on each side of the intended cut. The distance between seizings should equal the rope's diameter.

To make a temporary wire rope seizing, wind on the seizing wire uniformly, using strong tension on the wire. After taking the required number of turns as in step 1 in figure 7-26, twist the ends of the wires counterclockwise as in step 2. Grasp ends with endcutting nippers and twist up the slack (step 3). Do not try to further tighten the seizing by twisting. Draw up on the seizing as in step 4. Twist up slack. Repeat steps 4 and 5 if necessary. Cut the ends of the wire and pound them down on the rope as in step 6.

Mousing Hooks and Shackles

A hook is *moused* to keep slings, straps, etc., from slipping out of the hook and to strengthen the hook if there is danger of the load bending it. If the purpose of the mousing is to keep a strap or sling from escaping, marline or rope yarn may be used. If the purpose is to strengthen the hook, seizing wire or a shackle may be used. The proper method for both purposes is shown in figure 7-27.

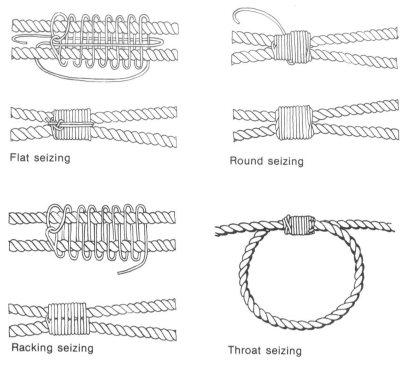

Flat seizing

Round seizing

Racking seizing

Throat seizing

Figure 7-25. Flat, racking, round, and throat seizings.

Shackles are moused whenever there is danger of the shackle pin working loose and coming out because of vibration. Several turns are taken through the eye of the shackle pin and around the shackle itself with seizing wire in such a manner that the pin cannot turn.

The Seaman's Tools

The tools a seaman uses as he works with line and rope are relatively simple instruments that require only a reasonable amount of care. Using the tools of his trade properly is, however, the most important element of that care. Tools that are mistreated and used for purposes other than that for which they were intended will not last long and will be more apt to fail, at what always seem to be particularly inopportune moments. Even worse, the life or limbs of the seaman are often placed in jeopardy if tools are used improperly or the wrong tool is selected for use.

The best knife for working with line is the one shown in figure 7-28. The blade has a straight cutting edge rather than a curved one, and the small spike on the knife is convenient for opening shackles and small turnbuckles and for working with certain knots.

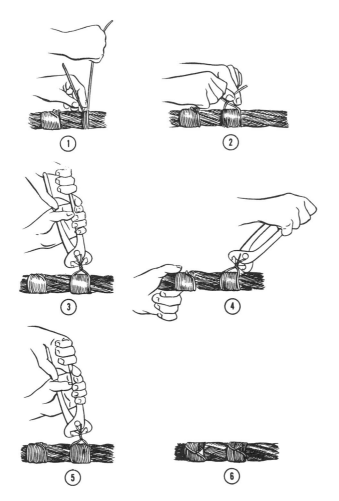

Figure 7-26. *Putting temporary seizings on wire rope.*

Figure 7-27. *Methods of mousing hooks and shackles.*

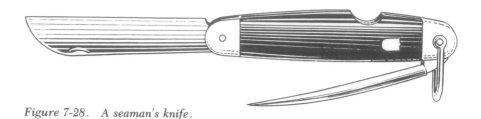

Figure 7-28. A seaman's knife.

A *fid* is a long, tapered, wooden tool used to open strands in line for splicing or other purposes. A fid should never be confused with a marlinspike nor used with anything other than fiber line. To properly use a fid, set the butt of the fid on deck, place the line to be separated on the fid's pointed end, and hammer the line onto the point. Never hammer the butt of a fid to drive it through. It splits or splinters very easily. (see figure 7-29.)

The *marlinspike*, as mentioned earlier, is a tapered steel tool that serves the same purpose with wire as a fid does with line. A good marlinspike should never be used as a crowbar or as a pin to open shackles. These wiresplicing spikes should be used exclusively for their designed purpose, and care must be taken to avoid bending or blunting their points. Unlike the fid, however, the butt of a marlinspike can be hammered to your heart's content.

A *serving mallet*, shown in figure 7-31, is another of the seaman's tools used to work with line or wire rope. It is a hammer-shaped wooden device that allows a serving to be bound tightly around a line or splice. A *serving* is a smooth finish or covering of marline or seizing stuff that when wound around a larger fiber line, wire, or splice, provides the rope greater protection from the weather or exceptionally hard use. Sometimes serving is used merely to make a line look neater.

All wire rope used as standing rigging is wormed, parceled, and served around splices, and other places where chafing is likely. Otherwise, it is left bare except for a coating of lubricant. *Worming* is accomplished by spiraling marline with the lay of the wire between the strands for the purpose of calking the inner part of the wire against moisture. *Parceling*, a spiral wrapping of canvas strips, is put on next (with the lay) to provide added waterproofing and to build up a symmetrical shape. The wire rope may then be served.

Knots, Bends, and Hitches

Among seamen, the landsman's all-inclusive term "knot" must give way to its more specific meaning and to the terms "bends" and "hitch-

Figure 7-29. Using the wooden fid.

es." In addition, seamen must know which knot, bend, or hitch will serve best in a particular circumstance.

Knots, bends, and hitches are defined by their use. *Knots* in the specific sense refer to fastenings in small line. They are tied with the idea that they will be permanent, and therefore they are characteristically hard to untie. *Hitches*, on the other hand, are relatively easy to tie and untie, and they are generally better adapted for use in rope than in small cord. The word hitch suggests a temporary rather than a perma-

Figure 7-30. The marlinspike.

nent fastening. A hitch is used to secure a rope to another object or to another rope, or to form a loop or a noose in a rope. The word *bend* is both a noun and a verb. As a noun, it describes knots that join the ends of two ropes. As a verb, it denotes the act of joining the ends of two ropes, or of attaching the end of a line or wire to some object; for example, to bend a messenger to a mooring line.

Figure 7-31. A serving mallet.

Figure 7-32. Worming with a marlinspike.

Appendix A contains those knots, bends, and hitches most often used aboard ship. There are several factors to keep in mind when selecting a knot. First, it must hold fast without slipping. Second, if it is a knot in general use and not an ornament, it should be easy to tie. Finally, the best knot, bend, or hitch is one that possesses both these characteristics and is easy to untie as well. A knowledge of when and how to use a particular knot is required of every mariner; often, in day-to-day operations, his life and those of his shipmates depend upon a particular knot doing the job for which it was designed.

Ornamental Work

The ornamental or "fancy" work created from rope and small stuff has long been a source of pride for the seaman. The intricate braids and coverings that can be constructed serve not only to improve a ship's or boat's appearance, but they may also serve the purposes of safety and habitability. Only a few types of ornamental work are described here; however, there are several encyclopedias on the subject that can be obtained through shipboard or local libraries.

Turk's heads: Usually thought of as strictly ornamental, but they serve many useful purposes, such as keeping protective leathers on lifelines.

Coxcombing: Used to cover handrails for ladders, etc. It looks smart and affords a more secure grip.

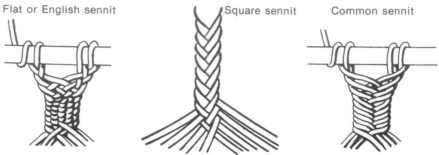

Figure 7-33. Ornamental work.

Cross pointing: Generally used on stanchions, but can also be employed in many other places where a round core is covered. It looks best on cores of fairly large diameter.

Fox and geese: This is a simple and fast way of covering a handrail or stanchion. It can be used any place coxcombing or crosspointing can be used.

Sennit or braid: Made of small cord, such as codline, sennits are used to form ornamental lines or lanyards. A well-known book of knots describes and illustrates close to 400 sennits, so don't be misled into believing the examples in figure 7-33 are the only ones, or even the basic ones.

Canvas and Leather

Canvas and leather have long been important in the seaman's life. Although the use of these materials is becoming less frequent with the advent of synthetics, they remain important elements in a branch of marlinspike seamanship.

Canvas and Synthetic Fabrics

Canvas, often called duck, is a general name for a class of strong, heavy plain cloth woven of cotton or linen. Canvas comes in different weights from no. 1, the heaviest, to no. 12, the lightest. Each number means a certain weight in ounces per square yard of cloth.

Canvas has been used extensively by boatswain's mates to make such things as protective coverings for equipment stored on the weather decks and awnings that are rigged when in port to keep the sun off the decks. Much of the canvas work aboard ship is done by hand with the aid of sail needles, palms for forcing the needle through the canvas by hand, sailmakers' or bench hooks for holding the ends of two pieces of canvas being sewn together, sail twine in a variety of weights, and beeswax for reducing the wear on sail twine and retarding its deterioration. Sewing machines are in most boatswain's lockers on destroyers and larger ships.

Much of the canvas issued in the Navy is treated to make it somewhat resistant to fire, water, weather, and mildew. Some is waterproof and oil-and gasoline-resistant.

Canvas is expensive; so learn how to care for it, and make sure you and your men never abuse it. New and unused canvas, spare covers, etc., should be stowed in a clean, dry storeroom. Never store canvas

Figure 7-34. Crosspointing.

where acid is (or has been) stowed; acid fumes are detrimental to canvas. Every effort should be made to provide a space free from rats, mice, and insects. Wet, painted, or oil-soaked canvas should not be stowed below deck. Occasionally it is necessary to scrub canvas that has become particularly dirty or stained by grease or oil. Use a mild soap solution, rinse thoroughly, and hang it up to dry.

Even with the best of care, however, canvas is relatively short-lived, and for this reason, the Navy is turning to synthetic fabrics. They are not only lighter and easier to stow, but resist rot and mildew.

Synthetics may or may not be available in your ship; if not, the supply officer can get them for you. Of course, like synthetic line, the original cost is much greater than for the natural fabric item. Because of this greater cost, you must be more selective in its use.

One type of synthetic fabric used extensively for tarps and awnings and for boat, winch, and reel covers is a nylon cloth with a vinyl film on both sides. (The smooth or face side is the side to expose to the

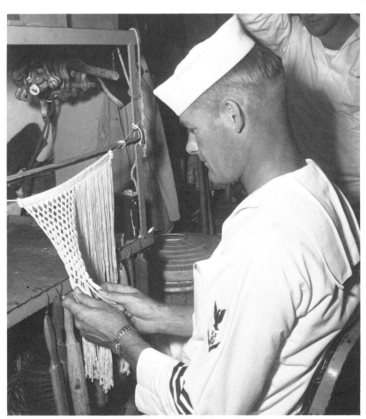

Figure 7-35. MacNamara lace is made by stripping the horizontal strands from canvas and then weaving them in intricate patterns.

Figure 7-36. A boatswain's mate applies the finishing touches to ornamental work of the captain's gig.

weather.) Different companies furnish this type of cloth under their own trade names. These white and grey materials are fire-, water-, weather-, and mildew-resistant.

Another type of cloth, a black, neoprene-coated material, is less suited for topside uses but has many below-deck applications, such as for blackout and welding curtains.

Generally, the same care should be accorded synthetic cloths as is given synthetic lines. When they are dirty, however, you should wash these fabrics with saddle soap, or any other mild soap and water; scrub with a soft bristle brush, using a circular motion; and rinse with clear water. In some instances, two cleanings may be necessary.

Most metal fittings that must be attached to canvas or synthetics are rings or *grommets* of some sort. Several different types of metal grommets are in use, but the two that are most familiar are pictured in figure 7-38. The one in sketch A is called the eyelet and ring type. Sketch B shows the spur type.

The cutting punches illustrated range in diameter from one inch down to seven-sixteenths of an inch in the double-bow type (sketch C), and from three-eights to one-eighth inch in a single-bow type (sketch D). When using these to punch holes in canvas, lay the canvas on a piece of heavy sheet lead, and they will cut a neat, clean hole.

The grommet-inserting punches and dies pictured in sketches E and F are available in sets in the same sizes as the grommets. The proper way to insert the spur-type grommet is to push the eyelet part of the grommet through the hole in the canvas. Place the eyelet on the die and the spur over the eyelet. The punch fits inside the eyelet and, when struck with a hammer, curls the edge of the eyelet down over the spur. Don't pound too hard on the punch; doing so causes the grommet to cut through the canvas, and later it may pull out.

The eyelet and ring type of grommet is used for awnings and sails. Properly used, this is the best of all types. The ring part is sewn to the canvas the same as the handmade grommet. Then the eyelet is placed in the ring and set with the punch and die.

Leather

Leather has very limited use aboard Navy ships today. Artificial leather is encountered more often since it is frequently used as flame-resistant upholstery. The guidelines for care of these materials are very much the same, however.

Leather is especially subject to mildew and rotting. It is also highly susceptible to accidental cutting, gouging, and abrading. Excessive heat causes it to shrink considerably, with consequent rending and cracking.

Leather exposed to the elements should be kept well oiled or waxed. Any oil that does not contain harsh chemicals is suitable, but the best is Neat's foot oil. Leather in such places as on lifelines may be kept well preserved by the application of paste wax. Saddle soap, an excellent preservative and cleaner, can be used on holsters, and on shoes, jackets, and other leather wearing apparel. If leather becomes badly

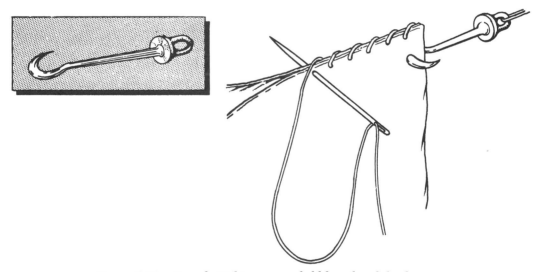

Figure 7-37. Round stitching canvas held by a bench hook.

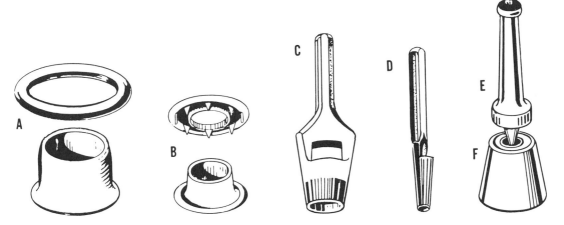

Figure 7-38.   Grommets, cutting punches, and inserting punch and die.

soiled and stained, wash it with a mild soap and water solution, rinse well, and dry in a place away from intense heat. After it is dry, apply saddle soap or Neat's foot oil to replace the natural oils of the leather.

Summary

Marlinspike seamanship and the broad field of knowledge associated with it are fundamental both to the Navy's seamen and to the officers who supervise them. Often an art in itself, marlinspike seamanship and those who practice it lend a ship greater operational capability, increase its safety and habitability, and allow pride in one's ship to be expressed through intricate and ornate fancywork.

8

Deck Seamanship—Mechanical Weightlifting and Cargo-Handling Rigs

Deck Seamanship

Deck seamanship means the rigging, operation, and maintenance of all the ship's equipment located on deck or aloft. A person versed in deck seamanship must know the purpose of everything topside, how it is rigged out for operation, how it is operated properly and safely, how it is rigged in and secured for sea, and how it is kept in proper working order. A ship's officers must have a solid, working knowledge of deck seamanship in order to supervise properly the activities of their men and to ensure that safe procedures are followed.

Rigging, in general, represents a large portion of deck seamanship. A ship's *standing rigging* consists of the nonmoving lines and wires supporting the masts, stacks, yards, and so forth. The lines and wires used in hoisting and lowering heavy weights or in positioning and operating the ship's movable deck gear are referred to as *running rigging*. The process of setting up an apparatus containing rigging is itself called *rigging*; for example, rigging booms or rigging cargo gear.

Blocks and Tackles

The block and tackle, or just plain tackle, is an important element in almost any type of running rigging. A block consists essentially of a wood or metal frame (or shell) containing one or more rotating pulleys called sheaves. A combination of line and blocks used to change the direction of an applied force or to gain a mechanical advantage constitutes a tackle (pronounced TAYK-el). If a line or wire (a fall) is rove (threaded) through a fixed or stationary block and force is applied at one end of the line to lift a weight at the other, we would have what is known as a *single whip*. This arrangement merely changes the direction of the force applied, with no gain in power. Usually, the purpose of a tackle is to multiply the force applied on the hauling part of the fall. The number of times it is multiplied (disregarding friction) is the theoretical mechanical advantage of the tackle. A tackle can sometimes be referred to as a *purchase*. The term purchase usually is applied to a tackle that has blocks with an equal number of sheaves and which has a decided mechanical advantage; for example, a twofold purchase or threefold purchase. (See figure 8–1).

Over the years blocks have changed little in general design, but their construction materials have frequently differed. Once wood was the principal material; now metal is more common.

The principal parts of a modern block are the shell, the sheave, the pin, straps, and such connections as a hook, shackle, or swivel. The shell or frame safeguards the sheave from damage and also keeps the line in place on the axle for the sheave, and transmits the load from the line to the straps and connections. The straps take the load from the pin and also hold the block together, while a connection permits fastening of the block to a support, to an object to be lifted, to a line, or to another block. Blocks with more than three sheaves are seldom used for tackles aboard ship.

Blocks receive different names according to their shape, purpose, or mode of application. Some of the blocks in use aboard ship are named after the particular lines or wires rove through them. Normally, however, a block assumes a name derived from its function or location in a particular rig. For example, regardless of type, a cargo block is usually named for its location in the cargo rig. The block at the head of the boom through which the whip runs is called the *head block*. One type of block used in a *fairlead* is called a *snatch block*. It allows a line to "round" a corner or change direction. A snatch block is hinged on one side and fitted with a hasp on the other. This permits the block to be

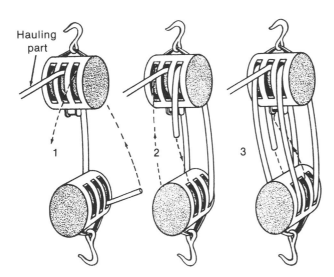

Figure 8-1. *Reeving a threefold purchase.*

opened and clasped on a line, rather than having to reeve the end of the line through it.

Snatch blocks used with manila line are usually made with a wooden shell; conversely, steel-plate snatch blocks fitted with a safety-locking clasp are universally used with wire rope. They are handy as portable fairlead blocks in hoisting boats or in heaving cargo into the wings (outboard parts) of the cargo hold.

The sizes of wood or steel blocks intended for fiber line are designated by the length in inches of the shell or cheek. The sizes of blocks intended for wire rope, usually made of steel, are designated by the diameter of the sheaves. Blocks are designed for use with a certain size of line; therefore, they are never to be used with a line of larger size, and rarely with a line of smaller size. Line that is too large for a particular sheave will be distorted and damaged when placed under a heavy load. A safe rule of thumb to find the correct block size to use with fiber line is to multiply the size of line by three to obtain the cheek size of the block. Another rule of thumb is that the diameter of the sheave must be no smaller than two times the circumference of the rope used.

On board ship, blocks are extremely important. A destroyer often carries from 60 to 75 blocks, and a cruiser will have more than 150. An

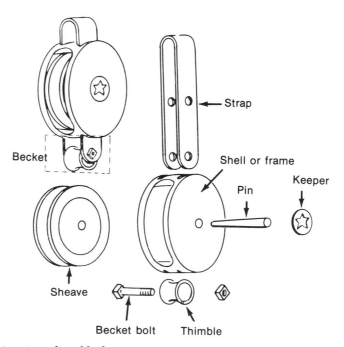

Figure 8-2. A modern block.

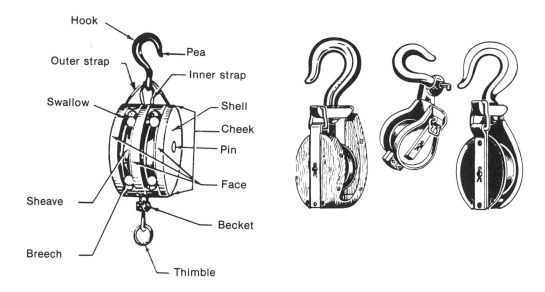

Figure 8-3. Snatch hooks.

amphibious ship of the Navy, such as an LKA or LPD, carries more than 400 blocks of many different types, varying greatly in size, weight, and number of sheaves. The huge cargo blocks of the heavy lift gear on an LPD, for instance, can run up to eight feet in length when the links and swivels are included. They are capable of lifting up to 75 tons. At the other extreme are the small metal blocks used for flag halyards, which are barely two inches long and weigh approximately 10 ounces.

Common Cargo Blocks

There are many kinds of cargo blocks; however, the three types most frequently seen on naval ships are the *diamond*, the *oval*, and the *roller bearing*. An example of a single sheave *diamond* block is shown in figure 8–4. Such a block can have more than one sheave depending on the use to which the block will be put. *Oval* blocks are built to the same specifications as diamond blocks, except the cheeks are oval instead of diamond shaped. These blocks are most commonly used as topping lifts of cargo booms.

Head, heel, and many fairlead blocks are of the *roller-bearing* type shown in figure 8-5. Roller-bearing blocks are used when a high-speed operation is essential. When manufactured for the Navy, these blocks have the following information stamped or cast on the shell: USN; safe working load; proof test; and size of rope to be used with the block. Roller-bearing blocks are commonly referred to as gin blocks.

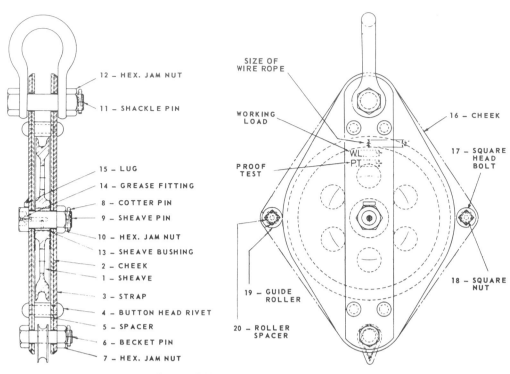

The labels in the figure are:

12 – HEX. JAM NUT
11 – SHACKLE PIN
15 – LUG
14 – GREASE FITTING
8 – COTTER PIN
9 – SHEAVE PIN
10 – HEX. JAM NUT
13 – SHEAVE BUSHING
2 – CHEEK
1 – SHEAVE
3 – STRAP
4 – BUTTON HEAD RIVET
5 – SPACER
6 – BECKET PIN
7 – HEX. JAM NUT

SIZE OF WIRE ROPE
WORKING LOAD
PROOF TEST
WL
PT
16 – CHEEK
17 – SQUARE HEAD BOLT
18 – SQUARE NUT
19 – GUIDE ROLLER
20 – ROLLER SPACER

Figure 8-4. A diamond block.

Mechanical Advantage of Tackles

As mentioned earlier, the mechanical advantage of a tackle is the term applied to the relationship between the load being lifted and the power required to lift the load. In other words, if a load of 10 pounds requires 10 pounds of power to lift it, the mechanical advantage is 1. If a load of 50 pounds requires only 10 pounds of power to lift it, then the mechanical advantage is 5 to 1, or 5 units of weight lifted for each unit of power applied.

The *theoretical mechanical advantage* of a simple tackle is determined by counting the number of parts of the falls at the movable block. Therefore, a gun tackle has a theoretical mechanical advantage of 2 because there are 2 parts of the falls at the movable block. (See figure 8–6.)

To ascertain the amount of power required to lift a given load by means of a tackle, determine the weight of the load to be lifted and divide that by the mechanical advantage.

For example, if it is necessary to lift a 600-pound load by a single luff tackle, we first determine the mechanical advantage gained by using this type of tackle. We count the parts of the falls at the movable block and determine that we have a theoretical mechanical advantage of 3. Therefore, by dividing the weight to be lifted, 600 pounds, by the mechanical advantage in this tackle, 3, we find that theoretically 200 pounds of power are required to lift a weight of 600 pounds when using a single luff tackle.

The more sheaves a tackle has, the greater the mechanical advantage it provides. Up to a point, that is. The factor of sheave friction limits the number of sheaves that can be used, making more than eight impractical in most cases.

A certain amount of the force applied to any tackle is lost through friction. Friction in a tackle is the rubbing of ropes against each other or against the frame or shell of a block, the passing of the ropes over the sheaves, and the rubbing of the pin against the sheaves. This loss in efficiency of the block and tackle must be added to the weight being lifted when ascertaining the actual power required to lift a given load. Roughly, 10 percent of the load must be added to the load for every sheave in the tackle. For example, when lifting a load of 500 pounds with a twofold purchase:

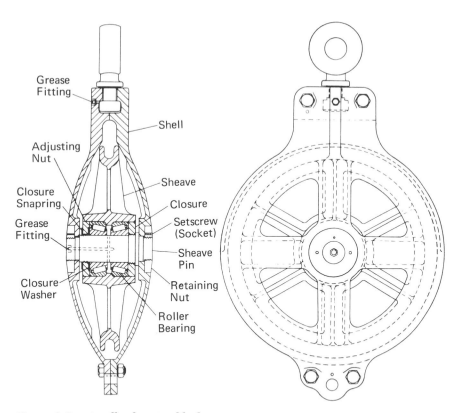

Figure 8-5. A roller-bearing block.

a) 10 percent of the load (500 pounds) is 50 pounds.

b) Four sheaves x 50 pounds = 200 pounds.

With four sheaves in the tackle, the weight that must be contended with due to friction is an additional 200 pounds.

c) 500 pounds (the original load) + 200 pounds (the frictional load) = 700 pounds (the actual load).

d) In the twofold purchase, the theoretical mechanical advantage is 4 (four pieces of fall at the movable block).

e) 700 pounds ÷ 4 (the theoretical mechanical advantage) = 175 pounds (the actual power required to lift the load).

Theoretically, it should take only 125 pounds (500 lbs. ÷ 4) to lift the load. But because of friction *more* power is actually required. Thus, the *actual mechanical advantage* of this twofold purchase is approximately 2.85. (500 lbs. ÷ 175 lbs. = 2.85)

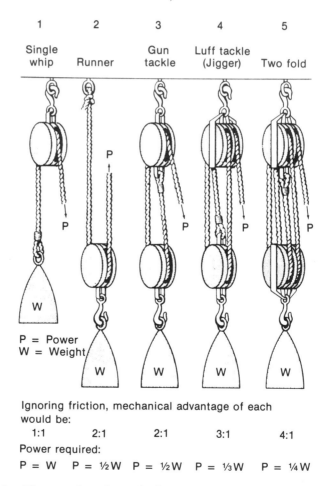

Figure 8-6. Theoretical mechanical advantage.

Breaking Strength and Safe Working Load

Any officer supervising people using line, wire rope, or blocks and tackles should know how to determine the safe working limitations of such equipment in addition to ensuring that the normal safety precautions are observed.

The manufacturer's data concerning the strength of a line is used when it is available, but if it is not, there are formulas or thumb rules for computing the size of line needed for a particular job. The boatswain will need to know what size of line to use in a given situation, and these thumb rules give results that approximate the figures in the manufacturer's tables. The definitions, symbols, and formulas used in these calculations are as follows:

Breaking strength (BS): The amount of weight or pull (in pounds or tons) required to break the line.

Safe Working Load (SWL): The maximum weight or pull (in pounds or tons) that a given line is expected to withstand with safety. In practice it is the greatest weight or pull that is expected to be put on a given line.

Safety factor (SF): The relationship between breaking strength and safe working load. A safety factor is simply a number by which the (BS) is divided to find the range in which it is safe and economical to operate the line.

Circumference (C): The circumference in inches of manila, nylon, and wire rope is used in calculations determining breaking strength (BS). Wire is measured by the diameter (D). To obtain the circumference (C) required in the formula, multiply D by pi (π), which is approximately 3.1416; $D \times \pi = C$.

Comparison factor (CF): synthetics to manila. The strength of manila has been taken as the standard by which to compare the strength of other line, and because of this fact, the basic formula is that for finding the BS of manila. With manila rated as 1, the strength of synthetics are as follows:

Nylon 2.5   Polypropylene 1.4
Polyester (Dacron) 2.0   Polyethylene 1.4

Breaking strength. The three most commonly used formulas for determining breaking strength are as follows:

Breaking strength of manila: $BS = C^2 \times 900$ pounds
Breaking strength of synthetics: $BS = C^2 \times 900$ pounds $\times$ CF
Breaking strength of wire rope: $BS = C^2 \times 8,000$ pounds

A note of caution is required concerning the formula for the breaking strength of wire rope. Since wire rope is manufactured in widely different types and of different materials, any formula to determine its BS, which is based on size alone, is likely to be inaccurate. For this reason, the best way to determine the strength of a wire rope is to refer to tables listing that particular type of rope. These tables are available in handbooks and manufacturer's catalogues.

Safe working load. Obviously, it is unwise to apply loads to line that approach the line's breaking strength. Hence, limits are necessarily set to provide a margin for safety. This is done by introducing into the problems elements called safety factors. In the case of line, the safety factor used depends upon the line's condition. The safety factors for fiber line have been divided into three categories:

	Manila	*Nylon, Polyester*	*Polypropylene, Polyethylene*
1. Best conditions (new line):	5	3	5
2. Average conditions (line used, but in good condition):	10	4	6
3. Unfavorable conditions (frequently used line such as running rigging or boat falls):	15	6	8

To compute safe working load, find the breaking strength and divide by one of these safety factors. $SWL = BS/SF$

Example: Find the safe working load of a new piece of 2-inch manila. Safety factor for new line = 5.
Breaking strength of manila = $C^2 \times 900$.
Safe working load for new 2-inch manila =
$$\frac{C^2 \times 900}{5} = \frac{4 \times 900}{5} = 720 \text{ lbs.}$$

Any block constructed by a reputable manufacturer will have a safe working load in excess of the safe working load of the line that will fit it. To determine the actual safe working load of a block, the appropriate tables in the manufacturer's catalogue are consulted.

The safe working load of a tackle is commonly accepted as being the safe working load of the line multiplied by the number of parts of the line at the moving block. The overall strength is therefore assumed to increase in direct proportion to the number of sheaves. This method of calculation overlooks the strength of the blocks that make up the tackle. Unfortunately, blocks are not always as strong as the new line that can be rove through them, and the strength of the block does not increase in proportion to the number of sheaves, as is often assumed. Despite this assumption, blocks themselves, although commonly overloaded, rarely fail completely. Damage to blocks from overloads normally shows up in the form of bent pins or binding sheaves, which require their premature repair or replacement.

Chain Hoists

Chain hoists, or chain falls as they are often called, provide a convenient and efficient method for hoisting loads by hand. The chief advantages of chain hoists are that one man can raise a load of several tons, and the load can remain stationary without being secured. The slow lifting travel of a chain hoist permits small movements, accurate adjustments of height, and gentle handling of loads. For these reasons chain hoists are particularly useful in machinery spaces, but many times they also come in handy on deck. There are three general types of chain hoists: the differential, the spur gear, and the screw gear. Figure 8–7 shows two of these types.

Differential chain hoist   Spur gear

Figure 8-7. Chain hoists.

The mechanical advantages of chain hoists vary from 5 to 250, depending on their rated capacities, which range from ½ ton to 40 tons.

Ordinarily, chain hoists are constructed with their lower hook as the weakest part of the assembly. This is a precaution so that the lower hook will start to spread open before the chain hoist itself is overloaded. Under ordinary circumstances, the pull exerted on a chain hoist by one or two men will not overload the hoist.

Chain hoists should be inspected at frequent intervals. Any evidence of spreading or excessive wear on the hook is sufficient cause to require its replacement. If the links of the chain are distorted, this is an indication that the chain hoist has been heavily overloaded and is probably unsafe for further use. Under such circumstances, the chain hoist should be replaced.

Shackles, Swivels, and Hooks

Most of the weight-lifting appliances and equipment thus far discussed are common to any kind of ship. The same is true for shackles,

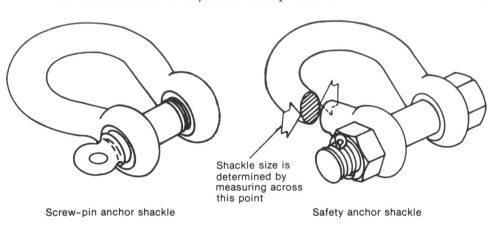

Shackle size is determined by measuring across this point

Screw–pin anchor shackle

Safety anchor shackle

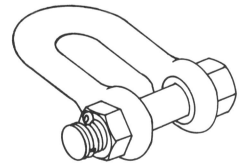

Screw–pin chain shackle

Safety chain shackle

Figure 8-8. Types of shackles.

swivels, and hooks. Their role in cargo handling can not be overlooked. Personnel versed in deck seamanship know that choosing the right shackle or hook or swivel is as important as using the proper line when lifting heavy loads.

Shackles

The uses of shackles in cargo handling and other shipboard applications are so numerous as to preclude mentioning more than a few. In general, shackles are used to connect objects—such as a hook to a block, a sling to a load, or a hook to a wire rope eye.

Shackle bales or eyes are manufactured in two forms. An *anchor shackle* eye has more spread at the curve of the eye than at the shackle-pin end, while a *chain shackle* eye is easily identified by its straight sides and uniform width. There are three types of anchor and chain shackles. The most common type used on board ship is the screw pin, whose pin is merely screwed into threads to secure it in place. The other types are the round pin shackle and the safety shackle. The pin of the round pin shackle is prevented from dislodging by a cotter pin, while the pin of the safety shackle is held in place both by threads and a nut and by a cotter pin. The round pin shackle and the safety shackle are more frequently used when a permanent shackle connection is required.

The following formula may be used to estimate the safe working load of a shackle (where D is the wire diameter of the shackle at the sides).

$$\text{Safe working load} = 3 \times D^2 \text{ (expressed in tons)}$$

Thus, for a one-inch shackle the safe working load is $(1)^2 \times 3$ or 3 tons.

When lifting extremely heavy loads, it is often desirable to substitute shackles for hooks, since a shackle is about five times stronger than a hook of the same wire diameter.

Swivels

Swivels are used together with shackles, blocks, and hooks in weight-lifting appliances. A swivel should be inserted in the makeup of a rig whenever a twist is possible in the rig or load. One type of swivel is illustrated in figure 8-10, Cargo hoist assembly. These are the most common types in shipboard use. Swivels are somewhat stronger than shackles of the same size.

Hooks

The hook of a block or cargo rig is customarily the point where the load is attached. Because of its open construction, the hook is usually the weakest part of a weight-handling appliance. A latch across the opening of a safety eye hook is installed to prevent a load from popping

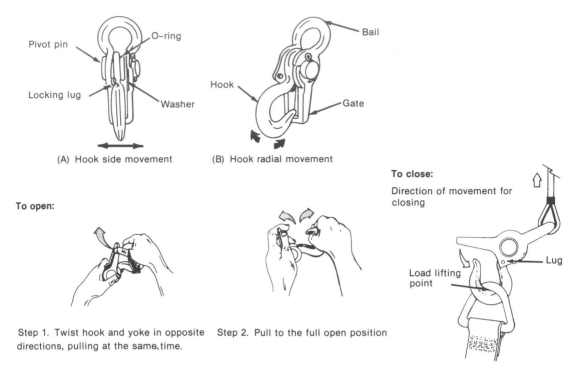

To open:

Step 1. Twist hook and yoke in opposite directions, pulling at the same time.

Step 2. Pull to the full open position

Figure 8-9. Operation of safety hook.

out or being jolted out of the hook if the strain is abruptly eased. Mousing a hook with marline or other small stuff, as described in the previous chapter, accomplishes the same thing. It should be pointed out, however, that mousing of the hook with line will do nothing to prevent the hook from opening under excessive strain. A formula for estimating the safe working load of a hook is given (where D is the wire diameter at the back of the hook below the eye.) as:

$$\text{Safe working load}—2/3 \ D^2 \ \text{(expressed in tons)}$$

Cargo Handling

The exigencies of the Second World War forcibly demonstrated the great need for personnel who possessed skills in the art of loading, unloading, receiving, storing, warehousing, and delivering materials to consuming activities in the field. To meet this need, the Navy created a complete organization that could, and did, do this tremendous job well. With the end of hostilities, the Navy retained its cargo-handling skills through a concentrated training program that kept her ships prepared for the logistic missions of later combat. Such training continues to this day.

The knowledge of equipment and the skills required to operate machinery used in handling cargo form a major portion of the deck seamanship practiced aboard amphibious and service-force ships of the U.S. Navy. Nearly every ship, however, performs some aspect of cargo handling from time to time. The next few pages introduce a number of the deck procedures and equipments that most naval personnel, officer and enlisted, come into contact with during their shipboard experience.

Cargo Gear

Cargo gear comprises the system of booms, guys, whips, winches, blocks, tackles, and other equipment used to handle and move cargo. Cargo loaded aboard ships is handled either by the ship's gear or by equipment independently operated from the dock or a floating crane.

Booms

The essential feature in any cargo gear or rig generally is considered to be the *boom*, the long spar from which a load is suspended. Booms were formerly made of wood, but on most cargo vessels are now made of tubular steel, reinforced in the middle. A cargo boom is usually supported by a ship's masts or by a strong, vertical, metal pillar called a *kingpost*. The lower end (the heel) of the boom fits into a socket near

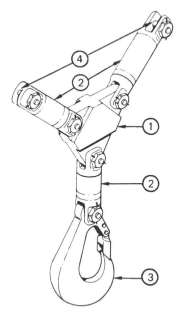

1. Tie plate
2. Cargo safety hook swivel
3. Cargo safety hook
4. Clevis pin sleeve

Figure 8-10.   Five-ton capacity cargo hoist assembly.

the foot of the kingpost (or mast), with its upper end connected to the top of the kingpost by means of a tackle, called the *topping lift*. The topping lift provides a means for raising and lowering the boom's upper end (the head). Horizontal boom motion—that is, from side to side—and steadying the boom head are accomplished by means of cables called *guys*, or *vangs*. (Guy is the naval term. Vang is the Merchant Marine term.) A guy usually consists partly of a wire pendant and partly of a tackle.

The wire used to lift cargo suspended by the boom is called a *whip* (sometimes a *runner*). The heavy hook that is shackled to the whip, and from which a load is suspended, is referred to as a *cargo hook*.

Another device used to aid in hoisting cargo is the *cargo net*, a net made of line, wire, or interwoven synthetic strips attached to bridles that fit over a cargo hook. To control the movements of a load suspended from a hook or in a cargo net a *lizard line* is often connected to the hook or load at a strategic point. Keeping the lizard line taut prevents a load from swinging wildly during transfer and aids in maneuvering heavy loads through open deck hatches.

Safety

Because topping and lowering a boom are perhaps the most dangerous operations performed during cargo handling, safety cannot be overemphasized. Men must be cautioned to stay out from under booms while the raising or lowering operations are in progress. Inexperienced men must be shown the danger of standing in the bight of a line. The deck should be kept as clear of obstructions and lines as possible. Insist on safety; don't invite injury.

Winches

Power for cargo handling is usually provided by winches, which may be driven by steam, gasoline, diesel fuel, or, as is more common today, by electricity. Although most modern winches are manufactured to operate on electrical power, steam-driven winches are still in use on some older ships, and new oilers have a number of them installed, since they provide smooth acceleration and a wide range of speed.

The control levers for a steam winch are normally located on the winch itself, dictating that the winch be placed so that the operator has an unobstructed view of the cargo hatch and deck. An electrically powered winch, on the other hand, may be placed where best suited for deck work, while its controls may be put in another location more advantageous to the operator. Another difference worthy of note is that electric winches are usually equipped with both electrical and mechanical brakes, the mechanical brake a precautionary measure intended

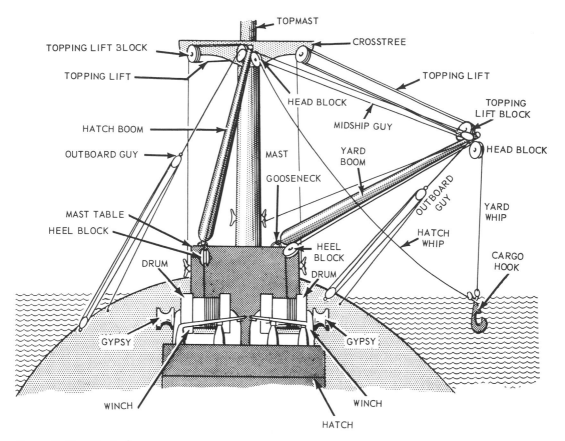

Figure 8-11. Typical cargo gear.

for use only if the electrical brake fails or when the winch is not energized.

Winches are classified not only by their source of power, but by their type. Types of winches include those with drums, those with gypsy heads, and combinations of the two.

Drum winches are those with cylindrical drums on which line is wound for raising, lowering, or pulling loads. Gypsy winches, also known as warping winches, have one or two horizontally mounted gypsy heads around which turns of line can be taken to pull or hoist a load. Gypsy heads are spools, smaller than drums, usually located on the ends of the winch motor shaft. They often have ridges or raised whelps which reduce a line's tendency to slip.

Operating Winches

It generally takes at least two winches and two winchmen to move

Deck Seamanship   **261**

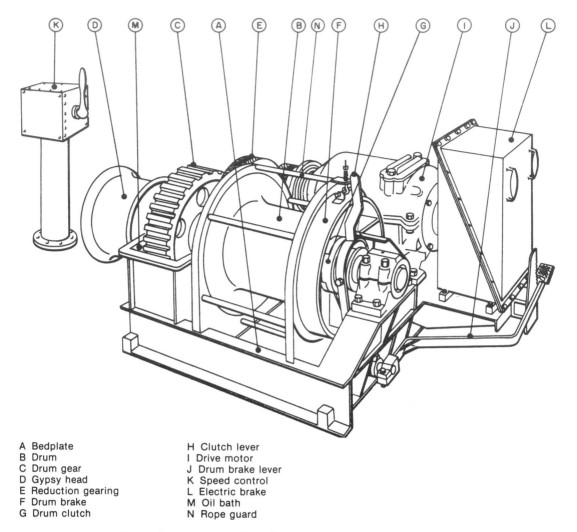

A Bedplate
B Drum
C Drum gear
D Gypsy head
E Reduction gearing
F Drum brake
G Drum clutch

H Clutch lever
I Drive motor
J Drum brake lever
K Speed control
L Electric brake
M Oil bath
N Rope guard

Figure 8-12. A typical winch.

cargo from one location to another. Coordination between the two winch operators is essential to avoid damage both to the cargo and to the rig. The manufacturer's instructions for the operation and maintenance of all winches should be carried out faithfully. Naval vessels are required to have operating instructions and safety precautions posted in the vicinity of each winch.

In simplest terms, cargo is handled in three distinct movements—hoisting, racking, and lowering. In *hoisting*, one winch and boom support the entire load, while the other winch maintains either constant tension or, in some rigs, is completely slacked. When the load or "draft" is sufficiently clear of the ship's side or the hatch coaming, it is carried across the deck by swinging the boom or, in other rigs, by winch control—that is, one winch pulls and one winch slacks. In this latter type of rig, however, both winches keep enough tension on the whips to support the load and to keep it clear of the deck. This movement of the load across deck is called *racking*. When a draft is in position for *lowering*, one winch and boom support the entire load, while the second winch is either held under constant tension or, with some rigs, is slacked. The draft is then lowered to the deck or through a hatch.

It is vitally important that the right amount of slack be left in the "nonworking" whip during the hoisting and lowering phases of any loading cycle. If the nonworking whip is kept too tight, the load will strike against the side of the ship or the coaming of the hatch. If the whip is allowed excess slack, loose turns will pile up on the drum of the winch, and these must be rewound before resuming operations.

When cargo is being hoisted or lowered, swinging should be avoided if possible. A wildly swinging draft often results in damaged cargo and endangers the lives of men working in the hold, on deck, or on the pier. Swinging usually can be prevented in the hold or on the pier by dragging or "touching" the load until it is directly under the head of the boom to be used for hoisting.

At least two steadying lines (lizard lines) should be attached to heavy or unwieldy loads. These should be manned by men in the hold until the load is hoisted above the coaming, then passed simultaneously to men on deck.

Safety

The key to top-notch winch operation is smoothness. Violent starts and stops must be avoided, for the resulting sudden stresses are many times greater than the weight of the draft and may carry away the runner, one of the blocks, or even the boom.

Never leave a winch unattended. When leaving the winch—even for a minute—replace the safety pin and lock the control handle in a neutral position. Otherwise, the handle may be jarred, throwing the winch into operation. Some winches, particularly old models with leaky valves or packing, have a tendency of creeping, even when the handle is pinned in a neutral position. When leaving such a winch, steam valves or electrical power should be shut off.

Signals to Winch Operators

Once a cargo hook has disappeared into a hatch or over the side of the ship, winchmen, in order to handle the winch controls properly, must depend on signals from other sailors who can see the hook and its suspended cargo. These signalmen advise the winch operators of the load's position and how the winches should be operated to complete lowering or hoisting.

The signalman is a key individual in any cargo-handling operation. Under the supervision of a safety officer, he is the director, or quarterback, in any loading or discharging operation, and all eyes look to him for cues. He must be level-headed, unexcitable, and able to foresee and avoid trouble. To understand the job of the winchman to whom he is giving signals, the signalman must, of course, be able to operate a winch capably. A conscientious, alert signalman and a capable winchman instill confidence in the men working the cargo and help greatly to increase the rate of loading or discharging.

Raise the hook

Lower the hook

Raise the boom

Lower the boom

Raise the hook, lower the boom

Raise the hook, hold the boom

Raise the hook, swing boom in direction hand points

Stop hook, stop boom

Rack

Figure 8-13. Hand signals for operating booms and winches.

Signals to winch operators must be distinct and easily understood. It is important that both the winchmen and the signalman be thoroughly familiar with the signals they need to use. The Navy has recently adopted a standard set of signals. Those illustrated in figure 8–13 should be adequate for most operations. These hand signals are described in the list that follows (right hand controls the boom; left hand controls the hook).

- Raise the hook (whip): Forefinger extended, pointed up, and circling. For faster speed, extend two or more fingers, depending on speed desired and speeds available. (The more fingers, the faster the speed.)
- Lower the hook: Same as for raise the hook, except finger (or fingers) points downward.
- Raise (lower) the boom: Fist closed, thumb extended, pointing in direction desired.
- Raise (lower) the boom; raise (lower) hook: One hand gives appropriate signal for boom; other hand gives desired signal for hook.
- Raise (lower) the hook; hold the boom: One hand gives a signal for boom just described; other hand is held on same side of body as first hand, fingers extended and together, back of hand toward winchman.
- Swing load: Arm held straight out, shoulder high, pointing in direction load is to be moved. Fingers should be extended, with palm toward winch operator.
- Stop: Upper arm held straight out, shoulder high; forearm straight up; fist clenched.
- Emergency stop: Rapidly swing fists back and forth, or rapidly pump fists up and down.
- Rack: Arm extended on side of body to load. Swing arm across body in direction load is to be moved.

Note: Winchmen have authority to move the load at their discretion only when the RACK signal is given. This authority terminates when the signalman gives another signal.

Although not all possible signals are described or shown, you should be able to figure out the correct combination for any signal if you remember that in this system the right hand controls the hook, and the left hand controls the boom. However, in a rig where the boom cannot move (yard-and-stay, for example) and there are two whips, each hand controls the corresponding whip.

Cargo Rigs

The Navy is continuously studying and experimenting to make all phases of cargo handling faster, safer, easier, and more economical. Consequently, many innovations will be found on newer types of naval ships that may not be on other cargo vessels. Also, there are many ships designed for specific tasks that have rigs peculiar to those tasks. For example, some heavy new replenishment ships are not equipped with cargo booms and the large hatches typical of ordinary cargo ships. Instead, cargo elevators are installed at one or both ends of the cargo holds; the hatches are just large enough to accommodate the elevators. On other ships, kingposts and booms have been replaced by M-frames and outriggers that provide more efficient methods of transferring cargo.

However, despite various hardware or equipment differences between ships and regardless of the Navy's continuing efforts to improve cargo-handling procedures, there are fundamentals of cargo handling and cargo-handling rigs that, for the most part, do not change. These fundamentals are best demonstrated in the operation of the two basic cargo rigs (common to the Navy and the Merchant Marine) that are described below.

Yard and Stay Rig

The *yard-and-stay* rig is most commonly used for loading and discharging medium-weight cargo of approximately one or one-half tons between ship and shore or from ship to boats and barges. Two booms are used in the yard-and-stay method. One is called the *hatch boom* and plumbs (is adjusted over) the hatch. The other is called the *yard boom*, which is rigged out to one side so that the head of the boom is over the point of pickup or delivery, a pier, a barge, or the like. The cargo whips, coming from different winches, are led through their respective heel and head blocks and are shackled to the same cargo hook. The hook is usually a triple swivel hook with a flounder plate, as shown in figure 8–14. The winch controls are located so that operators have a clear view of the hatch area.

A load is moved from a ship's hold to the pier in the following manner. The yard whip is allowed to hang slack as the hatch whip hoists the load out of the hold and clear of the hatch coaming. Then, by heaving around on the yard whip and paying out on the hatch whip, the load is racked (swung) across the deck and over the side. When the load is positioned under the yard boom, the hatch whip is slacked, and the yard whip lowers the load to the pier. Bringing cargo aboard is, of course, simply the reverse of this procedure.

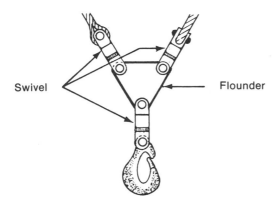

Figure 8-14. Triple swivel hook.

Single Swinging Boom

A modern *single swinging boom*, as shown in figure 8–17, consists of a single boom of five- to ten-ton lift capacity (or more) with powerful topping winches, most of which are capable of lowering or raising a fully loaded boom. The boom can be swung in a horizontal plane by the guys (vangs), one positioned on the starboard bulwark and one on the port. Fittings or *pad eyes* on each bulwark or on deck provide the attachment points for positioning the guys in the most suitable positions for an inboard or outboard swing of the boom. Single swinging booms are commonly used to hoist and lower landing craft on LPDs and LKAs.

In this operation the swinging boom is moved to a position directly over a landing craft in the water, and the hoisting winch lowers the hook for attachment to the lifting bridle on the boat. The loaded hook is then raised to clear the ship's bulwark or railing. Next, the boom is swung inboard by the guy or vang on the side opposite the landing craft to position the craft on deck. The operation is performed in reverse when discharging the landing craft from the ship to the water. Cargo, in nets or when attached directly to the hook, can be handled the same way.

Heavy Lift Booms and Cranes

Tanks, landing craft, large military vehicles, and other extremely heavy cargo required by our forces in the field present difficult problems in cargo-handling operations at advanced bases. At ports in this country, loading such heavy lifts is a relatively simple matter; however, at overseas bases, dockside equipment or floating cranes are not always

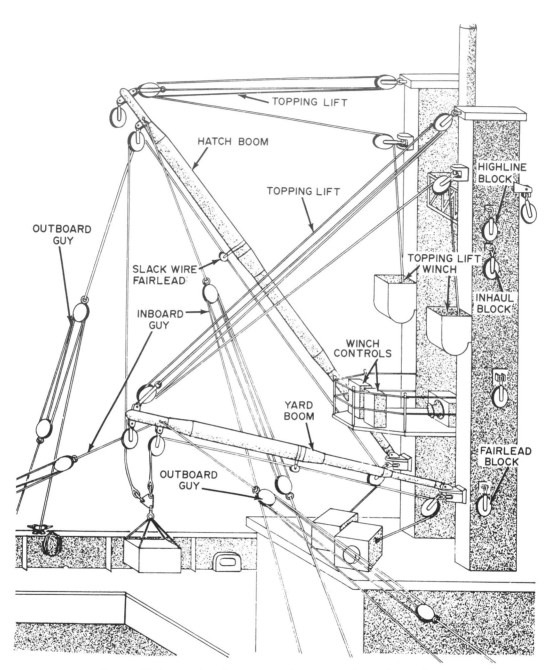

Figure 8-15. *Yard-and-stay rig with topping lift winches on kingposts.*

available. Often a ship's own gear must be used for off-loading. Because neither a yard-and-stay rig nor an ordinary, single swinging boom can support loads of this magnitude, a heavy lift (jumbo) boom or a large shipboard crane may have to be used.

Figure 8-16. A yard-and-stay rig at work.

Most modern Navy cargo and amphibious ships are fitted with a heavy lift boom or crane of up to 50-ton capacity. Some Navy ships are equipped with 70-ton booms to handle the largest LCMs. A jumbo or a crane is, for the most part, rigged and operated like a single swinging boom. One of the greatest difficulties in working with a heavy lift boom, however, is handling the guys.

Every change in position of the boom must be accompanied by an adjustment of the guys. When a boom is topped, the guys must be slacked off; when it is lowered, the guys must be taken in. To swing a boom, it is necessary to heave in one guy and pay out the other, and this requires marked coordination between the men handling the guys.

When a boom is swung outboard or inboard, one guy may be considered as a "hauling" guy, the other as the "following" guy. The latter is generally the troublemaker. Green hands often fail to ease off on this guy smartly enough, and it parts with disastrous results. It is good practice to allow a small amount of slack in a following guy, but never enough to permit the boom to slap about. Some of the newest heavy lift booms have eliminated this disadvantage by controlling the swing of the boom solely with topping lift tackles mounted between two kingposts. An error by a winch operator merely causes the boom head to move in the wrong direction without introducing dangerous opposing tensions.

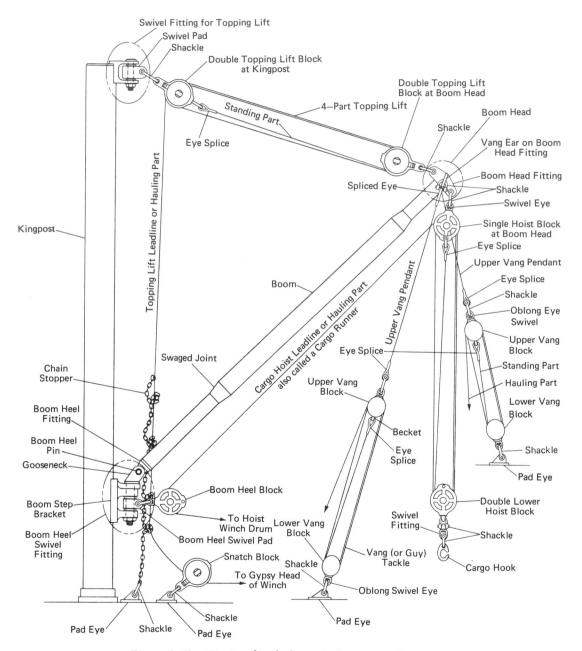

Figure 8-17. Rigging details for a single swinging boom.

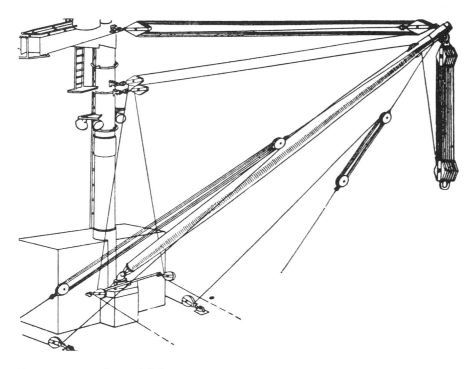

Figure 8-18.   A heavy lift boom.

Most modern cranes are either electric-hydraulic or straight electric. Electric-hydraulic cranes are installed where a wide range of speed, delicate control, and smooth acceleration and deceleration are required. Straight electric drives for cranes consist of electric motors that drive the hoisting and topping machinery of the crane. Cranes generally are more powerful and are more automated than conventional booms of equal size.

Cargo-Handling Safety

Cargo handling is full of dangers to careless personnel. It will be your job as a supervisor to see that safety precautions are strictly observed by all hands at all times. The following list contains some common-sense precautions that all cargo handlers must observe. Otherwise they will endanger themselves and their shipmates.

Open hatches in use should be cleared of any adjacent loose equipment that might fall into them and injure men below, or cause men on deck to trip.

Traffic about the hatch should be restricted to the opposite side from where cargo is being worked. The area over which the loads are traveling should be roped off to traffic.

Figure 8-19. A 30-ton crane on board an LPD.

Experienced seamen should supervise the topping and lowering of booms. Before making any repairs or replacing any of the gear, booms will be lowered to the deck. When lifelines are removed for any purpose, officers and petty officers concerned are required to ensure that emergency lines are rigged and that everyone is cautioned to keep clear. Sailors who help to operate such special equipment as winches or booms must be thoroughly indoctrinated in the safety precautions peculiar to their use. In general, loose clothing should not be worn when working around deck machinery. Safety precautions must be posted in the immediate vicinity of the equipment. Only the men who have been trained, and who have been specifically authorized to operate equipment by the first lieutenant, should be assigned to work with the ship's cranes, capstans, winches, and windlasses. Operation of the machinery must be supervised by a responsible officer.

Remember:

• Wear safe clothing and shoes. Do not wear trousers that are too long, and do not wear rings while at work.
• Climb ladders in the hold only when the hoist is not in motion.

- Do not engage in horseplay, practical jokes, or arguments. They are shortcuts to the hospital.
- Never stand on deck machinery.
- Stand in the clear away from suspended loads.
- When steadying a load, do not stand between the load and any fixed object. Always face the load and keep feet and hands in the clear.
- Be especially attentive when handling objects with sharp or rough edges.
- Report any defect in tools, materials, appliances, and gear.
- Learn to lift properly to prevent strains and sprains.
- Always use a light when entering dark places.
- Report all injuries and get immediate first aid or medical attention.
- And once again, manufacturer's tables should be consulted for the strength of shackles, hooks, and chain hoists. The following facts are noted, however:
    1. A shackle is always stronger than a hook of the same size.
    2. Shackles usually fail by the pin shearing.
    3. Hooks usually fail by straightening.
    4. Be skeptical of any formula based on size alone that purports to give the strength of a hook or shackle.

The best advice to preach, and to perform, is: Stop, look, and listen! Watch while a load is being moved, and keep every part of the rig under constant observation. Listen for any change in sound. A wire or fiber rope normally hums under strain, but when it starts to squeak or squeal, be careful. A faulty block may give warning by squeaking or groaning.

Keep unnecessary personnel out of the area. Those concerned with the operation must stay alert. Look alive and stay alive!

Inspecting Rigging

A weekly inspection of all booms, their rigging, and associated fittings should be conducted by the responsible officer of the deck department in accordance with requirements of the Planned Maintenance System (PMS). This system provides for the periodic tests, servicing, and inspection of all machinery and equipment throughout the ship. As a matter of practice, booms and rigging should also be inspected before each use.

Whenever a boom is to be used for hoisting or lowering a load equal to its rated capacity, as shown on the label plate for the boom, the first lieutenant must be notified. He will inspect the boom and its associated fittings and rigging before the lift is made. If the inspection indicates a dangerous condition or weakness of any component, the boom must not be operated until the problem is corrected.

Summary

Deck seamanship encompasses many skills, skills that are honed through experience. A knowledge of blocks, tackles, winches, booms, and their rigging components is vitally important to any deck officer or seaman. It is the responsibility of every individual involved with deck seamanship and cargo handling to become familiar with deck equipment and its proper operation to ensure that work on deck is done well and done safely.

9

Deck Seamanship—Underway Replenishment

Introduction to Underway Replenishment

Keeping a navy at sea for prolonged periods of time is of major importance both in peace and in war. A deployed fleet gives a nation the ability to extend its influence and to project power far from its own shores. To remain at sea, however, ships must be resupplied on a continuing basis.

The United States cannot rely on such logistic support being delivered through a network of overseas shore bases. Shore bases may be destroyed, or our ships may suddenly be denied entry to previously friendly ports. For these reasons the U.S. fleet must be self-supporting.

To appreciate the magnitude and the extent of this logistic undertaking, consider that the Sixth Fleet has been deployed in the Mediterranean Sea since 1946, relying almost completely on underway replenishment (UNREP) for support. Nearly all transfers of food, fuel, ammunition, mail, and repair parts are made at sea over a supply line extending some 4,500 miles back to the United States.

Underway replenishment is the broad term applied to all methods of transferring fuel, munitions, supplies, and personnel from one vessel to another while under way. The primary aim of underway replenishment is the safe delivery of the maximum amount of cargo and fuel in the minimum amount of time. This operation must be conducted, however, without interfering with the mission of the force.

Before the techniques of UNREP were developed, ships that ran low on fuel, supplies, or ammunition had to return to port or had to lie to while small boats brought supplies from the shore. The disadvantages of these procedures were obvious. The effectiveness of a fleet was reduced by every ship that returned to port, and a ship or small group of ships detached from the fleet was in greater danger of being sunk or captured. In addition, a fleet heading back to port merely left the way open for the enemy to accomplish his mission.

The first significant replenishment operation ever performed at sea by the U.S. Navy was in 1899, when the collier *Marcellus* transferred coal to the ship she was towing, the USS *Massachusetts*. Since that time many replenishment methods have been tried and abandoned.

Two general methods of UNREP are practiced today—vertical replenishment and connected replenishment. Vertical replenishment is carried out by helicopters over varying distances. Supplies are lowered to a ship in nets carried by the aircraft. Connected replenishment, on the other hand, calls for two ships to steam side-by-side connected by transfer lines and hoses. Thus, connected replenishment can involve both refueling and resupply.

Refueling at sea (FAS) is the mission of oilers (AOs) and replenishment oilers (AORs) and is one function of a fast combat support ship (AOE). Some large combatants also have the capability to refuel smaller ships. *Replenishment at sea* (RAS), a term formerly applied to all underway transfers, now refers to any logistic transfer other than refueling. Replenishment at sea is the primary mission of vessels such as the combat store ship (AFS) and the ammunition ship (AE), although frequently they too have the capability of transferring lesser amounts of fuel.

While this chapter is primarily concerned with underway replenishment and will seek to describe the various elements of UNREP, it would be negligent to fail to mention a closely related area of naval support operations known as *mobile logistic support*. Mobile logistic support involves the use of repair ships and other ships in an anchorage, where they function as floating bases for fleet units, providing operating forces with support that otherwise would have to come from shore facilities. Their greatest value lies in their ability to make repairs of considerable scope near the scene of action. Their availability in forward areas is an essential element in providing the means to carry out planned operations requiring limited support, and to make temporary repairs to ensure seaworthiness of ships that must return to rear areas for permanent repairs. When projected operations indicate that the use of an anchorage in a forward area is to be of a temporary nature, with no need for a build-up of shore installations, the use of mobile support ships represents a sizable conservation of resources.

Replenishment Ships

A variety of vessels are employed as underway replenishment ships. Some are single-product vessels that carry only one primary commodity, such as oil. Others are multiproduct types that can supply fuel, ammunition, and general cargo. The great advantage of the latter type is that the ship being replenished need make only one stop alongside the replenishing ship, thus eliminating the necessity of going alongside an oiler, then an ammunition ship, then a stores ship, etc. The multi-product ships themselves are replenished by single-product types.

An example of continuing efforts to improve logistic support of the fleet is the mini-multi concept, whereby a single-product ship is modified to provide a limited multiproduct capability. Ammunition ships in particular have been used in this new role. With holds modified to carry dry stores and an increased fuel cargo, and fitted with portable reefer boxes, ammunition ships can support a small force engaged in distant operations, as was done for a destroyer unit during an Indian

Figure 9-1. A replenishment group refueling a carrier task group.

Ocean deployment. Another example is that all Pacific Fleet Mobile Logistic Support force nonoilers have been fitted with fuel-delivery rigs.

Although most of the replenishment is done by ships of the service force described below, large combatants, such as aircraft carriers, periodically refuel (top off) escorting vessels in between their scheduled replenishments. This practice maintains the operational readiness of the force at a uniformly high level and serves as insurance against possible delays of scheduled FAS because of adverse weather. It should be noted, as well, that even the smallest ships occasionally transfer men, light freight, and mail by manila highlines.

Oilers (AO)

An oiler carries the complete range of Navy petroleum products and can carry some fleet freight. Ships of the *Neosho* class displace about 40,000 tons, are 655 feet long, 75 feet in the beam and have a draft of 36 feet. In addition to the fuel carried in the ship's tanks, bottled gases and drums of lube oil are carried on deck as cargo.

Some older AOs have been "jumboized" by adding an extra section of hull in the middle of the ship. This increases the payload and provides for an improved balance of cargo fuel products to meet the more recent demands placed upon the AO by the increase in fleet requirements for jet aircraft fuel.

Figure 9-2. USS Hassayampa (AO-145).

Figure 9-3. A jumbo version of an older AO.

Replenishment Oilers (AOR)

The AOR was designed to provide rapid replenishment of petroleum products to operating forces at sea, and additionally, to have a limited capability for replenishment at sea of provisions, fleet freight, and selected kinds of ammunition. It has a smaller load capacity and slower maximum speed than the AOE. In size it is similar to a jumboized oiler, but additional features in the design allow for more capacity and more variety in stores.

Store Ship (AF)

The main task of the AF is to deliver chilled and refrigerated stores. It is also used to replenish dry and general stores. The largest AF has eight transfer stations.

Combat Store Ship (AFS)

The AFS is a relatively new concept in design, providing within a single hull the triple logistic capability of handling general stores, dry stores, and refrigerated stores. It is designed for high-speed replenish-

Figure 9-4. A store ship (AF).

ment at sea, can maintain separation during replenishment of up to 200 feet, and can conduct vertical replenishment from its decks.

In addition to the conventional replenishment rigging, the AFS has a constant-tension wire highline system available at all transfer stations.

Ammunition Ship (AE)

Ammunition ships deliver ammunition, bombs, and missiles to ships at sea. Ships of the *Kilauea* (AE-26) class are 564 feet in length, with a beam of 81 feet and a draft of 30 feet. Displacement is about 20,000 tons. AEs also have a limited dry-cargo capability. The design of AEs incorporates a mechanical handling system for more rapid loading and unloading of ammunition. This includes such equipment as elevators in the holds, forklift trucks, and low-lift, power-operated transporters on the main deck for handling palletized ammunition from the elevators to the transfer stations. A tensioned highline system with improved electrohydraulic cargo winches provides rapid and reliable transfers. Ammunition ships also operate helicopters for VERTREP operations.

Figure 9-5. USS San Jose (AFS-7).

Fast Combat Support Ship (AOE)

The AOE is the largest and most powerful auxiliary ship ever built for the Navy. With a full-load displacement of 52,000 tons, a beam of over 100 feet, and a length of nearly 800 feet, the AOE is larger than most of our World War II battleships. Unlike other replenishment ships, it is designed to be operated as an integral unit of a fast task force rather than as a part of an underway replenishment group.

The AOE is a multiple-product ship that carries missiles, fuel, ammunition, general stores, and refrigerated stores. It has a cargo-fuel capacity greater than the largest fleet oilers plus a hold capacity nearly equal to the largest AE. It is able to service the smallest patrol craft or the largest aircraft carrier. The fuel hoses on the AOE are designed to permit an average ship separation of 200 feet during replenishment, instead of the normal 100 feet. This greater distance reduces the possibility of collision and makes increased replenishment speeds feasible. There are nine replenishment stations to port and six to starboard. A helicopter platform and hanger for launching and servicing two helicopters adds the capability of vertical replenishment.

Figure 9-6. USS Butte *(AE-27).*

Military Sealift Command Ships

Many former naval auxiliaries are now manned by Military Sealift Command (MSC) personnel. These ships are identified by the letter "T" as a prefix to their type classification, e.g., T-AF, T-AO, and are designated USNS vice USS. Fleet units often are replenished by MSC vessels.

NWP-14

Over the years as fleet units developed greater and greater expertise in underway replenishment, certain procedures were found to be most effective and most efficient. These procedures can be found in a Navy publication entitled *Replenishment At Sea* (NWP-14 series). This publication has evolved as a direct result of continuing fleet requirements to standardize procedures, to furnish rig make-up and operation guidance, and to attain the highest degree of professionalism and safety in underway replenishment evolutions. NWP-14 is often referred to as the "Bible of underway replenishment."

Although an individual ship's plans must at times be consulted to determine details of rigging peculiar to that unit, NWP-14 is designed both to establish standard practices and to provide specific, fleet-wide guidelines for all aspects of underway replenishment.

UNREP Planning

The overall efficiency of any underway replenishment is directly proportional to the degree of planning that precedes it. Even in the case of small or one-product UNREPs, thorough planning is required. When there is time, a prereplenishment conference is an excellent means of improving the operational performance of all the ships involved. Factors that lend themselves to discussion are the order or sequence of ships going alongside for replenishment, the type and number of rigs to be used, and the logistic requirements of each ship. These factors must be determined prior to beginning the replenishment operation. Crew and space limitations aboard replenishment ships require that cargo be "broken out" ahead of time and off-loaded in an orderly sequence. To do this, a replenishment vessel must know the order in which the ships requiring replenishment will approach. Cargo designated for a cruiser may still be in the hold if she pulls alongside before expected.

Much of the planning for an UNREP is the responsibility of the officer in tactical command (OTC). The OTC is generally the most senior commander in the force and, as such, is responsible for the

Figure 9-7. An AOE replenishing two ships.

Figure 9-8. The oiler USNS Taluga *(TAO-62) fights her way through heavy seas off the Philippines while replenishing the attack carrier USS* Constellation *(CV-64).*

execution of the entire replenishment operation. The OTC determines the time and location of the UNREP rendezvous, the direction of force movement during replenishment, and the replenishment speed. In making his decisions, the OTC should always consider the recommendations of the replenishment ship commander. If the replenishment force commander is the OTC, he should seek the recommendations of the commander whose ships are being supported.

The factors involved in making replenishment course and speed decisions will be addressed shortly.

Shipboard Preparation

Preparation aboard ship for any underway replenishment operation is critical. Special tools and equipment must be made ready, the fuel load must be redistributed in the tanks, computations made as to how much additional fuel is required, and plans must be made for storage and distribution of all supplies received.

Many of the ship's officers have special responsibilities prior to and during underway replenishment. For example, the officer of the deck is responsible for making sure his ship is at the rendezvous point or in the proper position in the formation to begin an UNREP. He is charged, also, to alert the appropriate department heads as to when UNREP preparations should begin. The OOD informs the commanding officer when the ship is completely ready to receive fuel or supplies. In addition to these duties, the officer of the deck supervises the use of prescribed flaghoist signals during the UNREP, and assists the conning officer in relaying orders to the helmsman and the lee helmsman. He also ensures that smoking is controlled in accordance with ship's regulations. This is especially important during refueling operations. A replenishment-at-sea checkoff list is often used by the OOD to ensure that all preparations have been completed.

On most ships, if the OOD plans to keep the conn during the UNREP, another officer temporarily assumes most of his responsibilities and the "deck." (The OOD is, in essence, relieved of control of the bridge to concentrate on maneuvering.) The maneuvering restrictions and inherent danger of collision during underway replenishment generally call for his undivided attention. In few other situations must a ship's conning officer exhibit greater shiphandling skill and foresight. (The details of UNREP maneuvering are discussed later in this chapter.)

During underway replenishment, the commanding officer normally views the overall conduct of the operation from the bridge while providing direct supervision to the conning officer. A ship's executive officer (XO) assists the CO in supervising the UNREP and is usually responsible for coordinating the transfer evolution. In addition, the XO ensures that intership communications via sound-powered telephone talkers are established and maintained throughout the UNREP.

The ship's engineering officer sees to it that the service suction tanks (those providing fuel to the ship at that time) are isolated from tanks to be refueled. Prior to receiving fuel, it is his responsibility to tell the oiler the pumping rate he requires and to have evenly apportioned his remaining fuel among the ship's tanks to maintain balance. He keeps the commanding officer informed of the progress of fueling. After fueling, he reports to the commanding officer the amount of fuel received and the total amount of fuel on board.

Along with the first lieutenant, the ship's weapons officer supervises the handling of deck gear, including transfer rigs, fuel hoses, and lines. He supervises the transfer of missiles and ammunition, including handling and striking down, and enforces special safety precautions. The first lieutenant prepares for underway replenishment by organizing deck personnel and by supervising the preparation and rigging of all deck equipment required. He ensures that the side of the ship designated for hookup to the replenishment vessel is ready to receive both fuel and stores at the appointed time.

During any underway replenishment, the operations department head ensures that an up-to-date tactical plot of other ships and their movements is maintained in CIC. This plot enables the ship to keep track of the replenishment schedule and allows the ship to anticipate changes in course, speed, and formation. Another department head, the ship's supply officer, is responsible for the storage and distribution of provisions and other material received during UNREP. He often works through the operations officer to alert the replenishment vessel of necessary changes required in the list of supplies to be received.

Finally, it is the responsibility of each of the ship's division officers to see that their respective *Watch, Quarter, and Station Bills* are up to date. Enlisted personnel consult this bill or an *Underway Replenishment Bill* to determine their individual assignments and duties during UNREP. The first lieutenant or the weapons officer, under the supervision of the executive officer, is responsible for maintaining this UNREP bill and for consulting with the appropriate division officer when personnel changes or reassignments are necessary.

Basic UNREP Principles and Procedures

The close coordination required to effect transfer of material, fuel, and personnel between ships under way can be achieved only by a clear understanding of the responsibilities of each ship. In the following description of these responsibilities, two basic sets of terms are used. The responsibilities relating to shiphandling are described in terms of the *control ship* and the *approach ship*. The control ship maintains the replenishment course and speed and serves as guide for the approach ship, which keeps station alongside during the UNREP. The responsibilities relating to the rigs that are passed between the ships are set forth in terms of the *delivery ship* and the *receiving ship*. The delivery ship furnishes and handles the rigs.

These sets of terms are independent, however, since either the approach ship or the control ship may be the delivery ship. Normally, though, the control ship is the delivery ship. Exceptions to this convention are infrequent. Generally, only in very rough weather (since it is desirable to have the more maneuverable ship make the approach) might the OTC require a delivery ship to be the approach ship.

Romeo Corpen and Romeo Speed

Abbreviated naval terminology and code designate the chosen replenishment course and speed as *Romeo corpen* and *Romeo speed*. As mentioned earlier, it is the responsibility of the officer in tactical command to select a suitable replenishment course and speed, taking into consideration the mission of the group and the condition of the sea.

Unless it is vitally important that the force continue moving along a specific heading, the direction and height of swells are the principal considerations in selecting Romeo corpen. Heavy seas adversely affect the replenishment operation and generally require that ships maintain greater lateral separation. Increased rolling and pitching, with high waves breaking over the sides and bow of a ship, add to the difficulties of station keeping and line handling and may cause excessive strain on rigs. During heavy weather, a course with the sea will moderate these adverse effects and may permit replenishment when it otherwise would be impossible.

Although not as significant as sea state, wind conditions too must be considered when selecting a replenishment course. Relative wind velocity should be kept as low as the tactical situation permits. High relative winds, especially in cold and rainy weather, will quickly fatigue exposed personnel and increase replenishment time. Therefore, a downwind heading may be preferable.

Under other conditions, heading into the wind may be more desirable. It may permit carriers to conduct flight operations at replenishment course and speed. Also, steaming with the wind one or two points on the port bow provides a lee for destroyer-type ships replenishing to starboard of larger ships.

Speeds between 12 and 16 knots are usually advisable for underway replenishment. However, weather conditions influence the selection of Romeo speed just as they do the selection of replenishment course. Under all conditions, a ship must make sufficient speed to maintain steering control. Speeds less than eight knots are not advisable because of reduced rudder effect. Replenishment speeds above 16 knots may be used if weather permits, but greater lateral separation must be obtained because of the increased venturi effect (explained later).

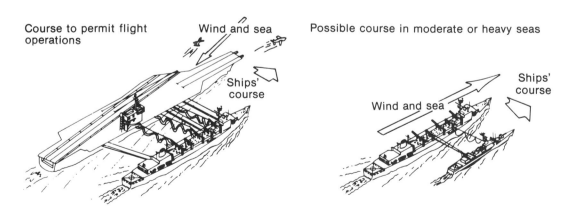

Course to permit flight operations   Wind and sea   Possible course in moderate or heavy seas

Ships' course

Wind and sea   Ships' course

Figure 9-9. Selecting Romeo corpen.

The Approach

As stated, basic UNREP principles generally stipulate that the delivery ship will assume and maintain the designated Romeo corpen and Romeo speed, while the receiving the ship makes an approach from astern, comes alongside the delivery ship, and adjusts course and speed as necessary to maintain that position during the operation. Prior to coming alongside, however, the receiving ship normally positions herself 300 to 500 yards astern of the delivery vessel. When the delivery ship is steady on replenishment course and speed, she so indicates by flying the Romeo flag at the dip on the side being rigged for replenishment. The receiving ship replies that she is ready to come alongside by showing the same signal, Romeo, at the dip, on the side rigged. When the delivery ship is ready for the approach, she hoists Romeo close up. The receiving ship then hoists Romeo close up and simultaneously commences her approach by increasing speed by three to ten knots, depending on ship type, over signaled Romeo speed (the speed of the control/delivery ship).

At a point determined by the surge rate of the approach ship, she slows her engines to replenishment speed. This should effectively slide the approach ship into a position alongside the delivery vessel. When the ships are in proper relative position, transfer rigs are passed and hooked up. As the first line is passed between them and secured, both ships haul down Romeo.

As long as the ships are replenishing, they will display at the yardarm the day shape or night lights indicating restricted maneuverability as required by the Rules of the Road. By day the display is one black ball over one black diamond over one black ball; the lights required at night are naturally red, over white, over red. When transferring fuel or ammunition, each ship flys the Bravo flag as well.

Because of the danger of collision during underway replenishment, it is important that sufficient distance be maintained between ships as they travel side by side transferring fuel and cargo. Adequate lateral separation must be ensured during the approach, particularly when the bow of the receiving ship passes the stern of the delivery ship. If the separation is not adequate at this stage, there is increased risk of collision, since a water-pressure differential causes the bow of the receiving ship to veer in toward the delivery ship. These areas of increased water pressure at the bow and stern of a ship and decreased pressure (suction) amidships are the result of the differences in velocity of the flow of water around the hull. When ships are alongside each other under way, this velocity differential (known as the *venturi effect*) is greater and becomes further complicated because of the interming-

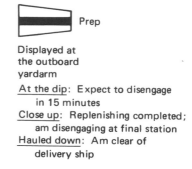

CONTROL SHIP

■✚ Romeo

Displayed on
fore yardarm
on side rigged

At the dip: Am steady on course
and speed and am preparing to
receive you on side indicated
Close up: Am ready for your
approach
Hauled down: First line secured

APPROACH SHIP

■✚ Romeo

Displayed on
fore yardarm
on side rigged

At the dip: Am ready to come
alongside
Close up: Am commencing
approach
Hauled down: First line secured

Prep

Displayed at
the outboard
yardarm

At the dip: Expect to disengage
in 15 minutes
Close up: Replenishing completed;
am disengaging at final station
Hauled down: Am clear of
delivery ship

BOTH SHIPS

◀ Bravo

Where best seen: Fuel or
explosives are being
transferred

Figure 9-10. Visual signals for underway replenishment.

ling of the pressure areas. The intensity of the venturi effect varies with the distance between the two ships, their size and configuration, their speed, and the depth of the water.

Adequate ship separation is even more vital at night and in poor weather, when reduced visibility impairs accurate distance and depth perception.

The distance or separation established between two ships during replenishment depends on a number of factors—including their size and ship type, their ability to maneuver while alongside, and, as noted previously, the replenishment speed and the prevailing wind and sea conditions. Primarily, however, lateral separation required between replenishing units is dependent upon the type of transfer rig used. A destroyer using a standard span-wire fueling rig, for instance, maintains a normal separation from the replenishment ship of between 80 and 100 feet; a carrier with the same equipment maintains a distance of between 100 to 140 feet. When the STREAM system is employed, all ships remain from 80 to 200 feet away from the support ship, but must maintain a separation of 140 feet during tensioning. The optimum lateral separation lies between these upper and lower limits.

Heavy fenders were once thought to be necessary on both delivery and receiving ships to protect their sides should failure to maintain proper lateral separation result in collision. Current guidelines, however, state that fenders provide little or no protection for ships engaged in underway replenishment, and they are no longer required.

Maintaining Station Alongside

Maintaining station alongside the replenishment ship requires precise maneuvering on the part of the receiving ship's conning officer. Steaming too close restricts maneuverability and increases the turbulence between the ships. In the case of some heavily laden oilers, this can throw seas into the tank deck and endanger personnel who must work there. Steaming too far apart puts an undue strain on the rigs.

Prior to going alongside, a ship's steering control must be checked in all modes of operation both from the pilot house and after steering. Gyro error must be determined as well as the operability of the standby gyro and associated alarms. Personnel assigned steering control stations must be highly qualified and thoroughly familiar with steering casualty control procedures. After steering must be kept continually informed of the progress of the evolution, with particular attention to course and speed changes. To this end, a sound-powered telephone circuit is used solely for ship control functions. While conducting UNREP operations, an officer or qualified petty officer must be

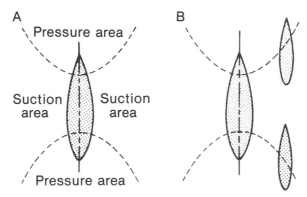

Figure 9-11. *Dangers of the venturi effect.*

assigned both to ensure that the helmsman follows the orders of the conning officer and to assist as necessary in the event of a steering casualty. The helm supervisor should have no other duties assigned.

Because of the venturi effect and the influence of both wind and seas, slight adjustments in the receiving ship's course and speed are needed throughout the replenishment evolution to maintain the same relative position alongside the delivery vessel. The delivery ship generally does not alter course or speed, and never does so without first informing the receiving ship of her intentions. Bridge-to-bridge phones are essential for this purpose, and it is imperative that communications and liaison be maintained between respective conning officers.

The conning officer of the approach ship must conn from a position where he can observe his own ship's heading, the rudder angle indicator if installed, and the relative motion of the two ships. Orders should be given to the helmsman by actual course, in degrees or in half degrees. This should enable the conning officer to maintain proper distance between ships and adjust his relative fore-and-aft position without resorting to radical changes in course or speed. It is important

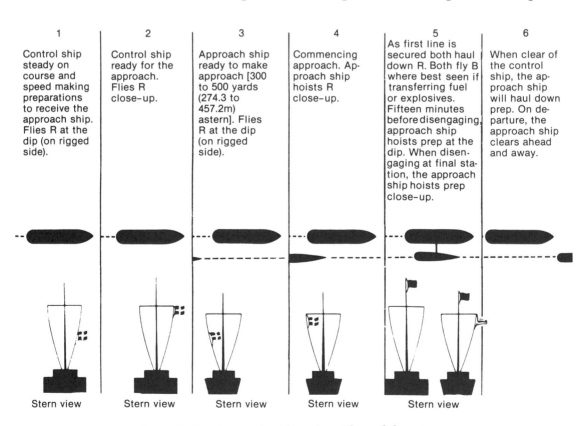

1	2	3	4	5	6
Control ship steady on course and speed making preparations to receive the approach ship. Flies R at the dip (on rigged side).	Control ship ready for the approach. Flies R close–up.	Approach ship ready to make approach [300 to 500 yards (274.3 to 457.2m) astern]. Flies R at the dip (on rigged side).	Commencing approach. Approach ship hoists R close–up.	As first line is secured both haul down R. Both fly B where best seen if transferring fuel or explosives. Fifteen minutes before disengaging, approach ship hoists prep at the dip. When disengaging at final station, the approach ship hoists prep close–up.	When clear of the control ship, the approach ship will haul down prep. On departure, the approach ship clears ahead and away.
Stern view	Stern view	Stern view	Stern view	Stern view	

Figure 9-12. Approach, riding alongside, and departure.

to reemphasize that he makes small adjustments, as necessary, to the ship's heading (in one or one-half degree increments) in order to keep the proper separation between ships. In like manner, he makes adjustments in speed (small RPM changes) in order to maintain a constant fore-and-aft position alongside.

To assist the conning officer in monitoring the distance between his ship and the delivery ship, a distance line is stretched between the replenishing units. Embedded in the polypropylene distance line are conducting wires for a sound-powered telephone circuit. The circuit provides a communication link between the bridges of the two ships.

This *phone and distance line*, as it is frequently termed, is among the first lines to be passed between the two ships. By watching it, the conning officer of the receiving ship will know immediately when his ship is moving in too close or going out too far. The distance line is marked with rectangles of colored cloth or painted canvas spaced 20 feet apart and numbered to indicate in feet the distance of separation. At night, red flashlights or fluorescent chemical markers are attached to the line at the appropriate points.

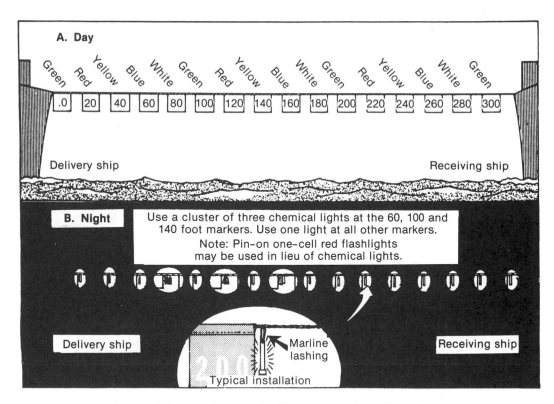

Figure 9-13. *A phone and distance line stretched between two ships. Note the zero end on the delivery ship and the color sequence of the distance markers.*

The distance line is generally passed by the receiving ship to the delivery ship. The zero end is secured at or near the rail of the delivery ship, and the other end is tended by hand on the receiving ship. The men tending it should keep the line as taut as possible and should particularly avoid stepping in bights of the line as it coils and uncoils on the deck when the distance between the ships changes.

A situation calling for especially close monitoring of the phone and distance line occurs when replenishment rigs are tensioned and detensioned. As replenishment lines and wires between two ships are mechanically pulled taut to support the transfer of hoses or cargo, the tremendous pull of tensioning will often cause the ships to move toward each other. The opposite is true when those lines are detensioned and the great strain on the wires and lines is released. During these brief periods of tensioning and detensioning, the conning officer and helmsman must be prepared to use more rudder to counteract the accompanying ship movement. One of the earliest indicators of this movement toward or away from the replenishment ship will be the phone and distance line.

Night Replenishment

Although it is often impossible to see clearly what is happening on the ship alongside, all ships can replenish at night. During night replenishment, darkened ship (no white lights showing) is the normal lighting condition. Limited lighting measures are prescribed to aid sailors in handling cargo and working rigs, but white lights are never used because of their blinding effect and, in certain situations, because of the need for security. Under darkened ship conditions, dimmed or low-powered red lights, called contour lights, are used to assist the receiving ship in coming alongside and maintaining station. The deliv-

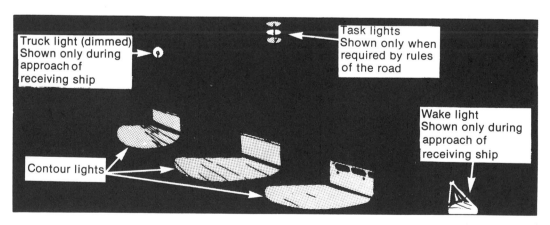

Figure 9-14. Approach and station-keeping lights.

ery ship displays two contour lights along her rigged side, a light on the truck (the highest part of the mast), and a fourth light aft that illuminates her wake. The truck and wake lights replace the Romeo flag. They are lit during the approach, indicating Romeo close up; when the receiving ship is alongside, they are switched off, indicating Romeo has been hauled down.

At each transfer station on both ships, a station-marker light box is set up to indicate the commodity being transferred. The side of the box facing the other ship has nine holes, each fitted with a red lens that can be covered by a hand-operated shutter. By opening some shutters and leaving the others down, the operator produces a recognizable pattern of lights. The day and night codes for indicating commodities are shown in figure 9–16.

The Replenishment Station

Ships usually have several replenishment stations at which they receive fuel or supplies. As noted, these stations are clearly marked so that a replenishment vessel can quickly see them.

Line-Throwing Guns and Bolos

As the receiving ship completes her approach and steadies alongside, *line throwing guns* or *bolos* are made ready on the delivery ship. By means of these devices, the first messenger lines are started over.* However, prior to the transfer of any lines during UNREP, a warning is passed on both ships over the general announcing system (1MC) or by electric megaphone (bull horn). This warning is as follows:

> *Firing Ship*: "On the (name of the receiving ship), stand by for shot lines. All hands topside take cover."
> *Receiving Ship*: "On the (name of own ship), stand by for shot lines at (station(s) concerned). All hands topside take cover."

As an additional safety measure, hand-held whistle signals are exchanged at each replenishment station before sending lines across. One whistle blast from a delivery-ship station indicates her readiness to throw a bolo or to shoot a line over. When prepared to receive the shot line, the opposite station on the receiving ship replies with two blasts. Before signaling, though, the receiving ship makes sure that all personnel have taken cover. Every effort is made to prevent accidental injury to personnel from a flying bolo or line-throwing projectile.

---

*Line-throwing guns are never fired toward carriers or other ships with aircraft on deck (such as an LPH). In these situations, the receiving ship would fire lines to the delivery ship.

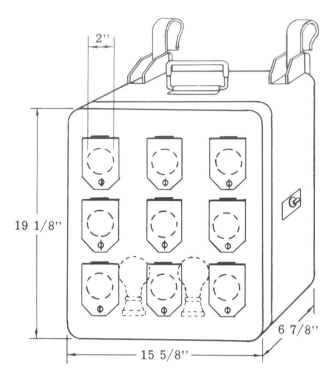

Figure 9-15.   Station marker box.

Line-throwing guns generally fire a plunger-like, rubberized projectile to which is attached a very light, synthetic shot line. The shot line, being relatively weak (6 or 9 thread), must be pulled with some care. It is to a shot line that heavier messenger lines are connected. The *messenger* is the main line used to assist in hauling any basic rig across between ships. Messengers allow phone lines, cargo transfer lines, the distance line, and span wires to be pulled over.

Bolos serve the same purpose as line-throwing guns but are used less frequently. Consisting of a leather or rubber-encased lead weight attached to a nylon shot line, a bolo is thrown by swinging it overhead several times to gain momentum and then letting it go. When well-aimed and thrown with enough strength, it reaches its mark. Bolos, although reliable enough for daytime use in good weather, are not practical at other times. They often require the receiving ship to approach the delivery ship much more closely to allow completion of the bolo throw.

Once in a while, the delivery ship has difficulty getting her shot lines across due to high winds or less than expert marksmanship. Rather than delay the UNREP further in order to prepare additional shot

COMMODITY TRANSFERRED	CODE		
	DAY 3-FT. SQ. BUNTING OR PAINTED AREA		NIGHT LIGHT BOX
MISSILES	INTERNATIONAL ORANGE		
AMMUNITION	GREEN		
FUEL OIL	RED		
DIESEL OIL	BLUE		
DIESEL FUEL MARINE (DFM)	RED & BLUE TRIANGLES		
AVGAS	YELLOW		
JET FUEL (JP-5)	YELLOW & BLUE TRIANGLES		
WATER	WHITE		
STORES	GREEN WITH WHITE VERTICAL STRIPES		
PERSONNEL AND/ OR LIGHT FREIGHT	GREEN WITH WHITE LETTER "P" CENTERED		
FUEL OIL AND JP-5	RED/YELLOW & BLUE TRIANGLES		
DFM AND JP5	RED/BLUE & YELLOW/ BLUE TRIANGLES		

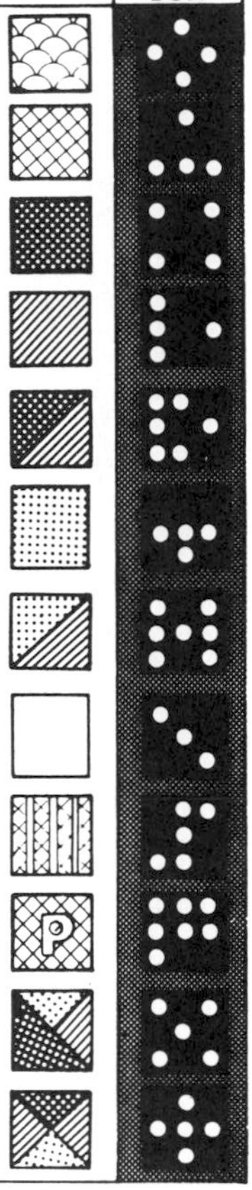

Figure 9-16. Day and night markers for transfer stations.

lines, the delivery ship may request that the receiving ship use her own line-throwing guns. For this reason, every UNREP station is required to have a line-throwing gunner standing by.

Communications

Communications between replenishing ships can be carried out by radio telephone, flashing light, flaghoist, semaphore, and by megaphone; but at the replenishment station itself, communications generally are provided by other means.

One of the first lines transferred at each replenishment station is a sound-powered telephone line. It is sent over connected to a messenger line and is then detached and hooked up to a sound-powered

Figure 9-17. "Stand by for shot line!"

telephone headset. This line provides verbal communications between the delivery ship and receiving ship stations. It is especially handy for passing pumping or rigging instructions and significantly enhances safety. Nevertheless, a phone talker attached to an intership station-to-station phone line must be cautioned not to fasten his headset neck-

Figure 9-18. Heaving a bolo.

strap. As ships surge together and then veer away from each other during alongside replenishment, phone lines suddenly may be pulled taut or extended to their limit. A talker with his neckstrap fastened could be pulled over the side before he could free himself.

Visual communications between replenishment stations are achieved by the use of hand-held, colored, paddle signals (colored flashlight wands at night). These signals are given by the replenish-

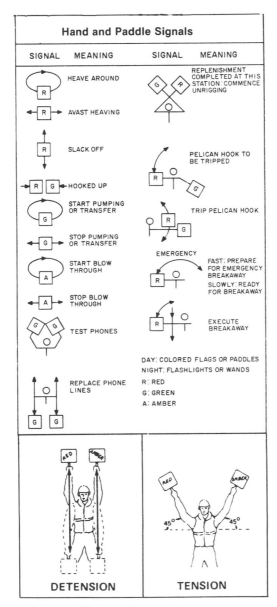

Figure 9-19. Hand and paddle signals.

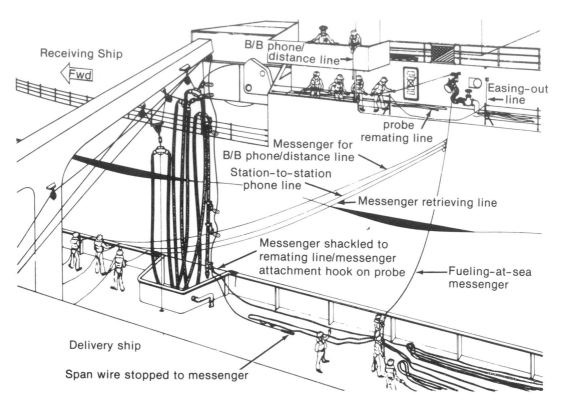

Receiving Ship

←Fwd

B/B phone/distance line→

Easing-out←line

probe remating line

Messenger for B/B phone/distance line

Station-to-station phone line

Messenger retrieving line

Messenger shackled to remating line/messenger attachment hook on probe

Fueling-at-sea messenger

Delivery ship

Span wire stopped to messenger

Figure 9-20. Passing the lines.

ment station signalman and are designed to parallel orders passed over the sound-powered telephones. Each ship signals the action it desires the other ship to take; for example, the receiving ship might signal the delivery ship to start pumping oil. If the other ship cannot comply, it initiates the avast signal, which is repeated by the first ship. (The ship initiating an avast signal must originate the next signal.) The various hand or paddle signals used during underway replenishment are shown in figure 9–19. Note that the color of the paddle used may be as significant as the paddle motion.

Replenishment Station Safety

Persons assigned to replenishment stations must be thoroughly schooled in safety precautions and should be so well trained that they observe such precautions almost automatically. Unfortunately, people tend to be careless, particularly when doing familiar tasks. For this reason, personnel at each station must be briefed on safety precautions before each replenishment exercise.

The supervisor or safety officer at each station must ensure that all replenishment personnel engaged in handling stores or lines (or anybody in the transfer area for any reason) wear properly secured, orange-colored, inherently buoyant, vest-type life jackets. A life jacket is a welcome article of apparel to anyone unfortunate enough to fall over, or be washed over, the side during UNREP.

In addition to the life jacket, a line-throwing gunner must wear a red jersey (or vest), and replenishment station signalmen must wear green jerseys (or vests). Jerseys are worn under life jackets, and vests over life jackets, thus permitting maximum visibility of the jacket should that individual fall overboard. A one-cell flashlight (or chemical light), whistle, and sea marker (fluorescent) also should be worn on the jacket to aid in spotting a man lost overboard during night replenishment. As a further safety precaution, both the delivery and receiving ship must station a life-buoy watch aft to deploy smoke floats and a ring buoy in the event of a man-overboard emergency. If the life-buoy watch sees or hears an individual in the water, he tosses the floats and buoy toward the man and immediately notifies the bridge via sound-powered telephone.

Topside personnel in the immediate vicinity of any replenishment station transfer area also must wear construction type (safety) helmets. These helmets not only protect the wearers but aid intership communications as well. The helmets are color coded, allowing rapid identification of key men from a distance. Replenishment station safety helmets are color coded as follows:

Helmet Color	*Worn By*
White	Officers/CPOs and supervisors
Yellow	Rig captains
Green	Signalmen/phone talkers
Brown	Winch operators
Purple	Repair personnel
Red	Line-throwing gunners (or bolo heavers)
White (with red cross)	Corpsmen
Blue	Deck riggers/line handlers
Orange	Supply personnel
Grey	All others

Other general replenishment safety precautions include the following:

• Personnel handling messenger lines, distance lines, and inhaul lines should use the "hand-over-hand" grip and may wear gloves.

- Line handlers must button sleeves and remove all loose objects to keep them from wrapping or fouling lines. However, personnel assigned to replenishment stations should carry an appropriate knife to be used in the event of an emergency. If caught in a bight or tangle of lines, a knife may be the only means by which an individual can quickly free himself.

- All personnel involved in cargo-handling operations on both the delivery and receiving ship should wear safety shoes and must keep clear of suspended loads.

- During fuel transfer the smoking lamp is out, except in authorized spaces. The smoking lamp should never be lighted on an oiler's weather decks.

Breakaway (Normal)

Fifteen minutes before the conning officer on the receiving ship expects to complete replenishment, he orders the Prep pennant hoisted at the dip to so notify the next ship scheduled to replenish.

On completion of the UNREP, all nets, slings, transfer lines, and hoses are returned to the delivery ship. When this disengagement has begun, the receiving ship hoists Prep close up. Messengers are passed back last to facilitate the delivery ship's preparations for transferring supplies to the next ship. Concurrently, the phone and distance line is passed back to the receiving ship. When the last line is clear, the Prep pennant is hauled down. This action lets other ships know that the replenishment is complete.

To move his ship away from the delivery vessel, the receiving ship conning officer increases speed moderately (3 to 5 knots) and directs his course outboard in small steps. These incremental changes are required both to ensure that his ship's stern does not swing into the delivery ship and to reduce propeller wash, which may adversely affect the delivery ship's steering control. When completely clear of the replenishment vessel, the receiving ship can manuever freely. It is rarely advisable, however, for a conning officer to cross ahead of the delivery ship, and the commanding officer should always be consulted about such a maneuver.

Emergency Breakaway

During underway replenishment, emergencies may arise that require ships to break away on short notice. Examples of such emergencies are: any equipment casualty that affects a ship's ability to maintain replenishment course or speed; an enemy threat in the vicinity; or the requirement to make an urgent aircraft launch or recovery. Other emergencies that might require breakaway include a man being lost overboard with no lifeguard ship or helicopter on station, a cargo or fuel rig parting and threatening to foul the ship's screws, and "tightlining" situations. Tightlining can occur when replenishing ships separate to the point where hoses appear to be in danger of parting, when separation distances cause wires to approach the last layer on winch drums, or when an equipment casualty puts undue stress on a line or hose.

An emergency breakaway is basically an accelerated normal breakaway using an orderly and prearranged procedure. Paramount in execution of an emergency breakaway is safety and the allowance of sufficient time for the ships to disconnect the rigs in an orderly manner. Fueling rigs in particular are subject to severe damage if not properly released at the breakaway signal—damage that may require vital hours to repair. The objective, then, is to disengage quickly without damaging the rigs or endangering personnel.

Shortly after station-to-station communications are established during UNREP, the officers in charge of the delivery ship transfer stations contact their receiving ship counterparts to review emergency breakaway procedures. Written instructions also accompany the first lines transferred. When bridge-to-bridge communications are established through the phone and distance line, the commanding officers may review the actions to be taken, as well.

In anticipation of an always-possible emergency, all lines brought aboard the receiving ship are faked clear for running, and emergency tools such as hammers, axes, and bolt cutters are kept ready. And although station-to-station phones and paddle signals are the primary means for ordering an emergency breakaway, the 1MC, bull horns, and voice radio circuits are also prepared should their use be necessary to ensure rapid ship-to-ship communications.

The order for an emergency breakaway may be given by the commanding officer of either ship. Once that order is given, however, and the danger signal (at least five short blasts) is sounded on the ship's whistle to alert other vessels in the vicinity to the emergency, the delivery ship assumes control of the breakaway. Instructions are sent over the station-to-station, sound-powered telephones, while delivery ship signalmen at the transfer stations each rotate a red paddle, flag, or wand in a semicircular arc overhead to indicate "prepare for emergency breakaway." The ship alongside acknowledges with the avast heaving signal and, when ready, responds with the emergency breakaway signal. On the originating ship, signalmen then lower their paddles from the overhead position to initiate the breakaway. Slacked wires and lines are disconnected at this point and rapidly pulled back to the delivery ship. Once all lines are clear, the ship with most maneuverability will pull away. Replenishment can be resumed after equipment or operational emergencies are resolved.

Summary

The success of any replenishment operation is determined, in large part, before a ship ever pulls alongside and transfers the first line. Adequate preparation is the key. Preparation is so important that memory alone can not be trusted, and many ships make use of replenishment checkoff lists to avoid overlooking critical steps or procedures.

The ability of men to work together smoothly is no less important in a replenishment operation than in bringing a ship alongside a mooring. Indeed, the need for adequate training in transfer operations is increased, because the crews from different ships are called upon to work as a team. Although replenishment during daylight and in fair seas is a comparatively simple operation, greater difficulties at night and bad weather require the services of highly trained men. Only thoroughly practiced crews with an awareness of safety can produce the high degree of accident-free coordination necessary for successful underway replenishment.

Deck Seamanship—Underway Replenishment Cargo and Personnel Transfer

Introduction

A replenishment ship loaded with cargo intended for delivery to a base or to a group of replenishment ships is said to be base-loaded; if carrying cargo intended for delivery to the combat fleet at sea, she is fleet-issue loaded. Base-loaded supply ships are loaded without particular attention to cargo accessibility. Fleet-issue-loaded ships, on the other hand, carry a variety of cargo stowed for quick access and easy handling during underway transfer. It is the cargo and personnel transfer methods employed by the fleet-issue-loaded vessels and the ships to which they deliver, that center in the following discussion.

Replenishment Methods

Fleet-issue-loaded ships are not loaded to full, cubic-foot capacity, but are loaded, instead, for cargo mobility. Much cargo space has to be sacrificed to provide passageways through the stacks of cargo, because each item must be constantly accessible. The efficiency of the replenishment operation depends on this cargo-loading plan and the equipment selected for transfer of the cargo.

Various methods can be used to transfer provisions and stores between delivering and receiving ships. Each has its advantages and disadvantages in relation to the size, structure, and rigging potential of the ships involved. The method to be used for a particular replenishment operation is selected on the basis of:

1. Type and quantity of cargo to be transferred.
2. Capacity of the rig and associated fittings.
3. Weight and size of heaviest or largest load.
4. Type and location of receiving station.
5. Weather and sea conditions.

It should be noted, however, that no rig can be operated at full capacity if the weather is bad or if the gear is not in perfect condition.

Maximum capacities on conventional transfer rigs are listed below.

Method	Maximum capacity per load (pounds)
Burton	6,000
Doubled-whip burton	12,000
Housefall	2,500
Double housefall	2,500
Modified housefall	3,500
Wire highline (wire outhaul)	3,500
Manila highline (5-inch)	600
Synthetic highline (4-inch)	600
Manila/synthetic highline (3-inch)	300
Missile/cargo STREAM	3,600

The Burton Method

Essential elements of the burton rig are a winch and a whip from each ship. The outer ends of the whips are shackled to a triple-swivel

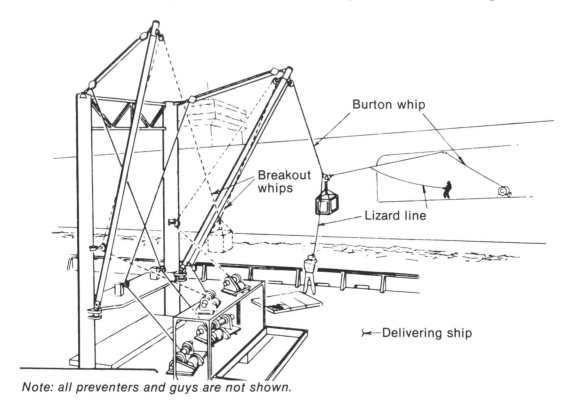

Note: all preventers and guys are not shown.

Figure 10-1. Burton rig.

cargo hook, and the load is transferred by one ship paying out on her whip while the other ship heaves in on hers. There are various ways of rigging the delivery ship for the transfer of cargo by the burton method. Normally, a boom to the engaged side is used for the actual transfer, and a boom on the opposite, or unengaged side, is employed to hoist loads from the hold.

In passing the lines, the ship's ordinary roles may be reversed, with the receiving ship sending over the bolo or gun lines. When the delivery ship has the bolo or gun line in hand, personnel on the receiving ship bend their end to the messenger, and the delivery ship personnel haul over the messenger, phone line, and burton whip. They shackle the whip to the triple-swivel cargo hook, and the rig is ready.

Actually, in the burton method a load is transferred in the same way as in the yard-and-stay method of cargo handling. That is, the load is hoisted clear of the deck by the delivery ship's whip; then the receiving ship heaves in on hers as the delivery ship pays out. Usually, when the load reaches the receiving ship, its weight is entirely on her whip, which she slacks to set the load down. Men tending the lizard line make sure that no load drops on another. When a load is unhooked, any empty nets or pallets are hooked on the rig and returned to the delivery ship.

Successful burtoning depends on teamwork between the winchmen of both ships. A constant tension should be maintained on each whip despite the relative movement due to rolling and yawing.

Line tensions may be reduced by keeping the load as low as practicable and hoisting it only high enough to clear the sides of the ships. As it crosses the water, the load should be lowered to trace a good catenary yet maintain the necessary height to prevent immersion.

During cargo transfer, the messenger is faked down on the delivery ship's deck, ready for return. Upon completion of the operation, when all nets and slings have been returned, the delivery ship attaches the distance line, telephone line, and burton whip to the messenger and returns them to the receiving ship. All lines are returned in the same manner in which they were received, but in reverse order. Time required for rigging on the delivery ship thus is reduced, and preparations are expedited for transferring supplies to the next ship to come alongside.

Doubled-Whip Burton Method

There are various ways of doubling up burton whips to handle loads up to 12,000 pounds. The basic doubled-whip rig is shown in figure 10–3.

Figure 10-2. Burton rig.

The Housefall Method

The basic housefall method of cargo transfer differs from the burton method in that all sources of power are located on the delivery ship. The delivery ship as a rule provides and controls the rig, while the receiving ship provides only the attachment point for the rig. Like the burton method, however, rigging can be done in several ways.

One of the most efficient rigs uses the housefall boom both to lift cargo from the hold and to transfer it to the receiving ship. After the load is raised clear of the delivery ship rail with the inboard transfer whip, a strain is taken on the outboard transfer whip. By gradually paying out the inboard whip, the load is worked over to the receiving ship.

On completion of the transfer operation, the lines are passed back to the delivering ship in the usual manner. This type of rig provides maximum flexibility for continuous transfer of cargo when the ship alongside does not keep good fore-and-aft position.

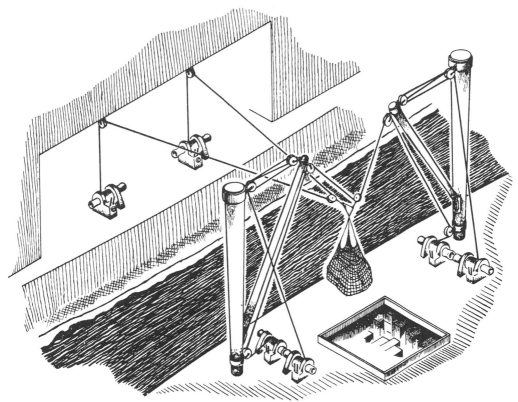

Figure 10-3. Basic doubled-whip burton rig.

Modified Housefall Method

When it is necessary to lift a slightly heavier load or to keep the load higher above the water than is possible with the ordinary housefall rig, a modified rig can be used. The rigging is the same as for the ordinary housefall, except that a trolley block is added and the suspension points for the transfer whips must be kept close together. As you can see, the trolley block rides on the outboard transfer whip. (See the trolley in figure 10–6.)

Double Housefall Method

The double housefall speeds transfer of goods to ships that, because of structural limitations, do not have enough suspension points to handle more than one (individual) housefall rig. Double housefalling is slower than housefalling to two separate receiving stations, but faster than housefalling to one station in the usual manner. In double house-falling, the delivering ship uses two adjacent housefall rigs attached to a

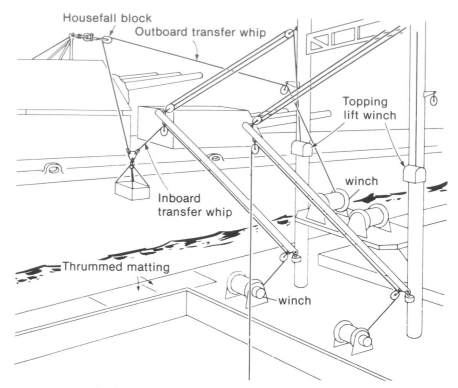

Figure 10-4. The housefall cargo transfer method.

single suspension point on the receiving ship. In passing lines, both housefall blocks are sent over simultaneously. Then, in operation, one housefall rig delivers a loaded net, while the other brings back an empty net. As shown in figure 10–7, the two nets pass each other, going in opposite directions, each time a load is transferred.

Wire Highline Method

The wire highline method of cargo transfer is seen less and less frequently in the fleet today since STREAM rigs are becoming the standard. However, the similarities between a STREAM rig with a manila outhaul and the basic wire highline rig are such that a brief discussion of the latter is warranted.

The wire highline method of transfer uses a highline traveled by a trolley. The highline extends from a winch on the delivering ship through an elevated block and across to a pad eye on the receiving ship (figure 10–8). The trolley is moved toward the receiving ship by either a wire or a manila outhaul line and is brought back to the delivering ship with a winch-operated wire inhaul line. If the receiving ship has the proper winch available, a ¾-inch wire outhaul may be used, in which

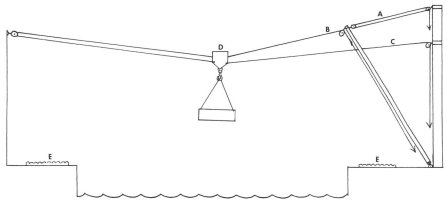

Figure 10-5. The modified housefall cargo transfer method. A. Topping lift; B. Outboard transfer whip; C. Inboard transfer whip; D. Trolley block; E. Trummed matting.

case 3,500-pound loads can be handled. If no winch is available, a manila outhaul must be used, which limits loads to 800 pounds.

As the delivery ship slacks the inhaul line, the receiving ship pulls the load across with the outhaul line. When the load is over the landing area, the delivery ship slacks the highline and sets the load on deck. It then retrieves the trolley (and empty nets) by reversing the process.

Manila/Synthetic (Nonwire) Highline Method

Nonwire highlines are similar to wire highlines except, of course, manila or double-braided spun polyester (Dacron) is substituted for wire. These highlines can be used in transferring provisions, ammunition, personnel, and light freight.

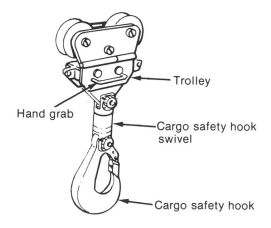

Trolley

Hand grab

Cargo safety hook swivel

Cargo safety hook

Figure 10-6. Modified housefall and highline trolley assembly.

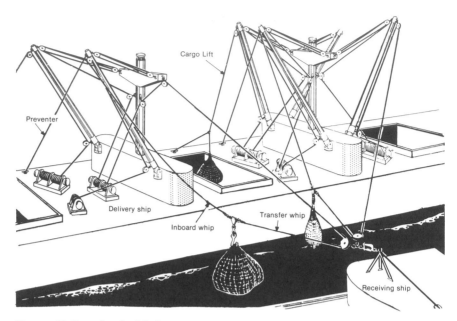

Figure 10-7. *The double housefall cargo transfer method.*

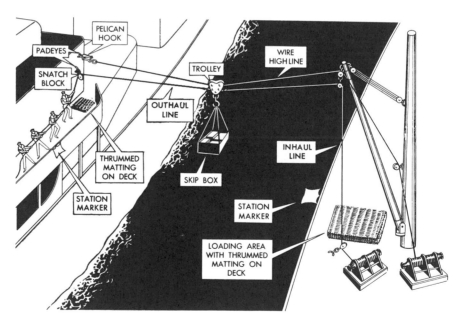

Figure 10-8. *Wire highline rig with manila outhaul.*

Preparations for nonwire highline transfer are essentially the same as for a wire highline. No boom is necessary on the delivery ship; a 12-inch snatch block (14-inch block for a 5-inch highline) attached to a pad eye at the delivering station is sufficient. The highline is rove through this block and any other blocks needed to provide a fairlead. It is tensioned and kept taut during transfers either by 25 to 50 men or by a capstan. A capstan, however, may not be used when personnel are transferred. The trolley which rides the highline is moved by hand-heaved inhaul and outhaul lines.

Although horizontal personnel transfer was until fairly recently permitted only with a manila highline, spun polyester (Dacron) line is now

Figure 10-9. Manila highline transfer in the boatswain's chair.

an acceptable replacement. It should be stressed, though, that with both the manila or spun polyester highline *all lines must be tended by hand*. Tending lines by hand, with a sufficient number of men standing by for an emergency, is the only means by which proper measures can be taken against highlines parting as a result of the sudden strains caused by rolling ships. It is because of this requirement that spun polyester or manila is always prescribed instead of wire; wire cannot be adequately or safely tended by hand.

Normally, personnel are transferred in a transfer chair as shown in figure 10–9. Persons unable to sit up may be transferred in an especially equipped Stokes litter.

During personnel transfer, safety is the primary consideration, and the following precautions must be taken:

  • Highlines that have been tended from a gypsy head or capstan must not be used for personnel transfer.
  • Personnel being transferred in the chair must wear orange-colored, inherently buoyant lifejackets.
  • They must be instructed on how to release the safety belt and get out of the chair if they fall into the water.

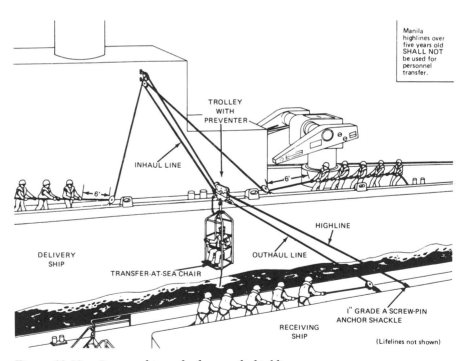

Figure 10-10. *Personnel transfer by manila highline.*

Missile Cargo STREAM Method

STREAM is an acronym for *Standard Tensioned Replenishment Alongside Method.* When using this method, cargo is transferred between ships by a trolley that rides on a constant-tensioned wire highline. The primary difference between this method and that used with a basic wire highline rig concerns the tensioning of the highline itself. As will be shown, the STREAM highline tension is not affected by the ships' motion and can allow ship separation up to approximately 300 feet.

Figure 10–12 shows a basic STREAM rig consisting of three winches, ram tensioner, highline, outhaul, inhaul, and trolley. The trolley block is moved between ships by varying tension on the inhaul and outhaul lines, which are on separate winches.

Attachment Points and the Cargo Drop Reel

There are several STREAM rigs that can be used, depending on the product being transferred, attachment points available, and equipment available in both the delivery ship and the receiving ship. All of the rigs, however, use a wire highline. It is pulled over to the receiving ship and then connected to an attachment point with a pelican hook.

Two common receiving-ship attachment points are the *sliding pad eye* and the *fixed pad eye.* A sliding pad eye is powered to move up and down in a guide track that may be permanently mounted on a king post or a bulkhead. The pad eye is lowered to a point near the deck and attached to the highline and then raised to the top for cargo transfer. When goods are received, the pad eye is lowered to the deck for unloading.

When the highline is attached to a fixed pad eye, it is kept at a single point above the receiving ship's load landing area. To lower the cargo brought over on the highline, a *cargo drop reel* (CDR) normally is used. (Although less desirable, tension/detension may be used to lower the load; that is, the delivery ship slackens the highline to set the load on deck.) Although the CDR does not provide the same degree of load control as the sliding pad eye, it does allow the load to be lowered under the control of the receiving ship. Two models are presently in use—the MK I CDR with a 4,000-pound capacity and the MK II CDR with a 5,700-pound capacity.

The Ram Tensioner

To keep a cargo load out of the water during ship-to-ship transfer with a conventional wire highline rig, and to keep the span wire (highline) from parting as the ship rolls from side-to-side, a highly trained, constantly alert winch operator is required. With a STREAM

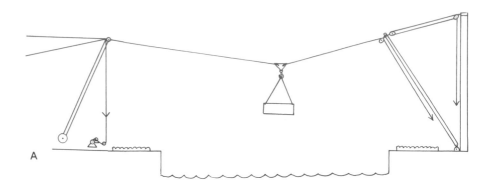

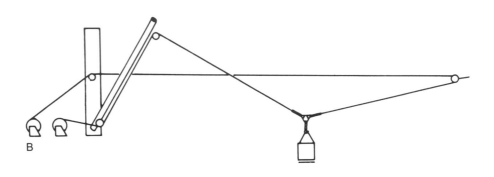

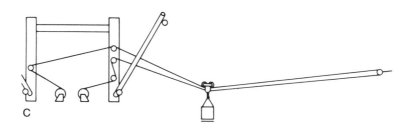

Figure 10-11.   A. Burton cargo rig; B. Basic housefall rig; C. Modified housefall rig; D. Manila highline rig; E. Wire highline rig; F. Missile/cargo STREAM rig.

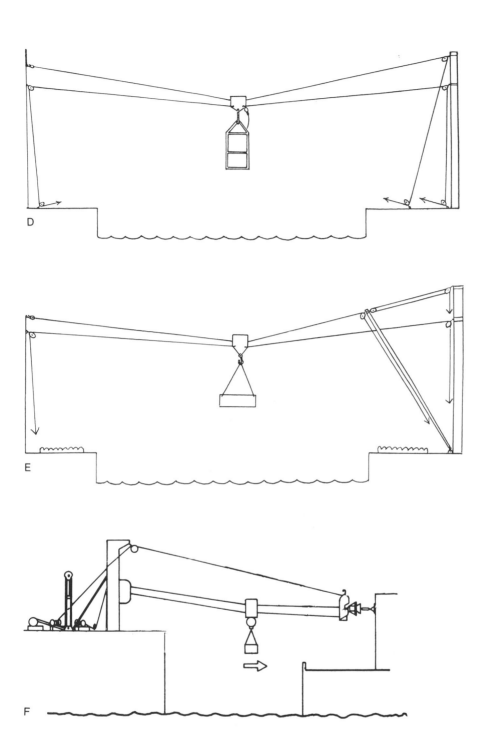

D

E

F

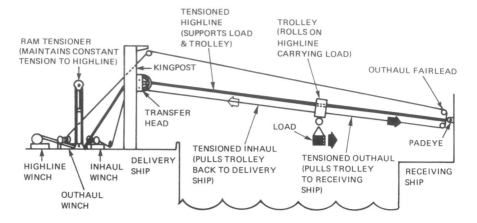

Figure 10-12. Missile/cargo STREAM rig.

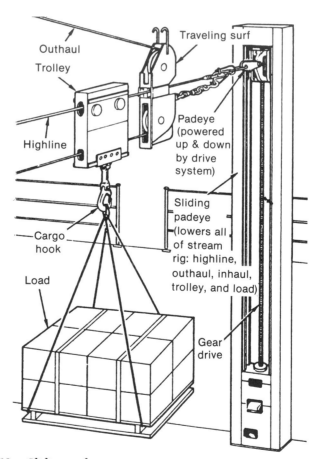

Figure 10-13. Sliding pad eye.

316   Seamanship

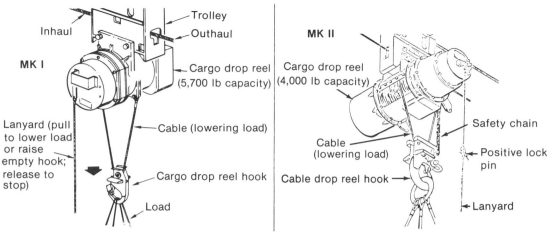

Figure 10-14. Cargo drop reel.

rig, however, much of the winch operator's job is done for him by a device designed to compensate automatically for the slackening and tensioning of the span wire due to the roll of the ship and the loading and unloading of heavy cargo on the trolley.* This device is the hydraulic *ram tensioner*. It consists of a ram cylinder, accumulator cylinder, air flasks, and an indicator assembly.

To make use of the ram tensioner, the highline or span wire is fairled from the boom or king post to blocks mounted on the ram and the ram cylinder and then to the winch. Air from the flasks maintains pressure on a piston in the accumulator cylinder, and this pressure is transmitted by means of oil to the ram. Thus, as the tension in the span wire is relaxed, lessening pressure in the system allows the ram to extend, taking up the slack in the span wire. Conversely, when tension increases and the ram is pushed back down, air is forced back into the flasks. A small wire cable transmits ram motion to the indicator assembly, and the ram's position is shown by a needle swinging across an indicator dial. One pound of air pressure on the accumulator causes about 10 pounds of line pull on the span wire. Thus, 900 psi in the air flasks maintains a tension of about 9,000 pounds on the span wire.

The Traveling SURF and STAR Latch Assembly

There are two means of running or fairleading the STREAM outhaul to the receiving ship. One means is the use of a Concord block; the other is the use of a standard UNREP receiving fixture (SURF). The Concord block can be used by ships having a burton winch and the capability to handle a burton whip. Since the highline and outhaul are

---

*Large variations require adjustments by the highline winch operator.

Figure 10-15. Missile/cargo STREAM. Cargo drop reel delivery to fixed pad eye.

transferred simultaneously with a Concord block, the rig is too heavy to be hauled in manually.

The use of a SURF is somewhat more common and has been made simpler with the addition, to many rigs, of a STAR (Traveling SURF-Actuated Remotely) latch assembly. The *Traveling SURF block*, with the outhaul reeved through and the *STAR latch assembly* bolted on, is hauled along the already tensioned highline to the receiving station by

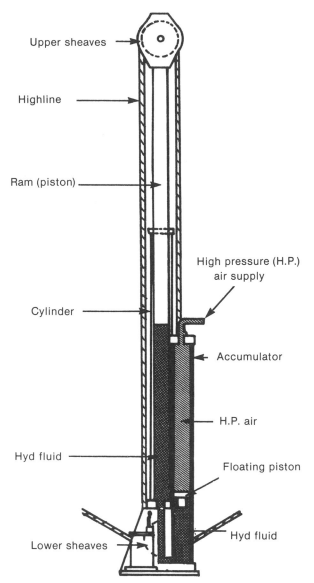

Upper sheaves

Highline

Ram (piston)

High pressure (H.P.) air supply

Cylinder

Accumulator

H.P. air

Hyd fluid

Floating piston

Lower sheaves

Hyd fluid

Figure 10-16.   Ram tensioner cross section.

messenger. (See figure 10–19.) The STAR latch assembly slides over the highline probe fitting, and the latches (inside the STAR latch assembly) strike the probe. As they come into contact with the probe head, the latches momentarily tilt open and then snap closed after they have passed the head of the probe. This indicates that the STAR rig is latched onto the probe. (To unlatch the STAR latching assembly, a strain is taken on the messenger releasing line until the latches tilt

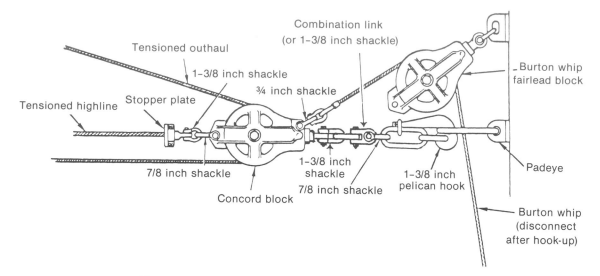

Figure 10-17. STREAM with Concord block.

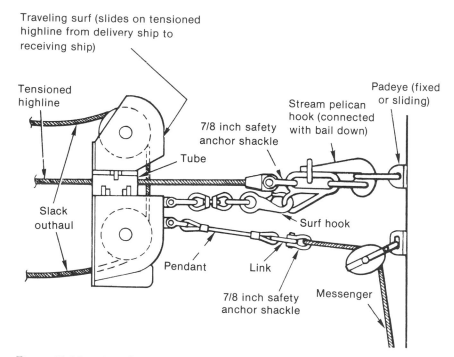

Figure 10-18. Traveling SURF hooked up to a fixed or sliding pad eye.

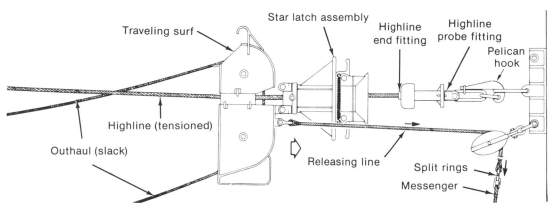

Figure 10-19. STREAM with messenger-rigged STAR hauled into receiving station.

open, indicating they are unlatched.) Next, the receiving ship slacks the messenger, the delivery ship tensions the outhaul, and the rig is ready for cargo transfer via the trolley.

Cargo is loaded on the trolley at the delivery station. A transfer head slides up and down on a track (like a sliding pad eye) inside the delivery ship's STREAM king post (or M-frame) to make the trolley more accessible. The transfer head contains the sheaves system for the highline and the inhaul wire. The outhaul block usually is mounted on the king post.

Each STREAM station is equipped with two electrohydraulic hauling winches: the inhaul winch and the outhaul winch. Each is equipped with a tension-sensing mechanism that causes the winch to heave in or pay out. The trolley and its load moves in the direction of the winch applying the most tension. STREAM, then, with constant tensioned inhaul, outhaul, and highline, provides positive control of the trolley and at the same time compensates for a ship's rolling motion to prevent tightlining and overstressing of the rig.

Standard UNREP Machinery

In order to reduce logistic and design problems and to simplify UNREP machinery maintenance and operation, the Navy is attempting to standardize the underway replenishment equipment used throughout the fleet. A long-range program has begun to develop improvements in all UNREP rigs and to install these improvements in virtually every replenishment ship now in service. All future ships constructed will receive the improved equipment. These improvements include the installation of highline antislack devices, standardized winches and ram tensioners, and the development of a standard, enclosed, UNREP rig-control station.

Vertical Replenishment

In vertical replenishment (VERTREP), helicopters are used to transport cargo and personnel from one ship to another. It augments or, in some cases, replaces connected replenishment. When conducted simultaneously with connected replenishment, VERTREP reduces the time normally required to replenish a force, reduces the time that screening ships are off station, and enhances the replenishment of dispersed units.

For small-scale replenishments VERTREP eliminates the approach, hookup, and disconnect time required in alongside transfers. It can be conducted with receiving ships steaming over the horizon in an ASW screen, while ships fire gunfire support missions, or even with ships at anchor.

While the VERTREP transfer rate is normally less than that for alongside RAS, by using two helicopters transfer rates of up to 180 short tons per hour can be achieved, depending on the type of receiving ship.

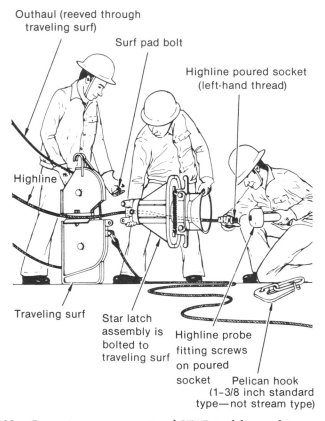

Figure 10-20. Preparing messenger-rigged STAR in delivery ship.

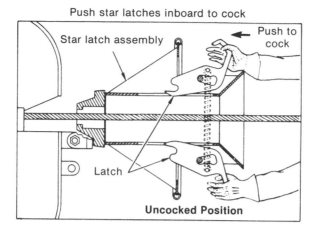

Star latch assembly

Push to cock

Latch

Uncocked Position

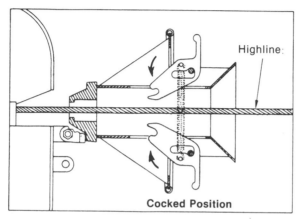

Highline

Cocked Position

Figure 10-21. How to cock STAR latches.

The bulk of this cargo is transported in nylon cargo nets by placing a loaded pallet on the center of the net and drawing the net up around the load. Nets used for VERTREP are made of 1½-inch nylon webbing with an overall size of 12 by 12 or 14 by 14 feet.

Delivery Ship Preparations and Procedures

VERTREP can commence within an hour after the order is given. Usually, however, one to three days before the scheduled day, the delivery ship begins to break out, strike up, sort, and palletize cargo to be transferred. With the exception of chilled and frozen items, as much material as possible is assembled into loads and staged near the VER-TREP area. Cargo is staged by destination and type within the specified area so as to be accessible to the hovering helicopter. It is important that like cargo be transferred load after load so that strike-down

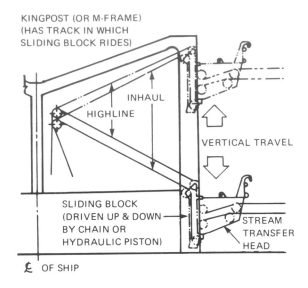

KINGPOST (OR M-FRAME)
(HAS TRACK IN WHICH
SLIDING BLOCK RIDES)

INHAUL

HIGHLINE

VERTICAL TRAVEL

SLIDING BLOCK
(DRIVEN UP & DOWN
BY CHAIN OR
HYDRAULIC PISTON)

STREAM
TRANSFER
HEAD

℄ OF SHIP

Figure 10-22. STREAM transfer head and track.

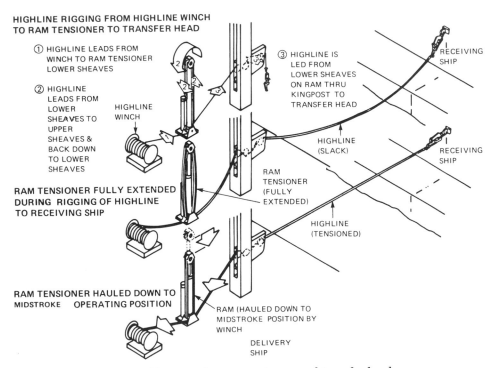

HIGHLINE RIGGING FROM HIGHLINE WINCH
TO RAM TENSIONER TO TRANSFER HEAD

① HIGHLINE LEADS FROM
WINCH TO RAM TENSIONER
LOWER SHEAVES

② HIGHLINE
LEADS FROM
LOWER
SHEAVES TO
UPPER
SHEAVES &
BACK DOWN
TO LOWER
SHEAVES

HIGHLINE
WINCH

③ HIGHLINE IS
LED FROM
LOWER SHEAVES
ON RAM THRU
KINGPOST TO
TRANSFER
HEAD

RECEIVING
SHIP

RECEIVING
SHIP

HIGHLINE
(SLACK)

RAM TENSIONER FULLY EXTENDED
DURING RIGGING OF HIGHLINE
TO RECEIVING SHIP

RAM
TENSIONER
(FULLY
EXTENDED)

HIGHLINE
(TENSIONED)

RAM TENSIONER HAULED DOWN TO
MIDSTROKE   OPERATING POSITION

RAM (HAULED DOWN TO
MIDSTROKE POSITION BY
WINCH

DELIVERY
SHIP

Figure 10-23.   Highline winch, ram tensioner, and transfer head.

324   Seamanship

crews on the receiving ships need not be shifted back and forth. Usually, chilled and frozen cargo is broken out last and transferred first.

Pallets and nets should be loaded as heavily as safety permits. Small and lightweight articles should be placed on top of heavier items and covered with tarps or otherwise secured to keep them from blowing away. All palletized loads should be strapped or banded as tightly as possible.

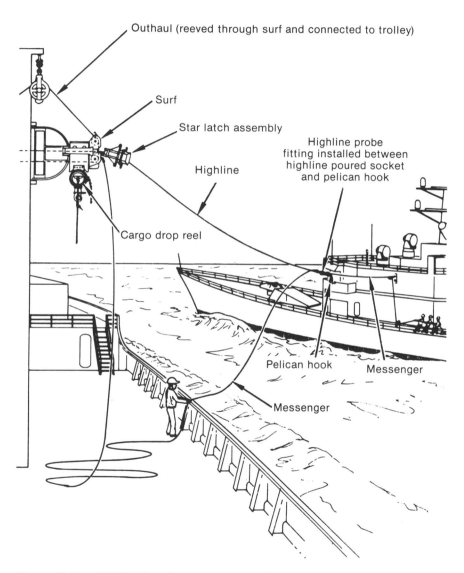

Figure 10-24. *STREAM with messenger-rigged STAR, passing the rig.*

Each load should be marked with its weight and destination. Because the most efficient load for helicopters presently being used for VERTREP is around 3,000 pounds, light loads should be stacked together and paired for delivery. As each load is picked up, its destination and weight are displayed on a hand-held blackboard from a position clearly visible to the pilot. Voice radio may be used as an alternate method of communicating such information, but especially during daylight hours, radio transmissions should be kept to a minimum.

When the helicopter nears the delivery ship cargo-staging area, its approach is announced over the 1MC. All hands clear the landing and pickup zone, except a hookup man, who takes a position alongside the load and holds up the pole (reach tube) of the hoisting sling pendant to show the location of the load to the pilot. Guided by hand or flag signals from the landing signalman and by instructions from a helicopter crewman, the pilot maneuvers the helicopter over the load. As the helicopter hovers there, the hookup man slips the loop of the pendant over the cargo hook. Then he clears the area directly under the helicopter, and the aircraft departs with its load.

Figure 10-25. Fourth generation highline winch with mechanical controls.

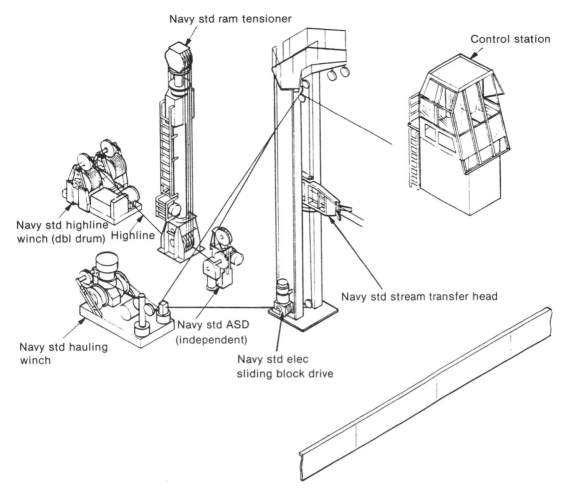

Navy std ram tensioner

Control station

Navy std highline
winch (dbl drum) Highline

Navy std stream transfer head

Navy std hauling
winch

Navy std ASD
(independent)

Navy std elec
sliding block drive

Figure 10-26. A standardized missile/cargo STREAM station.

Receiving Ship Preparations and Procedures

Vertical replenishment preparations on the receiving ship include the following actions:

• Clear the cargo-handling area of obstructions; cover and pad any fixed fittings; train gun mounts on the beam and depress the guns; unstep flagstaffs.

• Clear the VERTREP area of all loose gear such as trash cans, hats, loose clothing, empty boxes, sheet metal, and plywood. Sweep down to ensure that all small objects are removed. *Warning*: The powerful rotor wash of the helicopter can pick up a loose object and hurl it with sufficient force to injure a man or the aircraft.

• Ensure that the crash and rescue detail is on station with all required gear.

• Batten down all hatches in the area to keep burning fuel from pouring below should the helicopter crash.

• Man and equip the lifeboat for aircrew rescue.

• Station a signalman to direct the helicopter. Signal flags for him are optional.

• Ensure that all hands required to work in or near the VERTREP area are wearing goggles, lifejackets, and ear protectors.

Figure 10-27. Vertical replenishment by helicopter.

During the approach to the customer ship, the pilot lines up on the flight deck's VERTREP approach lines and flies high enough to keep the load from dragging on the deck. Guided by the landing signalman, but at the same time flying so that any obstruction can be seen and avoided, the pilot maneuvers the helicopter over the ship. Once over the drop zone, the pilot follows a crew member's directions to position the load over the landing spot. As soon as the load is on deck, the crew member informs the pilot and releases the cargo hook on signal or when the pendant slackens.

As soon as the helicopter departs, cargo handlers clear the area of cargo. If no pallet trucks are available or they cannot be used, assigned personnel release the pendant hooks, open the net or cargo wraparound, and cut bands or unbuckle straps. Other personnel then move in and carry boxes from the zone. The last of them removes the pendant, empty pallet, and loose debris from the drop zone and places them in a staging area. Pallets are stacked and nets are folded to be returned later.

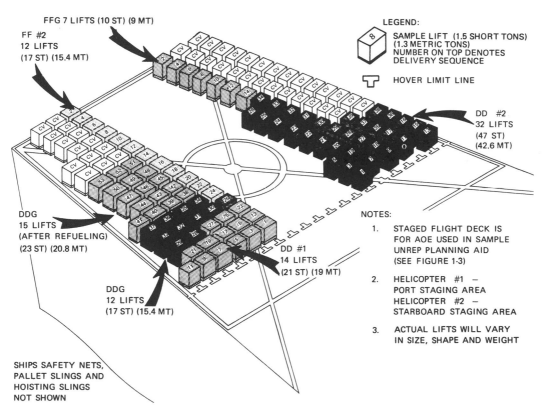

Figure 10-28. Typical VERTREP cargo staging.

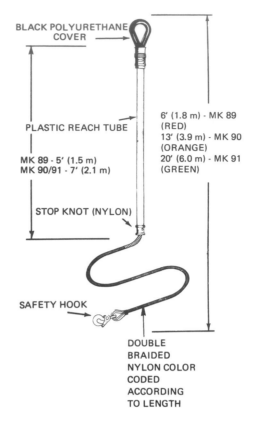

BLACK POLYURETHANE COVER

PLASTIC REACH TUBE

MK 89 - 5' (1.5 m)
MK 90/91 - 7' (2.1 m)

6' (1.8 m) - MK 89 (RED)
13' (3.9 m) - MK 90 (ORANGE)
20' (6.0 m) - MK 91 (GREEN)

STOP KNOT (NYLON)

SAFETY HOOK

DOUBLE BRAIDED NYLON COLOR CODED ACCORDING TO LENGTH

Note

SAFE WORKING LOAD
4,000 POUNDS (1,814 KG)

Figure 10-29. Hoisting sling Mk 89, 90, or 91.

Ship Maneuvering for VERTREP

For best flight characteristics during VERTREP, a helicopter takes off, approaches, and hovers into the relative wind. High relative wind reduces the power required for a helicopter to conduct such maneuvers, especially hovering. Thus, the main task of the OOD during VERTREP is to keep the ship in a favorable position relative to the wind. A relative wind of 15 to 30 knots from 30° on either bow is optimum, but other similar winds are acceptable, depending on various conditions. Downwind helicopter approaches and departures with an external load are dangerous and should be avoided if possible.

On the receiving ship, the landing signalman is stationed at the landing area to assist the pilot in positioning the load for release. The executive officer directs the overall operation on the receiving ship, usually from the after part of the bridge.

During transfer operations, the receiving ship hoists the flag signal Hotel One (meanings are as indicated).

Signal Position	*Meaning*
At the dip	Am preparing to receive helicopter transfer
Close up	Helicopter may close now
Hauled down	Transfer completed

When a ship is not ready to receive the helicopter (even though Hl may be closed up), she displays a red flag (or light) in the landing area; otherwise, she shows a green flag (or light). Similarly, colored wands

Figure 10-30. Hand signals to helicopter pilot (use of flags is optional); amber wands are used at night.

A MINIMUM OF
FOUR WOOD OR
SIX METAL PALLETS
WITH FOLDED NETS
ON TOP IS REQUIRED
IN ORDER TO PROVIDE
SUFFICIENT WEIGHT FOR
LOAD FLIGHT STABILITY.

NETS AND PALLETS

Figure 10-31. Preparation of nets and pallets for return to the UNREP ship.

are waved in overhead circles at night. A flag or numeral following Hl indicates the type of helicopter transfer being accomplished; for example; Hl-M for mail, or Hl-P for personnel.

As indicated earlier, VERTREP can be conducted with widely dispersed receiving ships. The ideal VERTREP formation or ship stationing, however, is for receiving units to be positioned within 1,000 yards of the delivery ship. This enables helicopters to transfer cargo more efficiently, since they can deliver to a number of ships with less flying time. Another advantage to this procedure is that it avoids delays resulting from a ship's failure to quickly clear her flight deck of previously received VERTREP cargo. With a number of ships close at hand, VERTREP helicopters can establish a delivery sequence that allows each ship sufficient time to have cargo handlers clear the drop area.

Night VERTREP

Although night VERTREP procedures are essentially the same as those conducted during the day, not all ships are certified to conduct night operations, except in emergencies. The final decision to conduct night VERTREP, even for certified ships, is left to the pilot.

Night cargo pickup and delivery require increased care and precision, and a wider flight pattern under low visibility conditions. Delivery rates, therefore, are lower than they are during daylight. Other limiting factors are that the pilot's depth perception and visual reference are reduced, and crew fatigue is increased because of the extra vigilance required and the constant transition between visual flight and instrument flight.

At night the landing signalman uses amber wands to direct the helicopter. The hookup man uses a green wand to show the point of pickup, or he may tape a one-cell flashlight to the top of his helmet. This procedure leaves both of his hands free to hook up the loads and makes it less likely that he will drop the light and lose it among the loads.

Information on the weight and destination of loads is transmitted to the pilot by radio, but no transmissions should be made to him by outside sources while he is hovering over the ship. Such transmissions will interfere with directions from his aircrewman at the cargo hatch.

During night VERTREP, only the shortest hoisting sling pendants should be used to hook loads to the helicopter's cargo hook. Using only pendants of one length makes it easier for the pilot to use the same reference points for hovering while he picks up or drops successive loads. The shortest pendants are preferable, because it is more difficult to hover at the higher altitudes required with the longer pendants.

Figure 10-32. Simultaneous VERTREP and connected replenishment.

Deck Seamanship—Cargo and Personnel Transfer   **333**

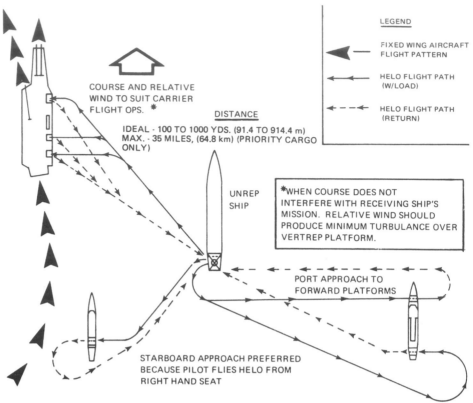

LEGEND

◄─── FIXED WING AIRCRAFT
FLIGHT PATTERN

◄─── HELO FLIGHT PATH
(W/LOAD)

◄─ ─ ─◄ HELO FLIGHT PATH
(RETURN)

COURSE AND RELATIVE
WIND TO SUIT CARRIER
FLIGHT OPS. **∗**

DISTANCE

IDEAL - 100 TO 1000 YDS. (91.4 TO 914.4 m)
MAX. - 35 MILES, (64.8 km) (PRIORITY CARGO
ONLY)

UNREP
SHIP

∗WHEN COURSE DOES NOT
INTERFERE WITH RECEIVING SHIP'S
MISSION. RELATIVE WIND SHOULD
PRODUCE MINIMUM TURBULANCE OVER
VERTREP PLATFORM.

PORT APPROACH TO
FORWARD PLATFORMS

STARBOARD APPROACH PREFERRED
BECAUSE PILOT FLIES HELO FROM
RIGHT HAND SEAT

Figure 10-33. Typical ship stations for VERTREP.

VERTREP Safety

Preparation, organization, and the observance of all pertinent safety practices are, of course, essential to all shipboard evolutions. However, many nonaviation ships involved with helicopter operations are not fully aware of hazards peculiar to VERTREP operations. The rotor wash of a hovering helicopter, for example, can pick up all loose objects, including a 40- by 48-inch wooden pallet, in the vicinity of the drop area and turn them into dangerous, even lethal, missiles. All personnel involved in VERTREP, therefore, must be thoroughly indoctrinated in safety procedures.

The following precautions are among those that must be observed:

• The helicopter hookup person must wear a lifejacket and helmet with chin strap, goggles, and eye and ear protection. Loose articles of clothing should not be worn.

• All personnel in the vicinity of the helicopter must remove their hats while the rotors are turning.

• Personnel must be instructed concerning the shrapnel effect caused when rotor blades strike a solid object and shatter. Spectators

Figure 10-34. Maneuvering for flight quarters.

must be kept clear of the pickup or delivery area while VERTREP is in progress.

    • Men on deck must not attempt to steady loads swinging under a helicopter.

    • Communications on the VERTREP radio net should be kept to a minimum to prevent pilot distraction.

    • Never attach a helicopter's hoist to the ship.

Summary

Cargo on replenishment ships is fleet-issue-loaded for quick, easy access and handling for underway transfer. A number of rigs may be used to carry out this transfer. The rig to be used for a particular replenishment operation should be selected after taking into account the type and quantity of cargo to be transferred, the type and location of the receiving station, weather and sea conditions at the time of transfer, and several other factors.

Vertical replenishment provides a capability for augmenting and enhancing alongside replenishment and also permits increased flexibility and considerable latitude in replenishment, particularly regarding time and location of the UNREP operation. As with all UNREP operations, though, safety is the primary consideration.

11

Deck Seamanship—Refueling at Sea

Introduction

A U.S. Navy ship at sea is supplied with fuel by means of hoses suspended between itself and a delivery ship. During the fuel transfer, lubricating oil (in drums), industrial gases (in metal bottles), water, personnel, and cargo may also be transferred. This chapter details the methods and rigs used for transferring fuel between ships of the U.S. Navy. Some deviations in procedures and equipment may be demanded by design features or circumstances peculiar to a specific ship; however, such alterations should be kept to a minimum. If questions arise, the weapons officer or first lieutenant should consult NWP-14.

Fueling Preparations

Fleet auxiliary ships with a primary refueling-at-sea mission generally rig six to seven replenishment stations to deliver petroleum products. Oilers usually are rigged for fueling large ships to port and destroyers to starboard. If necessary, however, they can replenish almost any type of ship from either side. CVs, LHAs, and LPHs, though, are always fueled to port.

Most ships have a number of large fuel tanks. As fuel is consumed, ships may ballast these tanks with seawater or redistribute their fuel load in order to maintain their stability and liquid-protection characteristics. Prior to each replenishment, therefore, it normally is necessary for a ship to deballast tanks or shift some fuel so that additional petroleum products may be taken on board.

A number of fuel-hose fittings or couplings may be used by U.S. Navy ships, and all require some degree of preparation. Fuel transfer methods employed by Navy ships also require that rigs be set up by a ship's deck division personnel prior to going alongside. The general UNREP preparations discussed in chapter 9 are, of course, made before any connected replenishment.

Fueling-at-Sea Couplings

A variety of fueling-at-sea couplings are required to provide increased compatibility among the Navy's several different fueling rigs.

The various couplings that may be found in use today are described in the following paragraphs.

Single-Probe Coupling

The single-probe fueling coupling consists of a delivery ship fueling probe and a receiving ship receiver as shown in figure 11–1. The probe itself was inspired and modeled after that used to refuel aircraft in flight. The probe is mounted on a metal tube and trolley-block assembly which connects directly to a fuel hose. The trolley-block assembly is hinged (like a snatch block) so that it can be attached to a span wire without disassembling the parts. This trolley-block assembly rides on the span wire and supports the probe as it travels from the delivery ship to the receiver on the ship being refueled.

The probe has a built-in sliding sleeve valve which opens on proper engagement with the probe receiver and automatically closes upon disengagement. A latching mechanism in the probe holds it in the receiver during fuel transfer and works to prevent the probe from accidently being dislodged. It takes a pull of nearly 2,500 pounds to forcibly unseat the probe once it has engaged.

The coupling's funnel-shaped probe receiver is supported by a swivel fitting mounted on the receiving ship. [A 7-inch-diameter rubber hose (wire-reinforced) connects the receiver to a fuel riser leading into the ship's tanks.] A pelican hook, used as the attachment point for the span wire, is an integral part of the swivel fitting. Since the receiver is mounted on the swivel fitting, it is kept directly in line with the span wire and with the probe. This arrangement provides excellent align-

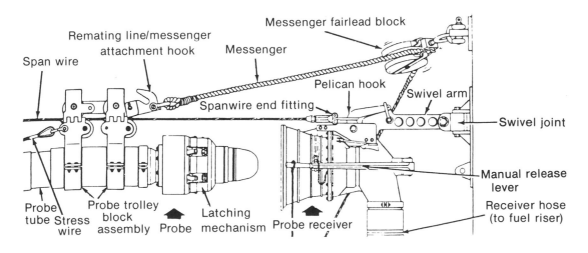

Figure 11-1. Single probe and receiver.

Figure 11-2. Rigging the fuel probe connection.

ment during connect-up of the probe and the receiver and attempts to maintain the alignment regardless of the relative positions of the ships.

As the probe engages, visual indicators mounted on either side of the receiver rise to the vertical, then drop back to a position approximately 30 degrees above the horizontal. These flags or *rabbit ears*, as they are commonly called, indicate when the probe is properly seated. The usual way to disengage the probe after completion of fueling is to pull on the manual release lever mounted on the side of the receiver.

Double-Probe Coupling

The double-probe coupling consists of a double fueling probe and a double receiver as shown in figure 11–3. The probes and receivers are identical to, and interchangeable with, those used in a single-probe coupling. The only significant difference is the double-probe coupling's lower attachment point location for the receiving ship's inhaul messenger, the line with which the probes are pulled to the receivers. One of the primary advantages to this coupling is that it allows two different types of fuel to be sent simultaneously to a single replenishment station on the receiving ship. The different fuels are, of course, routed to separate tanks by the receivers.

Combined Quick-Release Coupling and Valve

The *combined quick-release (Robb) coupling* and valve (figure 11-5) consists of a female and a male end. The male end, rigged on the receiving ship, is a slightly tapered tube with a flange at one end. Near the other end is a machined groove (1). A spring-tensioned ball race (2) in the female end lines up with the groove, and a spring-tensioned sleeve (3) on the outside forces the balls down into the groove, holding the two ends together. When the sleeve is forced back by hand or, as usually is necessary, by pry bars, tension on the ball race is released and the male end can be withdrawn. Slots (4) are cut into the sleeve to permit the insertion of pry bars between the sleeve and end ring (5).

A valve located in the female end (6) is normally closed and held in place by a heavy spring (7). A gasket (8) ensures a tight seal. Another gasket (9) provides a tight joint when the two ends are joined. A ring-shaped actuating cam (10) in the male end is linked to an operating

Figure 11-3. A close look at a probe receiver.

lever (11). When the lever is turned to the OPEN position, the cam is thrust forward, opening the valve (12).

Both 6-inch and 7-inch adapters (13 and 14) are available for the female end. Therefore, the coupling can be used with either size of hose.

Despite the name, the Robb coupling does not qualify as a quick-release device, because uncoupling is virtually impossible when the fitting is under strain. For this reason, any strain must be taken by the riding line, and to connect or disconnect, the ends must be lined up perfectly. To provide for emergency breakaway, a breakable spool is inserted between the receiving ship's manifold and the male end.

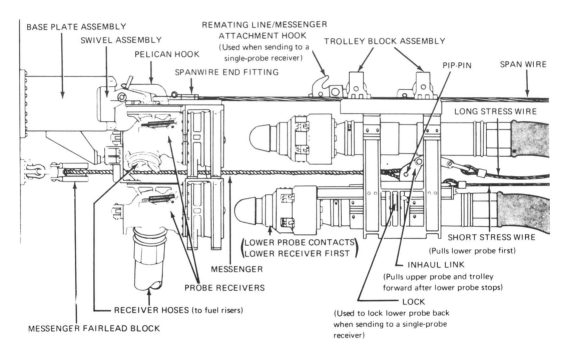

Figure 11-4. Double probe and receiver.

Breakable-Spool Quick-Release Coupling

The *breakable-spool quick-release coupling* (figure 11-7) is used in fueling operations with NATO and MSC ships that are not equipped with a probe receiver. It is also used with the Robb coupling. It consists of an A-end and a B-end. The A-end, rigged on the receiving ship, is a cast-iron spool with a standard hose flange on one end and a slotted flange on the other. It is weakened by a groove machined around the spool. This groove is easily broken in an emergency by a blow from a sledge hammer.

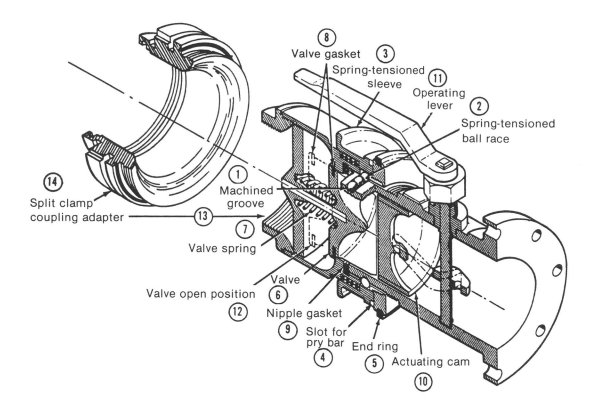

Figure 11-5. Inside the Robb coupling.

The B-end is a similar spool with a standard hose flange on one end and a special floating-ring flange with drop bolts on the other. The floating-ring flange can be rotated to bring the drop bolts quickly in line with the slots in the A-end. A gasket mounted in the outboard end of the B-end ensures an oiltight fit. A blank flange is attached to the B-end when the hose is being passed to prevent oil from spilling and water from entering the hose.

Trunk Refueling Connection

Neither probe nor quick-release couplings can be used on a few old ships still in service. The ship receiving fuel merely has an open trunk on deck leading to the fuel tanks. In that instance, the delivery ship sends over the standard hose without a coupling, substituting a soft rubber hose called a *pig tail* on the end of the hose to facilitate directing the fuel into the trunk. When the hose is lashed in place, the receiving ship signals the delivering ship to begin pumping.

Fueling at Sea Transfer Methods

Replenishment ships normally can conduct fueling at sea using more than one transfer method. Their choice of method is governed primarily by the type of ship to which they are delivering and the conditions under which replenishment takes place. The methods used differ mainly in the way by which the fueling hose is extended or transferred to the receiving ship.

The Conventional Span-Wire Method

In the conventional span-wire method of fueling at sea, the fuel hose is carried between the delivery ship and receiving ship on a span wire. The hose hangs from trolley blocks that ride along the span wire. Saddle whips position the hose while fueling and serve to retrieve the hose after the fueling operation is completed.

The span-wire rig permits ships to open to 140 to 180 feet. Such distance is reasonably safe and makes it fairly easy to maneuver and keep station. These factors not only allow commanders a wider latitude in choosing a fueling course, but they also facilitate the use of antiaircraft batteries should the need for them arise. Additionally, the high suspension of the hose affords fair protection for it in rough weather.

Ordinarily, in the span-wire method, saddle whips and the retrieving line are of wire; but when the necessary winch drums are not available and winches with gypsy heads are available, 3½ inch, double-braided nylon line may be substituted for one or more of the whips. A

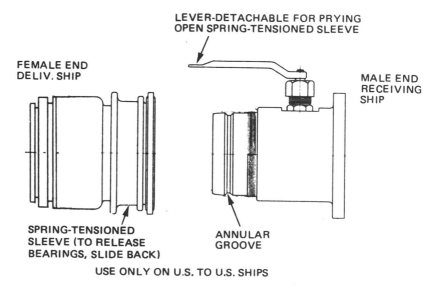

Figure 11-6. Combined quick-release (Robb) coupling valve.

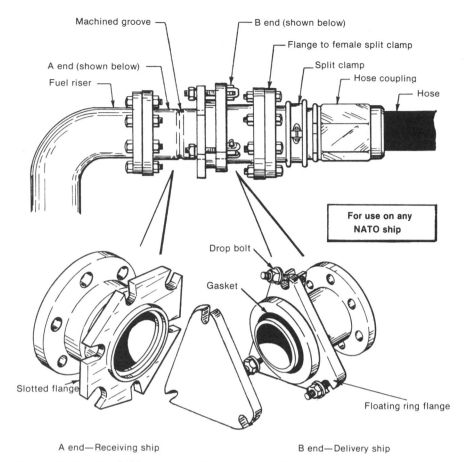

Machined groove

B end (shown below)

Flange to female split clamp

A end (shown below)

Split clamp

Fuel riser

Hose coupling

Hose

For use on any
NATO ship

Drop bolt

Gasket

Slotted flange

Floating ring flange

A end—Receiving ship

B end—Delivery ship

Figure 11-7. Breakable-spool, quick-release coupling.

wire rope retrieving whip is mandatory in double-probe rigs. Figure 11-8 illustrates a typical span-wire rig.

As the receiving ship completes her approach and steadies alongside, lines from line-throwing guns are sent over from each station on the oiler to corresponding stations on the receiving ship. By means of these lines, the messengers are hauled aboard. When a messenger reaches the receiving ship, it is secured to the line rove through the messenger snatch block.

The messenger is heaved in, and when the end of the span wire comes aboard, its pelican hook is secured to the receiving ship's pad eye. The oiler then begins to tension the span wire, and an easing-out line is rigged to the span wire by the receiving ship.

Next, the receiving ship continues heaving in on the hose messenger and when the end of the hose comes aboard, it is coupled to the fuel riser. When refueling has commenced, the messenger and the shot line are returned to the delivery ship.

When enough fuel has been received, the delivery ship is signaled to stop pumping. The delivery ship will then determine the need for blowdown of the fuel hose. In a *blowdown*, low-pressure air (approximately 80 psi) is injected into the fuel hose to remove excess oil. This final step of blowing excess oil into the receiving ship's tanks requires about three minutes to complete, and the receiving ship must not disconnect the FAS coupling or remove the pigtail from the fueling trunk until the blowdown is completed. Receiving ships must also leave valves and tank vents open during blowdown so that the oil and air may move through the hose.

A second method used by delivery ships to remove fuel from the hose is commonly referred to as a *back suction*. This term is misleading, as fuel is removed by gravity flow combined with a venturi effect. Delivery ships cannot reverse their large centrifugal pumps that run in one direction only. The delivery ship allows fuel to cycle through a line passing the hose piping manifold. As the fuel in this by-pass line flows to the fuel tanks, a slight suction is created at the piping manifold. This

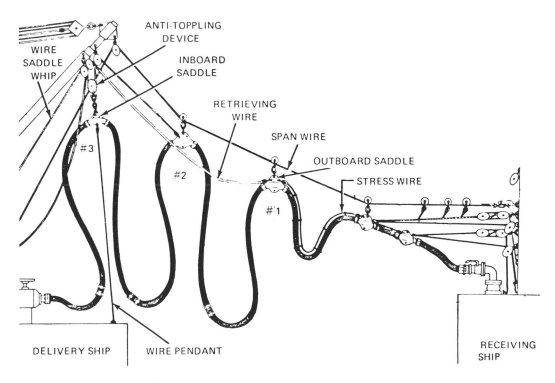

Figure 11-8. Conventional span-wire rig, single hose with Robb coupling.

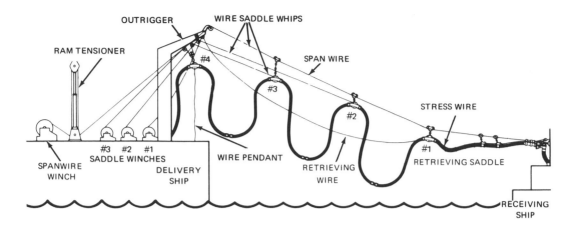

Figure 11-9. Fuel STREAM, single hose with probe.

method normally consumes considerably more time than the blow-down method.

Upon completion of the blowdown or back suction, the receiving ship disconnects the hose coupling and the oiler heaves in on the saddle whips. When the hose has been retrieved, the delivery ship slacks the span wire. The receiving ship then trips the span-wire pelican hook and eases the wire over the side with an easing-out line. The oiler recovers the span wire from the water and prepares for the next ship alongside.

The Fuel STREAM Method

With fuel STREAM (standard tensioned replenishment alongside method), the fuel hose is carried between two ships on a ram-tensioned span wire. As with the conventional span-wire rig, the hose is suspended from the span wire by trolley blocks. The fuel STREAM rig, however, allows ships to open out to a greater distance than is possible with other fueling rigs (200 feet), minimizes the possibility of tightlining and parting of the span wire, and provides for improved personnel safety.

The STREAM transfer procedures are essentially the same as those for the conventional span wire. As the receiving ship comes alongside, the delivery ship sends over the gun lines from each transfer station to the corresponding station on the receiving ship. Remember, however, that in all cases where a CV, LPH, LHA, or other ship with aircraft on deck is either the delivery ship or the receiving ship, she will send the lines. These lines are used to haul in the sta/sta phone line, the phone/distance line, and the messenger. Each line must be clearly marked to identify its function.

After detaching the phone line, etc., the receiving ship continues to heave in on the span wire and hose messenger. When the span wire comes on board, it is connected to the pelican hook on the probe receiver. (Most STREAM rigs have probe couplings, although other types may be employed.) The receiving ship then releases the hose messenger from the span wire and begins to heave in the hose and probe. At this point the delivery ship starts tensioning the span wire.

After the probe is engaged in the probe receiver, the receiving ship's remating line is attached to the probe, pumping begins, and the hose messenger is disconnected and returned to the delivery ship along with the shot line.

As can be seen, the STREAM rig also operates essentially like the conventional span-wire rig. The fact that the span wire is kept under a constant, ram-tension is the major difference between these transfer methods. Blowdown, back suction, and disconnect procedures are the same.

The Close-In Method

The close-in method of fueling is used when the delivery ship is not equipped with a span-wire rig or the receiving ship does not have a pad eye strong enough to hold a span wire.

In the close-in rig, the hose is supported by whips leading from the hose saddles to booms, king posts, or other high projections on the delivery ship. When the rig is used to fuel ships as large or larger than destroyers (which is rare), the outboard bight of hose also may be supported by an outer bight line (figure 11-10) leading from the outboard saddle to a high point on the receiving ship. The outer bight line is passed to the receiving ship by means of the hoseline messenger.

On the receiving ship, the same preparations are made as for receiving the span-wire rig except that an additional 12-or 14-inch snatch block must be shackled to a high, convenient, and adequately tested point above the point where the hose will come aboard. Such other blocks as are necessary to fairlead the bight line to a winch also must be rigged. A small pendant should be rove through this set of blocks to haul the outer bight line quickly through the blocks and to the winch. The outer bight line is used to help haul the hose to the receiving ship and, once the hose is secured, is tended in the same manner as are the saddle whips.

Ordinarily the close-in rig is used to refuel minesweepers and ships of similar size. This method of fuel transfer is done at a distance of approximately 60 to 80 feet.

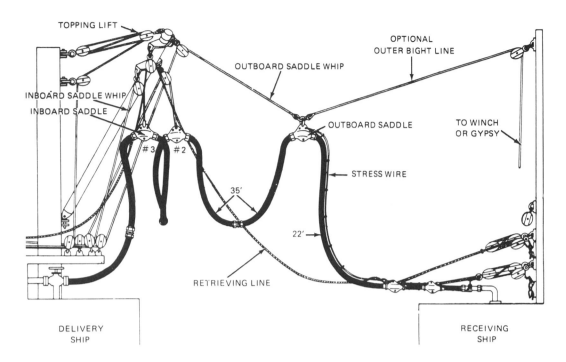

Figure 11-10. Close-in rig.

Table 11-1. Distance between Ships for Various Rigs.

Type of Replenishment Rig

Ship Type	Missile/ cargo STREAM*	Burton, housefall, modified housefall, wire highline, manila highline	Fuel STREAM**	Conventional span-wire fueling rig	Close-in fueling rig
DD types and smaller	80'–200' normal 300' max	80'–100' normal 180' max	80'–180' normal 200' max	80'–100' normal 180' max	60'–80'
Larger ships	80'–200' normal 300' max	80'–120' normal 200' max	80'–180' normal 200' max	80'–120' normal 200' max	
Carriers	100'–200' normal 300' max	100'–140' normal 200' max	80'–180' normal 200' max	100'–140' normal 200' max	

* Minimum separation of 140 feet required during tension/detension transfer method.
** 300-foot heavy-weather rig.

The Astern Fueling Method

The astern fueling method normally is not employed by ships of the U.S. Navy. Agreements between NATO nations, however, require that all escort-type vessels be capable of receiving fuel from designated merchant tankers by both the alongside and astern methods. Astern fueling has the advantages of simplicity and ruggedness of equipment and adaptability of the rig to all the different types of escort vessels. But the alongside method is superior in connecting up, passing fuel, and disconnecting the rig.

In the astern method of fueling, a single 6-inch hose rig is streamed astern of the delivery ship with a pickup buoy secured to it by a 310-foot messenger (of 1-inch double-braided nylon). On the port side of the tanker another small position buoy is deployed and towed about 400 feet astern. Some variations of this fueling astern equipment are used, but all have a close resemblance to the rig shown in figure 11-11.

To refuel, a receiving ship approaches the hose messenger pickup buoy from astern at three to four knots over Romeo speed. A grapnel is then heaved across the delivery ship's hose messenger to catch it and haul it on deck.

After the messenger and the refueling hose are pulled aboard, the hose is connected to the forward replenishment-station fuel riser using the NATO breakable spool coupling. As fueling begins, the receiving ship adjusts her position to the starboard quarter of the delivery vessel opposite the tanker's towed position buoy. By keeping station on the position buoy, the receiving ship is able to maintain a safe distance astern of the tanker.

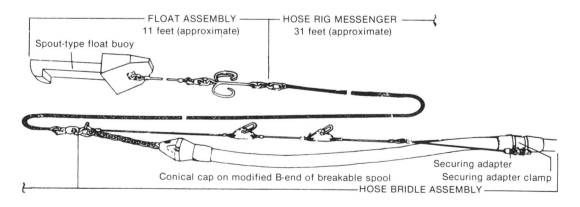

Figure 11-11. Float assembly, hose rig messenger, and hose bridle assembly details.

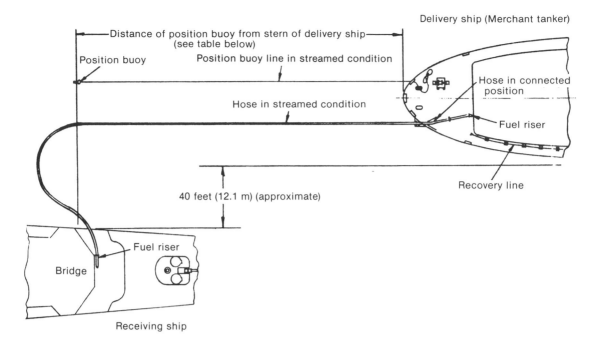

Distance of Position Buoy from Stern of Delivery Ship			
Fair Weather	NATO Vessels	480 feet	146.2m
	U.S. Destroyer Types	400 feet	121.9m
Foul Weather	NATO Vessels	690 feet	210.3m
	U.S. Destroyer Types	610 feet	185.9m

Figure 11-12. Typical astern fueling station keeping.

Upon completion of fueling, the hose is cleared of all remaining oil. This cleanout is accomplished from the delivery ship by propelling a polyurethane projectile, called a *pig*, through the hose with air pressure. The pig pushes out the remaining fuel and is itself caught and retained at the end of the hose in a strainer. The hose, the messenger, and the buoys are then pulled back to the tanker.

Astern fueling is carried out at speeds of 8 to 15 knots, with the best speed normally being 12 knots. In all cases, it is the responsibility of the tanker to maintain a steady course and speed as prescribed by the OTC.

Because no sound-powered telephone line is passed from the delivery ship to the receiving ship, all station-to-station communications during astern fueling are carried out by visual means. Colored flags are used to convey control signals during daylight; colored wands are used at night. These flag signals and their meanings are detailed in NWP-14.

Fueling at Sea Safety

Precautions normally taken to assure the safety of rigs and personnel during UNREP are, of course, stringently observed when fueling at sea. A few precautions directly associated with refueling are reviewed below.

- The smoking lamp is always out while refueling except in authorized areas.
- Receiving ships will not release a span wire prior to the delivery ship's retrieval of the fueling hose. Serious damage to the fueling coupling can result.
- Fuel rigs and hose pressures should be monitored continuously on the delivery ship to detect leakage instantly.
- Crew members must make every effort and take every precaution to prevent environmental damage resulting from spillage of petroleum products.

Summary

The need for working at close quarters during fueling at sea makes ship maneuvering a critical operation. In addition, the combustible and environmentally damaging nature of the product being transferred calls for considerable caution on the part of delivery and receiving ship crews.

The use of the various rigs and transfer methods available to replenish ships requiring fuel should be governed by a ship's design characteristics, the receiving ship's size and draft, rig availability, and existing weather and sea conditions. Detailed operating procedures and special ship requirements are furnished in NWP-14.

12

Shipboard Damage Control

Basic Damage Control

A ship's ability to accomplish its mission may someday depend on its crew's damage control capability and response. It has been said that 90 percent of the damage control needed to save a ship takes place before the ship is damaged and only 10 percent can be done after the damage has occurred. In spite of all precautions and preparations that are made before damage, the survival of the ship will often depend upon prompt and correct damage control measures after the damage occurs.

What is damage control? Damage control is the measures and techniques used to preserve and reestablish the watertight integrity, stability, or offensive power of a ship after damage from any source. The main objective of damage control is to maintain the maximum offensive power of the ship at all times. It is necessary, therefore, to train all shipboard personnel in damage control procedures.

Shipboard Damage Control Organization

The engineering officer is designated in the ship's organization as damage control officer. He is responsible for establishing and maintaining an effective damage control organization to minimize the effects of hull damage, fire, and flooding. He reports directly to the commanding officer concerning the readiness of the damage control organization and systems.

There are two types of damage control organizations. One is a vital function of the ship's engineering department, and the other is the damage control battle organization, which varies from ship to ship, depending on size, type, and mission.

Damage Control Assistant (DCA)

The damage control assistant works under, and reports to, the engineer officer. He is responsible for preventing and repairing damage, training the crew in damage control, and maintaining the machinery, drainage, and piping assigned to the organization.

The damage control assistant (DCA) is responsible specifically for:

a. The prevention and control of damage.

b. The training of the ship's personnel in damage control.

c. The operation, care, and maintenance of auxiliary machinery, piping, and drainage systems not assigned to other departments or divisions.

The damage control assistant's general quarters station is in damage control central (DCC), where he is the directing force of the damage control organization.

Heads of Department

As previously stated in chapter 1, the shipboard head of a department is the representative of the commanding officer in all matters that pertain to the department. He is responsible for maintaining his department in a maximum state of *battle readiness* at all times. He must keep the commanding officer and the executive officer advised concerning all casualties, deficiencies, and anticipated difficulties that may significantly affect the operational readiness of the ship. He must ensure that sections of the ship for which he is responsible are secured for sea before leaving port and ensure proper maintenance and repair of damage control machinery, equipage and equipment within his department.

Division Officers

The division officer's duties and responsibilities concerning damage control readiness cannot be overemphasized. As previously stated in chapter one, a division officer is an officer regularly assigned by the commanding officer to supervise a division in the ship's organization. Division officers are responsible to the department head and, in general, act as his assistants. The division officer must understand the mission of his ship, and at the same time he must concentrate on a great many specific details regarding his assigned division. Each division officer is charged with the responsibility for conducting periodic hull, safety-device, and damage control inspections for cleanliness, state of presentation, watertight integrity, and proper operation of safety and damage control equipment. *Even though specific officers are assigned various responsibilities in damage control shipboard readiness, the control of damage, either due to enemy action or accident, is an all-hands responsibility.*

Division Damage Control Petty Officers

On all ships, a qualified senior petty officer is assigned as the division's damage control petty officer (DCPO). This petty officer coordinates the relieving, qualifying, training, and duties of division damage control personnel as directed by the DCA. Division duty section leaders are designated as duty DCPOs outside normal working hours in port. Divisional DCPOs and duty DDCPOs normally serve three months. They are assigned to the DCA on a collateral basis and are assigned various duties in damage control administration and maintenance pertinent to their respective divisional spaces.

DCPOs and their duty counterparts specifically accomplish the following:

• Supervise all phases of the division's damage control fire fighting and precautionary procedures.

• Instruct division personnel in damage control, fire fighting, and nuclear-biological-chemical (NBC) warfare defense procedures.

• Maintain compartment checkoff lists and set specified damage control material conditions within their division spaces.

• Maintain portable carbon dioxide (CO_2) bottles, inspect and test damage control and fire fighting equipment and ensure that battle lanterns, dog wrenches, spanners, and other divisional damage control equipment are maintained and properly stowed.

• Inspect division spaces daily for fire hazards and cleanliness.

Damage Control Battle Organization

When the ship is at battle stations, reports from damage control units are coordinated by damage control central (DCC). Damage control central assesses the damage and decides which area is most in need of repairs. DCC also reports to, and receives direction from, the commanding officer concerning matters affecting buoyancy, list, trim, stability, watertight integrity, and NBC defensive measures. Damage control central is normally the battle station for the damage control assistant (DCA).

Damage control central uses a variety of administrative tools to monitor a casualty. These include:

• Charts and diagrams that show the subdivisions of the ship and its systems.

• A casualty board to visualize the damage sustained and the corrective action in progress from the on-the-scene repair party.

• A stability board to show liquid-loading, the location of flooding boundaries, the effect of list and trim, and the corrective action taken.

• A list of access routes for ready shelter, deep shelter, electronic casualty control, and battle dressing.

• Graphic displays to record corrective damage control and electrical systems.

• Deck plans to indicate areas contaminated by NBC agents, the location of battle-dressing stations and decontamination stations, and safe routes to them.

Repair Party Function and Organization

Repair parties are the DCA's representatives at the scene of the casualty or damage. They are the primary units in the damage control organization. Parties may be subdivided to let personnel cover a greater area more rapidly, and to prevent loss of the entire party from a single hit.

The number and ratings of men assigned to a repair party, as specified in the battle bill, are determined by: the location of the station, the size of the area assigned to that station, and the total number of men available for all stations.

Each repair party will usually have an officer or chief petty officer in charge, a scene leader to supervise all on-scene activities (he also functions as the assistant repair-party leader), a phone talker, and OBA men and messengers. Additional men assigned will include petty officers and nonrated men from various departments, such as electrician's mates (EMs), hull technicians (HTs), storekeepers (SKs), and hospital corpsmen (HMs).

Repair parties and teams are designated as follows:*

Repair 1: Main deck repair. Comprised of deck petty officers and nonrated men, storekeepers, radiomen (RMs), electrician's mates, hospital corpsmen, and aviation details (except on aircraft carriers). Engineering petty officers may also be required.

Repair 2: Forward repair. Comprised of petty officers of the deck and engineering branches, electrician's mates, storekeepers, hospital corpsmen, and nonrated men.

Repair 3: After repair, Similar to Repair 2.

Repair 4: Amidship repair. Similar to Repair 2.

Repair 5: Propulsion repair, Comprised of an electrical officer or senior electician's mate and a broad cross section of engineering ratings. Assignment to this unit is based more on fireroom/engine-room takeover qualifications than on damage control qualifications.

Repair 6: Ordnance repair. Comprised of gunner's mates, fire control technicians, and electrician's mates. This party is sometimes divided into forward and after groups.

*A small combatant such as an FF will normally use Repair 2, 3, and 5 only.

Repair 7: Gallery deck and island structure repair. This unit is used primarily on aircraft carriers and other ship types where it is needed. It consists of personnel from air, engineering, damage control, and other areas.

Repair 8: Electronics repair. Comprised of electronics, sonar, and fire control technicians—ETs, Sts and FTs—as well as electrician's mates. This party works within the electronics casualty control organization.

Aviation fuel repair teams and *crash and salvage teams* are peculiar to aircraft carriers and ships equipped for manned helicopter operations. On carriers the teams consist of air department personnel. On ships equipped for helo operations, the appropriate deck, engineering, and damage control personnel are assigned.

The *ordnance disposal team* is made up of specially trained personnel, deployed aboard ships as required. The team is administered as a unit of the weapons department.

All ships except submarines, patrol and yard craft, minecraft, and small auxiliaries maintain at least one at-sea *firefighting team*. A smaller ship whose complement is not large enough to warant formation of such a team may organize a fire party as appropriate.

Functional teams within each repair party include: hose teams; dewatering, plugging, and patching teams; investigation teams; shoring, pipe repair, structural repair, casualty power, IC communications repair, and electrical repair teams; radiological monitoring, biological sampling, chemical detection, and NBC decontamination teams; and stretcher bearers.

Every man in the repair party should be able to perform effectively on any team.

In general, repair parties must be:

• Capable of controlling and extinguishing all types of fires.
• Capable of giving first aid and transporting the injured to battle dressing stations without seriously reducing the damage control capabilities of the party.
• Capable of detecting, identifying, measuring dosage and intensity of radiation, and carrying out decontamination procedures.
• Organized to evaluate and report correctly on the extent of damage in its area.

In addition to the above functions, certain repair parties are also responsible for:

• Maintaining watertight integrity.
• Maintaining the ship's structural integrity and maneuverability.

- Maintaining the ship's propulsion protecting ordnance and magazines, and maintaining deck and hangar bays in aircraft carriers, plus the crash and salvage team and the explosive ordnance disposal (EOD) team.
    - Maintaining electronics equipment on certain ships.
    - Protecting exposed ordnance (EOD team).

Damage control central (DCC) holds continuing drills in fire fighting, flooding, battle damage, collision, and comunications during general quarters.

The repair party leader is responsible for:

- Assigning personnel of his repair party to form an effective damage control and damage repair group.
- Instructing repair party personnel in damage control duties and the operation and use of damage control equipment.
- Ensuring that the performance of his repair party is in accordance with current applicable instructions and safety precautions.
- Ensuring that repair party equipment is kept in the proper state of stowage, cleanliness, and maintenance.
- Ensuring that training records of repair party personnel with respect to damage control training are properly maintained.
- Ensuring that all status boards and message logs at the repair station are properly maintained and that damage control central is kept informed.
- Coordinating the efforts of his repair party with other repair parties.
- Striving to correct any damage sustained and to maintain the ship in fighting condition by using personnel assigned and equipment provided in the most effective manner.

The on-scene leader is the assistant repair party leader and is in charge of the repair locker in the absence of the repair party leader. (An alternate on-scene leader should also be designated.) The on-scene leader:

- Takes charge of all actions at the scene, directing the efforts of the repair party personnel effectively against fires, flooding, and structural damage.
- Keeps the repair party leader informed of all items of damage discovered and action taken.
- Ensures that all personnel in his charge observe all safety precautions and use standard procedures in the performance of all evolutions.

• Ensures that all equipment is used correctly, and that safety precautions are observed.

Compartmentation

The success of damage control depends partly on the proper use of watertight-integrity equipment. Each ship is divided into compartments to control flooding, to withstand NBC attacks, to segregate activities, to provide underwater protection with tanks and voids, to strengthen the structure of the ship, and to maintain buoyancy and stability.

Every Navy ship is divided by decks and bulkheads, both above and below the waterline, into as many watertight compartments as possible. In general, the more extensive a ship's compartmentation, the greater her resistance to sinking will be. The original watertight integrity, which is established when the ship is built, may be reduced or destroyed by enemy action, storms, collisions, or negligence.

Material Conditions of Readiness

These refer to the degree of access into an area and the system of closing hatches and other openings to limit the damage. Maximum closure is not always maintained because it would interfere with the normal operation of the ship. For damage control purposes, Navy ships have three material conditions of readiness, each representing a different degree of tightness and protection. They are X-ray, Yoke, and Zebra. These titles are used in all spoken and written communications concerning material conditions.

Condition X-ray provides the least protection. It is set when the ship is in no danger of attack, such as when she is at anchor in a well-protected harbor, or secured at home base during regular working hours. During this condition all closures marked with a black X are secured; they are also closed when setting Conditions Yoke and Zebra.

Condition Yoke provides somewhat more protection than Condition X-ray; Yoke is set and maintained at sea. In port, it is maintained at all times during war, and at times outside of regular working hours during peacetime. Yoke closures, marked with a black Y, are secured during Conditions Yoke and Zebra.

Condition Zebra is set before going to sea or when entering port during war. It is set immediately, without further orders, when general quarters stations are manned. Condition Zebra is also set to localize and control fire and flooding when not at GQ stations. When Condition Zebra is warranted, all closures marked with a red Z are secured.

Material conditions of readiness and special category markings of various damage control fittings are summarized in figure 12-1.

Table 12-1. Types of Watertight Fittings

Condition	Circumstances	Close fittings marked
X-Ray	In well-protected harbors; at home base during regular working hours.	X, Ⓧ. These fittings are kept closed at all times except when actually in use.
Yoke	At sea; in port outside of regular working hours.	X, Ⓧ, Y, Ⓨ. Ⓧ and Ⓨ fittings may be opened for access, to pass ammunition, for inspection, etc.
Zebra	General quarters; fire or flooding; when entering or leaving port in war-time.	X, Ⓧ, Y, Ⓨ, Z, Ⓩ. Ⓩ fittings may be opened to permit distribution of food, use of sanitary facilities, and ventilation of vital spaces. Must be guarded when open.

Markings	Purpose
W (William)	Classification W is applied to sea suction valves that supply water to the condensers and fire pumps, and to other fittings and equipment necessary for fire protection and mobility. These fittings are normally open or running.
Circle W	Ventilation fittings and certain access openings are marked Ⓦ (circles are black.) Normally open, these fittings are closed only to prevent NBC contamination or smoke from entering a vent system.
Red Circle Z (Zebra)	Special fittings marked Ⓩ (circles are red) may be opened during long periods of general quarters to allow for preparation and distribution of food or for cooling vital spaces such as magazines. When open, these fittings are guarded so that they can be closed immediately if necessary.
Black circle X and Y	Fittings marked with Ⓧ or Ⓨ permit access to battle stations, are used for transfer of ammunition, or are part of vital systems. They may be opened without special permission, but must be kept closed when not actually in use.
Dog Zebra	Ⓩ is applied to accesses to weather decks that are not equipped with light traps or door switches that will turn lights off when the access is opened during darkened ship conditions.

Once the material condition is set, no fitting marked with a black X, black Y, or red Z may be opened without permission of the commanding officer (through the DCA or OOD).

Additional fitting markings for specific purposes are modifications of the three basic conditions, as follows:

Circle X-ray fittings, marked with a black X in a black circle, are secured during Conditions X-ray, Yoke, and Zebra. *Circle Yoke* fittings, marked with a black Y in a black circle, are secured during Conditions Yoke and Zebra. Circle X-ray and Circle Yoke fittings may be opened without special authority when going to or from general quarters, when transferring ammunition, or when operating vital systems during GQ. The fittings must be secured when not in use.

Circle Zebra fittings, marked with a red Z in a red circle, are secured during Condition Zebra. These fittings may be opened during prolonged periods of general quarters, when the condition is modified. Opening these fittings enables personnel to prepare and distribute battle rations, open limited sanitary facilities, ventilate battle stations, and provide access from ready rooms to the flight deck. When open, these fittings must be guarded for immediate closure if necessary.

Dog Zebra fittings, marked with a red Z in a black D, are secured during Condition Zebra and during darkened ship condition. The Dog Zebra classification applies to weather accesses not equipped with light switches or light traps.

William fittings, marked with a black W, are kept open during all material conditions. This classification applies to vital sea suction valves supplying main and auxiliary condensers, *fire pumps*, and *spaces* that are manned during Conditions X-ray, Yoke, and Zebra. It also applies to vital ship valves that, if secured, would impair the mobility and fire protection of the ship.

Circle William fittings, marked with a black W in a black circle, are normally kept open (as William fittings are) but must be secured against NBC attack.

It is the responsibility of all hands to maintain the material condition in effect. If it is necessary to break the condition, permission must be obtained (from the OOD or damage control central). A log is maintained in DCC at all times to show where the existing condition has been broken; the number, type, and classification of fittings involved; the name, rate, and division of the man requesting permission to open or close the fitting; and the date the fitting was opened or closed.

The number of times and circumstances in which DCC may give permission to break watertight integrity is determined by the commanding officer.

Watertight Integrity

The purpose of damage control is to keep the ship watertight. She may sustain a great deal of damage, but with proper watertight integrity, the ship will remain afloat.

Doors, hatches, and manholes giving access to all compartments must be securely dogged (closed down). Manhole covers to double bottoms should always be bolted except for inspection, cleaning, or painting. They must never be left open overnight or when men are not actually working.

Watertight (WT) doors and hatches will work longer and require less maintenance if they are properly closed and opened. When closing a door, first set up on a dog opposite the hinges, with just enough pressure to keep the door shut. Then set the other dogs evenly to obtain uniform pressure all around. When opening a door, start with the dogs nearest the hinges. This procedure will keep the door from springing and make it easier to operate remaining dogs.

When the ship sustains damage, watertight doors, hatches, manholes, and scuttles should be opened only after making sure that the compartment is dry or has little flooding, so that there won't be more flooding when the closures are opened. They should never be opened without DCC permission. Extreme caution is always necessary in opening compartments below the waterline, near any damage.

Types of Closures

The strongest doors are classified as *watertight (WT) doors*. They are used in watertight bulkheads or lower-deck compartments and are designed to resist the same amount of pressure as the bulkheads. Some doors have dogs that must be individually closed and opened. Others, known as *quick-acting* watertight doors have handwheels that operate all dogs simultaneously (See figures 12–1 and 12–2.)

Nonwatertight doors (NWT), used in nonwatertight bulkheads, usually do not have dogs.

Airtight doors (AT) are also flame-tight and fire-retarding. When used in air locks, they usually have lever-type, quick-acting closures. Others usually have individually operated dogs.

Passing scuttles may be placed in doors through which ammunition must be passed. These are small, tube-like openings, watertight and flashproof.

Spraytight doors are used topside in vessels with low freeboard, to prevent spray and seawater from getting in.

Joiner doors are ordinary shore-type metal doors used to provide privacy for staterooms, wardrooms, etc.

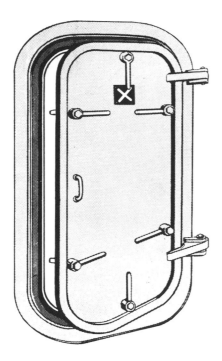

Figure 12-1. The individually operated dogs on this watertight door are in the closed position, but would have to be opened before the door can be closed.

Hatches are horizontal doors used for access through decks. A hatch is either set with its top surface flush with the deck, or on a coaming raised above the deck. Hatches usually are not quick-acting, but must be secured with individually operated dogs.

An *escape scuttle* is a round opening with quick-acting closures that can be placed in a hatch, bulkhead, or deck to permit rapid escape from a compartment (figure 12–3).

Bolted manholes normally provide access to water, fuel tanks, and voids. They are sections of steel plate which are gasketed and fastened over deck openings where access may be required. They are seldom used by ship's personnel. Manholes are occasionally placed in bulkheads.

Most closure devices depend on a rubber gasket, which is usually mounted in the covering part to close against a fixed-position knife edge for their tightness. Gaskets of this type are either pressed into a groove or secured with retaining strips held in place by screws or bolts. These gaskets should never be painted and should be replaced when worn excessively.

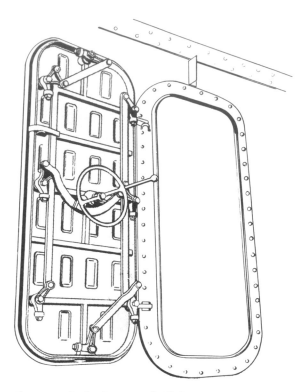

Figure 12-2. The control wheel operated all dogs at once on the quick-acting WT door.

Fire Protection

Fire is a constant potential hazard aboard ship. All possible measures must be taken to prevent the occurrence of fire or to bring about its rapid extinguishment. In many cases, fires occur in conjunction with other damage as a result of enemy action, weather, or accident. Unless fire is rapidly and effectively extinguished, it may easily cause more

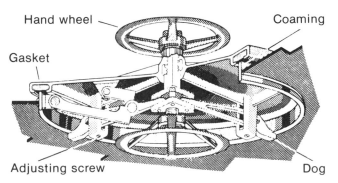

Figure 12-3. This cutaway section of an escape scuttle shows quick-acting hand wheels above and below.

damage than the initial casualty. In fact, fire may cause the loss of a ship even after the original damage has been repaired or minimized.

Classes of Fires

Fires have four classifications, indicating the type of material burning and the agents and methods required to extinguish them.

Class A fires involve solid substances—wood, cloth, paper—that usually leave an ash. Explosives are in this category. Water is the usual means of extinguishing Class A fires. Carbon dioxide may be used on small fires but not on explosives. A large fire usually requires knocking down (cooling) the flames with fog, then usually a solid stream to break up the material for further cooling.

Class B fires involve flammable liquids—oil, gasoline, paint, etc. For small fires or in confined spaces, CO_2 is a good extinguisher. For large fires, other agents such as water and fog foam must be used. Never use a solid stream on Class B fires. The steam only penetrates the fuel's surface, scatters the fuel, and spreads the fire.

Class C fires are those in electical/electronic equipment. The primary extinguishing agent is CO_2. Fog is used only as a last resort. Foam should not be used because it will damage the equipment and may be a shock hazard. A solid stream should *never* be used. If possible, the equipment should first be de-energized.

Class D fires involve combustible metals such as magnesium, sodium, and titanium. These metals are used for building certain parts of aircraft, missiles, electronic components, and other equipment. An example is the magnesium aircraft parachute flare, which can burn at a temperature above 4,000 degrees F., with a brilliancy of 2 million candlepower. Water coming in contact with burning magnesium produces highly explosive hydrogen gas, so use only low-velocity fog on this type of fire. One important safety precaution: welder's goggles with very dark (No. 6) lenses should be worn to protect the eyes from the intense light of the fire. Table 12-2 summarizes the classes of fires.

Fire Prevention Rules

Nobody can win against a fire. It can be fought effectively, but some property will be destroyed, productive work interrupted, and additional effort and materials will be required to clean up the mess. *The objective, therefore, is to prevent fires from starting.*

All shipboard gear should be stored properly—clean, shipshape, and in their proper places. Flammable products (gasoline, oily rags, paint, etc.) should be kept away from fire-starting articles (such as torches, cigarettes, and sparking equipment.)

Table 12-2. The Classes of Fires and Recommended Extinguishing Agents Are Listed in Order of Priority

Combustible	Class	Extinguishing agent
Woodwork, bedding clothes, combustible stores	A	Fixed water sprinkling, high-velocity for, solid water stream, foam, dry chemical, CO_2.
Explosives, propellants	A	Magazine sprinkling, solid water stream, or high velocity fog, foam.
Paints, spirits, flammable liquid stores	B	CO_2 (fixed system), foam, installed sprinkling system, high-velocity fog, PKP, CO_2.
Gasoline	B	Foam, CO_2, (fixed), water sprinkling system, PKP.
Fuel oil, JP-5, diesel oil, kerosene	B	Foam, PKP, water sprinkling system, high-velocity fog, CO_2, (fixed system).
Electrical and radio apparatus	C	CO_2 (portable or hose reel), high-velocity fog, fog foam or dry chemical (only if CO_2 not available).
Magnesium alloys	D	Jettison overboard, low-velocity fog.

The correct fire-fighting equipment should be kept in the right places and maintained in good condition. If a fire does start, the right equipment must be on hand, ready to go into operation. If a fire cannot be prevented, it is critical that it not be allowed to get out of control.

Some fire prevention rules for each class of fire:

Class A fires: All smoking materials should be handled carefully and extinguished completely in the appropriate container. Smoking in bunks is not authorized. Extreme caution should be exercised in the stowage and disposal of rags and oily paint-smeared cloth and paper. During welding or burning operations, Class A materials should be protected against flame and hot droppings. Additionally, opposite bulkheads should be continually inspected and a fire watch maintained.

Class B fires: Expect that all low places such as bilges, tanks, and bottoms may have an accumulation of potentially flammable liquid oil vapors. Only nonsparking tools should be used in areas where Class B substances have been or are stored. Sparking materials such as matches, lighters, rings, keys, and metal buttons should not be carried or worn in the presence of gasoline or oil vapors. Only lamps, flashlights, or electrical equipment that are certified as spark proof should be used where flammable oil vapors can accumulate.

Class C fires: Paint, oil, grease, or solvents should not come in contact with electrical insulation or wires. All frayed or worn wires as well as all sparking contacts, switches, or motors should be immediately reported to cognizant maintenance personnel. All portable electrical equipment such as grinders, drills, sanders, and deck polishers must be checked for electrical safety periodically by the electrician's mates and tagged as such in accordance with ship's regulations.

Class D fires: Class D fuels should be protected from welding and burning operations. Class D fuels should not be stored in areas that are susceptible to intense heat. Some of these fuels are extremely volatile and do not require flame for ignition.

Firefighting Equipment

All firefighting equipment is located in readily accessible positions and is inspected frequently to ensure its reliability and readiness for instant operation.

The firemain system is designed to deliver seawater to fireplugs and sprinkler systems. It has a secondary function of supplying water to flushing systems and auxiliary machinery as a coolant.

The piping usually is four inches in diameter and is either a single line running fore and aft near the centerline (on small ships), or in a loop system (on larger ships) running along each side of the ship inside protective bulkheads or armor. In both systems the main is located on or below the damage control deck. There are many cross-connection points and shutoff valves throughout the system to allow any damaged sections of piping to be isolated or "jumped." Risers lead from the main to fireplugs throughout the ship.

Aboard larger ships most fireplug outlets are 2½ inches in diameter. A wye gate provides two 1½-inch outlets, or a reducing fitting can be used to provide a single 1½-inch outlet. On destroyers and smaller ships, fireplug outlets are 1½ inches throughout the ship (figure 12-4).

The standard Navy fire hose has an interior lining of rubber, covered with cotton jackets. It comes in 50-foot lengths with a female coupling at one end and a male coupling at the other. The female coupling is connected to the fireplug. The male coupling is connected to another length of hose or receives a nozzle.

Destroyers and smaller ships use 1½-inch hose. Larger ships use 2½-inch hose on the weather decks and 1½-inch below deck and in the superstructure.

One or more racks are provided at each fireplug for stowing the firehose. The hose must be faked on the rack so that it is free-running, with the ends hanging down so that couplings are ready for instant use. On large ships, each weather-deck fire station has 100 feet of 2½-inch hose faked on a rack and connected to the plug. Below deck, 200 feet (two lines) of 1½-inch hose are stowed by each plug, but only one line is connected to the plug. One smaller ships, 100 feet of 1½-inch hose are faked on the racks, with 50 feet connected to the plug. A spanner wrench for tightening connections and one or two applicators are also stowed at each fire station. Spare lengths of hose are rolled and stowed in repair lockers.

The all-purpose nozzle (figure 12-5) can produce a solid stream of water, high-velocity fog, or low-velocity fog. It is available for both

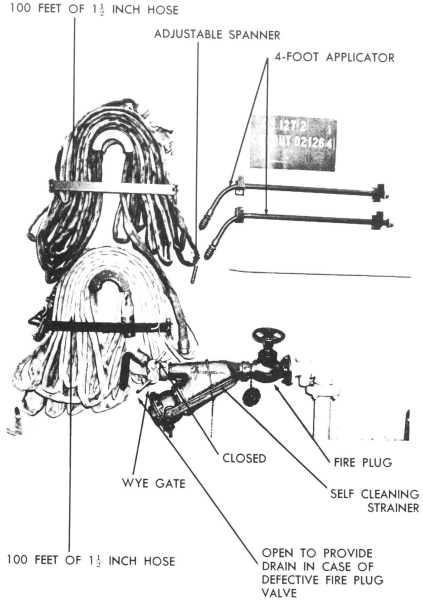

100 FEET OF 1½ INCH HOSE

ADJUSTABLE SPANNER

4-FOOT APPLICATOR

CLOSED   FIRE PLUG

WYE GATE   SELF CLEANING STRAINER

100 FEET OF 1½ INCH HOSE   OPEN TO PROVIDE DRAIN IN CASE OF DEFECTIVE FIRE PLUG VALVE

Figure 12-4. *In a standard shipboard installation of the fire plug, strainer, and hose sections, note that the lower valve on the wye gate is open to provide drain in case of a defective fire plug valve.*

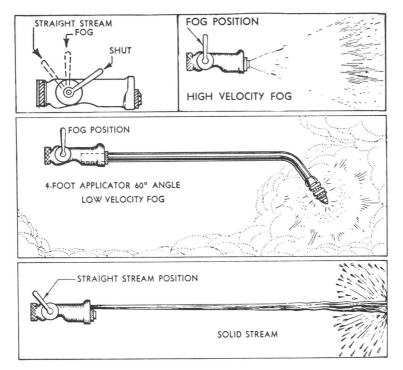

Figure 12-5. The all-purpose hose nozzle is used for high-velocity fog, low-velocity fog, and a straight stream.

1½-inch and 2½-inch hose. The nozzle can be adjusted easily and quickly by a handle. Never pick up a charged hose by the handle of the all-purpose nozzle. The handle could easily move to the fog or open position and the high water pressure (about 100 psi) could make the hose whiplash dangerously.

Foam-Producing Equipment

Foam, a frothy mixture of air, water, and chemicals, is used to fight Class B fires. The foam provides a blanket that floats on top of the burning liquid and smothers the fire. Mechanical or protein foam is nontoxic, and once the fire is out, can prevent a reflash for up to 24 hours. Foam will not damage surfaces, but it should not be used on Class C fires because of the obvious cleanup problems. It is not used, unless absolutely necessary, on either Class A or C fires.

Mechanical foam is produced by mixing a foam concentrate with water under pressure. A proportioner puts in the correct mixture (6 percent concentrate, 94 percent water). Two types of proportioners may be used.

Easiest to use is the straight-type proportioner. The mechanical nozzle is a 21-inch length of 2-inch diameter flexible metal or asbestos hose, with a suction chamber (the proportioner) and an air port at the pump end (figure 12-6). The pickup tube siphons the correct amount of foam concentrate into the water stream. As the stream crosses the air port, air is mixed with the solution to produce the foam. Foam concentrate comes in five-gallon cans; each can lasts 90 seconds and produces 660 gallons of foam.

The FP-180 water-motor proportioner consists of a foam liquid pump driven by a water motor. It has 2½-inch connections at both the inlet and outlet sides, and uses two half-inch pickup tubes. When the foam valve is in either of the two foam positions, the pump injects foam liquid into the water stream. With the valve in the "off" position, no foam is delivered, and the fire line can be used for conventional firefighting.

Water-Motor Proportioners. These come in two sizes—60-180 gallons per minute, and 1,000 gallons per minute. The larger unit is used with high capacity foam systems on hangar decks. Both types have foam liquid pumps driven by positive displacement water motors. Flow through the water motor causes the foam pump to inject a metered amount of liquid foam into the firestream, depending on the position of the foam valve. Proper use of this unit requires a ready supply of cans of foam. A sight tube lets the operator know when to shift from one foam can to another to maintain a steady stream of foam. The smaller unit can supply sufficient foam to operate three one and one-half inch hose lines equipped with mechanical foam nozzles. These smaller units are also found semipermanently installed on smaller ships having helicopter hangars which require foam sprinkling systems.

High Capacity Foam Systems. These systems have 1,000 gallon per minute water-motor proportioners equipped with built-in foam liquid tanks. The proportioners deliver foam to special sprinkling systems or to large three and one-half inch nozzles installed on aircraft hangar decks (figure 12-7).

The foam chemical comes in five-gallon containers. The cylinder is divided into upper and lower chambers. There are two sets of filling shafts—water shafts and siphon tubes—one set extending into the lower compartment and the other into the upper compartment. Water enters the manifold at the top of the cylinder where it exerts pressure on the foam solution, forcing it up through a siphon tube from the bottom of the compartment in use to the top of the cylinder. Just enough solution is fed into the stream to produce a good foam.

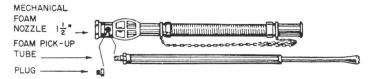

MECHANICAL
FOAM
NOZZLE 1½" →
FOAM PICK-UP
TUBE ————→
PLUG ————→

Figure 12-6. Mechanical foam nozzle and pickup tube.

These machines are built to close tolerance, and should only be used by trained men. After each use, the foam liquid pump must be thoroughly flushed with water. The oil level in ball-bearing reservoirs and drive-unit housing must be checked, drained, and refilled every six months. The valves and strainers must also be cleaned and checked periodically.

Light Water

Light water is a fluorochemical agent known as aqueous film forming foam (AFFF). It is a 6 percent concentration (that is, 6 parts of light water mixed with 94 parts of water) and, when mixed with water, produces a foam. As the water drains from the foam, a vapor-tight film is formed.

Light water is used in combination with a dry chemical to extinguish fires. The dry chemical is potassium bicarbonate (similar to baking

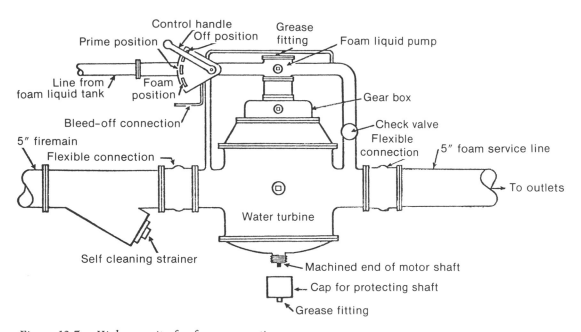

Figure 12-7. High-capacity fog-foam proportioner.

Figure 12-8.   Two views of the twinned agent unit.

soda), called purple-K powder, or simply PKP. PKP cannot prevent reflash of a fire, because it has no vapor suppression capability. Neither can PKP be used with protein (mechanical) foam, as it causes the foam to break down. It is fully compatible, however, with light water.

A light water/PKP combination will extinguish a fuel fire one and one-half to three times faster than protein foam. The PKP beats down the fire, and the light water prevents its reflash by forming a film on top of the fuel.

Aircraft carriers have a portable light water/PKP system mounted on a truck (figure 12-10), known as a twinned agent unit (TAU). The TAU has a sphere containing 200 pounds of PKP, and a cylinder containing 80 gallons of light water concentrate. Nitrogen is used for pressurization. Discharge hoses are 1-inch for light water and ¾-inch for PKP. They are joined together near their nozzles, and may be operated independently or concurrently by one man.

A fixed TAU installation has been developed for shipboard use and is being installed in each machinery space as ships go into a yard for overhaul. The CO_2 hose reel system will no longer be used except in certain ships having a heavy concentration of electrical equipment, such as those with electric propulsion. Protein foam also is being phased out in favor of light water.

Sprinkler Systems

Sprinkler systems installed in magazines, missile- and gun-handling rooms, turrets, stowage spaces for flammable materials (such as pyrotechnics and film lockers), and hangar spaces usually take water from the fire main. Most systems are equipped with remote-control valves which can be operated by hand, electricity, hand-operated hydraulic units, or the system may start automatically by heat-actuated devices.

Fixed Fog-Spray Installation. These are used aboard carriers, transports, and cargo ships where there is great danger of gasoline fires, and consist of overhead fixed piping, equipped with fog heads, and connected to the fire main. The system is not automatic.

Steam Smothering. Oil and gasoline fires in some machinery spaces can be extinguished with steam, which smothers the fire in much the same way as water fog does. However, steam will scald and suffocate trapped men, and raise temperatures, so it is used only in the bilge areas of some machinery spaces.

Carbon Dioxide (CO_2) Extinguishers

These are used mainly in putting out electrical fires. They are also effective on any type of small fire, including fuel oil, gasoline, alcohol, or paint. These pour a smothering layer of carbon dioxide (CO_2) gas over a fire. CO_2 will not burn, is heavier than air, and puts out a fire by cutting it off from the air. It is quick to use and leaves no mess, but can be blown away by wind or draft. While not poisonous, it will not support life, and can smother men as well as fires in confined spaces. It gives no warning of its presence. CO_2 is best used on small fires in low

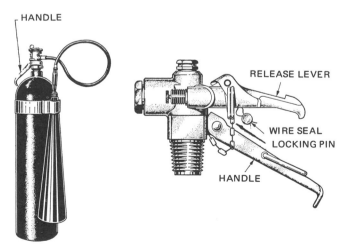

Figure 12-9. The portable CO_2 extinguisher, with detail of handle, release lever, and locking pin.

places and is particularly valuable for electrical equipment, because it will not damage wiring or delicate parts.

The portable extinguisher (figure 12–9) has a squeeze-grip type release valve. To operate, pull out the locking pin and squeeze the release lever.

CO_2 released from the container expands rapidly to 450 times its stored volume. This rapid expansion causes the temperature to drop to 110° below zero. Most of the liquid carbon dioxide is vaporized, but some of it forms "snow." If it touches the skin, it will produce painful blisters.

When using CO_2, keep the compartment closed, and secure ventilation. Except in an emergency, do not open a compartment flooded with CO_2 for at least 15 minutes after it has been flooded—a precautionary measure to give burning substances time to cool below ignition temperatures and prevent re-ignition when air is again admitted.

Monitoring Equipment

Combustible Gas Indicator (figure 12–10). The Navy type E explosimeter is designed to detect miscellaneous flammable gases and vapors. It can be used to test tanks or compartments where flammable gases

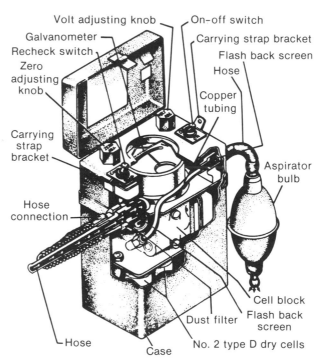

Figure 12-10. Combustible gas indicator type B or E.

and vapors may be present, including gases and vapors associated with gasoline, alcohol, acetone, hydrogen, and acetylene in mixtures with air or oxygen.

Flame Safety Lamp. The flame safety lamp (figure 12–13) is intended solely for the detection of oxygen deficiency in the atmosphere in which men must work. The flame safety lamp will also detect the presence of flammable vapors, but its intentional use for this purpose in atmospheres suspected of containing flammable or explosive gases or vapors is very dangerous and is *expressly forbidden* except in extreme emergency when the lamp is the only device available for testing the atmosphere. Using the flame safety lamp to test for the presence of flammable or explosive vapors is particularly dangerous in atmospheres that may contain acetylene or hydrogen.

The flame safety lamp should not be used until *after* tests with the combustible gas indicator have indicated that the space does not contain flammable or explosive vapors or gases.

When atmospheric conditions are normal, the flame of the safety lamp looks like an ordinary flame. When the atmosphere undergoes certain changes, the appearance of the flame is altered. If the oxygen in the atmosphere becomes lower than normal, the flame of the safety lamp grows dim. If the oxygen content becomes less than 16 percent by volume, the flame of the lamp is extinguished. If the lamp is placed in an atmosphere that contains flammable or explosive gases, some of the gas inside the lamp nearest the flame will burn, thus causing an increase in the length of the flame. If the concentration of explosive gas in the atmosphere is at or above the lower explosive limit, an explosion will take place in the lamp but the cooling effect of the gauzes will keep the explosion from being transmitted to the surrounding atmosphere. However, the lamp will *not* give protection against explosive mixtures of hydrogen or acetylene; if used in such an atmosphere, a serious explosion could result.

Caution: Never light or relight a flame safety lamp in a compartment that is suspected of containing any flammable or explosive vapors. Do not use the lamp at all in any space that may contain acetylene or hydrogen.

When making tests, hold the lamp in a vertical position so that it is upright at all times. It is very important to move the lamp *slowly* while it is in the space under test. Rapid movement of the lamp may cause the flame to be drawn through the wire gauze, thus igniting any gas that may be present.

The condition of the flame in the flame safety lamp indicates the condition of the atmosphere, as follows:

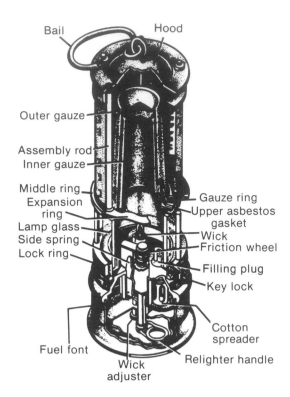

Bail · Hood · Outer gauze · Assembly rod · Inner gauze · Middle ring · Expansion ring · Lamp glass · Side spring · Lock ring · Gauze ring · Upper asbestos gasket · Wick · Friction wheel · Filling plug · Key lock · Cotton spreader · Fuel font · Wick adjuster · Relighter handle

Figure 12-11. Flame safety lamp.

1. If the flame dies out, there is less than 16 percent oxygen by volume.

2. If the flame goes out with a slight pop, there is an explosive concentration of gases or vapors.

3. If the flame flares up brightly, there is a lean concentration of explosive gases or vapors.

4. If the flame flares up and then goes out, there is a rich concentration of explosive gases or vapors.

When making a test with the flame safety lamp, keep the flame under constant observation. Hold the lamp steady for several seconds in each part of the space being tested; test all parts of the space, including any bays or other irregular areas. Use an airline mask or a breathing apparatus or else allow the flame safety lamp to precede you far enough in advance so that you can be sure the atmosphere contains enough oxygen to support life.

The flame safety lamp is currently being phased out of shipboard use in favor of a device called the Oxygen Analyzer. The lamp cannot indicate a minimum oxygen content of 20 percent as required by a recent change to Naval Ships Technical Manual, Chapter 074. Ships not having an authorized oxygen indicator must use respiratory equipment (OBA) for personnel requiring entry into a potentially oxygen-deficient space.

Protective Clothing and Equipment

Any clothing that covers the skin will protect it from flash burns and other short-duration flames. In situations where there is a likelihood of fire or explosion, one should keep covered as much as possible, and protect the eyes with antiflash goggles.

If the clothing catches fire, one shouldn't run. This fans the flames. One should lie down and roll up in a blanket, coat, or anything that will smother the flames. If nothing is available, roll over slowly, beating out the flames with the hands. If another person's clothes catch fire, throw him down and cover him (except his head) with a blanket or coat.

Asbestos suits do not burn, but they conduct heat. Such suits offer only short-term protection against flames. The wearer should be heavily clothed before putting one on.

Anyone wearing an asbestos suit should not be sprayed with water while working on a fire because the suit becomes soaked and heavy. If it becomes necessary to do this, do not stop the stream of water until the man is clear of the fire and the suit has cooled. If the water is stopped after the suit is wet and while still hot, the water will turn to steam and scald the wearer.

The proximity fire-fighting suit, which consists of a one-piece coverall, gloves, hood, and boots, is made of glass fiber and asbestos. It has an aluminized surface and is designed to replace the asbestos suit. Its hood provides a protective cover for the OBA (see below) which is normally worn with it. It is lightweight and resists penetration of liquids. The suit allows men to enter overheated or steam-filled compartments and to make crash fire rescues.

Oxygen Breathing Apparatus (OBA)

The Navy uses Type A-3 *oxygen breathing apparatus* (OBA). A new and improved OBA, Type A-4, is currently being put into fleet use after several years of testing. Since distribution is not complete, only the Type A-3 will be discussed here. The self-contained unit is designed to protect the wearer in an atmosphere lacking oxygen or containing harmful gases, vapors, smoke, or dust. The wearer breathes in a closed system in which oxygen is supplied by chemicals in a canister that purifies exhaled air. (See figure 12-13.)

Figure 12-12.   Proximity fire-fighting suit.

Figure 12-13.   Type A-3 oxygen-breathing apparatus.

The wearer's breath is circulated through the canister of chemicals, which react with the carbon dioxide and the moisture in his breath to produce oxygen. The process continues until the oxygen-producing capacity of the chemicals is used up—in about 45 minutes, depending on the amount of physical labor involved.

Survival Support Device (SSD)

A new *fire escape mask* consists of a transparent plastic head covering that can be donned in 20 seconds. Each mask carries a cartridge of compressed air—enough for eight minutes—which should enable the wearer to escape from any part of a ship to topside. It is especially designed to protect against smoke inhalation.

This type of fire escape mask is known as the Survival Support Device (SSD). (See figure 12–14.) The SSD is *not* designed for fire fighting.

Flooding—Key Concepts

Stability

Stability is the ability of a ship to return to an upright position when being acted on by outside forces. When stability has been impaired due to damage, speed, maneuverability, cruising radius, and seaworthiness are reduced. Therefore, stability plays a major part in damage control.

Buoyancy

Buoyancy is the ability of an object to remain afloat. The force of buoyancy is the sum of the vertical components of the hydrostatic pressure on the underwater body of a ship. It is also equal to the weight of the water displaced by the underwater body. The force of buoyancy also keeps the ship afloat, but it may be overcome and the ship may be sunk if too much weight is introduced—as is the case when too many compartments are flooded due to damage, and the damage is not controlled or repaired. A flooded compartment presents a serious hazard to the safety of the ship and its crew; any hole that lets water into the ship must be plugged or patched as soon as possible.

Figure 12-14. Survival support device.

Ballasting

To change the trim, or to regulate the stability of a ship is ballasting. It is often necessary to ballast in order to maintain proper list, trim, draft, and stability. Usually after battle damage or damage from grounding or collision, flooding is encountered in the area of the damage. In order to keep the ship trim and on an even keel, it is necessary to ballast. This is usually accomplished by flooding with saltwater from the sea or from the firemain system.

Solid Flooding

The term *solid flooding* refers to a compartment completely filled (from deck to the overhead, with every available cubic foot of the compartment occupied) with flooding water. A compartment must be vented in order to flood solidly. Venting may take place through an air escape, through an open scuttle or vent, or through fragment holes (damage) in the overhead. Solid flooding affects the stability of a ship only because the flood water constitutes an added weight.

Partial Flooding

Flooding is used to describe the situation in which the surface of the flooding water lies somewhere between the deck and the overhead of a compartment, that is, if the ship is on an even keel. The compartment is partially, but not completely, filled. Partial flooding of a compartment with its boundaries intact (an expression meaning the deck and the bulkheads remain watertight) affects the stability of the ship because of (1) the effect of added weight, and (2) the effect of free surface.

Free Surface Effect. If a ship's compartment, tank, or void is damaged and is only partially flooded (full), the liquid contents may "slosh" back and forth with the motion of the ship. This effect is known as *free surface*. There is little excuse for much free surface. Tanks partially full should be ballasted. Free surface should be avoided, since it always causes a reduction in the overall stability.

Free Communication

Thus far, the discussion has been concerned with loose water that is confined within the ship. If, because of an opening in the hull, the flooded area is open to the sea, there is an additional effect to be considered, called *free communication*. The effects of free communication will be superimposed on all other factors, such as added weight and free surface, which affects the stability of the ship. Free communication effect is only present when the flooded compartment is off the centerline of the ship. The effect of free communication can best be understood by assuming that the flooding is instantaneous and that the opening to the sea is then closed. The ship will sink to a new waterline because of the added weight of the new water in the ship. Further, the ship will take on a list because of the off-center weight of the water, which will result in another new waterline. Free communication and free surface with the sea are, when combined, the deadly enemies of stability.

Effects of Flooding

Flooding is one of the primary causes of loss of a ship after damage. This loss can be incurred for one of three reasons or from combinations of these reasons.

First, the ship can sink. This will occur when the weight of the flooding water becomes greater than the ship's reserve buoyancy. If this happens, the ship will sink on a nearly even keel. Second, the ship can capsize if there are shifts of weight such that transverse stability is lost. These weight shifts can be caused by flooding, shifting of cargo, improper loading, or any combination of events that result in a concentration of weight off the centerline. The result is that the ship rolls over and sinks. Finally, the ship can be lost by plunging. If flooding water is concentrated in either end of the ship and the weight of the water overcomes the ship's longitudinal stability, the ship will sink by either the bow or the stern.

Since it is impractical to assume that the entry of flooding water can be immediately prevented following damage to the hull, and since removal requires time, the most practical means of resisting loss by flooding is to limit the amount of flooding water admitted. This is done by providing watertight transverse and longitudinal bulkheads and watertight decks which serve to limit the entry of flooding water after damage, as discussed previously in this chapter.

Dewatering Equipment

Pumps

There is presently available a portable gasoline-driven pump called the P-250 (see figure 12-15). This pump is designed for use in fire-fighting or dewatering operations. For fire fighting, it is used to draw water from the sea or other sources and to pump it through suitable hoses and nozzles at high pressure. For dewatering, it is used to draw large volumes of water from flooded compartments. The P-250 pump has a capacity of 250 gallons per minute and is self-priming to a suction lift of between 16 and 20 feet.

MANUAL PRIMING BOWL

POWER HEAD

PRESSURE REGULATOR

DISCHARGE

STARTER

INTAKE

OPERATING CYLINDER

FIRE PUMP

EXHAUST OUTLET

Figure 12-15. P-250 portable pump.

An important part of damage control equipment is the portable electric submersible pump. Portable electric submersible pumps are used for dewatering compartments that are not drained by regularly installed drainage systems. The submersible pumps are rated to deliver 140 gallons per minute against a maximum head of 70 feet for the A.C. unit or 60 feet for the D.C. unit (see figure 12-16).

Eductors are jet-type pumps that contain no moving parts. An eductor moves liquid from one place to another entraining the pumped liquid in a rapidly flowing stream of water. Eductors are also used for pumping liquids that cannot be handled directly by the portable pumps. Eductors can handle a liquid that contains fairly small particles of foreign matter. There are two types of eductors available for shipboard use (figure 12-17 and 12-18)—the S-type and the single-jet eductor. Both types have a 4-inch discharge: Since the operating medium of an eductor is water under pressure, eductors can be actuated by discharging pressure from a pump or by connecting a 2½-inch hose from a fire plug to the eductor.

Investigating and Reporting Damage

Investigating and reporting damage is one of the most important factors in damage control. In order to make a complete and thorough investigation, you must know your ship. There are three basic principles of investigation. They are:

1. *Be cautious*
   —Each investigation team should consist of two or more people.
   —Toxic or combustible gases may be present.
   —Do *not* lose control of any watertight fittings.
   —Use safety equipment.
2. *Be thorough*
   Determine:
   —What hit.
   —Where it hit.
   —How it hit.

   Damage to look for:
   —Loss of electrical power
   —Presence of smoke
   —Presence of *explosive* material
   —Wreckage
   —Flooding
   —Fires
   —Damage to vital equipment
   —Damage to piping system
   —Condition of compartments surrounding the damage area
3. *Reporting damage*
   —Report damage to Repair Party Headquarters accurately by the quickest means possible.
   —Reports of *no damage* are also required by D.C. Central and Repair Party Headquarters.

NBC Warfare Defense

In the event of nuclear, biological, or chemical attack upon a naval vessel, there is much that could be done by the ship's crew to minimize

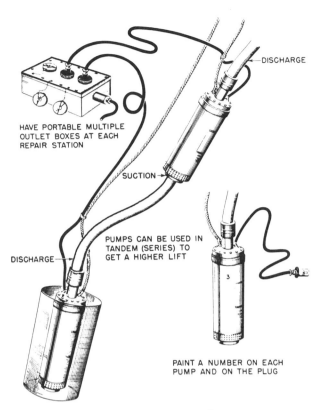

DISCHARGE

HAVE PORTABLE MULTIPLE
OUTLET BOXES AT EACH
REPAIR STATION

SUCTION

PUMPS CAN BE USED IN
TANDEM (SERIES) TO
GET A HIGHER LIFT

DISCHARGE

PAINT A NUMBER ON EACH
PUMP AND ON THE PLUG

Figure 12-16. Portable submersible pumps in tandem.

casualties and damage. For those ships located at or near ground zero in a nuclear attack, or in the areas of highest biological or chemical agent concentrations, casualties and damage would, of course, be very great. However, proving-ground tests have shown that those vessels not receiving the direct effects of such attacks would have a very good chance of survival with relatively few casualties and with weapon systems intact. Since naval formations are generally widely dispersed, the probabilities are that nearly all of the fleet units would escape the direct effects of an NBC attack.

The defensive actions taken by a ship, as in nearly all damage control actions, are divided into (1) preparatory measures taken in anticipation of attack and (2) active measures to commence immediately following an attack. Since preparatory measures taken must be timely, heavy reliance is laid on intelligence sources to warn the fleet of imminent attack.

Some preparatory measures involve design changes in our older ships to provide them with gas-tight envelopes and topside water washdown piping. One can well imagine the difficulty in providing for a

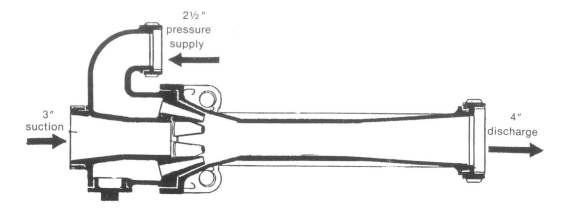

Figure 12-17. Cross-sectional view of perijet eductor.

gas-tight envelope that would completely shield the crew from outside NBC contamination. This problem exists in particular for any ship propelled by fossil fuels and breathing large amounts of air to support combustion. However, design accommodation can be made to minimize this defect and provide adequate protection from contamination.

Perhaps the most effective preparatory measure is thoroughly to indoctrinate and train the ship's force. The crew must know the nature of NBC agents, what to expect, and how best to handle the decontami-

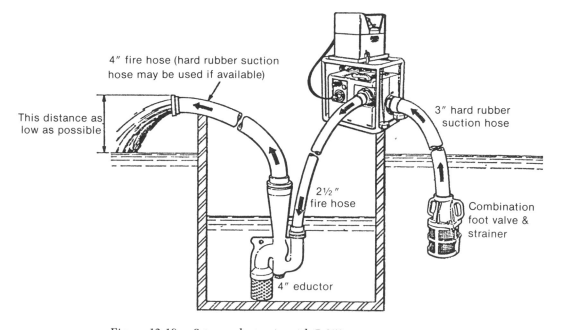

Figure 12-18. S-type eductor in with P-250 pump.

nation of the ship. Removal of porous material that easily becomes contaminated with radioactive, toxic, or pathologic organisms and particles is one of the most important first steps. This subject will not be covered directly here but will become obvious when various NBC defense equipments are studied.

The preparatory measures taken when attack is declared imminent are generally described as follows:

1. Go to general quarters to "button up" the ship. Conduct a preattack washdown of all topside areas using the water washdown system. Maintain the entire outer surface of the ship wet so that NBC contaminants will tend to wash overboard and not adhere to the external surfaces of the ship.

2. Close all nonvital openings of the ship in order to maintain as nearly complete a gas-tight envelope as possible or as the design of the ship will allow. Personnel manning general quarters stations below decks who must breath air conducted directly into the ship during an attack should be provided with gas masks. These areas are generally in firerooms, diesel-generator rooms, and other main propulsion spaces that require large volumes of air to support combustion.

3. All topside exposed personnel don protective clothing and masks. All personnel would then be issued detectors that would indicate to what kind of NBC agent the wearer had been exposed.

The extreme effectiveness of some bacteriological agents, the toxicity of chemical agents, and the danger of radiological fallout dictate that protective clothing and gas masks be carefully designed. It is mandatory that all personnel be periodically retrained in the use of protective clothing and masks.

Protective clothing used by the U.S. Navy in NBC defense is of four types:

1. Ordinary work clothing is effective in initially preventing droplets of chemical or bacteriological agents from making easy contact with the skin but will quickly become contaminated and must be discarded.

2. Foul weather clothing, including parka, trousers, rubber boots, and gloves, protects the skin against penetration by liquid chemical agents and low energy radioactive particles but retains contamination as does work clothing and must be discarded when hosing down of the garments will no longer decontaminate the material.

3. Permeable protective clothing has been treated with chemicals that neutralize blister-agent vapors and aerosols. It becomes unable to neutralize these agents when soaked down and is not effective for long-term protection.

4. Impermeable protective clothing has a rubberized outer covering and hence will not permit air or water to pass through. Needless to say, this clothing is hot and uncomfortable in warm climates. Nevertheless, it will provide the best overall protection against BW and CW agents and alpha particles. Gamma and high-energy beta radiation will penetrate, however.

Figure 12-19 shows a man completely dressed in a suit of impermeable protective clothing.

There are several protective masks available for general use in the Navy and some have application to NBC defense. Masks are generally of two types. The first type includes all masks that do not provide oxygen to the user. This type of mask employs a filtering system of mechanical and chemical filters that removes solid or liquid particles and absorbs or neutralizes toxic and irritating vapors.

The MK V gas mask is a good example of this type. As can be seen in figure 12-20, the mask fits over the head and face and has no hose or other encumbering fittings. This mask will protect against the inhalation of some nerve, blister, choking, vomiting, and tear agents. It will not protect against carbon monoxide, carbon dioxide, ammonia, and many fuel gases or vapors. This mask is not used in connection with fire fighting or smoke, or in an atmosphere containing less than 20 percent oxygen, which is necessary to support life. If, however, one should be trapped in a smoke-filled space with no other means to protect the lungs, then this mask is better than nothing at all. The danger is that an uninformed user may mistakenly believe he has full protection and remain in the space. It should only be used during escape to fresh air, as the filtering device will provide some protection from smoke particles. Plastic escape hoods having a short supply of oxygen stored in a bottle are available to personnel located some minutes away from fresh air.

Various other masks will provide some protection against NBC agents, but only for short periods of time and only if air supplies to them are kept uncontaminated.

As one can imagine, the detection of NBC agents that are generally invisible, odorless, tasteless, and give no other hint of their presence to the senses requires special equipment and training. While it is beyond the scope of this book to describe all of the methods used in NBC detection, some of the general-issue equipments will be described.

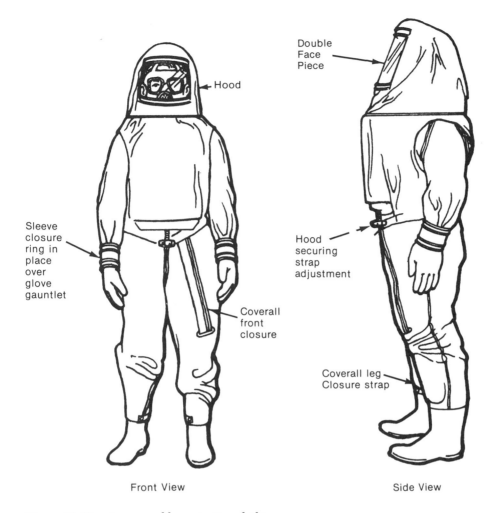

Front View

Side View

Double
Face
Piece

Hood

Sleeve
closure
ring in
place
over
glove
gauntlet

Hood
securing
strap
adjustment

Coverall
front
closure

Coverall leg
Closure strap

Figure 12-19. Impermeable protective clothing.

Radioactive particles betray their presence by giving off several kinds of radiation. Some types of radiation contain no detectable mass or charge and are classed as high-energy electromagnetic radiation called gamma rays. Other types have charge and/or mass and are further classed into neutrons, electrons, alpha particles, neutrinos, and other subatomic particles too numerous to mention. The ionizing radiations—alpha particles, beta electrons, and gamma waves—are the easiest to detect. The three primary types of radiation can be detected by instruments known as radiacs, an acronym for radiation, detection, indication, and computation. These instruments use a Geiger tube that contains various gases that ionize when subjected to one or more of the three types of readily detectable radiation. Since the military needs

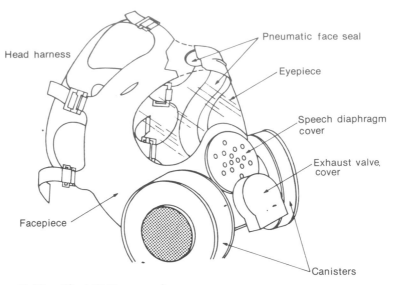

Figure 12-20. The MK V gas mask.

knowledge of the presence of these injurious radiations, radiacs are provided to all ships and stations. Depending upon their specific internal configuration, they are used as intensity meters for measuring the highly penetrating gamma radiation or the less penetrating beta and alpha radiation, as survey meters detecting alpha particles, or as dosimeters for measuring the total amount of radiation an individual has received during an attack. Whenever nuclear attack is considered probable, the ship will issue a dosimeter to each member of the crew. The present device is known as the DT-60/PD. This is a high-range non-self-reading dosimeter consisting of a special phosphor glass between lead filters encapsulated in bakelite. It is worn around the neck on a chain. It is read by the CP-95/PD computer indicator and records accumulated whole-body gamma radiation from 10 roentgens to 600 roentgens. Film badges are also available for issue and are nonself-reading indicators of whole-body beta and gamma radiation.

From tests and careful extrapolation from Japanese atomic bomb casualties, it has been determined that with a whole-body dose of 450 roentgens received in a short interval of time, 50 percent mortality will occur. This, however, is a relatively large dosage; if early detection of the radiation is made, with prompt decontamination effected and with removal of radiation hot spots from the ship, many lives can be saved and much radiation sickness avoided.

The detection of pathogenic organisms and chemical warfare agents generally takes longer than that of radioactive fallout. In the case of biological detection, samples must be taken, cultured, and subjected to thorough laboratory testing before the agent can be identified. This is slow, exacting work, and if viruses are used, they can greatly augment the difficulty of agent identification. Since identification is difficult, by the time the BW agent has been identified, many people could already be casualties. Much research is currently under way to provide civil as well as military agencies with rapid, reliable test procedures.

Chemical agents are somewhat easier to detect, but no one test procedure will detect all of the chemical agents known to exist. Some of these agents are lethal in extremely small concentrations and hence could be deployed upwind over a very great area with devastating results.

As BW and CW agents tend to neutralize the effectiveness of military forces and the general population as well without causing physical destruction of the target area, they should be taken very seriously in the civil-defense planning of the nation. A number of devices including air sampling kits, papers, testing tubes, and indicator solutions are in general use. This is a most difficult area in detection; hence stocks of antidotes and vaccines have been prepared against the more common agents.

Monitoring and surveying of ships and stations is a vital part of NBC defense. The location of the hazard, isolation of the contaminated areas, recording of the results of the survey, and the reporting of the findings up the chain of command are the functions of any military unit encountering contamination.

On board ship, two more types of survey would be required after an NBC attack. A gross survey would be taken to include weather decks, interior spaces, machinery, and so on, to discover the location of obvious contamination. Personnel decontamination would start as soon as the decontamination area itself was ready.

Detailed instructions for making monitoring surveys cannot be specified for all situations, but generally after a gross survey had been made, gross decontamination would begin. This would entail flushing the contaminated surfaces with copious amounts of water with the water washdown system for external surfaces. For internal contamination, firehoses and manual scrubbing could be used. Steam is a useful agent for gross contamination, especially if BW agents are suspected or the contamination is lodged in greasy or oily films.

Detailed decontamination would be the next step, its purpose being to reduce the contamination to such a low level that no significant hazard would remain. There are three general procedures: surface decontamination reduces the agent without destroying the utility of the object; aging and sealing allows the contaminant to decay or lose its potency through evaporation or dissolution; disposal removes contaminated objects and materials to a place where they can do little harm.

NBC defense doctrine assumes that no completely overpowering dosage would afflict the ship. Heavy concentrations of radioactivity, lethal chemicals, or biological agents could wipe out any crew. However, dispersal and timely intelligence concerning a planned attack would do much to mitigate the dosage and allow units not receiving the highest concentrations to survive to fight another day.

Summary

This chapter has discussed the shipboard damage control organization that includes the various responsibilities and duties assigned to officer and enlisted personnel in maintaining maximum damage control readiness. The importance of maintaining watertight integrity through the proper maintenance of material conditions cannot be over emphasized. The junior officer must be thoroughly familiar with the operation of the various types of damage control equipment, with particular emphasis on fire-fighting and dewatering devices. It has been repeatedly demonstrated that effective preparation before damage occurs is the key to the ultimate survivability of the ship and its crew after damage occurs. This preparation not only involves proper maintenance of installed and portable damage control equipment, but constant training in its purpose and use. Above all, proper damage control procedures are an *all hands responsibility. Your life may depend on it.*

The Special Sea Detail

Getting Under Way and Returning to Port

1. *Purpose.* To establish policies for assignment of personnel to stations and duties during periods when the ship is being handled in restricted waters, and to provide uniformity of procedures in preparation for getting under way or returning to port.

2. *Responsibility for the bill.* The navigator, under the supervision of the executive officer, is responsible for maintaining this bill.

3. *Information.* The special sea detail supplements the regular steaming watch. In some instances, special sea detail personnel will relieve the regular watch. In situations where the primary maneuvering sound-powered circuits are overcrowded when special sea details are set, consideration should be given to the use of the auxiliary maneuvering circuits.

4. *Procedures and responsibilities.*
   a. Heads of departments shall:
      (1) Ensure that division officers assign qualified personnel to all ship and engine control stations in accordance with the provisions of this bill.
      (2) Initiate having reports of readiness for getting under way for their departments made to the officer of the deck thirty minutes before the ship is to get under way. A report of "ready to get under way" shall mean that the department is secured for sea as prescribed in NWP 50 and that all navigational and ship or engine control equipment that is the responsibility of the department is in commission and ready to function.
   b. The officer of the deck shall:
      (1) Be responsible for calling away the special sea detail.
      (2) Supervise the procedures outlined in the bill except as otherwise indicated herein.
   c. The navigator shall ensure that the gyros used in navigating the ship are started at least six hours prior to getting under way. After the master gyro has steadied, an azimuth shall be taken if practicable.

Procedure for Getting Under Way

Time	Event	Responsibility
6 hours	(1) Start gyros.	Navigator, Duty IC man
3 hours	(1) Verify underway schedule; light off boilers.	Engineering officer
2 hours	(1) Ascertain from the executive officer: a. If any variation in standard time of setting Special Sea Detail; b. Time of heaving in to short stay; c. Disposition of boats; d. Instructions concerning U.S. and Guard Mail; e. Number of passengers, if any, and expected time of arrival.	OOD
	(2) After obtaining permission from the executive officer, start hoisting in boats and vehicles when no longer required.	OOD
	(3) After obtaining permission from the executive officer, rig in booms and accommodation ladders not in use and secure them for sea.	OOD
	(4) Have word passed giving the time the ship will get under way.	OOD
	(5) Energize and check all CIC equipment.	CIC officer
	(6) Conduct radio checks.	Comm officer
1 hour	(1) Set material condition YOKE (material condition ZEBRA in reduced visibility).	Division officers
	(2) Clear ship of visitors. Chief master at arms make inspection for stowaways.	
	(3) Energize radars.	
45 minutes	(1) Pass word "All hands shift into uniform of the day."	OOD
	(2) Muster crew on station.	Division officers
	(3) "OC" and "R" divisions man after steering and pilot house; test	Navigator

steering engine, controls, communications, and emergency steering alarm.

	(4) Test engine order telegraph and revolution indicator.	Engineering officer
	(5) Test anchor windlass.	Engineering officer
	(6) Test running lights.	Engineering officer
30 minutes	(1) Pass word "Station the Special Sea Detail."	OOD officer
	(2) Test fathometer and sonar equipment.	Navigator/ASW officer
	(3) Adjust bridge PPI radarscope.	CIC officer
	(4) Check navigation equipment on bridge. Check gyro repeaters against master gyro.	Navigator
	(5) Test sound-powered communication circuits. Check harbor radio circuit.	OOD
	(6) Receive departmental reports of readiness to get under way, including material condition YOKE/ZEBRA.	OOD
	(7) Test complete steering system and engine order telegraph.	OOD
	(8) CMAA make report of inspection for stowaways.	CMAA
	(9) Record fore-and-aft draft of ship.	DCA
	(10) Direct engineering control to report when main engines are ready for testing. Upon receiving this report, obtain permission to test main engines from the commanding officer and direct be on the bridge when engines are tested.	OOD
	(11) Disconnect utility lines to pier and stow.	Engineering officer
	(12) Pass the word "The officer of the deck is shifting his watch to the bridge." All heads of departments report readiness for getting under way to the OOD.	OOD

15 minutes	(1) Report ready for getting under way to the executive officer who will report to the commanding officer.	OOD
	(2) If moored to a buoy, take in chain or wire, and ride to manila lines when ordered. Record draft of the ship fore and aft.	OOD
	(3) When directed, test the ship's whistle.	OOD
	(4) When directed, rig in brow.	First lieutenant
	(5) As boats are hoisted or cleared away, rig in booms and davits.	First lieutenant
	(6) Check ship for smart appearance.	OOD
	(7) Obtain permission to get under way from SOPA, or appropriate authority.	
	(8) Have pilot escorted to the bridge when applicable.	JOOD
10 minutes	(1) Pass word "All hands not on watch, fall in at quarters for leaving port."	OOD
	(2) Check sides of ship to ensure they are clear of all lines, ladders, and cables except mooring lines. Check again for smart appearance.	First lieutenant

Immediately prior to getting under way, warn engineering control to stand by to answer all bells.

Procedure for Entering Port

Time	*Event*	*Responsibility*
Prior to entering restricted waters		
	(1) Deballast, as required.	Engineering officer
	(2) Man fathometer.	Navigator
1 hour	(1) Ascertain time of anchoring (mooring) from the navigator and notify engineering officer, weapons officer, first lieutenant, and engineering control.	OOD
	(2) Pass word "Make all preparations for entering port. Ship will anchor (moor_____ side to) at about _____."	OOD

	(3) Ascertain time for quarters for entering port from the executive officer.	OOD
	(4) Check smartness of ship for entering port.	OOD
	(5) Obtain information concerning boating from executive officer and inform weapons officer.	OOD
	(6) Lay out mooring lines if required.	First lieutenant
	(7) Prepare anchors for letting go.	First lieutenant
	(8) Pass word "All hands shift into the uniform of the day."	OOD
30 minutes	(1) Blow tubes on all steaming boilers. Set material condition YOKE. (Set material condition ZEBRA in restricted visibility.)	OOD
	(2) Station the special sea detail.	OOD
	(3) Obtain from the navigator information on depth of water at anchorage, and from commanding officer, anchor and scope of chain to be used and inform first lieutenant. When mooring to a pier, inform weapons officer and first lieutenant as to range of tide and time of high water.	OOD
	(4) Place propeller locks on torpedoes, and secure otherwise is required.	Weapons officer
20 minutes	(1) Complete setting of all Special Sea Detail.	OOD
	(2) Ensure smart appearance of ship.	OOD
	(3) Direct chief master-at-arms to inspect upper decks to see that crew is in proper uniform.	OOD
	(4) Swing lifeboat in or out as necessary.	First lieutenant
	(5) Request permission to enter port from proper authority prior to anchoring or mooring.	OOD
	(6) Pass word "All hands to quarters for entering port."	OOD

15 minutes minutes (prior to mooring or anchoring)	(1) Station quarterdeck watch.	SWO
	(2) Assemble on the quarterdeck the guard mail petty officer, mail clerk, movie operator, shore patrol, or other details leaving the ship in the first boat.	Inport OOD
	(3) If mooring to a buoy, lower boat with buoy detail as directed.	First lieutenant
	(4) Stand by to receive tugs if previously requested and if required in going alongside.	First lieutenant

Upon anchoring or mooring

	(1) Rig out boat booms and lower accommodation ladders.	First lieutenant
	(2) Lower boat as directed.	First lieutenant
	(3) Record draft of ship fore and aft.	DCA
	(4) Secure main engines as directed by the commanding officer.	Engineering officer
	(5) Secure the Special Sea Detail. Set in-port watches.	OOD
	(6) Pass word: "The officer of the deck is shifting his watch to the quarterdeck."	OOD
	(7) Secure gyros only if permission is obtained from the commanding officer.	Navigator

Knots, Bends, and Hitches

Bending Two Lines Together

A *bend* ordinarily is used to join the ends of two lines together. The *square knot*, also called the *reef knot*, is the best-known *bend* for joining two lines together. The uninitiated trying to tie a square knot frequently ends up with a *granny* as shown in figure B-1. A granny knot will slip under strain and fall into two half hitches.

Figure B-2 shows how to tie a square knot. A square knot is indispensable when a bundle, or anything of that nature, is to be bound up and secured. It is the most convenient way to tie two cords together when there is tension on both of them; however, it can jam if the tension is very great, making it very difficult to untie.

B-1. Granny knot.

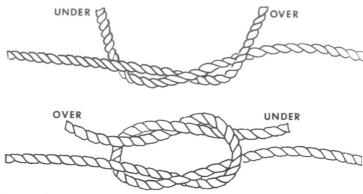

B-2. Square knot.

A *becket bend*, also called a *sheet bend*, is considered as good a bend as the square knot and is much easier to untie after being under strain, although it will jam. On the whole, it is the most generally useful bend for the many kinds of miscellaneous needs encountered aboard ship. It is strong, secure, and easy to tie and is especially good for bending together two lines of different sizes. Figure B-3 details the steps in tying a becket bend, single or double.

When one ship is towing another, there is an extremely heavy strain on the towing hawser. If two hawsers must be bent together, a *double carrick bend* should be used (figure B-4); otherwise, when the tow is completed, the two hawsers will have to be cut apart. A double carrick, with ends seized down as shown, cannot jam, because it never draws

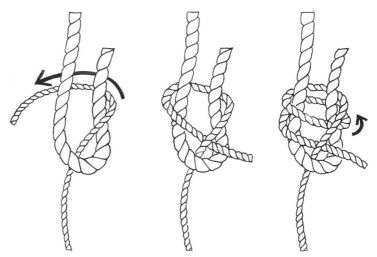

B-3. A becket bend, single and double.

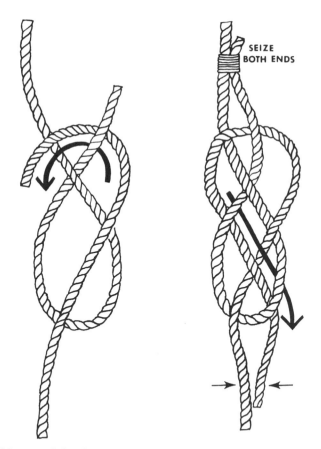

B-4. Double carrick bend.

up tight. There is also a *single carrick bend*, but it has no advantages over a square knot or becket, and jams under even a moderate strain.

Frequently it is necessary to bend together two lines that must reeve around a capstan or winch drum. The best knot for this purpose is the *reeving line bend*, which is shown in figure B-5. As you can see, it consists of taking a half hitch with the end of each line around the standing part of the other and seizing the bitter ends. The seizings must be tight or the knot might pull out.

A *bowline* (figure B-6) is a method for putting a temporary loop in the end of a line. Two bowlines can be used to bend two lines together. Though it is convenient, the sharp kinks of a bowline may cause the line to part much sooner than if it were bent with a square knot or a becket bend. The bowline neither slips nor jams, yet it ties and unties easily. It is the best knot to use for bending a heaving line or messenger to the eye of a hawser, because it is quick to tie and easy to get off.

B-5. Reeving line bend.

Knots to Form a Loop or Eye

The *single bowline on a bight* (figure B-7) is a knot that comes in handy whenever an eye in the center of a line is needed. It can be tied quickly and does not jam. Further, an end of the line is not needed in order to tie it. A single bowline on a bight is a good knot to use for making equipment or cargo secure.

The *double bowline on a bight* gives two loops instead of one, neither of which slips. It is used to hoist a man, chair-seat fashion, out of a lifeboat or hold while not unduly constricting him. Figure B-8 shows how to tie a double bowline on a bight. Note that to start, the line is doubled.

A *French bowline* serves the same purpose as a bowline on a bight. It gives two loops that can be adjusted for hoisting a man. One of the loops is adjusted under the man's hips, the other around his chest and under his armpits, and the knot at his chest is drawn tight. Even an unconscious man can ride safely in a properly secured French bowline. The method of tying a French bowline is given in figure B-9.

The *Spanish bowline* (figure B-10) can be used wherever it is desirable to have two eyes in the line. Its primary use, however, is as a substitute for the boatswains's chair, a chair used to work aloft. Many prefer it to the French bowline, because the bights are set and will not slip back and forth, as they do in the French bowline when the weight is shifted.

A *running bowline* (figure B-11) is merely a slipknot or a lasso and consists of a bowline tied around the line's standing part. It is the most useful temporary running knot and can be used to throw a noose around a bollard, for instance.

Bending a Line to a Ring or Spar

In securing a line to a hook, ring, or another line, the use of *hitches* is usually employed, although one bend, the *fisherman's bend*, is well suited for this job. The name of this "bend" is considered by some to be a misnomer, because a bend is normally thought of as a knot used to join the ends of two lines together in a permanent or semipermanent fashion. Therefore, according to the previously stated guidelines and on the basis of its more common usage, a fisherman's bend might more logically be called a fisherman's hitch. The fisherman's bend is a knot used to bend a line to a ring or spar as shown in figure B-12. Like the

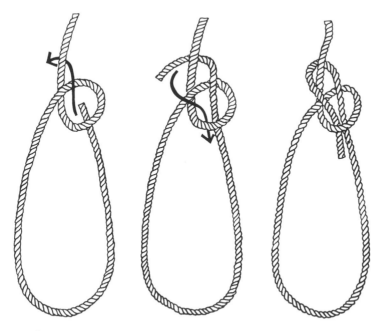

B-6. Bowline.

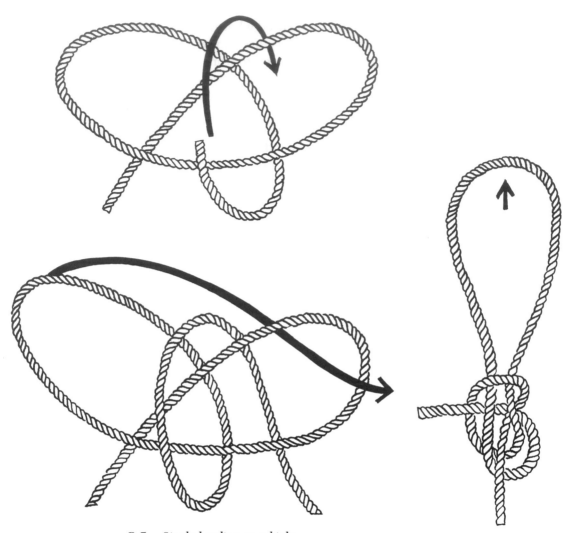

B-7. *Single bowline on a bight.*

bowline, it is also frequently used to bend a messenger to a mooring line. It is a good example of a knot having both simplicity and strength.

The *rolling hitch* (figure B-13) is one of the most useful and most important hitches. It is used, for example, to pass a stopper on a mooring line when that line is shifted from the capstan to bitts. In like manner, it is to stop off a boat fall when shifting it from a winch to a cleat. It also may be used to secure a taut line back on itself. If tied properly, it holds as long as there is a strain on the hitch. It also has little inclination to slide as long as the second turn remains jammed against the first, which will last as long as tension is continuous.

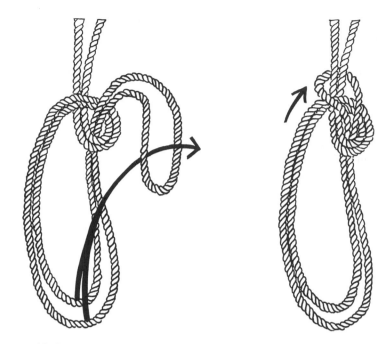

B-8. *Double bowline on a bight.*

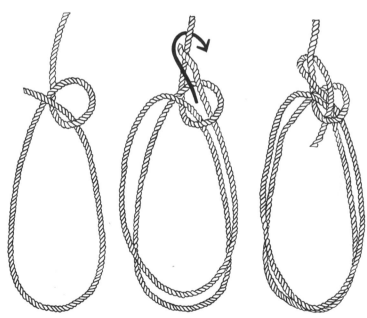

B-9. *French bowline.*

The best all-around knot for bending to a ring, spar, or anything else that is round or nearly round, is a *clove hitch* (figure B-14). A clove hitch will not jam and will rarely pull out. A slack clove hitch, as on a boat painter, however, might work itself out. For that reason, it is a good idea to put a *half hitch* in the end as in figure B-15. A half hitch, by the way, never becomes a whole hitch. Put another one on, and you have two hitches, as shown.

The slight defect of a clove hitch is that it can slide along a slippery spar when the strain is along the spar. The knot that cannot slide this way is the *stopper hitch* (figure B-13). This knot is especially useful for bending a boat painter to a larger line whose end is unavailable. It jams on a hard strain, however.

A hitch that requires no detailed explanation is the *marline hitch* (figure B-16). This hitch is used on furled sails and awnings, doubled up mooring lines, and hammocks.

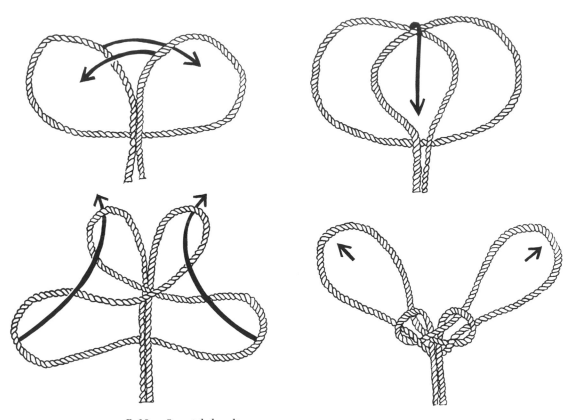

B-10. *Spanish bowline.*

B-11.   Running bowline.

B-12.   Fisherman's bend.

B-13. *Rolling hitch.*

The *round turn with two half hitches* is a combination that may be used in a ring, pad eye, or on a spar. It is particularly useful on a spar, because it grips tightly, and holds it position (figure B-17).

The *barrel sling* (figure B-18), which may be used to hoist almost any bulky object, is particularly useful in hoisting barrels, drums, and boxes, with or without tops. The part of the hitch surrounding the

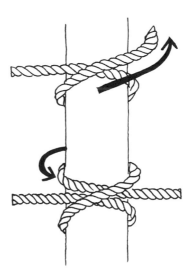

B-14. *Clove hitch.*

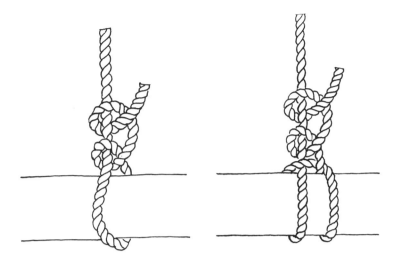

B-15. *Two half hitches and a clove hitch with two half hitches.*

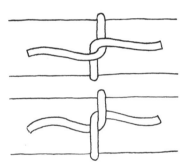

B-16. *Difference between a marline hitch and a half hitch.*

object should always be located above the center of gravity. A bowline is tied at the top to make certain that the hoisting part comes out of the eye. The first overhand knot should be looped down low to keep the hitch from slipping from under the bottom. The second overhand knot is looped near the top. If the center of gravity is near one end of the object, that end should be at the bottom, if possible.

Closed barrels, drums, and boxes, as well as numerous other items, can be hoisted by means of the *bale sling* (figure B-19). A temporary sling may be fashioned simply by knotting the ends of a line together with a square knot or a becket bend as shown.

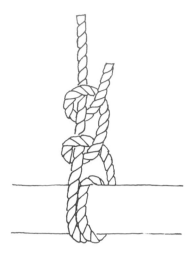

B-17. Round turn with two half hitches.

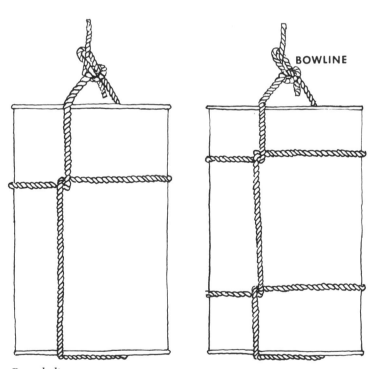

BOWLINE

B-18. Barrel sling.

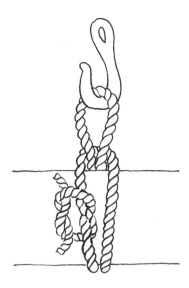

B-19. Bale sling.

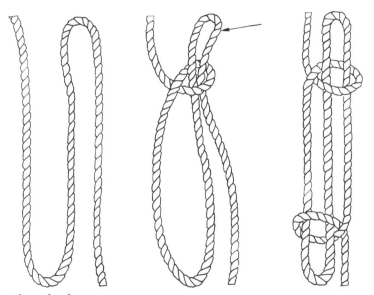

B-20. Sheepshank.

Miscellaneous Knots

The *sheepshank* knot is generally thought of as merely a means to shorten a line, but in an emergency it can also be used to take the load off a weak spot in the line (figure B-20). When used to take the load off a weak spot, it is essential that the spot be in the part of the line indicated by the arrow in view 2.

To *shorten a sling*, the procedure followed is as illustrated in figure B-21. This also forms a knot, sometimes called a *miller's knot*, used to tie the tops of bags. it can also serve as a handcuff knot or be used to lash two spars or piles together. When properly tied and pulled tight, it will not slip.

B-21. Shortening a sling.

Introduction

Safety is a job for all hands, 24 hours a day. Some danger exists in every single operation on board a naval vessel. Going to sea involves working with powerful machinery, high-speed equipment, steam that has intensely high temperature and pressure, volatile and exotic fuels and propellants, heavy lifts, high explosives, stepped-up electrical voltages, and the unpredictable forces of weather. It is the responsibility of everyone on board ship to observe all safety precautions.

Safety precautions for each piece of equipment used in the Navy are available and should be read and understood. The Navy Ships Technical Manual (NAVSHIPSTECHMAN), the Ship's Organization and Regulations Manual (SORM) for a ship, and numerous bureau and systems manuals all contain written safety regulations.

Another important part of safety is the regular maintenance of equipment and systems. Maintenance involves much more than just cleaning and painting. For safety and efficiency, every item aboard ship—from the simplest valve to the most complicated electronic gear—must be kept operable.

The following general instructions, listed alphabetically and not covered elsewhere in this text, serve as an introduction to the most important principles regarding shipboard safety.

Aircraft Operations

During aircraft operations, only those actually involved are allowed in the flight-deck area. All other personnel remain clear or below decks. People engaged in flight operations must wear appropriate safety equipment.

Passengers must be led to and from a helicopter or aircraft by a member of the transfer crew, handling crew, or flight crew. All loose gear in the flight-deck area must be stowed elsewhere or secured to the deck. Personnel must be instructed on the shrapnel effect caused when rotor blades or propellers strike a solid object. Be careful around props and helo rotors. When turning, they are nearly invisible. A helicopter's rotor tips cover a wide area, and they often will dip close to the deck when the helo lands.

Engine noise of the plane you are watching will drown out the noise of ones you are not watching. Don't move without looking in all directions and don't direct all your attention to a single aircraft.

Also beware of jet blast. Any place within 100 feet of a jet engine is dangerous. A jet blast can burn a man, knock him to the ground, or blow him over the side.

Ammunition Handling

Everyone required to handle ammunition must be instructed in safety regulations, methods of handling, and storage and uses of all ammunition and explosives. Only careful, reliable, mentally sound and physically fit sailors are permitted to work with explosives or ammunition.

Anyone knowing of defective ammo or other explosive ordnance, defective containers or handling devices, rough or improper handling, or willful or accidental violation of safety regs must report the facts to his immediate superior.

All persons supervising the inspection, care, preparation, handling, use, or disposal of ammunition or explosives must see that all regulations and instructions are observed, remain vigilant throughout the operation, and warn subordinates of the need for care and constant vigilance. Supervisors must also ensure that subordinates are familiar with the characteristics of the explosive materials involved, the equipment to be used, safety precautions to be observed, and the hazards of fire, explosion, and other catastrophies which the safety regs are designed to prevent. Supervisors must be alert to hazardous procedures, or symptoms of a deteriorating mental attitude, and take immediate corrective action when these are found.

Smoking is not permitted in magazines or near the handling or loading operations.

Crews working with explosives or ammunition are limited to the minimum number required to perform the operation properly and safely. Unauthorized personnel are not permitted in magazines or in the immediate vicinity of loading operations, except for authorized inspections.

Electrical and Electric Equipment

Electrical equipment includes generators, electrically powered machinery and mechanisms, power cables, controllers, transformers, and associated equipment. Electronic equipment includes radars, sonars, power amplifiers, antennas, electronic warfare equipment, computers, and associated controls. The most important precaution with all such equipment is to never work alone.

No one shall operate, repair, or adjust any electrical or electronic equipment unless he has been assigned that duty, except in definite emergencies, and then only when no qualified operator is present. (Electric light and bulkhead electric fan switches are exempted.)

No one shall operate, repair, or adjust electrical and electronic equipment unless he has demonstrated a practical knowledge of its operation and repair and applicable safety regulations, and then only when duly qualified by the head of the department.

Electric equipment should be de-energized and checked with a voltage tester or voltmeter to ensure that it's de-energized before servicing or repairing it. Circuit breakers and switches of de-energized circuits must be locked or placed in the "off" position while work is in progress, and a suitable warning tag attached. If work on live circuits or equipment is required, it is done only when specific permission has been received from the commanding officer.

Lifelines, Ladders, and Safety Nets

No one shall lean, sit, stand, or climb on any lifeline in port or under way. Men working over the side in port may climb over lifelines when necessary, but only if they are wearing life jackets and safety lines that are tended.

No lifeline shall be dismantled or removed without specific permission of the first lieutenant, and then only if temporary lifelines are promptly rigged.

No person shall hang or secure any weight or line to any lifeline unless authorized by the CO.

Ladders must not be removed without permission from the department head in charge. All access must be carefully and adequately roped off, or suitable railings installed. Work on ladders must, when possible, be performed when there is the least traffic.

No one may enter a flight-deck safety net or cargo net, except as authorized. The parachute-type safety harness is worn by all working aloft or over the side. The following components are used: safety line with dynabrake shock absorbers, nylon working line (wire when doing hot work), and nylon tending line.

In heavy weather additional inboard life and safety lines are rigged when personnel are required to be on weather decks.

Men Working Aloft

No person may climb the masts or stacks without first obtaining permission from the OOD, and then only to perform necessary work or duty. Before authorizing men aloft, the OOD must ensure that all power on radar and radio antennas in the vicinity is secure when they are aloft. Controls and related equipment are tagged "SECURED! MEN ALOFT." Main engine control is notified to refrain from lifting safety valves and, if men are to work nearby, to secure steam to the whistle. The OOD ensures that men assigned to work near the stack gases wear protective breathing masks and remain there for only a short time. The OOD determines that wind and sea conditions will not endanger men aloft, and he ensures that men wear parachute-type safety harnesses with safety lines attached to the ship's superstructure at the same level.

All tools, buckets, paint pots, and brushes must be secured by a lanyard when used in work on masts, stacks, upper catwalks, weather decks or sponsons that overhang areas where the personnel may be.

Personnel Protection

Avoid wearing clothing with loose ends or loops when working on or near rotating machinery. Suitable leather, asbestos, or other heavy-type gloves must be worn when working on steam valves or other hot units. Keep the body well covered to reduce the danger of burns when working near steam equipment.

Goggles or helmet and leather welding jacket must be worn when brazing, welding, or cutting. Fire watches *must* wear protective goggles. Protective goggles should also be worn whenever working with substances corrosive to the eyes, such as acid, alkali, monoethemolamine, and vinyl paint. Water in plastic squeeze bottles or other containers should be readily and quickly available.

When using an oxygen-breathing apparatus (OBA), two men normally work together. An insulated line may be attached to the men using the OBA, but the line is used only to signal, not to pull. The OBA is not authorized aboard submarines.

Plastic face shields must be worn when handling primary coolant under pressure, and suitable eye protection—a shield, goggles, or safety glasses—must be worn when buffing, grinding, or doing similar operations hazardous to the eyes.

Fumes from burning teflon are very dangerous. There should be no smoking where work can produce teflon chips or dust. Precautions should be taken when working in abestos dust, such as when lagging is being removed.

Portable Electric and Pneumatic Tools

The rated speed of a grinding wheel cannot be less than that of the machine or tool on which it is mounted. Grinders are not operated without wheel guards. Face shields or safety goggles are required for all types of grinding, chipping, or scaling. Automatic securing devices, such as dead-man switches, must be tested for satisfactory operation before they're used.

Radiation Hazards (RADHAZ)

The power generated by electronic equipment can result in biological injuries. Where such danger is possible, an r-f (radio frequency) radiation hazard exists, and warnings must be posted.

No visual inspection of any opening, such as a wave guide, that emits r-f energy is allowed unless the equipment is secured for inspection.

When there may be exposure while the antenna is radiating, someone must be stationed topside, within view of the antenna (but well out of the beam), and in communication with the operator.

Radiation warning signs must be posted and used to restrict access to certain parts of the ship where equipment is radiating.

Safety Tags

DANGER, CAUTION, OUT-OF-COMMISSION and OUT-OF-CALIBRATION tags and labels must be posted to ensure the safety of personnel to prevent improper operation of equipment. Posted safety tags must not be removed without proper authorization.

Smoking

There is no smoking in holds, storerooms, gasoline-tank compartments; gasoline pump rooms, voids, or trunks; in any shop or space where flammable liquids are being used; in the ship's boat; in bunks or berths; in magazines, handling rooms, ready service rooms, gun mounts or turrets; in gasoline control stations, oil relay tank rooms, and battery and charging rooms; in the vicinity of motion picture stowage; in the photo lab; anywhere there is bleeding oxygen; in any area where vinyl or saran paint is being applied; on the flight deck, flight-deck catwalks, and gun platforms; or in hangar and galley spaces open to the hangar.

No smoking is permitted alongside when ammunition is being handled; in any part of the ship when receiving or transferring fuel oil, diesel oil, aviation gasoline, or other volatile fuel, except in spaces designated as smoking areas by the commanding officer.

There is no smoking during general quarters, general drills, or during emergencies except as authorized by the CO. And there is no smoking when the word "the smoking lamp is out" is passed.

Tanks and Voids

No one is permitted to enter any closed compartment, tank, void, or poorly ventilated space aboard a naval or Navy-operated ship until the space has been ventilated and determined to be gas-free. In an emergency, if a space must be entered without gas freeing, a breathing apparatus, such as airline mask, must be worn. In all cases at least two persons must be present when such space is occupied. One acts as tender or safety observer.

Additional precautions: the space entered should be continuously ventilated; a reliable person must be stationed at the entrance to keep count of the number of persons inside as well as to maintain communications; suitable fire-extinguishing equipment must be at the scene; non-sparking tools will be used; and persons entering will not carry matches or lighters, or wear articles of clothing that could cause a spark.

Use of Life Jackets

Life jackets must be worn by the crew when the possibility exists that a man will slip, fall, be thrown or carried into the water. The safest life jacket, when properly worn, is the Navy nylon inherently buoyant vest (figure C-1). Other types that require inflation are subject to puncture. They also require that the wearer be conscious, because he will have to inflate the preserver. Sailors working over the side of the ship, both in port and at sea, must wear life jackets and lifelines tended by someone on deck. The term "over the side" means any part of the ship outside the lifelines or bulwarks. Men handling lines or other deck equipment must wear life jackets and helmets during such evolutions as transfers between ships, fueling under way, and towing. The crews being raised or lowered in the ship's boats, sailors entering boats from a boom or Jacob's ladder, and sailors in boats under way in rough water or low visibility must wear life jackets. Ring buoys with a line and light attached should be available when a sea ladder or a Jacob's ladder is being used (figure C-2). Men being transferred by highline or helicopter will don life jackets before they get into a transfer seat or sling. Any man crossing weather decks during heavy weather, even when exposed only for a short time, is required to wear a life jacket when going from one station to another. The word "all hands wear life jackets when on the weather decks" should be passed frequently during heavy weather. This information should also be included in the plan of the day.

C-1. A life vest properly tied. All the straps have to be secured if the vest is to be effective. The leg straps prevent the jacket from riding up over the head. Without leg and chin straps, the vest could force a man's head under water.

Welding and Burning

Welding or burning is not permitted without permission of the CO or the OOD. The area of "hot work" must be cleared of flammable matter before work begins.

Various synthetic materials yield toxic gases when burned or heated. Use caution when burning or welding vinyl resin-coated surfaces. Vinyl coating must be chipped or scraped clear of work area whenever

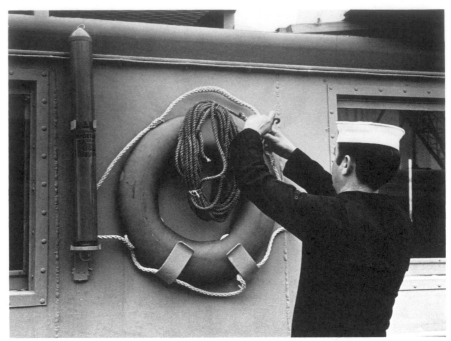

C-2. *A typical ring buoy and floating light.*

possible; welders, fire watch, and others required to be in the immediate area will be equipped with line respirators; and a local exhaust ventilation will be provided in the work area and must have a minimum capacity of 200 cubic feet per minute for each three-inch suction hose.

Although the ship's force normally doesn't weld on the hull, if such work is required, proper precautions must be taken. An X ray of the hull must be taken at the first opportunity.

When they are cutting galvanized material, ship's personnel in the area wear air-line respirators. The area must be adequately ventilated to avoid illness caused by toxic fumes.

A shipboard fire watch is assigned for the purpose of detecting, and immediately extinguishing, fires caused by welding or burning operations. Usually at least two persons are assigned—one with the operator, the other in the space behind, below, or above the site of the cutting, grinding, or welding. Remember, heat generated by welding or burning passes through a bulkhead or deck and can ignite material on the other side. A fire watch must remain alert at all times, even though the assignment may become boring and dreary. When the ship is undergoing a shipyard overhaul, for example, the ship's firemains may be inoperative. If the watch is "goofing off" or is absent from the watch station, a fire could gain considerable headway before the arrival of the firefighting crew—resulting in extensive, and unnecessary, damage to the ship and possibly in casualties to the crew.

When the hot-work operation is completed, the fire watch inspects both sides of the work area and remains on station for at least 30 minutes to be sure that there are no smoldering fires or sparks left and that the hot metal has cooled to the touch.

The fire watch should obtain safe and workable equipment and know how to operate it before going on watch. The watch inspects the work site with the hot-work operator and indicates a thorough understanding of the requirements of the assignment. The watch should be familiar with the location of all installed fire-fighting equipment in the work space and adjoining spaces and know how to use it. The watch must know where and how to sound the fire alarm and know all the assigned escape routes from the space. The watch returns all fire-watch equipment at the conclusion of the watch.

Working Over the Side

No work is done over the side without the permission of the OOD. Men working over the side on stages, boatswain's chairs, and on work floats or boats along the side of the ship must wear buoyant life preservers and shall be equipped with parachute-type safety harnesses with safety lines tended from the deck above. When another ship comes alongside, or if the screw is to be rotated, all men working over the side should be cleared.

Division officers have the responsibility for instructing personnel in all safety regulations and ensuring that they are qualified before allowing them to work over the side. Responsibility for ensuring that a competent petty officer is available to supervise also rests with the division officer.

All tools, buckets, paint pots, and brushes used over the side must be secured by lanyards to prevent loss overboard and injury to personnel below.

No person may work over the side while the ship is under way without permission of the commanding officer.

Typical Lessons Learned from Accidents That Should Never Have Happened.

A PO3 was descending a ladder and lost his balance due to excessive ladder movement. The fall resulted in a broken left wrist. Investigation revealed that the upper pins of the ladder had not been replaced after the ladder was cleaned the previous day. *Lessons learned*: Always ensure that locking or safety devices are reinstalled after maintenance has been performed.

A seaman was riding a conveyor from the pier to the ship. When he reached deck level, he moved his leg in preparation for getting off the conveyor. He did not move fast enough, and his leg was caught between the conveyor belt and rollers, resulting in a severe contusion. This man had been previously cautioned about the dangers of riding a conveyor belt. *Lessons learned*: Personnel must never ride conveyor belts.

A 110-volt electrical junction box was left uncovered with two bare wires sticking out and twisted together. The wires fell and brushed across the arm of an SN who was dozing in his bunk. He received a mild electrical shock. The wires then struck his bunk, scorched the paint, and created an abundance of sparks. *Lessons learned*: The circuit should have been de-energized and tagged out until repairs had been completed.

Two SNs were assigned to spray-paint a compartment without proper respiratory and facial protection. Proper ventilation was not rigged. They attempted to use MK 5 gas masks and then tried light plastic surgical masks. Both proved inadequate. Their supervisor checked their progress several times during the day and encouraged them to get protection, but did not *stop* the work. The two men decided to take turns and finish the job without protection. They both eventually left the space and became unconscious. Both men required hospitalization. *Lessons learned*: The supervisor failed in the performance of his duties. Even though he recognized the hazardous situation, he failed to take action. The two men involved also were aware of the hazards and failed to use proper personal protection.

Safety Postscript—Minute Wise, Hour Foolish

"I haven't got time." "Don't worry about that, we've always done it this way." "You can't always go by the book, it takes too much time." "Listen, let's hurry up—I've got other things to do." "Don't bother with that—we're in a hurry."

In a 24-hour span, we only have so much time. We can accomplish only a limited number of tasks properly. When we try to do more, or rush in order to finish, we don't "save" time, we misuse it. And we gamble with safety.

And even though the odds might not be too bad, the possible penalties (injuries and damage) are not too good.

Often, safety precautions only take a few minutes. Wearing protective equipment might slow you down somewhat for various jobs. But you have to save a lot of minutes to make up for the loss that results from an accident.

Here are examples of some recent "time-saving" shortcuts:

A petty officer doesn't want to miss the ship's evening movie, but he's stuck with a last-minute job, cleaning up in one of the voids. He knows he should check for the presence of toxic fumes before going in—it only takes 5 minutes—but he hurries in anyway and is knocked unconscious by fumes. He misses 5 days of work.

Two airmen working on an aircraft aboard a CV find they need a workstand. They figure it would take 10 minutes to get one and position it, while there's an aircraft tow tractor handy right across the hangar bay. When one airman tries to drive the tractor up to the plane, his foot slips off the brake, and the tractor crunches into the aircraft. Result: damage requiring 80 man-hours to repair.

A petty officer needs to do a minor welding job against a compartment bulkhead. The job itself won't take more than five minutes, but there's no fire watch around. He doesn't bother to get one, does the welding, and leaves. He doesn't realize he has started a fire on the opposite side of the bulkhead. The burned out compartment and saltwater damage to equipment take 500 man-hours to repair.

Two seamen are assigned to finish a painting job over the side. This assignment is given out just prior to liberty call. A quick analysis shows that this has all the ingredients for a "hurry up" accident. Sure enough, both seamen decide that the job will only take a few minutes and they will still make liberty call—that is if they don't have to rig safety nets, etc. The decision is made to use just a bosun's chair and finish off the

small area. The results of a parted line: one man drowned and one with a broken arm.

These are only a few examples of how the timesaving gamble doesn't pay off. The pressures on our time in a modern Navy dictate fewer and fewer personnel to get the job done, meet flight schedules, and keep our ships moving. We must take the time to save the countless hours lost due to accidents. Hurry is hasty action, or unthinking action, and too frequently it is touched by confusion, agitation, and inaccuracy. Hurry has no place in the Navy. Hurry is so unnecessary, and the business of getting hurt because we think there isn't time to work correctly isn't very smart.

Abaft   Behind; toward stern from.

Abaft the beam   Any direction between the beam and the stern.

Abeam   A position 090° or 270° relative to a ship or aircraft heading.

Accommodation ladder   A portable flight of stairs rigged over a ship's side.

Aft   A position to the rear or the rear extremity of a given object.

Aground   When any part of a vessel is resting on the bottom. A ship runs aground or goes aground.

Aloft   Above the decks. On the mast or in the rigging.

Amidships   Toward the center of a ship.

Anchor Buoy   A small floating marker attached with a line to the anchor, marking the location of the anchor on the bottom.

Anchor detail   Specific crew of sailors assigned to activities associated with anchoring, mooring, and entering or leaving port.

Anemometer   Instrument for measuring wind velocity.

Aneroid barometer   A no-fluid or "dry" barometer, as distinguished from a mercurial barometer.

Annual variation   A change in the earth's magnetic lines of force, varying in different localities.

Arm   That part of an anchor located between the crown and the fluke. Upright or nearly upright strength member of a davit. The act of plastering tallow into a recess in the bottom of a sounding lead; called arming the lead, and done for the purpose of bringing up a specimen of the bottom.

Astern   A position or location behind a ship or aircraft.

Athwartships   Direction 90° relative to the fore-and-aft reference, meaning across ship.

Avast   Stop; cease; as "Avast heaving."

Awash   Condition whereby the seas are flowing over the surface of an object.

Aweigh   The anchor's aweigh means the anchor is just clear of the bottom. This means a ship is considered to be under way as defined in the Rules of the Road.

Backing and filling When a sailing craft repeatedly catches and loses the wind from her sails, so as to be unable to make headway. Extended to cover the "fits and starts" of a person who cannot make up his mind. Also the backing and going ahead of a ship in casting or turning in confined waters.

Backstay Piece of standing rigging leading aft.

Barge Motor boat assigned as transportation for admirals.

Bathythermograph "BT"—A form of buoy used to measure record and transmit water temperature at various depths.

Beam Measured dimension of a ship at its widest point.

Bearing Used to define the direction of an object or a course from a particular point.

Becket The fitting on a block to which the dead end of the fall is attached.

Belay The act of securing a line to a cleat, set of bitts, or any other fixed point. In connection with an order or announcement, expresses the idea of "to disregard," as "Belay that last order."

Boatswain (Bosun) Usually a warrant officer in charge of the deck division.

Boatswain's chair A chair used to transfer personnel between ships via highline.

Bollard Strong cylindrical upright on a pier, around which the eye or bight of a ship's mooring line is placed.

Boom A free-swinging spar used to secure boats or to handle cargo, boats, or aircraft.

Boot topping An outside area on a vessel's hull from bow to stern between certain waterlines, to which special air, water, and grease-resisting paint is applied; also the paint applied to such areas.

Bow Forward extremity of a ship—referred to by slang term "pointed end."

Bow hook Seaman responsible for tending the bow on a boat. He hooks on to accommodation ladders and piers, and he serves as a lookout for the coxswain.

Break The point at which upper decks are discontinued.

Bridge Portion of a ship containing steering, power control, and navigation facilities. Commanding officer's battle station.

Broach The act of breaking through the surface and rising out of the water. Sometimes called porpoising.

Broadside Firing ship's armament or receiving hostile fire perpendicular to ship's course.

Brow A gangplank, ladder, or walkway leading from the ship to the pier.

Bulkhead Traditional nautical term for a wall or partition on a ship.

Bulwarks   A structural extension of ship's sides above upper deck.

Buoy   A floating (buoyant) marker anchored to the bottom, used to indicate a specific location or navigational hazard along a waterway.

Capstan   A powered vertical drum or spool used to pull or lift loads by winding rope or cable.

Cathead   See Gypsy.

Catwalk   A narrow, overhanging walkway providing utilitarian access to exposed operational areas of a ship.

Cavitation   Formation of a partial vacuum and resulting air bubbles along tips of propeller when it rotates at high speeds.

Centerline   The longitudinal axis of ship.

Chain pipe   Also called "spill pipe," it is the pipe through which the anchor chain passes into the chain locker.

Check   Expresses the general idea of "to slow." To check a line running out under a strain means to allow only enough of it to render around the bitts to prevent the line from parting.

CIC   Combat Information Center. Area on a ship that plans and controls offensive and defensive tactical operations.

Class   Vessels of the same type built to a common basic design.

Cleat   Stationary metal fitting on which a line or cable is secured.

Close up   The act of hoisting a flag to, or in, its highest position.

Cockle   Kink in an inner yarn of rope, forcing the yarn to the surface.

COD   Carrier On-board Delivery. Aircraft used to transport supplies and personnel to and from a carrier at sea.

Cofferdams   Void or empty spaces separating two or more compartments for the purpose of insulation or to enhance watertight integrity.

Collision bulkhead   The foremost transverse watertight bulkhead in a ship that extends from the bottom of the hold to the main deck.

Commissioning pennant   Traditional flag flown at the peak of all "in commission" U.S. Navy ships.

Companionway   Enclosed stairway or ladder for personal access between deck levels on board ships.

Conn   Abbreviation for control, used to refer to the ship's control station and the act of controlling a ship.

Coxswain   The man in charge of a boat; he maneuvers the boat.

Crown   Rounded part of an anchor below the shank. A knot in the end of a line made by interlacing the strands. In plaited line, the highest part of a pair of strands.

Darken ship   Procedure for extinguishing or screening all white light sources that would be visible from surrounding ocean area.

Davit   The steel arms and associated equipment used to raise a boat or lower it into the water.

Deck   Horizontal surfaces of ships, used for same purpose as floors in other structures.

Deviation   Magnetic compass error caused by the magnetic properties of a vessel. It is expressed in degrees east or west.

Dinghy   A small boat, sometimes equipped with a sail, but more commonly propelled by outboard motor or oars.

Dip rope   The rope used to haul an anchor chain out to a mooring buoy. It is also used to swing a suspended anchor under the bow and away from the side of a ship.

Displacement   The weight of water displaced by a ship.

Dog watch   One of the two 2-hour watches in a dogged 1600 to 2000 watch.

Dolphin   A piling or a nest of piles off a pier or beach or off the entrance to a dock used for mooring.

Double bottom   Type of ship construction with voids between outer and inner hulls. Used for fuel, ballast, stores, etc.

Down by the head (Properly, *By the head*).   Said of a vessel when her draft forward is deeper than her draft aft.

Down by the stern (Properly, *By the stern*).   Said of a vessel when her draft aft is deeper than her draft forward.

Downhaul   Any line, wire, or tackle that applies a downward pull.

Draft   The ship's vertical extension below the waterline at various points along the ship's entire length measured in feet and inches. Traditionally measured at the stern, bow, and amidships.

Drogue   A sea anchor

Dunnage   Any material used to separate layers of cargo, create space for cargo ventilation, or insulate cargo against chafing. Usually refers, however, to cheap wood boarding used for these purposes.

Ease   Relax the strain.

Ensign   Nautical term for the national flag. Flown from mainmast when under way, from stern jackstaff when moored or anchored.

Fairlead   A block or other fitting that provides a more convenient passage for a line or rope.

Fake   The act of disposing a line, wire, or chain by laying it out in long, flat bights, one alongside the other.

Falls (boat)   The blocks and tackle that are lowered from a ship to the boat in the water to pick it up. The boat hooks up to the boat falls.

Fantail   Term used to identify stern deck area of ships.

Fender   An item used as a bumper to minimize shock between ship and dock.

Fid A tapered wooden tool used by seamen to separate the strands of fiber line.

Fish hook A broken end of wire protruding from a wire rope.

Fittings Closures, doors, hatches, scuttles, vents, drains, valves, etc. used in the setting and maintenance of material conditions of readiness; e.g., X-ray, Yoke, Zebra.

Flag locker Space in vicinity of signal bridge for signal flag stowage, also known as "flagbag."

Flank Used in ship-control language to indicate maximum speed ahead. Also means position aft starboard or aft port.

Flash plate Line of plates between the anchor windlass and the chain pipes and hawsepipes over which the anchor cable runs.

Flemish A line coiled flat on deck so that the coils form a concentric spiral. (Flemish can be used both as a noun and a verb.)

Flight deck Deck used for launching and recovering aircraft. LAMPS platform.

Flotsam General term for articles that will float if jettisoned. Floating debris left on the surface by a sunken ship.

Fluke The piece of the anchor that is designed to catch in the bottom.

Flying bridge A light self-supporting structure extending from the side of ship's bridge.

Foc'sle Vernacular for forecastle.

Foot Rope Line by which the foot of a hammock is secured to a billet hook. The lowermost line of a set of lifelines (also called footline).

Forecastle A forward upper deck extending to bow.

Forestay Piece of standing rigging leading forward.

Forward Toward the fore part of a vessel or aircraft. Movement of an object in that direction.

Foul anchor Anchor with chain wrapped about a fluke or the stock, or with some other encumbrance entangled about it.

Foul deck A condition, for whatever reason, whereby the flight deck is not physically available for landing aircraft. (Also known as "red deck.")

Frame Main lateral bulkhead structure of a ship, spaced 4 feet apart from the stem to the sternpost.

Frapping lines Lines used to draw tight or to secure; for example, the lines passed horizontally around boat falls back to the side, to prevent the boat falls from swinging, are called "frapping lines."

Freeboard General term indicating the distance vertically from the mean waterline to lowest open deck area.

Gaff Small horizontal bar high on the mainmast from which the halyard for the national ensign is led.

Galley Traditional nautical name for a kitchen or any place where food is prepared.

Gangway Any ladder or stairway providing ship-to-dock or ship-to-boat access.

Gig Nautical term for motor launch assigned for use of ship's captain and his guests.

G.Q. General Quarters. Traditional Navy order to man all assigned battle stations. Personnel proceed up and forward on starboard side and down or aft on port side.

Green deck Opposite of Foul Deck. Recovery area prepared to land aircraft. Indicated by green light.

Grimes Term used for rotating aircraft identification lights. Adopted from name of company manufacturing original equipment used.

Gunwale Upper edge of a vessel's or boat's side.

Guy Any line, wire, or tackle that provides athwartships support or motion for a boom head or the head of a gin pole. (See Shroud).

Gypsy (Gypsy head) Cylindrical device at the end of the shaft on a winch or horizontal shaft windlass, on which the turns of a line or wire are taken for heaving. Also called cathead.

Halyards Light lines used in hoisting signals, flags, etc.

Handsomely To do something steadily and carefully, but not necessarily slowly.

Hatch Opening in a deck.

Hatch boom Cargo boom plumbed over the cargo hatch. (Yard-and-stay rig).

Hawse pipes Tubes leading anchor chains from deck down and forward through bow plating.

Hawser Any line over five inches in circumference.

Head The stem. The upper end of a lower mast, boom, or gin pole. The upper edge of a four-sided- fore-and-aft sail. A compartment containing toilet facilities.

Heave around Haul in on a line, wire, or chain by means of a power-heaving engine. The call on a boatswain's pipe, which is the signal to start heaving around.

Heave right up Order given to heave the anchor up into the hawse. May be given as "Heave right in."

Heave short The act of heaving in the cable until the anchor is at short stay. The order usually is given as "heave round to short stay."

Heave to The act of stopping the headway of a vessel or reducing headway to just enough to maintain steerageway.

Helm The mechanism for steering a ship; wheel or tiller.

Hitch　A knot used to bend the end of a line to a ring or to a cylindrical object usually is designated as some form of hitch.

Hoist　To move an article upward by means of some hoisting rig.

Holiday　A gap or space not covered during the application of paint.

Hull down　Said of a vessel when, because of distance and the curvature of the earth, only the superstructure is visible.

Inhaul　In general, a line used to recover any piece of gear.

In step　Said of a towing vessel and her tow when both meet and ride over seas at the same time.

Irish pennant　A loose end of line carelessly left dangling.

ISE　Independent Ship Exercise. Period at sea for practice of individual ship maneuvering and on-board drills.

Island　Carrier superstructure extending above the flight deck on starboard side; houses funnel, bridge, Pri-fly, flag plot, signal bridge, radar antenna, etc.

Jackstaff　Short, demountable mast used to fly the union jack at the bow of a ship while not under way.

Jacob's ladder　Rope ladder suspended from a horizontal boom or rail, a method for access to small boats.

Jumbo boom　Heavy-duty swing derrick for handling extra-heavy lifts.

Jury rig　Any makeshift device or apparatus rigged as a substitute for gear regularly designed for the desired purpose. The act of setting up a jury rig.

Keel　Main longitudinal structural member of ship, located at extreme bottom. Frames and stringers attach to this structure.

Keel, bilge　A fin fitted on the bottom of a ship at the turn of the bilge to reduce rolling.

Keel Block　One of a line of blocks along a drydock bed; used to support the keel or docking keel of a vesssel in drydock.

Keelhaul　Ancient form of summary punishment whereby man was hauled under keel from one side of ship to the other.

Kingpost　A strong upright supporting a boom.

Knife edge　A smooth, unpainted edge of a closure fitting; for example, a hatch, against which the gaskets in the door are pressed when closing the fitting. The result is a watertight seal.

Knock off　Expresses the idea of "to cease or desist."

Ladder　General term for any portion of ship's structure used for personnel access from one deck level to another.

Lanyard　Any short line used as a handle or as a means for operating some piece of equipment, as a firing lanyard on a gun. Also any line used to attach an article of equipment to a person, as a knife lanyard, pistol lanyard, or a call (boatswain's pipe) lanyard.

Launch   Action of propelling an aircraft from a deck. Also term for a type of motor-driven personnel boat.

Lay   Expresses the idea of "to move oneself"; as "Lay (yourself) aft." As a noun, refers to the direction of twist of the strands in a line or wire, as right lay or left lay.

Lazy guy   See Midship guy.

Leeward   In the direction that the wind is going or the downwind side of the object.

Left-handed   Counterclockwise. Extended to mean "not the right way" or "backwards."

Left-laid   Refers to line or wire in which the strands spiral along in a counterclockwise direction as one looks along the line.

Lifeguard   Term used for positioning a destroyer or a helicopter aft for rescue purposes while fueling or supplying ship at sea.

Lifeline   In general, the lines erected around the edges of decks. Specifically, the top line. From top to bottom, the lines are named: lifeline, housing line, and foot rope.

Lift   Term applied to any load to be hoisted.

Line   In general, sailors refer to fiber rope as line; wire rope is referred to as rope, wire rope, or just wire. More exactly, line refers to a piece of rope either fiber or wire, which is in use, or has been cut for a specific purpose, such as lifeline, heaving line, lead line, etc.

List   Transverse inclination of a vessel.

Lizard   A piece of line used to retrieve the end of a sea painter or to control the movement of a suspended cargo.

Log   A ledger used to record important daily data and occurrences.

Longitudinals   A term applied to the fore-and-aft girders in the bottom of the ship.

LSO   Landing Signal Officer. Pilot assigned duty of observing and assisting landing aircraft from after end of flight deck.

Luff tackle   Purchase containing one single and one double block.

MAA   Master-At-Arms. Naval designation for person responsible for discipline and housekeeping in crew area.

Mae West   Term for an inflatable type of water survival vest.

Main deck   Uppermost complete continuous deck of a ship. Areas below this are watertight. On a carrier, this is the hangar deck.

Marline   Two-strand, left-laid, tarred hemp small stuff.

Marlinspike   A tapered steel tool used to separate the strands in a wire rope.

Mechanical advantage, theoretical   The number of times (excluding loss due to friction) that the applied power is multiplied by a purchase or other machine.

Meet her   Check the swing of a vessel by putting on opposite rudder.

Mercurial barometer   Barometer that indicates atmospheric pressure by the height of a column of mercury.

Mess deck   Location of crew's eating area.

Midship guy   Guy between boom heads in a yard-and-stay rig. Also called a schooner guy or lazy guy.

Moor   Keep a ship in place by means of lines or cables fastened to the shore or to a buoy.

Mousing   To seize or bind the opening of a hook from the end across to the shank to prevent the hook from disengaging.

Movable block   Block in a purchase that is not a fixed block. Block to which the load is applied.

Muster on stations   Method of daily accounting for all assigned personnel. Routine roll call method at sea to economize on time involved.

Navy anchor   Old-fashioned anchor. Anchor with a stock.

Nothing to the Right (Left)   Order given to the helmsman not to allow the ship to come to right (left) of the course because of some danger lying on that side of the course.

On station   Term to denote presence of aircraft or ship at the assigned location.

OOD   Officer of the Deck.

OTC   Officer in Tactical Command.

Outer bight line   Line sometimes used in the close-in method of fueling. It extends from the receiving ship to the outboard saddle.

Outhaul   In general, a line used to haul a piece of gear from a ship. (See inhaul.)

Overhaul   In fire fighting, breaking up and raking over debris caused by the fire, to make sure there are no smoldering embers.

Overhead   Nautical term for ceiling of an area.

Painter   Line used to make fast a boat's bow.

Parceling   Wrapping a line in the direction of its lay with overlapping strips of canvas.

Passageway   Nautical term for a corridor or aisle on board ships.

Pelican hook   A hook to provide an instantaneous release. It can be opened while under strain by knocking away a locking ring that holds it closed.

Pelorus   Device for taking bearings; consisting of a movable ring, graduated like a compass card, and a pair of sighting vanes.

Pendant   A single part of line or wire used to extend the distance spanned by a purchase. A single part of line or wire whose purpose is to provide a means for connecting or disconnecting, as an anchor buoy pendant or a hauling pendant.

Pennant   Small triangular flag flown from ship to indicate "in commission" and for communication purposes.

Pier   A structure, usually built on piles, extending out into the water and providing a means for vessels to moor alongside.

Pigstick   Familiar term for a small staff bent to the truck halyards to which the commission pennant is attached.

Pillar or Stanchion   A vertical member or column giving support to a deck.

Pitch   Vertical rise and fall of a vessel's bow and stern caused by a head sea or a following sea.

Plane guard   Destroyer or helicopter assigned responsibility for rescue of crews during launch or recovery operations.

Plan-of-the-day   The daily published schedule of occurrences on board ship. Considered to be a direct order from the commanding officer.

Platform   A partial deck below the lowest most complete deck.

Port   Traditional nautical term denoting left side. Also a harbor for ships. Also a circular window in ship's hull.

Preventer   Any line, wire, or chain whose general purpose is to act as a safeguard if something else carries away.

Quarter   Position relative to ship, i.e., port quarter would be a bearing between 180° R and 270° R.

Quarterdeck   Traditional ceremonial area of a ship. Usually the space at head of officers' gangway.

Radial davit   One of a set of davits of the type that swings out a boat one end at a time by rotation of the davits. Also called a round bar davit.

Rail   Fencelike structure around edge of open ship's decks to provide personnel safety and restraint.

Rake   Angle from the vertical ascribed to the bow or masts of a ship.

Range   The distance an object is from the observer. A navigational range consists of two markers, some distance apart, located on a known line of true bearing. An area designated for particular purpose, such as a target range or a degaussing range. In regard to tide, the total rise or fall from low water to high, or vice versa.

Rat guard   A hinged metal disk that can be secured to a mooring line to prevent rats from using the line to gain access to the ship.

Ratline   Three-strand, right-laid, tarred hemp used chiefly nowadays for snaking on destroyer-type vessels.

Reeving   Passing a cable around or through a sheave or a series of sheaves.

Relative wind   Wind direction based on vector solution involving actual wind and ship's movement. Relative to ship's bow.

Releasing Hook   Hook on the lower block of a boat fall, which remains closed as long as there is weight on it, but tumbles and rejects the hoisting eye as soon as the weight is taken off. Usually called an automatic releasing hook.

Replenishment   Act of resupplying a ship with stores, fuel, ordnance, etc.

Rigging   Collective term for ropes and chains employed to support masts, yards, and booms of vessels.

Right-laid   Refers to line or wire in which the strands spiral along in a clockwise direction as one looks along the line.

Roller chock   A chock fitted with one or more rollers to reduce friction on mooring lines.

Rope   A term for all cordage over 1¾ inches in circumference, constructed by twisting wire or fiber. In U.S. Navy Ships, "rope" is generally used to refer to wire, whereas fiber rope is called line after it has been taken out of its original coil.

Running light   Any one of the lights required by law to be shown by a vessel under way. Not restricted to the side lights, as many sailors believe.

Samson post   In boats, a square post attached to the bow to which mooring and towing lines may be secured.

Scope   Expresses the idea of "the number of fathoms out" with regard to an anchor cable or a towing hawser.

Scupper   The waterway along the gunwales. Opening in the side through which waste water from a head or galley is discharged. Extended to cover any type of drain opening.

Scuttle   Small openings in hatch covers that allow access through the deck without undogging the hatch. They usually are provided with quick opening and closing covers. A sliding cover that closes the opening over a certain style of companionway. The act of deliberately sinking a vessel.

Scuttlebutt   Nautical term for water fountain. Also, applied to all rumors and gossip, said to originate around the water barrel.

Sea anchor   Any device streamed from the bow or stern of a vessel for the purpose of creating a drag to hold her end-on to the sea.

Sea ladder   Metal ladder secured to the ship's hull.

Sea state   State of the sea regarding wave action and height of swells.

Seizing   The use of small stuff to bind rope for various purposes. Seizings are named according to their use; for example, "throat seizing" where two parts of a line are seized side by side to form a permanent bight.

Serving Continuous turns of small stuff around parceling.

Set The direction toward which the resultant of the forces of wind and current is acting—is tending to set the ship, in other words.

Sheave A grooved wheel used to change direction on a cable; a pulley.

Sheer Longitudinal upward or downward curvature of deck or gunwale.

Sheer strake The topmost continuous strake of the shell plating, usually made thicker than the side plating below it.

Shore A timber or metal member used as a prop. The act of setting up shores to support or steady an article is called shoring up that article.

Short stay The situation when the anchor cable has been hove in just short of causing the anchor to break ground.

Shot A short length of chain, usually 15 fathoms, made up of links and detachable links.

Shrouds Athwartships lines or wires of the standing rigging used to support a mast.

Side light One of the colored lights required by law to be shown by a vessel underway. The starboard side light is green and the port side light is red.

Single up Take in the extra parts of doubled-up mooring lines, so that only a single part of each line remains on the dock. The act of returning a doubled-up cargo purchase to the status of a single whip.

Skids Wooden resting places on deck for boats.

Slack The opposite of taut; loose. Allow a rope or chain to run out, or feed it out.

Sling Mechanism for lifting stores, equipment, personnel, etc., using a hoist.

Small stuff Small cordage designated by a popular name—ratline stuff, roundline, marline—or by the number of threads—nine-thread, twelve-thread, etc.

Smart Sharp, seamanlike; smartly means to carry out an order quickly.

Smoking lamp Traditional nautical term for period or condition during which personnel are authorized to smoke.

Snaking Netting stretched between the deck and the housing line or the foot rope to prevent personnel and objects from being washed overboard.

Snatch block A single-sheaved block with a hinged strap that can be opened and the bight of a rope inserted, making it unnecessary to reeve the end of the rope through the block.

SOPA   Senior Officer Present Afloat. Certain responsibilities and authority are assigned to this status.

Sound   Determine the depth of the water.

Spanner   Wrench for tightening couplings on a fire hose.

Spar Buoy   Buoy consisting of a floating spar, or of metal shaped like a spar.

Spill pipe   The pipe through which the anchor chain passes into the chain locker.

Spot   Locate or place, as spotting boom heads for yard-and-stay transfer.

Spring   Go ahead or astern on a spring line to force the bow or stern in or out when mooring or unmooring.

Spring lay   A rope consisting partly of wire and partly of fiber.

Spring line   A mooring line leading forward or aft.

Standard rudder   The amount of rudder angle required to cause a ship to make a turn within a certain (standard tactical) diameter.

Starboard   Nautical term indicating the right side or in the direction toward the right.

Stays   The wires or lines of the standing rigging that support the masts fore and aft.

Steerageway   Nautical term for minimum forward speed that will provide safe steering capability or directional control.

Stem   Extreme forward line of bow.

Stern   The rearmost area of a ship. Opposite of bow.

Stern hook   The sailor resposible for tending the stern of a boat.

Stern post   The main vertical post in the stern frame upon which the rudder is hung.

Stern sheets   After passenger space in a boat.

Stockless   Refers to an anchor without a transverse piece perpendicular to the shank, designed to prevent an anchor from rolling on the bottom, thus improving its holding characteristics. Anchors without stocks have the advantage of being much easier to stow.

Stop off   The act of attaching a stopper to a line, wire, or chain under a strain to hold the strain temporarily while the rope or chain is being belayed.

Stopper   A line or chain or a patented device (such as a chain stopper) used for stopping off a rope or chain.

Stow   The act of packing articles into a storage space, or cargo into a cargo space.

Strain   Tension.

Strake   A term applied to a continuous row or range of plates.

STREAM   Standard Tensioned Replenishment Alongside Method.

Strut   Brace supporting the propeller shaft.

Superstructure   Structure built above a ship's hull.

Surge   To slack off a line by allowing it to slip around the object to which it is secured. The act of holding turns of a line on a gypsy in such a manner as to allow the gypsy to rotate without heaving in on the line. Sudden strain on a towing hawser caused by the pitching, sheering, or yawing of the tow and/or the towing vessel.

Swing   Progressive change of heading caused by an angle on the rudder, or by a ship circling around her anchor.

Taut   Under tension; the opposite of slack. A taut ship is one which is in a high state of discipline and efficiency.

Topping lift   Line, wire, or tackle used to hoist, lower, and support the head of a cargo boom or the outboard end of a sailing boom or boat boom.

Topside   Exposed or semiexposed, nonwatertight areas of a ship.

Top up   Raise a boom to a working angle by means of its topping lift.

Towing spar   A spar or other wooden device towed astern by ships in formation when visibility is poor to assist in station keeping.

Transverse   At right angles to the ship's fore-and-aft centerline.

Trough   The valley in the ocean formed between the crests of two adjacent swells.

Two-block   Raising a flag signal to the yardarm, which is the "Prepare to execute" signal.

Unlay   Untwist and separate the strands of a rope.

Unmoor   The act of letting go a mooring buoy, letting go mooring lines, or if a ship is moored with anchors, reconnecting each anchor to its own chain and heaving in the anchors.

UNREP   Short name for underway replenishment.

Up and down   The situation where the anchor cable and the shank of the anchor lead up and down, and the crown of the anchor still is on the bottom.

Vang   A tackle fitted with one or two wire pendants.

Variation   Magnetic compass error caused by the difference between the magnetic pole and the geographic pole and certain local conditions. It is expressed in degrees east or west.

Veer   Allow a line, wire, or chain to run out by its own weight, as to veer cable by slacking the brake on a disengaged windlass.

VERTREP   Vertical Replenishment. Operational technique developed for resupply at sea by helicopter.

Waist   The amidships section of the main deck.

Wake Formation of water turbulence and air bubbles left by a moving vessel.

Wardroom Shipboard space where officers' meals are served. Wardroom lounge is adjacent for social activities.

Warp Move one end of a vessel broadside by heaving on a line secured on the dock.

Warping winch Winch on the main deck aft, used to warp in the stern when mooring alongside.

Watch, Quarter, and Station Bill Posted listing of personnel duty stations for all ship's routine and emergency activities.

Weather deck An external passageway or space that is partially protected from the elements.

Weigh anchor Hoist the anchor clear of the bottom.

Wharf Same as pier.

Wherry A pulling boat similar to a dinghy, except that it cannot be rigged for sail.

Whip A rig consisting of a fixed block and line rove through it, as in yard whip or stay whip.

Wildcat The sprocket wheel in a windlass that catches the links of an anchor chain.

Winch A machine having one or more barrels or drums on which to coil a rope or cable for hauling or hoisting.

Windward In the direction that the wind is coming from or the upwind side of an object.

Wire diameter Refers to the diameter of a chain measured at the end of a link a little above the centerline.

Worming To spiral marline with the lay of wire rope between the strands to prevent moisture from penetrating to the core, generally accomplished before parceling.

X-Ray Damage control material condition. (Minimum condition.)

Yard-and-stay rig A method of transferring a load from one point to another by means of whips or tackles spanning the two points.

Yard boom Cargo boom plumbed over ship's side (yard-and-stay rig).

Yaw To veer suddenly and unintentionally off the course.

Yoke Damage control material condition. (Steaming and in-port at night condition.)

Zebra Damage control material condition (Battle condition).

Bissell, Oertel, Livingston. *Shipboard Damage Control*. Annapolis, Maryland: Naval Institute Press, 1976.

Boatswain's Mate 3 & 2 (NAVEDTRA 10120-F). Washington, D.C.: U.S. Navy.

Crenshaw, R.S., Jr. *Naval Shiphandling*, 4th ed. Annapolis, Maryland: Naval Institute Press, 1975.

Fathom, Fall 1978. Washington, D.C.: Naval Safety Center.

Hull Maintenance Technician 3 & 2 (NAVEDTRA 10573). Washington, D.C.: U.S. Navy.

Jacobsen, Kenneth C. *The Watch Officer's Guide*, 11th ed. Annapolis, Maryland: Naval Institute Press, 1979.

Navigation and Operations. Fundamentals of Naval Science, vol. 3. Annapolis, Maryland: Naval Institute Press, 1972.

Noel, John V., Jr. *Naval Shiphandling*, 4th ed. Annapolis, Maryland: Naval Institute Press, 1977.

Replenishment at sea (NWP 14). Washington, D.C.: U.S. Navy.

Seamanship. Fundamentals of Naval Science, vol. 2. Annapolis, Maryland: Naval Institute Press, 1972.

Ship Organization and Personnel. Fundamentals of Naval Science, vol. 1. Annapolis, Maryland: Naval Institute Press, 1972.

Standard Organization and Regulations of the U.S. Navy (OPNAVINST 3120.32). Washington, D.C.: U.S. Navy.

Surface Ship Operations (NAVEDTRA 10776-A). Washington D.C.: Naval Education and Training Command, U.S. Navy.

Wedertz, Bill. *The Bluejacket's Manual*, 20th ed. Annapolis, Maryland: Naval Institute Press, 1978.